MINA & JACOB

Holocaust survivors of nine camps

Freda Widawski and Adele Abraham

לזכרם של יעקב בן שמואל ומרים בת משה

(To the memory of Yaakov, son of Szmuel,
and Miriam, daughter of Moshe)

SYDNEY JEWISH MUSEUM
WHERE HISTORY HAS A VOICE

Community Stories

© Freda Widawski and Adele Abraham
Sydney, 2019
All rights reserved.

Without limiting the rights under copyright reserved above, no part of this publication may be reproduced, stored in or introduced into a retrieval system, or transmitted in any form or by any means (including but not limited to electronic, mechanical, photocopying, or recording), without the prior written permission of the copyright owner.

ISBN: 978-0-6485682-3-0

A catalogue record for this book is available from the National Library of Australia.

Cover and text design by compu-vision.

בס"ד

*Dedicated to the memory
of our beloved parents
Mina and Jacob*

———•◆•———

Preface

It is around 3am on the night of 31 October 2004. The phone rings. It is Adele with the news of Mum's passing. Dad stands in the corridor, crying uncontrollably. He knows what the news is, without hearing the actual words. Adele and her husband come and get us, and we hurry through the night to the hospital, to say our goodbyes, before the men from Chevra Kadisha come to take away our beloved Mum and Jacob's soulmate, the centre of his being, his heart and soul.

That phone call ended a fifty-eight-year union of two people who had met when they were young and devastated by the ravages of war and the brutalities visited upon them. It was in each other that they found the strength to rebuild their shattered lives.

This book is our attempt to honour their memory and the memory of our family members who perished in the Holocaust. It has also been written out of our desire to celebrate our parents' humanity, their love of life and indomitable spirit: to never give up, even in the face of overwhelming horror and deprivation.

We also wish to pay homage to the faceless millions killed in the Holocaust and to the Jews who for centuries leading up to World War II created a vibrant culture in countless Polish towns and shtetls. Although their presence is now no longer felt in these places, those of us who are their descendants continue to honour and glory in their achievements and to carry kernels of that culture within us.

The Holocaust is slowly becoming a distant event, with the

eye-witnesses to this horror now into their late nineties. There are those attempting to re-write history: to deny or minimize this crime perpetuated against the Jewish people, against humanity.

We, the descendants of the survivors, have a duty to remind the world and future generations of the dangers posed by extremist views. Ethnic cleansing, racism, bigotry and antisemitism must be called to account so humankind will never again witness such horror, death and the destruction of innocent lives.

Freda Widawski
Adele Abraham

Contents

PART 1: THE EARLY YEARS 1
    Map of Poland 1939 2
  1 Jacob 3
    Jacob's Family Tree 14
  2 Mina 18
    Mina's Family Tree 38

PART 2: THE WAR YEARS 43
    Map of Poland 1939/41-45 44
  1939-40: Invasion 45
  3 Occupied Wieruszów 47
  4 Galicia Invaded 60
  5 Occupied Kraków 64
  1941 77
  The Ghettos 77
  6 The Kraków Ghetto 81
  7 The Wieruszów Ghetto 99
  The Camps 106
  8 The Poznań Camps 110
  1942 120
  9 The Kraków Ghetto Liquidated 121
 10 Kraków's Amidah 141
 11 Bełżec 157
  1943: Death in the Camps 162
 12 Guttenbrunn (Kobylepole) 163
 13 Auschwitz 179
 14 Płaszów 199
 15 Skarżysko-Kamienna 223

16	Freüda in Pionki	248
	1944	252
17	Janinagrube	253
18	Mina in Leipzig	278
	1945: Death Marches	302
19	Jacob's Death March	304
20	Jacob's Liberation	320
	Map of Jacob's Journey	335
21	Mina's Death March	337
22	Mina's Liberation	346
	Map of Mina's Journey	354

PART 3: TOGETHER 357

	Map of Poland Post-World War II	358
	Aftermath	359
23	Brzeg: The Meeting Place	362
24	Life in Wrocław	375
25	Recreating Culture	399
26	Emigration	417

PART 4: AUSTRALIA 429

27	The Journey	430
28	Settling in Sydney	439
29	Finding a New Community	454
30	Zachor: To Remember	470
31	The Golden Years	488
32	Visiting the Past	510
	The Descendants	525

PART 1

The Early Years

———•◆•———

Map of Poland 1939

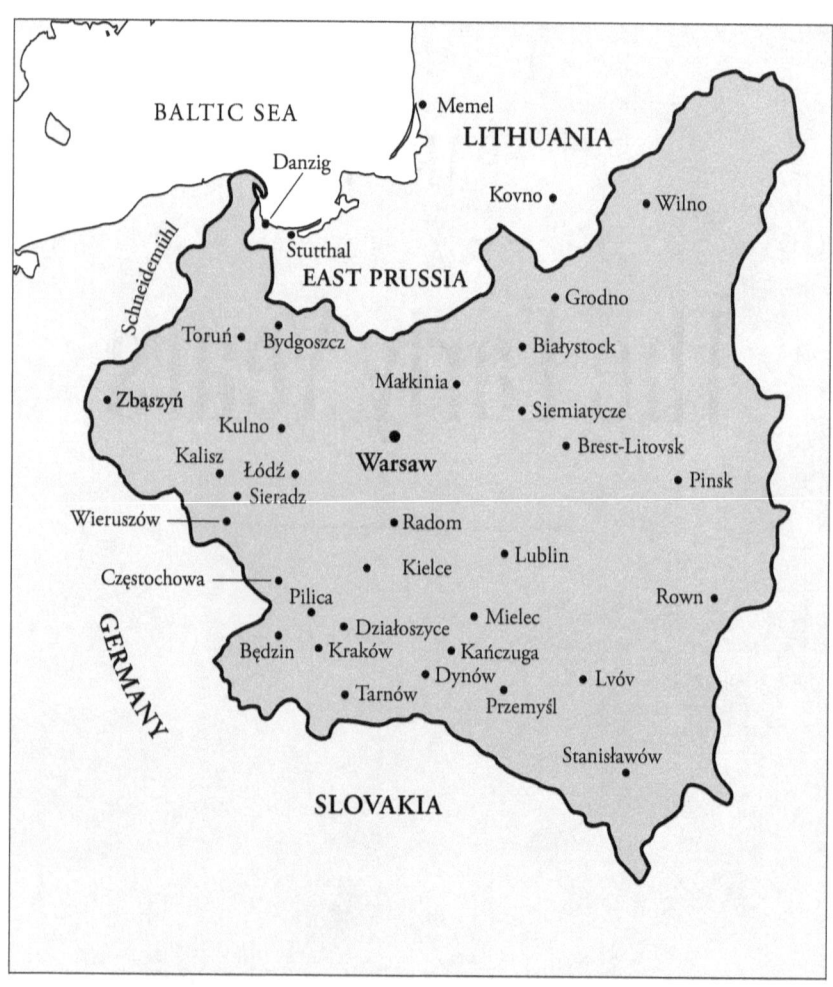

1
Jacob

Our father Jacob was born in western Poland in the little town of Wieruszów, which had some 4,000 inhabitants. He recalled:[1]

> Half of us were Jews; half were Catholics. The nearest town to us was Wieluń, which was a little bit bigger. The largest city in our region was Łódź, but that was quite far—about 120 kilometres away. We were a working class family of traders: there were four boys, mum and dad and we had a grandmother living with us, Ester Bajla. I was the youngest of the boys. There was Berek (Baruch), Abram (Awrum) and Majer. My father, Szmuel, was a worker, just a labourer; my mother Bracha (Brucha) didn't work.

Jacob was born on 21 May 1921 to Brucha (nee Jakubowicz) and Szmuel Widawski. They named their seventh and last child after his paternal grandfather, but affectionately called him Jankel in Yiddish. To his Polish friends he was Janek or Kuba. Three other children, Chaja Seisel, Dwora and Ajzyk died in infancy.

Wieruszów lies on the Prosna River. Before 1939, apart from agriculture, its other main industries were tanning and flour milling.[2] It was founded in the fourteenth century and attained the status of a town by the mid-fifteenth. The ancient amber route ran through it, contributing to its development as a centre of craftsmanship as well as trade.[3]

Jewish settlement commenced at the end of the fifteenth century and was connected with this development, as well as the tolerance shown by Tomicki (the town's owner) to non-Catholics. Jews banished from nearby Wieluń were allowed to settle there around 1585.[4]

By 1765 there were seventeen Jewish families in Wieruszów, totalling eighty-two people.[5] Records show that by 1792 Jews owned property. They were not, however, permitted to own small agricultural holdings, and so focused on crafts and trade. By 1794 Jews represented 11.5 percent of the total number of craftsmen. Tailors dominated but there were also carpenters, bakers, a candy maker, butchers, weavers and glaziers, among others.[6] The wealthier Wieruszów Jews in the seventeenth and eighteenth centuries were engaged in trading between Poland and greater Germany. They exported agricultural products and imported coal, iron and chemicals. The poorer traders made their living from commerce at local markets, fairs and from peddling around the villages.[7]

In 1815, the Vienna Congress established a border on the Prosna River and Niesób, dividing Wieruszów into two parts. The western part, Podzamcze, was incorporated into the Prussian Annexation and the eastern part into the Polish Kingdom.[8]

A law enacted in 1858 allowed Jews to live in certain parts of town. A Jew who intended to purchase a house had to produce a certificate issued by local authorities verifying that he was honest, of good conduct and known as a man of substantial means. In line with official requirements, these people had to be 'civilized' and send their children to Polish public schools. Wieruszów Jews had no difficulty receiving such certificates from the local magistrate.[9]

By the beginning of the nineteenth century the Jewish population had increased considerably, to some 1600, or 36 percent of the total.

By 1921, when Jacob was born, that number had reached 2,000 or 50 percent of the whole.[10]

Records indicate that Jacob's family was living in Wieruszów in the early nineteenth century. The marriage of his mother's paternal grandparents, Boruh Jakubowicz and Ruchla (Haj/Haia) Buranowa, took place on 8 March 1836. Boruh was twenty-three years old and Ruchla twenty-seven, so their approximate dates of birth would have been 1813 and 1809.[11]

Jacob's paternal grandparents, Jakób Widawski and Ester Bajla (nee Szwartz), were married on 28 (or 20) December 1865, when they were twenty-four and twenty-five. Ester's birth record shows that she was born on 24 October 1840, while Jakób was born sometime in 1841 (no record exists). Between them they had five children: Marjem (1866-1917), Mordka (1869-?), Lej Abraham (1877-?), Leiser (1878-1969) and Szmuel (1881-1934).

The families on both sides were primarily traders and artisans. Brucha's father was a tailor and her mother's family were wheat merchants. Ester Bajla's father, Szmul Szwartz, was a tailor, while Jakób, like his father Ejzyk, was a merchant.

Our father recalled:[12]

> I shared a room with my brothers; we were always together. We didn't fight, although I was a bit of a naughty boy at times. Sometimes I would fight with my older brother, when he started to grow up; probably I was jealous. I was maybe ten years old, and he was the eldest. There was thirteen years' difference between us, so he was already a grown man. He worked as a shoemaker, bringing money home to mum. When we had lunch on Saturday and I started to needle him, he would give me a knock! My father would say: 'Will you leave my child alone?' Years later my brother Berek reminded me:

'You were a naughty fellow when you were small.'

Of my other brothers, one was a hat maker and the other a shoemaker, making the tops of shoes. We were all working class people, craftsmen. When I was seven years old, I started to go to a Jewish cheder (religious school). After that I went to a Polish public school.

My grandmother lived with us until her death at ninety-five. I don't remember much about her because I was very young. She liked to walk and I would walk with her until our little town reached the river. After World War I, the town belonged to the Russians, while the other side of the river, Podzamcze, belonged to Germany. My grandmother had a friend, a doctor, living there, an elderly man she liked to visit. Every Sunday I would go with her. They had a good time together, a chat over coffee. Her eyesight was still good and I don't remember her wearing glasses—but maybe her hearing wasn't so good, so I would take her by the hand to walk with her. We had to cross two bridges. I would be given some lollies and would sit and play. After they had finished chatting, I would take my grandmother back home. I was around seven or eight years old at that time.

My grandmother was active until her last moment. She simply went to bed. I remember it was winter time and in Poland at that time we didn't have big homes. If you had a kitchen and two rooms, you were middle class! My grandmother had her own room and one morning my father came home from the synagogue and she was still asleep—which was unusual. He asked my mother: 'What has happened, Brucha? Is my mother not up?' My father went into her room and found that she was cold and dead. She had died in her sleep.

One of Ester Bajla's great-granddaughters, Myriam, who migrated to France in 1930, recalled that a year before they left, her great-grandmother was still working in the marketplace, aged ninety-five. Myriam spent time with her regularly and was ten at the time she left.[13]

Describing his religious life, Jacob recalled:[14]

> We were orthodox Jews. In Poland before the War there were few non-orthodox Jewish families. My father went to synagogue every morning for prayers and when I was a little boy I went with him. When I grew bigger, sometimes I went with him, other times not.

Jacob would often reminisce about Shabbat (Sabbath) dinners and how special they had been. This was primarily because most of the week the family ate mainly vegetables, with some fish. It was only on Shabbat that Brucha prepared meat, even if only small portions for each person. Their neighbour, Mrs Frankowski, would come in and light the stove for the family to cook, which also warmed the house. Travellers who were on the move on Friday nights would seek shelter with a Jewish family or sleep in a farmer's barn, rather than risk breaking the Sabbath.

All the holy festivals were special. Jacob would often laugh that even the poorest of the poor would have something new for Pesach (Passover), perhaps a new patch on an old pair of pants. Their Gentile neighbours were familiar with the food restrictions of Yom Kippur (Day of Atonement), but the butcher's wife would often 'take pity' on Jacob and slip him a piece of sausage, saying: 'Eat something, you poor child.' He kept this transgression secret from his parents and older brothers.

In 1821, an independent kahał (Jewish community) had been established in Wieruszów. Up until then, the Jews of Wieruszów had belonged to the one in the nearby town of Kępno.[15] The Wieruszów community built a synagogue, a mikva (bathhouse) and a cheder, a school, freeing families from having to hire private teachers. The funds for these projects came partially from collections and partially by advance selling of permanent seating places in the synagogue. The community also used its funds to provide assistance to the handicapped and feed the poor at Passover.[16]

While most of the community were orthodox Jews, the Hassidim were represented by the Gur and Aleksandrov sects.[17]

Max Procel, a contemporary of our father, recalled:[18]

> Wieruszów was a very Jewish town. I went on a visit to one of the big rabbis in Ger (Góra Kalwaria), about forty kilometres from Warsaw.[19] I used to go there for festivals about once a year. The Ger rabbi once came to our town for the wedding of his grandson, who was also one of my teachers. On the way, all the trains were packed, people travelling on the roof to accompany the rabbi. And when they got to our town, there wasn't enough room for everybody in the hotels, because there weren't many—so people were sleeping on the streets. They wanted to be close to the rabbi. For me that was the most exciting happening: when the rabbi came to our town with Jews from all around who had come to witness.

In 1904, Zionist activity began in Wieruszów. There were local branches of the Mizrachi, and Po'alei Zionist groups founded a Hebrew kindergarten and a public library. Girls studied in a government elementary school opened before World War I, while the boys were in religious schools.[20]

In the 1930s, Zionist parties, Communists as part of the trade unions, and Agudath Israel were all active in the Wieruszów Jewish community. As well as seating delegates in the Town Council, Agudath Israel also set up the Tzeirei Agudath Israel; the Bnot Yaacob school for girls; and a yeshiva named Sfatei Tsedek. Three hundred youngsters joined the Chofetz Chaim preparatory kibbutz. Zionist youth organizations such as Hanoar and Dror established clubs and libraries and held evening classes in Hebrew. The sports union Bar Kochba had a drama circle.[21]

Jacob recalled:[22]

> **I belonged to Hashomer Hatzair. This was a left-wing Zionist movement, organized like the scouts. I belonged to it from a very young age, when I was about ten, until the War broke out. We had a good time there. We were children, so every Saturday we had some Israeli folk dancing, like the hora. And we had a little theatre, a dramatic group, and I belonged. I liked to perform a lot: singing, acting. We used to put on the plays of famous Jewish writers such as Sholem Aleichem and others in Yiddish.**
>
> **We spoke Yiddish at home, and I learned Polish at school and in the street. I was born there: how could I not speak the language? It was the language of our country.**

After World War I and well into the 1920s and 30s, many Jews suffered poverty from the downturn in the economy, and chose migration.[23] One of Jacob's uncles, Leiser (aka Louis) went to the United States around 1910, while other relatives migrated to France in the early 1930s.

Jacob recalled that his father reportedly also travelled to the United States with the idea of bringing the family over once he was established, but returned to Poland after a year. It is not clear whether this was before or after Jacob's birth.

Jacob recalled:[24]

And then—it must have been in 1934—my father died. He had been ill with cancer. I was just twelve years old. After he died, we decided that I had to leave school to learn a trade. It was unusual at that time, but I couldn't afford to go to school any longer. We didn't have to pay for school but I had to earn a living, to help my mum. My cousin, my mother's brother's son, had a little tailoring workshop for menswear. The workshop had five or six people working in it. So I became an apprentice tailor and worked for him for five years, until the beginning of the War in 1939.

I worked full days, ten hours a day, six days a week, with a day off on Saturday. They taught me tailoring and I was quite good. After two years, the first payment I brought to my mother was nine złotys! This was a lot of money at that time in Poland. With it, my mother could buy food for the household for a whole week. My brothers still lived at home. Everyone was working and everyone brought home all their wages—to the last penny! When my mother saw that she had enough to pay the rent and feed us, the elder brothers got a little bit of pocket money. But I was still too young; she didn't bother too much with me. But sometimes I would get, say, fifty groszy (cents) from my mother to pay the monthly membership for my organization.

Sometimes during the summer, we used to go with it to camps. This was not easy, because to join in I had to pay two or three złotys per week, and my mother would say: 'Where will I get these three złotys?' But somehow, she managed it and I accompanied the other kids. We would play sport—I played a bit of soccer—and sing and dance. You know, it wasn't particularly luxurious: not much food and not too fancy.

The philosophy of the Zionist movement was for Jews to go to Israel, to Palestine. People went to Haksharah (agricultural preparation centre), where they learned to work in the fields, to prepare them for work in the kibbutzim. I wasn't so lucky. I was probably too young and, in any case, I didn't want to leave my job and go there for a year.

Antisemitism was everywhere in Poland, but I personally didn't suffer it. Up until today I have a Polish Christian friend, Józio Frankowski. We grew up together, he and his brother Zenek, side-by-side, sharing one house. It belonged to their grandmother, and our family rented the upstairs half from them. These people were really good to me: the boys were like brothers and we lived together in harmony, like a family. We played together and swam and fished in the Prosna River. Often all three of us were washed in the same bath by one or the other mother and put to bed together. Their life wasn't much different from ours. Maybe economically they were a little bit better off, because they had some land—not much but a few acres—so they had their own bread and a few potatoes. But they were good people, very good people. They helped me a lot during the War.

A Polish resident of Wieruszów, Sigmund Józefowski, recalled:[25]

There were many Jews living in the town prior to the War, and relations between us were good. For example, they were involved in jointly administering the town together with the Christian residents.

Max Procel recalled it differently:[26]

> **By the 1930s, antisemitism was growing and growing. I didn't experience it much at school, where there were mostly Jewish boys. We weren't scared of them, the Gentiles. They were more scared of us.**

This was the Widawski family's life on the eve of World War II. Jacob was learning to be a tailor and he, Majer and Abraham were living at home with their mother. When Berek married Hindy Fajlewicz, he established his own home. By 1939 they had two sons, the youngest, Szmuel (named after Berek's father), born on 30 December 1938.[27]

MINA & JACOB

Top: The only remaining photograph of Jacob as a small boy. It was given to him in Paris in 1994 by one of his cousins. From left: mother Brucha, brother Majer, grandmother Ester Bajla, brother Berek, father Szmuel and Jacob, 1926.
Bottom: Jacob's parents, Brucha and Szmuel. This photo was also sent to Jacob's brother by the French cousins and appears to have been taken in the mid-1920s.

MINA & JACOB

Jacob's Family Tree: Jakubowicz and Widawski (Wieruszów)

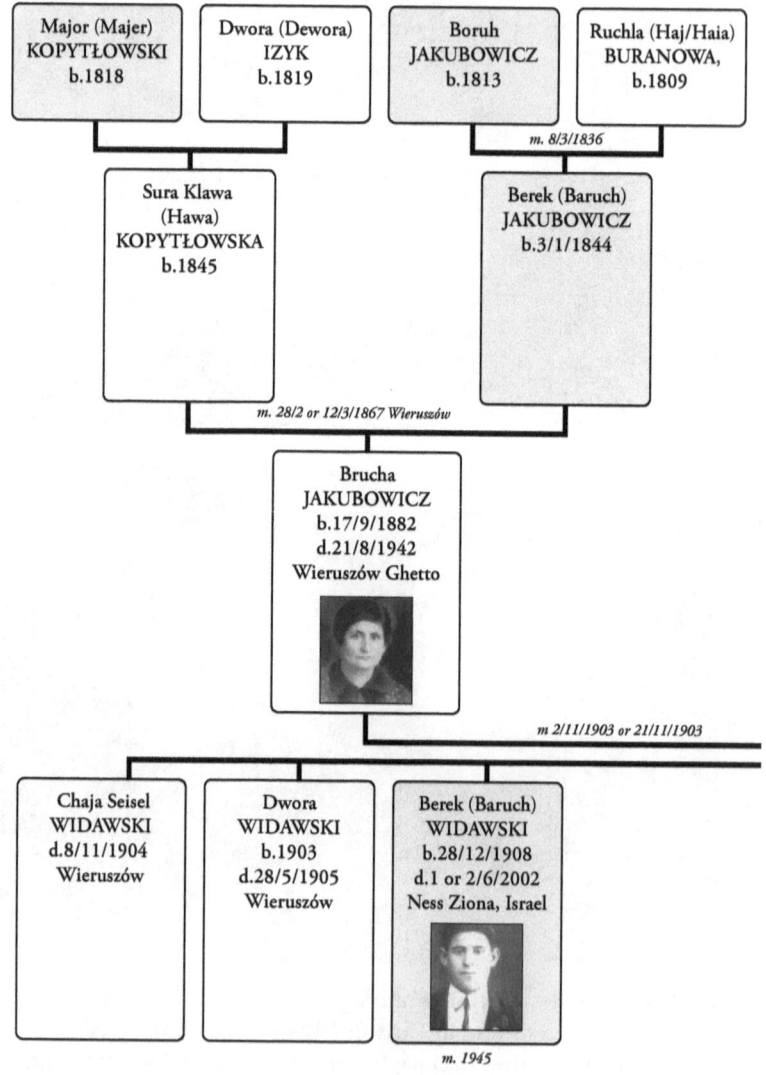

MINA & JACOB

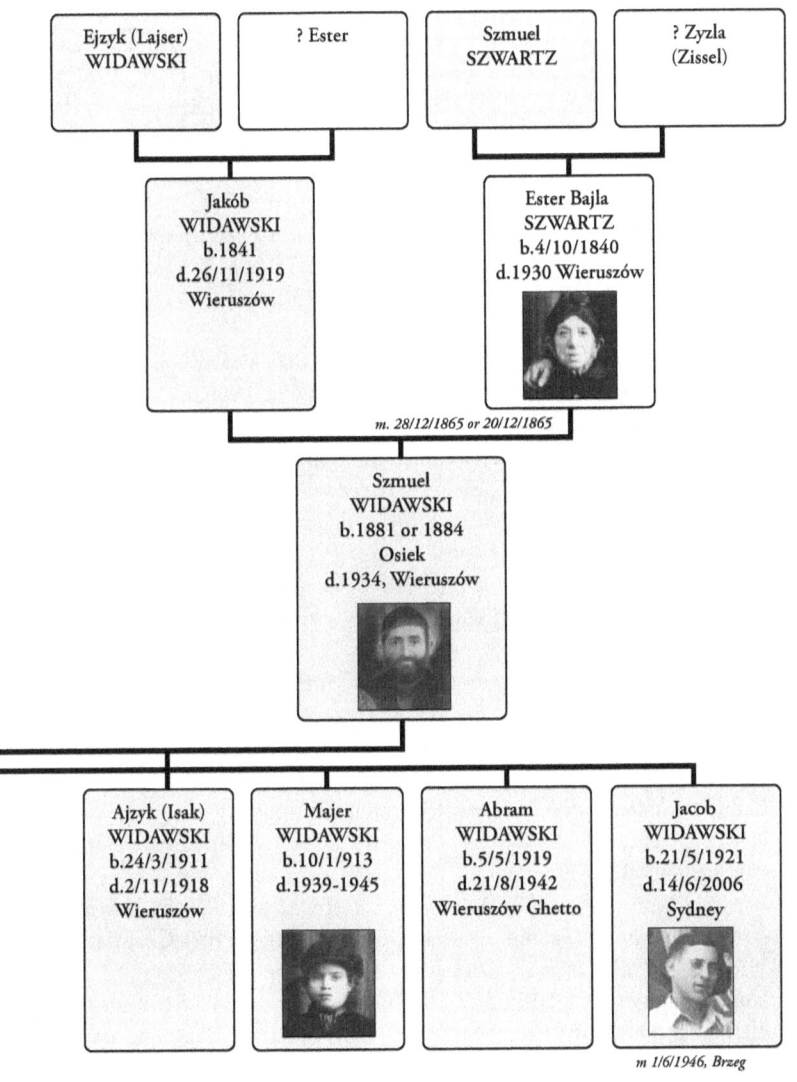

- Ejzyk (Lajser) WIDAWSKI
- ? Ester
- Szmuel SZWARTZ
- ? Zyzla (Zissel)

Jakób WIDAWSKI
b.1841
d.26/11/1919
Wieruszów

Ester Bajla SZWARTZ
b.4/10/1840
d.1930 Wieruszów

m. 28/12/1865 or 20/12/1865

Szmuel WIDAWSKI
b.1881 or 1884
Osiek
d.1934, Wieruszów

Ajzyk (Isak) WIDAWSKI
b.24/3/1911
d.2/11/1918
Wieruszów

Majer WIDAWSKI
b.10/1/913
d.1939-1945

Abram WIDAWSKI
b.5/5/1919
d.21/8/1942
Wieruszów Ghetto

Jacob WIDAWSKI
b.21/5/1921
d.14/6/2006
Sydney

m 1/6/1946, Brzeg

Notes

1. Jacob Widawski, transcripts of interviews conducted at the Consulate-General of the Federal Republic of Germany, 1974, 1975, Sydney; transcripts of testimony given at trial against Heinrich Niemeyer, 1978, 1982, 1989, Indictment StA Hannover 11 Js 5/73, Hannover; audio testimony for the *12th Hour Project of Oral Testimonies* (Sydney: Australian Institute for Holocaust Studies, 1990); video testimony, 1995 (Sydney: USC Shoah Foundation Institute), code 2528
2. The United States Holocaust Memorial Museum *Encyclopedia of Camps and Ghettos 1933-1945* (Washington: 2012) Vol. 3, Pt A, 115; Jack Kugelmass and Jonathan Boyarin, *From a Ruined Garden: the Memorial Books of Polish Jewry* (New York: Schocken Books, 1983), App. 2
3. Beit Hatfutsot (Museum of the Jewish People) (Tel Aviv, Israel: 1996) Unit Id# 73076; Wieruszów Commune publication (Wieruszów: 2010)
4. Jakub Goldberg, *Społeczność Żydowska w szlacheckim miasteczku: Żydzi w dawnym Wieruszowie* (A Jewish Community in a Noble Town: Jews in Ancient Wieruszów) (Warsaw: Biuletyn 59 Żydowskiego Instytutu Historycznego, 1966) (Bulletin 59 of the Jewish Historical Institute), 4; http://www.sztetl.org.pl/en/city/wieruszow/
5. Goldberg, *Społeczność Żydowska* (A Jewish Community), 4; www.wielun.org.il; www.sztetl.org.pl/en/city/wieruszow
6. Goldberg, *Społeczność Żydowska* (A Jewish Community), 12-13
7. Goldberg, *Społeczność Żydowska* (A Jewish Community), 12-13; Beit Hatfutsot, Unit Id# 73076
8. Wieruszów Commune publication
9. Goldberg, *Społeczność Żydowska* (A Jewish Community), 7-8
10. Goldberg, *Społeczność Żydowska* (A Jewish Community), 4; www.wielun.org.il; Urząd Stanu Ciwilnego/USC (Registry Office): Wieruszów, Poland; www.sztetl.org.pl/en/city/wieruszow
11. Archives Poland: Kalisz, Poland *Aktów Małżeństwa za Rok 1836 Dla Wyznań Niechrzescijańskich* (Records of Marriages after 1836 for non-Christians); USC: *Wieruszów, Przy Zarzgdzie Migksim w Wieruszowie: Syg 2, Akt 2*
12. Jacob Widawski, testimonies, German Consulate-General; transcripts, Hannover trial; *12th Hour Project* 1990; USC Shoah Foundation, code 2528
13. Myriam Salomonowicz, interview with Gerard Najman, 2014, Paris
14. Jacob Widawski, testimonies, German Consulate-General; transcripts, Hannover trial; *12th Hour Project*; USC Shoah Foundation, code 2528
15. Beit Hatfutsot, Unit Id# 73076; Goldberg, *Społeczność Żydowska* (A Jewish Community), 17-18

16 www.wielun.org.il; www.sztetl.org.pl/en/city/wieruszow; Goldberg, *Społeczność Żydowska* (A Jewish Community), 18-20
17 Shmuel Spector, ed., *The Encyclopedia of Jewish Life: Before and During the Holocaust* (New York: New York University Press, 2001), Vol. 3, 1,445
18 Max Procel, video testimony, 1997 (Melbourne: USC Shoah Foundation Institute), code 30561
19 Abraham Lewin, *A Cup of Tears: A Diary of the Warsaw Ghetto* (London: Fontana/Collins, 1990), 7
20 Beit Hatfutsot, Unit Id# 73076; Spector, *The Encyclopedia of Jewish Life*, 1,445
21 Guy Miron, ed., *The Yad Vashem Encyclopedia of the Ghettos during the Holocaust* (Jerusalem: Yad Vashem, 2009), Vol. 2, 929; Beit Hatfutsot, Unit Id# 73076
22 Jacob Widawski, testimonies, German Consulate-General transcripts, Hannover trial; *12th Hour Project* 1990; USC Shoah Foundation, code 2528
23 Spector, *The Encyclopedia of Jewish Life*, 1445
24 Jacob Widawski, testimonies, German Consulate-General; transcripts, Hannover trial; *12th Hour Project* 1990; USC Shoah Foundation, code 2528
25 Sigmund Józefowski, interview with Freda Widawski, Wrocław, 2010
26 Max Procel, video testimony, 1997
27 Urząd Stanu Ciwilnego/USC (Registry Office): Wieruszów, Poland, Księga U.M.Z. number 1939, Akt 5 (Register of Birth, Deaths, and Marriages); Księga Urodzeń 1927-1939 (Register of Births), Akt 5

2
Mina

A baby girl was born to Eidel (nee Sand) and Moses Laub on 9 November 1921, in Kańczuga, a district of Galicia in the southeast of Poland. They named her Mirla, after her maternal grandmother Miriam, but she was always called Mina. She was their seventh and last child.

Mina's mother and her family came from Kańczuga, and her father and his family from Dynów, twenty-three kilometres north.

Eidel and Moses were married in Kańczuga, and all their children, including Mina, were born there. Urząd Stanu Cywilnego (USC), the Registry Office, holds the birth record for Eidel (or Eidela), plus the marriage record dated April 1906 for Eidel and Moses. At the time of their marriage, Moses was twenty-seven years old and Eidel twenty-six. Moses' parents are listed as Jonah (Jones) Laub and Freüda; Eidel's parents as Mechel and Mirlimat (Mirla) Sand (nee Zwanzinger), merchants.

The marriage produced seven children: Mechel Baruch, Israel, Wolf, Osias, Freüda, Izaak (Izio) Mayer and Mirla. Also found was the death record for Osias, which stated that he died at home, aged six months.

Moses' occupation is described as kramarz, a market trader.

Galicia was the eastern outpost of the Austro-Hungarian Empire. Created in 1772 with Lwów (Lemberg, Lviv) as its capital and covering some 32,000 square kilometres, it was the largest single province in the Empire. It was populated by diverse cultural and linguistic groups: Germans, Poles, Ruthenians (Russians), Ukranians and Jews. The official language changed from German in the eighteenth century to Polish in the nineteenth.[1] A handful of aristocratic families dominated Galician society and its economy, while the vast majority of the population was poor, mostly illiterate peasants.

The province was mostly made up of small towns, almost villages, with few resources to feed their people.[2] In the latter part of the nineteenth century, 50,000 people were dying each year as a result of near-starvation conditions. Galicia was worse off than Ireland at the start of the potato famine. In the twenty-five years leading up to World War I, more than two million people left the region for France, Germany or the United States.[3]

Despite the unpromising conditions, culture flourished in Galicia. The Jagiellonian University of Kraków and the University of Lemberg earned worldwide reputations. There were learned societies, libraries, museums, publishers, bookshops, theatres, coffee-houses, and numerous journals and newspapers.[4]

On 3 November 1918, the Austro-Hungarian Empire was dissolved and Galicia, incorporated into the newly-independent Polish Republic, was re-named Mała Polska (Little Poland).[5]

By the eighteenth century, when the first records of Mina's family appear, 225,000 Jews lived in Galicia, most of them in the east. Western Galicia was dominated by royal towns such as Kraków, which had a right to 'de non tolerandis Judaeis', meaning Jewish settlement was severely restricted. In 1900, 70 percent of the 800,000 Jews in Galicia lived in towns, in some cases representing 50-75 percent of the population.

In the nineteenth century, the Jews of Galicia were predominantly engaged in commerce, as merchants, innkeepers or licensees.

The community was divided between the orthodox and the conservatives and the uneducated poor. A number of modernist intellectuals were associated with Haskala (the Enlightenment) and combined worldly knowledge with studying the Torah.[6]

During the second half of the nineteenth century there was a rise in Polish antisemitism, along with a rapid spread of Zionist ideology. In 1897, Zionists from Tarnów established the first Galician Jewish colony in Palestine.[7]

1904 saw the establishment in Galicia of the Jidysz Socjalist-Demokratische Arbeiter Partaj or Poalej Syjon (Jewish Social-Democratic Working Party or Workers of Zion), which combined Socialist and pro-Zionist principles.[8]

By the beginning of the twentieth century, around 141 Jewish kehillot (congregations) existed in Galicia, the largest being Lwów (57,000). Kraków had 32,000 and Tarnów 15,000. Hundreds of towns and villages had smaller Jewish communities: 1,273 Jews lived in Dynów and 967 in Kańczuga.[9]

In both Dynów and Kańczuga, Jews were present from the mid-sixteenth century. Dynów, with no industry, suffered long periods of impoverishment throughout its existence.[10] Kańczuga, situated at the crossroads of trade routes between Poland and Hungary and to the east towards Russia, prospered and developed.[11]

A great circular synagogue was built in Dynów in the eighteenth century, and by 1889 the Jewish population stood at 1,241, out of a total of 2,784, almost 50 percent. During World War I the town was badly damaged, and in the 1920s-30s, there were a number of antisemitic incidents.

As in other parts of Galicia, the Jewish young of Dynów and Kańczuga joined various Zionist groups, and a number supported the illegal Communist Party.[12]

Although not much information survives about Jewish life in Kańczuga, we know the community built a synagogue and a cemetery.

From her childhood, Mina remembered stories that were also passed down to her American cousin Seymour about Moses Laub's family in Dynów. Unfortunately, no records for Dynów's Jewish community exist, as these were destroyed during the War. However, records found in Kańczuga indicate that Moses' father, Jonah Laub, was born in Dynów in 1851. Jonah's parents are named as David and Golda Chaya (maiden name not known). Jonah married Freüda Jarc, who died in 1899 when she was in her forties. They had nine children: Mendel, Miriam (or Mirel), Annie, Sarah, David, Rebecca, Irving, Feigela and Moses. All the children, with the exception of Moses, like thousands of their compatriots in the early 1900s fled from the misery of Galicia. They settled in New York and other east coast American cities.

Seymour Feiler (Sarah's son) recalled:[13]

Jonah had his own cheder in Dynów. He was tall, over six feet, with red hair.[14] His wife Freüda sold scarves in the marketplace. He had a stroke when he found his grandchildren saying Kaddish in synagogue for their father David, who had died in Pittsburgh. Jonah had not been informed of his son's death.

The only surviving pre-World War II records relating to the Laub family are a few addresses contained in the Rejestra Mieszkanców Gminy Dynów (Register of Dynów's Residents), now stored in the Dynów Public Library. They contain three entries for Rynek No. 23, in the name of Laüb: Freile (born 5 November 1911), Naftali Hersh (born 1 February 1916), and Osias (born 12 June 1917), father David.[15]

The earliest Kańczuga records show that Mina's maternal great-

great-grandmother, Ginendla, was born in Kańczuga in 1799 and her husband, Aron Zellerkraut, in 1800. All the following generations were born, married and died in Kańczuga and all were merchants.

Mina recalled the family owning a shop in Kańczuga. This is supported by the 1929 Kańczuga Business Directory,[16] which lists M. Laub as one of three men dealing in building materials. He may have been her father. Further, her middle brother Wolf's Dowód Osobisty (Identity Card), issued by the Municipal Council of Kańczuga on 15 October 1929, shows his place of residence as Kańczuga. It would appear that there was still some family connection with Kańczuga at that time.

Mina had extended family members living in Tarnów before World War II. Unfortunately, no records of them exist, but she fondly remembered her cousin, Henryk Sand, who would visit from Tarnów. Her eldest brother, Mechel, also lived with his wife and young son in Tarnów, where he managed the local flour mill. As a girl she would visit during her school holidays and loved riding in a horse-drawn buggy and being fussed over by her big brother and his employees. The beloved little sister!

Tarnów, located some seventy kilometres east of Kraków, is one of the most important towns in Galicia. A Jewish presence was first mentioned there in 1445. By the middle of the eighteenth century, the Jewish population had reached 900, with infrastructure including their own craft guilds and kosher butchers. In 1855 they gained full citizenship rights, and by 1867 Jews represented 45 percent of the total population.[17]

The city was an important centre of religious life, with a well-organised kahal, two large synagogues and forty prayer houses. There were cultural institutions, sporting clubs, schools (including a Hebrew language school) and charitable organizations.[18] The community also established a library which housed some 20,000 books in Polish, Hebrew, Yiddish and German. In 1928, the first issue of the Polish language *Tygodnik Żydowski* (*Jewish Weekly*) appeared.[19]

In 1939, Tarnów had a population of 56,000, of whom about 45 percent were Jewish.[20]

Kraków, the city which in 1032 became Poland's royal capital and continued as the royal seat until, in the early seventeenth century, the capital was moved to Warsaw,[21] was located in Western Galicia. It had been founded on the banks of the Wisła River in the seventh century. It was the home of the Laubs until World War II broke out.

Kraków was prosperous. It lay on the amber route, with merchants carrying amber from the Baltic to southern Europe and Byzantium. The golden age of the city was under the Jagiellonian dynasty of kings (1385-1527), during which the renowned University was established and Kraków became an intellectual centre, housing some of the greatest humanists in Europe.[22]

Jews were present in Kraków from 1176, and by 1304 there was an established 'Jewish street' near the main market square. In 1335, King Kazimierz III (the Great), founded the town of Kazimierz for Jews to inhabit.[23]

By the mid-fourteenth century, Jews had established an organized community. Records reveal a mikveh and cemetery by the 1350s. Blood libels and mob attacks against Jews broke out in 1407 and 1423. Following the fall of Constantinople, on 12 April 1463, crusaders gathered in Poland and marched toward Kraków, where they attacked the Jewish population; 30 Jews were murdered and many wounded. Following on from that, in 1485, Jews signed an agreement barring them from most branches of commerce.[24]

After a fire in 1494 destroyed parts of the city including the Jewish quarter, the king in 1495 ordered the Jews expelled from Kraków and resettled in Kazimierz. Thereafter Kazimierz become an exclusively Jewish town, although Jews were permitted to continue to trade in Kraków itself.[25]

From the fifteenth to the eighteenth centuries, Kraków became one of the greatest Jewish spiritual and scholastic centres in Poland and played a vital role in Jewish commercial and intellectual life in Eastern Europe. The Jewish community established six main synagogues: the Alte Schule; the Remuh Synagogue and Old Cemetery; the High or Tall Synagogue; Popper's; Izaak's; and the Kupa. The city was the home of celebrated physicians and rabbinical scholars, a centre of both Hasidism and Enlightenment scholarship.[26]

In 1795, following the partition of Poland, Kraków and Kazimierz were annexed to Austria. When an independent Polish Republic was established after World War I, Kraków became part of Polish territory. By then the Jewish community had grown to represent a third of the total population. This grew to a quarter by 1939.

Kraków's Jewish community was part of the fabric of the city and as heterogeneous as were its non-Jewish neighbours. There was a new class of intelligentsia: doctors, pharmacists, journalists and politicians, all university-educated. While most Jews lived in Kazimierz and the majority of them were poor, the more affluent also lived in Stradom and across the Wisła in Podgórze.[27]

The Laubs settled in Stradom, into an apartment on ulica/ul. (street) Jasna 10, a small leafy street of solid, well-maintained apartment blocks.

As Mina was growing up during the inter-war years, Kraków's Jews established political, educational, social and cultural institutions. Both religious and secular people were involved in them. They attempted to integrate into Polish society while at the same time honouring their Jewish identity. Cultural influences on Mina would have included various versions of Zionism and politics; Yiddish culture; traditional religious orthodoxy and Reform Judaism.

Like many Jews throughout Poland, those in Kraków were trilingual, speaking Yiddish, Hebrew and Polish. However, Kraków's Jews were much more polonized than those living in the towns of the former Tsarist Emperor, such as Warsaw, Łódź or Wieruszów.[28]

Mina's family reflected this move towards polonization. While she spoke Yiddish, she was always more proficient in Polish.

The family kept Shabbat and celebrated the Jewish holidays. Moses attended shul (synagogue) every Shabbat (most likely the reform Tempel Synagogue, given the families' progressive leanings) and insisted that his sons accompany him. The girls helped their mother prepare the meal: the plaiting of the challah, which would then be taken to the local bakery for baking; cooked gefilte fish; chicken soup; and cholent, a traditional Jewish stew which is usually simmered overnight for twelve hours or more and eaten for lunch on Shabbat. The family gathered around the festive table in the company of perhaps a poor and lonely person Moses had brought that evening from shul to share in their Friday night meal, while Eidel lit the Shabbat candles.

Mina recalled:[29]

> Our household was traditional, but not fanatically religious. My parents were believers, and the children were brought up with a sense of tradition. However, my father often said: 'Be a Jew at home and a Pole in the street.'
>
> He worked as a secretary in a large flour mill. Two of my brothers, Wolf and Izaak Mayer, were also working, so on the whole we were reasonably well off and were taught to share with the less fortunate.

The Laubs had cousins who lived in Podgórze in Kraków, and extended family members in Przemyśl, Kańczuga, Dynów, Tarnów and Lwów. Mina would often reminisce about the flurry of activity and extensive preparations that went on prior to high holidays such as Pesach, and her excitement over relatives' visits. When her eldest brother Mechel married and moved to Tarnów, his visits with his wife and baby son were the highlight of the year for her and the rest of the family.

Mina recalled those times with sadness:[30]

> **Now, when we celebrate Jewish festivals, I cry, particularly around Passover, since I remember how it was at home before the War. I remember the gathering of our extended family and the strong and beautiful ties between us.**

Mina's father, a qualified accountant, strongly encouraged education for his children. He grew up in a home were learning was valued, his father having been a teacher who ran a cheder in Dynów. During the inter-war years, Jewish children had a choice between Polish public schools or private schools, Jewish or Polish. The majority of Jewish children attended public schools, but many also received some form of private Jewish education and participated in Jewish cultural activities outside their schooling.

Mina recalled:[31]

> **My days at the girls' primary school were very happy. I was ambitious and a good pupil. My older sister Freüda was in the same school, so she looked after me.**
>
> **My sister and I attended school until the age of thirteen. After that I didn't go to high school but took evening classes. The universities were extremely expensive, so we couldn't afford higher education for everyone, because we were a big family. The decision was made that higher education would**

be for the older boys, while my sister and I went to a college where we learned embroidery, sewing and dressmaking—practical skills. As students, we were given reduced train and bus fares, which made me very happy. Whenever I wanted to travel to visit my family during the holidays, I knew cheap fares were available. So, I was treated like a student, learned some skills and prepared for the future I expected. But my brothers told me they always regretted that I didn't go on to further study.

I went to college in the evening, and during the day I helped my mother, because we were a large family. Altogether we were eight people, so there was a lot to do for everybody. My sister and I used to take lunch to our father at the mill.

It is probable that Freüda and Mina attended their evening classes at the Szkoła Zawodowa Towarzystwa Ogniska Pracy w Krakowie (Girls' Vocational School of the Centre of Work Association in Kraków), located some 1.5 kilometres from where they lived. It offered courses in dressmaking, embroidery, knitting and home economics.[32]

The arrival in 1897 of Dr Ozjasz Thon as rabbi of the Tempel Synagogue had introduced new political and ideological ideas to the city, especially on Zionism. He was the most significant Jewish political leader to come out of Kraków. A gifted orator, writer and scholar, he was the Tempel's rabbi until his death in 1936, and founding editor of the newspaper *Nowy Dziennik* (*New Daily*). A close associate of the father of Zionism, Theodor Herzl, from 1923 he served on the Executive Committee of the World Zionist Organization. A national Jewish leader, he was a Member of Parliament and served as deputy to the Sejm, the Lower House of Parliament of the Second Republic of Poland, from 1919 until 1935.[33]

Mina was part of this milieu. Jewish Kraków supported a myriad of political parties with their affiliated youth organizations. The vast majority of young people joined Zionist groups: Hashomer Hatzair, Hashachar, Bnei-Akiva, Gordonia, Massada and Betar. The Agudath Yisrael represented the orthodox community, and the Bund was the party of the Jewish working class.[34]

Much of Mina's social life centred around her involvement with the Zionist youth organization Akiva.

She recalled:[35]

> From the time I turned thirteen, a whole group from my class were members of Akiva, which was the largest Zionist organization in Kraków and Western Małopolska. There we met our peers from other schools: the Hebrew Gymnasium, the School of Crafts and pupils who attended Polish high schools. Akiva bonded us more than school.
>
> The Zionist movement was very strong, with most young people belonging to an organization. Ours wasn't as religious then as it is in its current form; we were closer to Hashomer Hatzair and our hero was Dr Theodor Herzl. Because my youngest brother Izio also belonged to Bnei, my parents allowed me to attend.

The Kraków branch of Agudath ha-Nor ha-Ivri Akiva (The Akiva Union of Hebrew Youth) was founded at the beginning of the 1920s. It was a scouting-type Zionist movement which distanced itself from orthodox Judaism. However, its educational principles stressed respect for, and knowledge of tradition and religion, principles that Mina fully supported.

Akiva also prepared young people to go to Palestine, by teaching Hebrew; conducted lectures and discussions on life there; and involved its members in farm activities. It also organized summer and winter camps, promoted physical education and had a choir which sang on high holidays in the Tempel. Mina was a proud member.

Akiva also organized demonstrations and street parades. For example, on 19 March 1935, it arranged a live tableau mounted on flat trailers, depicting *The Productivity of Palestine*. The procession moved through many Kraków neighbourhoods and streets, including Mina's ul. Jasna.[36]

Mina recalled this event:[37]

> Purim was a huge celebration. The streets were very crowded and well lit. People put on fancy dress and sang in the streets late into the night. The Poles knew about this festival, since we celebrated it every year, so nobody bothered us.
>
> We rode in a procession of ten big carriages through the streets. The carriages were adorned with lamps and colourful decorations and were called 'od lo jada'. Every carriage illustrated a different aspect of life in Israel. Ours showed the kibbutzim: harvest, factories and so on. It was the last carriage in the procession and it carried the choir. We were all very proud to be singing in Hebrew, dressed in special uniforms.
>
> We rode down ul. Jasna and stopped outside the building where our patron, Dr Ozjasz Thon lived, across the street from our house. He came out on his balcony to greet us, surrounded by his family and friends, activists, people who belonged to our organization. They greeted all the young people. For us, it was a really beautiful event. When you are young and were allowed to stay up until 12 o'clock at night, this was something special. The band played Hatikva and the choir sang. Everyone applauded us. It was a memorable

occasion.

Jewish boys and girls often joined their own sports clubs, which competed with Polish ones. The Makkabi and Jutrzenka (Morning Star) soccer clubs were specifically for Kraków's Jews. The sports ground of the Makkabi Club, at the end of ul. Dietla (close to Mina's street), housed football matches in summer and ice-skating in winter. On state holidays and the Jewish feast of Lag B'omer, the orchestra of the Hebrew school, with its blue-and-white flag, led the entire school into the stadium, where there were exhibitions of gymnastics and other sport events for both boys and girls.[38]

Mina recalled:[39]

> I remember as a child that my brothers took me to the Makkabi ice skating ring. I started to try and skate and I fell down and started to cry. This is my main memory of sport. My youngest brother Izio was a very good sportsman, and he belonged to the Makkabi Club.

A number of reading rooms and Jewish community libraries existed to supplement Jewish education. Films were shown at the Promien picture house, and the Warszawa cinema hall, which was also occasionally used for community meetings. In 1935, the Revisionist Zionist leader, Ze'ev (Vladimir) Jabotinsky, spoke there. The Słowacki Theatre showcased a varied repertoire, mainly light performances and vaudeville, but also plays by Shakespeare and Bernard Shaw, and the Polish classics. A Yiddish language theatre thrived. It put on some original Yiddish plays as well as works translated from Polish, German and English.[40]

There were many Jewish restaurants, bars and famous cafes such as Feniks and Jama Michalika in the Market Square or the Cyganeria on ul. Szpitalna, which also offered music and dancing. Mina's cousin, Henryk Sand, was a violinist who often played at Feniks. Since he lived in Tarnów, he stayed with Mina's family whenever he came to Kraków to perform. Mina recalled his visits with great joy and loved to listen to him practise. She loved violin music all her life. Feniks still operates today as a restaurant and dance venue.[41]

The Jewish press available to Mina and her family consisted of both Yiddish and Polish-language publications. With Polish the dominant language, the main source of information for Kraków Jews was the Polish language newspaper, *Nowy Dziennik*, which reported on events in Poland, Palestine and the wider world. The Yiddish language press was represented by *Dos Yiddishe Vort (The Jewish Word)* and *Di Post (The Post)*. Zionist groups and youth organizations also put out publications, for example Akiva's *Diwrej Akiva (The Sayings of Akiva)* and *Ceirim (Youth)*, the latter usually published in Polish, with short sections in Hebrew.[42]

Mina recalled:[43]

> On a personal level, I didn't experience much antisemitism. Maybe there was a little bit of jealousy from my fellow students because I was a very good student. My neighbours' children were friendly with me because I would help them with their homework. And if we couldn't understand our mathematics lessons, my father was always there to help us.
>
> I do remember one incident when I was very little. I was out with my brothers when somebody threw a rock at us, which hit me on the head. It was a terrible injury and I bled badly. My brothers were terrified that I was going to die. I still have the scar.
>
> I did notice a lot of things that I didn't like: the treatment of other girls, the treatment of other Jews. We were always

afraid that somebody might attack us. But whenever I was going home from Akiva, I had my brother Izio as my protector. He was always waiting to walk me home. He was a good sportsman, so he wasn't afraid.

By the late 1890s, as many as 20 percent of students at the Jagiellonian University in Kraków were Jewish. There were also Jewish university professors. Despite their numbers, however, discrimination and violence were becoming part of university life. There were restrictions on the number of Jewish students who could be admitted to the various faculties (the 'numerus clausus') and this restricted what courses Jewish students could undertake. Once they enrolled, they often faced outright hostility, and there was violence directed at them from fraternities associated with the far right. The situation deteriorated further following Hitler's rise to power in 1933, and with the introduction of a 'seating ghetto'. Ghetto ławkowe (ghetto benches) was a form of official segregation in the seating of students in Polish universities, beginning in 1935 at Lwów Polytechnic and adopted by most other universities by 1937. Under this system, Jewish students were forced, under threat of expulsion, to sit at the left-hand side of the lecture halls in a section reserved for them. This official policy of enforced segregation was often accompanied by acts of violence directed against Jewish students.[44]

The most dangerous periods were the so-called 'autumn manoeuvres' at the start of each new academic year. For days and sometimes weeks, there were antisemitic demonstrations outside the University. The Endeks (members of a far right National Democratic Party), attacked anyone who looked like a Jew, both men and women, using clubs, knuckledusters and razor blades concealed in their palms. Their opponents fought back and running skirmishes took place around the Planty Gardens.[45]

MINA & JACOB

Mina recalled:[46]

> When my brothers and cousin attended the University, they had a fight on their hands. They were taunted and called Yids. And then came an order that Jews would have to sit separately. We were all depressed about this. My brother came home and said: 'Can you imagine that we even have to sit separately, somewhere else?' They started to feel as if they were in a ghetto.
>
> My cousin Henryk Sand was a very muscular young man and he wore a large signet ring. On one occasion, when the antisemitic students, the Endeks, started to attack Jewish students, my brothers were reluctant to fight. But this cousin stood up to them. He said: 'Do you think because I'm a Jew that I'm afraid of you?' Once he hit them with the hand on which he wore his ring—and blood flowed. After that, because they were sitting together, my brothers with my cousin, nobody attacked or abused them.

In the early to mid-1930s, Jewish students weren't the only ones targeted. There were calls for economic boycotts of Jewish businesses and restrictions of their civil liberties increased. There were also numbers of bombings of Jewish institutions. The buildings that housed the Association of Jewish Trade Unions and the editorial offices of *Nowy Dziennik* were two of those attacked.[47]

Despite this threatening atmosphere, the Jewish community continued to flourish and was a strong presence in the city. Jews owned factories, businesses and shops throughout Kraków. On ul. Floriańska, in the heart of the Market Square, there were many fashionable Jewish-owned boutiques, high-end china and porcelain shops and art galleries.[48] A second-hand book market owned by Jews stood on ul. Szpitalna. At the beginning of each school year, crowds of students enjoyed buying, selling and bartering old books for new.[49]

The bustling markets of Kazimierz provided the colour and atmosphere; the theatres, cafes and libraries the intellectual stimuli; and the Planty Gardens encircling the city were a peaceful place in which to stroll on warm summer evenings. Mina recalled with great pleasure many afternoons and summer evenings with her friends or family in the Planty.

Soon Mina's family's life of relative peace and prosperity was to change. On 28 October 1938, Polish Jews residing in Germany were ordered to leave.[50]

Mina recalled:[51]

> In 1938 a very close friend of my father came to visit us. He told us 'after so many years in Germany, we have to leave: whoever was born in Poland will be deported back to Poland.' He spent the whole night talking with my parents. We in Poland didn't have any idea of the extent of what was going on elsewhere. The friend told my father about the book that Hitler had written, *Mein Kampf*, and described his ideology.
>
> When the friend left, my father said: 'I heard what is going on and what Hitler is prepared to do with us.'
>
> My parents considered preparing a hiding place should Nazi forces invade. Many families started building hollow double walls to hide in. My father was a realist, but also a proud Jew. He said: 'A Jew should take pride in standing up and not hiding. Besides, it's useless. If they find your hiding place, they will torture and kill you.'
>
> So the only thing we did in preparation was to buy some gold coins, which later on helped me a lot. We also stored all our belongings, our clothes, fur coats and many other

valuables, including family photo albums, with our neighbours, a Polish Christian family. My mother thought that afterwards, we would be able to come back and collect our things. We knew these neighbours well, since we had lived in the same building with them for many years, and we trusted them.

Film director Roman Polanski wrote of this period:[52]

Once while my father and I were strolling in the Planty, we came across a hawker selling prints which, when folded in a certain way, transformed the faces of four men into the likeness of a pig. My father told me that the cartoons were of Hitler, Himmler, Goebbels and Göring. This was symptomatic of a new tension in the air, of fears that war was imminent. All over town, novel forms of activity could be observed: trenches were dug in the Planty and windows and store-fronts criss-crossed with adhesive anti-blast paper.

At the outbreak of World War II, the Jewish population of Kraków was over 60,000, almost a quarter of the total, in a city of which they had been an integral part for seven centuries. They had played an important role in the city's development, contributing not only to its flourishing commercial life, but also to its reputation as a cultural and intellectual centre.[53]

Mina's pre-war years were lived in an atmosphere of love and protection: a home full of warmth, vibrant conversation, laughter and music. Outside she went happily to school, sang in the choir, participated in activities with her Akiva friends and siblings; took trips to the country to visit relatives, and strolled through the Market Square window-shopping with her girlfriends. She dreamed of a bright future.

MINA & JACOB

Mina recalled:[54]

I was seventeen, almost eighteen in 1939 when the War broke out. Before then, because I was the youngest, my brothers and sister had spoiled and protected me. If life was hard before, at least the older children looked after the younger ones. My eldest brother, Mechel, used to remind me how he had mothered me, carried me in his arms and cherished me when I was little. Ours was a very warm and loving family. So when Hitler invaded our country and the Occupation came, I was not prepared for the tragic life to come.

MINA & JACOB

Top: (l-r) Mina's grandfather Jonah Laub, father Moses and mother Eidel Sand.
Centre: (l-r) Mina's brother Wolf, sister Freüda and brother Izaak.
Bottom: The earliest existing photograph of Mina, 15 August 1940 and
(right) 1929 Kańczuga Business Directory. Kańczuga, 2010.

MINA & JACOB

Mina's Family Tree: Sand (Kańczuga) and Laub (Dynów)

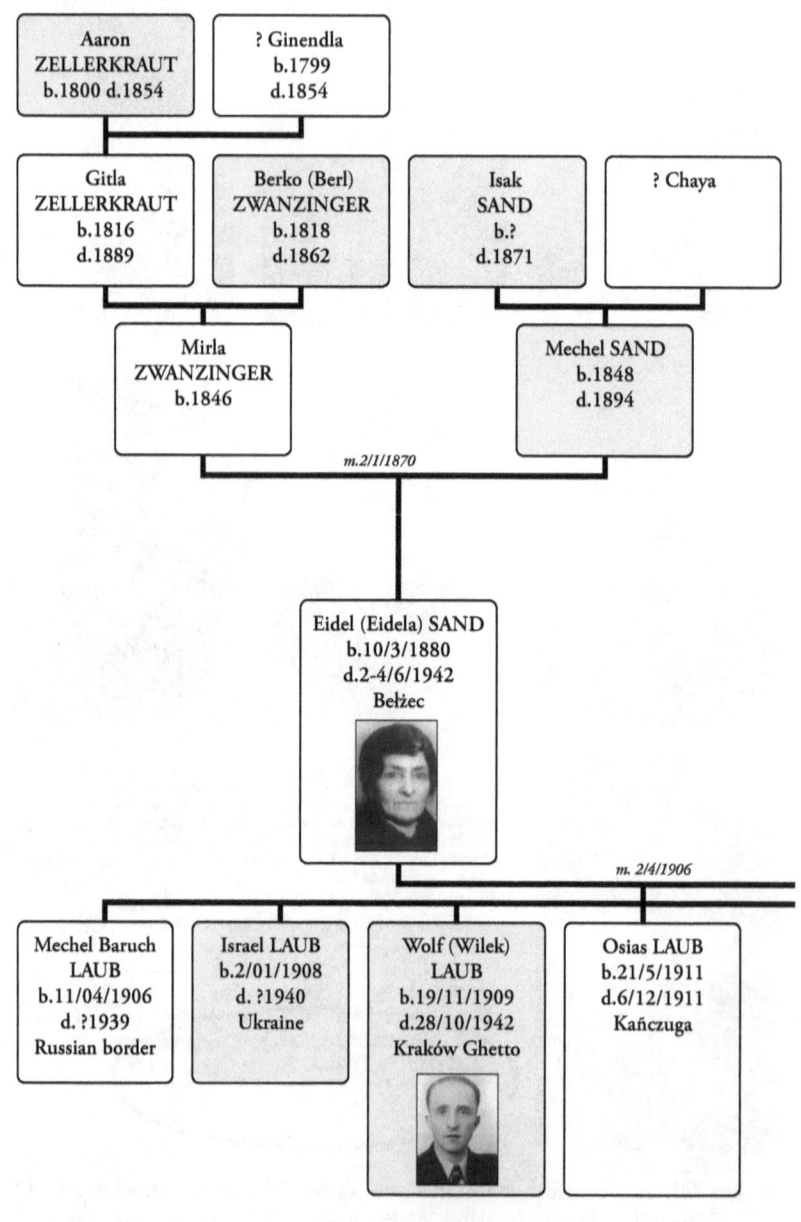

MINA & JACOB

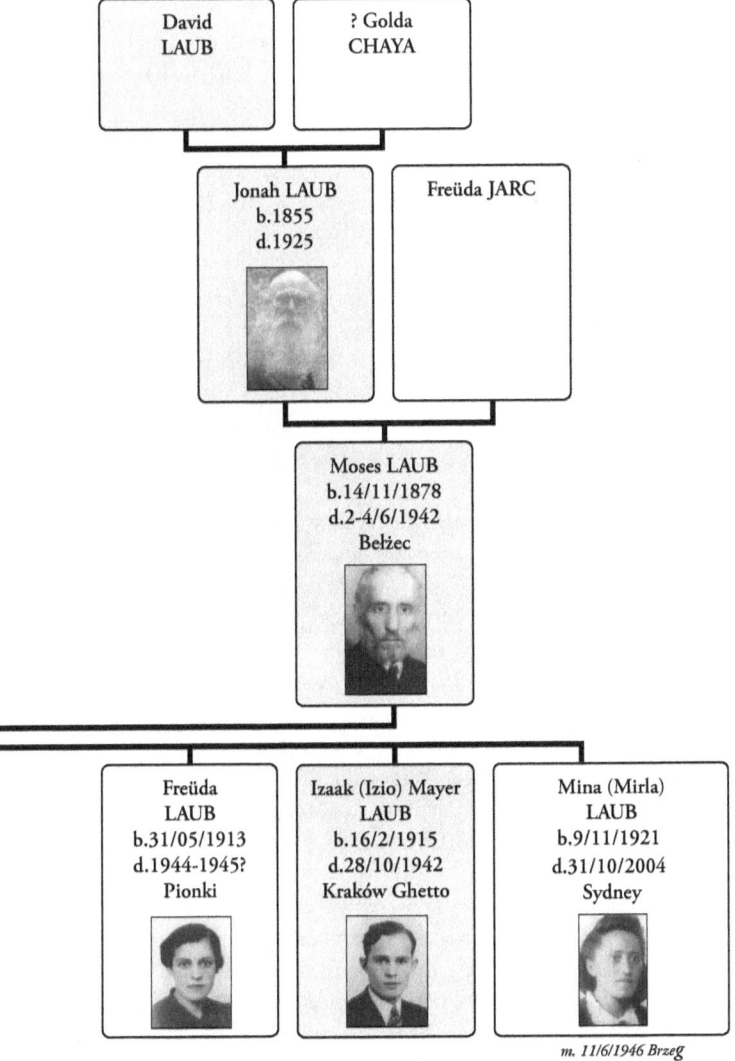

m. 11/6/1946 Brzeg

Notes

1. Norman Davies, *God's Playground: A History of Poland* (New York: Oxford University Press, 2005), Vol. 2, 102, 105; Zbigniew Fras, *Galicja* (Wrocław: Wydawnictwo Dolnośląskie, 2002), 6, 8, 19
2. Fras, *Galicja*, 58, 67; Davies, *God's Playground*, 104, 105
3. Davies, *God's Playground*, 2, 106
4. Davies, *God's Playground*, 114
5. Davies, *God's Playground*, 116, 117; voice recording, Galician Museum, Kraków, Poland, 2010; Edmund de Waal, *The Hare with Amber Eyes: A Hidden Inheritance* (London: Vintage Books, 2010), 200
6. Fras, *Galicja*, 58; 75-76; 210-11; Ruth Ellen Gruber, *Upon the Doorposts of Thy House* (New York: John Wiley & Sons, 1994), 268; Celia Heller, *On the Edge of Destruction: Jews of Poland between the Two Wars* (New York: Columbia University Press, 1977), 30, 31
7. Fras, *Galicja*, 214, 215
8. Fras, *Galicja*, 215; Saul Friedländer, *When Memory Comes* (New York: Farrar, Straus and Giroux, 1979), 5
9. Fras, *Galicja*, 215 75-77; voice recording, Galician Museum; de Waal, *The Hare with Amber Eyes*, 118; Kazimierz Bańburski, et al., *Żydzi w Tarnowie: Świat którego nie ma* (The Jews of Tarnów: A World which no longer Exists), (Tarnów: Muzeum Okręgowe w Tarnowie, 2003) (Museum in the Round in Tarnów), 21
10. http://www.dynow.pl/lf-4.html; Mieczysław Krasnopoloski, and Grzegorz Szajnik, *Dynów w okresie drugiej wojny światowej* (Dynów during World War II), (Kraków: CLICO, 2006), 7
11. http://en.wikipedia.org/wiki/Ka%C5%84czuga; http://www.kanczuga.pl/asp/pl_start.asp?typ=14&menu=36&strona=1
12. Shmuel Spector, ed., *The Encyclopedia of Jewish Life: Before and During the Holocaust* (New York: New York University Press, 2001), 348-49
13. Seymour Feiler, interview with Freda Widawski, 2012, Oklahoma City, USA
14. Eliot Feiler, interview with Freda Widawski, 2012, Oklahoma City, USA
15. Rejestra Mieszkanców Gminy Dynów (Register of the Residents of Dynów) Miejska Biblioteka Publiczna w Dynowie (Regional Public Library), Dynów, Vol. 1, 85
16. http://kehilalinks.jewishgen.org/kolbuszowa/kanczuga/Kanczuga35.html
17. Lucjan Dobroszycki, and Barbara Kirshenblatt-Gimblett, *Image Before My Eyes: A Photographic History of Jewish Life in Poland, 1864-1939* (New York: Schocken Books, 1977), 299, Table 1; voice recording, Galician Museum, 2010, Kraków Poland; Bańburski, *Żydzi w Tarnowie*, 5, 7-8, 16-17, 19-22, 25

18 Voice recording, Galician Museum; Bańburski *Żydzi w Tarnowie*, 34-35
19 Bańburski, *Żydzi w Tarnowie*, 32-33
20 Dobroszycki, *Image Before My Eyes*, 259, Table 1; Galician Museum; Bańburski, *Żydzi w Tarnowie*, 34
21 Jack Kugelmass, and Jonathan Boyarin, *From a Ruined Garden: The Memorial Books of Polish Jewry*, (New York: Schocken Books, 1983), 266; Gruber, *Upon the Doorposts*, 191-92
22 Michael Moran, *A Country in the Moon: Travels in Search of the Heart of Poland*, (London: Granta Books, 2009), 167-68, 170; Gruber, *Upon the Doorposts*, 192
23 Moran, *A Country in the Moon*, 178; Gruber, *Upon the Doorposts*, 192-93; www.jewishvirtuallibrary.org/jsource/vjw/Cracow.html; Martin Sean, *Jewish Life in Cracow 1918-39*, (London, Portland: Vallentine Mitchell, 2004), 31
24 Simon Wiesenthal, *Every Day Remembrance Day*, (New York: H. Holt, 1987), 90; www.jewishvirtuallibrary.org/jsource/vjw/Cracow.html
25 www.jewishvirtuallibrary.org/jsource/vjw/Cracow.html; Wiesenthal, *Every Day Remembrance Day*, 142; Dobroszycki, *Image Before My Eyes*, 50; http://www.yivoencyclopedia.org/article.aspx/Krakow/Krakow_before_1795
26 Gruber, *Upon the Doorposts*, 194, 203-04, 211-12; www.jewishvirtuallibrary.org/jsource/vjw/Cracow.html; Dobroszycki, *Image Before My Eyes*, 50; Kugelmass, *From a Ruined Garden*, 266
27 Martin, *Jewish Life in Cracow*, 31, 48-49; International Cultural Centre, *Świat przed katastrofą* (A World before a Catastrophe) (Kraków: 2007), 12, 62; voice recording, Galician Museum
28 Voice recording, Galician Museum; Martin, *Jewish Life in Cracow*, 10, 48-49; International Cultural Centre, *Świat przed katastrofą*, 62, 127
29 Mina Widawski, nee Laub, audio testimony for the *12th Hour Project of Oral Testimonies* (Sydney: Australian Institute for Holocaust Studies, 1990); video testimony (Sydney: USC Shoah Foundation Institute, 1995), code 2526
30 Mina Widawski, *12th Hour Project*, USC Shoah Foundation, code 2526
31 Ibid.
32 Martin, *Jewish Life in Cracow*, 186-87; International Cultural Centre, *Świat przed katastrofą*, 50, 71
33 Martin, *Jewish Life in Cracow*, 37-39; International Cultural Centre, *Świat przed katastrofą*, 37, 57-58; Gruber, *Upon the Doorposts*, 194, 203-04, 211-12
34 Rafael F. Scharf, *Poland what have I to do with thee?* (London; Portland: Vallentine Mitchell, 1998) 57, 66; Martin, *Jewish Life in Cracow*, 43, 197
35 Mina Widawski, *12th Hour Project*, USC Shoah Foundation, code 2526
36 International Cultural Centre, *Świat przed katastrofą*, 77
37 Mina Widawski, *12th Hour Project*, USC Shoah Foundation, code 2526

38 Martin, *Jewish Life in Cracow*, 209; International Cultural Centre, *Świat przed katastrofą*, 50
39 Mina Widawski, *12th Hour Project*, USC Shoah Foundation, code 2526
40 International Cultural Centre, *Świat przed katastrofą*, 60; Martin, *Jewish Life in Cracow*, 111, 209-12; 222
41 Scharf, *Poland what have I to do with thee?*, 25-26; Scharf, *Kraków—Blessed its Memory*, contained in Stanisław Markowski, *Krakowski Kazimierz: Dzielnica Żydowska 1870-1988* (*Kraków's Kazimierz: Jewish Suburbs 1870-1988*) (Kraków: Wydawnicwo ARKA, 1992), 10; International Cultural Centre, *Świat przed katastrofą*, 62; http://feniksklub.com
42 Scharf, *Poland what have I to do with thee?* 28; Martin, *Jewish Life in Cracow*, 21, 54, 57, 69, 97
43 Mina Widawski, *12th Hour Project*, USC Shoah Foundation, code 2526
44 Voice recording, Galician Museum; David Crowe, *Oskar Schindler* (Boulder: Westview Press, 2004), 88; https://en.wikipedia.org/wiki/Ghetto_benches
45 International Cultural Centre, *Świat przed katastrofą*, 63-64
46 Mina Widawski, *12th Hour Project*, USC Shoah Foundation, code 2526
47 International Cultural Centre, *Świat przed katastrofą*, 63-64; Martin, *Jewish Life in Cracow*, 86
48 International Cultural Centre, *Świat przed katastrofą*, 60
49 Scharf, *Kraków—Blessed its Memory*, 10-11; International Cultural Centre, *Świat przed katastrofą*, 59
50 Gerald Reitlinger, *Chronology of the Final Solution, the Attempt to Exterminate the Jews of Europe, 1939-1945* (London: Vallentine Mitchell, 1953), 568-80
51 Mina Widawski, *12th Hour Project*, USC Shoah Foundation, code 2526
52 Roman Polanski, *Roman* (New York: William Marrow and Company, 1984), 7
53 Moran, *A Country in the Moon*, 178; Gruber, *Upon the Doorposts*, 192-93; Israel Gutman, ed., *Encyclopedia of the Holocaust* (New York: Macmillan, 1990), 830; Polanski, *Roman*, 12
54 Mina Widawski, *12th Hour Project*, USC Shoah Foundation, code 2526

PART 2

The War Years

The German Partition of Poland 1939/41-1945

1939-40

Invasion

Following the annexation of Austria and Czechoslovakia, Nazi Germany set its sights on Poland. Hitler's Foreign Minister, Ribbentrop, raised territorial demands with regards to Gdańsk (Danzig) and the Polish Corridor.[1]

At 4.45am on 1 September 1939, the first shot was fired in Gdańsk and German armies moved into Poland. Their aircraft bombed Polish cities and warships bombarded naval installations and dockyards on the Polish-Baltic Coast. In response, Britain and France declared war on Germany on 3 September 1939, but provided no military aid to the Poles. On 6 September, Warsaw Radio announced the removal of the government to the east.[2]

On 17 September, in accordance with the Molotov-Ribbentrop treaty, the Soviet Army invaded Poland from the east and the Polish government fled to England. Poland surrendered on 27 September 1939.[3]

World War II had begun.

Notes

1. Walter Laqueur and Richard Brietman, *Breaking the Silence* (New York: Simon and Schuster, 1986), 58; Joanna Wiszniewicz, *A jednak czasem miewam sny: historia pewnej samotności* (And yet, at times I have dreams: a history of a certain loneliness) (Wołowiec: Wydawnictwo Czarne, 2009), 26
2. David Crowe, *Oskar Schindler* (Boulder: Westview Press, 2004), 69; Martin Gilbert, *Never Again: A History of the Holocaust* (London: HarperCollins Illustrated, 2002), 49; *Apocalypse: The Rise of Hitler* (Sydney: SBS TV, 29 November 2015); Wiszniewicz, *A jednak czasem miewam sny*, 26
3. Gilbert, *Never Again*, 50, 52-53; Malvina Graf, *The Kraków Ghetto and the Płaszów Camp Remembered* (Tallahassee: Florida State University Press, 1989), 8

3
Occupied Wieruszów

On the eve of World War II, some 2,400 Jews lived in Wieruszów.[1] Jacob recalled:[2]

> A week before the War broke out there were already rumours that the Germans were going to invade Poland. At that time the country wasn't like now, where everybody has a TV. In my whole town before the War there were two radios! One of them was owned by the guy who operated the cinema. The entire town came out to listen to the radio broadcasts. We heard the chief of the Army say: 'Yes, we are at war.' So whoever could ran away.
>
> Wieruszów was very close to the German border. The furthest border was about eighteen kilometres away and the closest only about nine kilometres. The War started on 1 September 1939 and the Germans walked into my town on the 2nd.

In the pre-dawn hours of 1 September, the citizens of Wieruszów were woken by the thunderous sound of bombing and artillery fire hitting nearby Wieluń. Wieruszów also came under heavy fire. The bridge over the Prosna River was blown up, the residents ordered to leave, and the town set on fire. Many Jews fled, among them Jacob and his friend Max Procel.[3]

Jacob recalled:[4]

By the time the Germans invaded my town I had already run away to Warsaw, approximately 220 kilometres from Wieruszów. I was a young boy and I ran with a few other boys from my town. My mother wanted me to run away, although she stayed behind. The elderly people stayed. They said: 'Where will we run? But you kids go!' I took only the clothes on my back. Nothing else.

I walked the whole way and there were a lot of other people walking on the roads too, running away from the front. Half of these were killed by the Germans flying overhead and shooting from their planes, because they were walking with the soldiers of the Polish Army, who were retreating.

When I got to Warsaw, I had nowhere to go. Thousands of people were on the run from towns in the surrounding districts, all coming into Warsaw. I slept in the cinema. I was there till 25 September, when the Germans took Warsaw. This was about three weeks later. The Germans bombarded the city with heavy artillery and thousands of people were killed. There was no food; there was no running water. If you wanted water you had to go down to the Wisła River with a bucket. And many were killed by shrapnel while carrying buckets of water.

The cinema in which I was staying was in the Jewish quarter, where later the Ghetto was established. One day I left the cinema and went into town, and there I met a Polish guy from Wieruszów. 'Jacob, what are you doing here?' he asked me. 'What am I doing? I'm dying.' He said to me 'I can't give you bread because we haven't got bread ourselves.

But come with me.' He was one of the cooks for the Army and he gave me half a bag of rice. In the block next to the cinema lived a Jewish family. So I went to them and said: 'Can you let me cook a little bit of rice?' The wife gave me water and allowed me to use her stove and I gave her some rice in exchange. For eight days I at least ate some cooked rice and that's how I survived.

Then one day, around midday, I met a Jewish friend from my town. He asked me where I was staying. I told him: 'I'm just here on the corner, in Leśnia, in that cinema.' He said: 'What are you doing there by yourself, among the Christians? There are a lot of Jewish people in the Twarda Synagogue. [The Zalman and Ryfka Nożyk Synagogue was the largest in Warsaw before the War.] Come there.' So, I said: 'All right—I'll come this afternoon.' An hour later, however, we heard that a bomb had fallen on the synagogue and my friend had been blinded. I said to myself: 'Oh my God, look how he saved me! If I had gone there, maybe I would no longer be alive.' A lot of people were killed there.

When the Germans occupied Warsaw, I thought: it's time to return home. But it wasn't as easy as that. The Germans were already catching people for labour, particularly Jews. My home district of Poznań belonged to Germany before World War I, and many of Poznań's people were half-German. Even in Wieruszów there were Volksdeutsche (ethnic Germans) and many people who were familiar with the German language. So, when the Wehrmacht (German Army) stopped us on the road and asked for our work papers, I said that I didn't have any documents: I was just a boy. They asked me: 'Where are you from?' I told them in German that I was from Poznań. If I was from Poznań, I must be half-German—so they let me go! They didn't know who I was. The first question they had asked was: 'Who are you—Pole or Jew?' If you told them you were a Jew, they took you away. They kept captured Jews on the outskirts of Warsaw for another couple of weeks doing forced labour, before they let them go. Their parents didn't know what had happened to them. They thought they had been killed.

I made it back home—another 220 kilometres, mostly on foot. Sometimes if I was lucky, I got a lift from a farmer who was going from one town to another on his horse, but mostly I walked. So I arrived home on foot.

Max Procel recalled his family's experience:[5]

We ran away—the whole family. We even took my grandmother, who was ninety-four years old. She walked with us up to Pabianice, some 120 kilometres away.[6] When we got there, she said: 'You're running—but the Germans are behind us. I want to go home because Rosh Hashanah (Jewish New Year) and Yom Kippur (Day of Atonement) are coming, and I want to go to shul. So we went back. Many of the non-Jews in the town were Volksdeutsche and they yelled out to the Germans: 'Here is a Jew!'

Thousands jammed the roads escaping from the capital. On Monday 25 September at six in the morning, the bombardment of Warsaw began. Two days later it was over. Poland had surrendered.[7]

On 28 September 1939, the Soviet Union and Nazi Germany divided Poland between them. The Soviets took control of Belarus, Ukraine and Lithuania in the east, while western and central Poland, with a population of some twenty-two million, came under German

rule.⁸ The territories occupied by Germany were divided into two parts:
1. The Wartheland, territories in the west which included the province of Poznań. Almost the entire Łódź province (including the cities of Łódź, Katowice and Jacob's Wieruszów) were annexed into the Reich. Around 385,000 Jews lived in this area.⁹
2. The rest of the country was to be organized as a protectorate under German administration, the *Generalgouvernement* or General Government for the Occupied Areas of Poland, with Hans Frank as Governor-General and headquarters in Kraków. The territory of the *Generalgouvernement* would serve primarily as a source of forced labour, as well as a dumping ground for Poles and Jews. Millions were deported from neighbouring states such as Romania and Ukraine to the *Generalgouvernement*. Its total area covered some 95,743 square kilometres, with a population of around twelve million, of whom approximately two million were Jews.¹⁰

This division of Poland altered age-old patterns of Jewish settlement and uprooted ancient Jewish communities. Some 330,000 Jews, one-tenth of the Jews in Poland, became homeless refugees.¹¹

Hitler's two major goals when he unleashed the War were world domination via the Thousand-Year Reich, and the destruction of the Jews. This linkage of the Jews with the War not only exploited existing antisemitic prejudice, but also provided him with a dynamic, messianic purpose. The second goal fed the first. The plunder of Jewish property following their forcible deportation financed Germany's War effort, and the expropriation of industries and infrastructure in occupied Poland, including coal mines, munitions factories and power stations, provided the material. Jewish forced labour serviced these stolen assets.

In the very first days of the invasion, German troops entering

Polish towns subjected the Jews to similar patterns of violent bullying: kicking, cutting off the beards of orthodox Jews, severe beatings and murder. Each day saw new executions with thousands killed during the invasion and immediately afterwards.[12]

This pattern was repeated in Wieruszów, where some twenty-four Jews were rounded up and executed in the first days of the Nazi occupation.

Zenon Szacfajer recalled:[13]

> Immediately following the entry of the Germans into Wieruszów on 2 September, the persecution of Jews began—they were thrown out of their homes and their properties were seized. From November everybody had to wear a yellow armband; in December they were ordered to wear a Star of David.

Yosef Eisen wrote:[14]

> On 3 September, the SS seized twenty Jews in the frontier town of Wieruszów, took them to the market place and lined them up for execution. When the daughter of Israel Lewi, one of the condemned men, ran up to her father to say farewell, a German ordered her to open her mouth for her supposed impudence, then fired a bullet into it. Then the twenty men were executed.

Houses were burnt down and searches were accompanied by beatings. Shopkeepers were ordered to open their stores, which were plundered by the occupiers as well as the local Poles and Volksdeutsche. Other Jews were rounded up and taken to the railway station, where they witnessed a bonfire of Jewish religious items: prayer shawls, tefillin and holy books. Then nineteen men were taken away to bury the victims of the street murders.

Local Jews were also used for propaganda purposes. For example, some eighty Jewish men with the rabbi at their head, all dressed in religious garb, were loaded on to trucks and photographed beside a sign: 'These are the Jews who shot our soldiers.'[15]

The Germans created a *Judenrat* (Jewish Council) shortly after they entered the town. Its first assignment was to register all Jews. As in Germany after August 1938, the name 'Israel' was attached to every male and 'Sara' to every female on the list.[16]

The *Judenrat* established a Jewish police force and supplied food. They were also required to provide lists of people for forced labour.[17] Unlike in other towns, Wieruszów's *Judenrat* was on the whole respected by the populace, and its *Juden-Alteste* (Chairman) 'enjoyed the confidence of the majority of fellow Jews'.[18]

As the refugees trickled back into town, they were appalled by the scene. Most of their homes had been destroyed, and the remaining population was huddled in the ruins. The persecution of the Jews grew day by day.[19]

Jacob recalled:[20]

> When I got back home, my town was already occupied by the Germans. One-third of the town had been bombed out on Occupation. This was the usual German procedure in Poland, before they marched into any little town, especially those near the border: they bombed it, to destroy the people morally, straight away!
>
> So now I had to think how I could make a living. I was the only breadwinner left at home, since we didn't know where my brothers were. Not only did I have my mother to care for, but also my brother Berek's family: his wife and two children.

First of all, every Jewish person except for children had to go to work every day. Because three-quarters of our town was burned out, the Germans took the Jewish people to clear up the bricks, the rubble. But I registered myself as a tailor, so I only had to do the clean-up work a few hours a day. I did whatever was possible. One way was to use my tailoring skills to barter for food. I knew a lot of local farmers who were willing to exchange a chicken, a bag of potatoes, some eggs or a slab of butter for a pair of trousers. The problem was finding the material to make them.

Our neighbours, the Frankowski family, were very good people. They helped me a lot during the War. Their mother had a fabric shop. Under the German occupation, material was rationed. Every year they allocated a specific amount of fabric for working clothes, and another quota for better clothing which you could not get any more. Everybody had coupons with a number of points. Mrs Frankowski would cut off these points when somebody bought some material from her. She then glued them to a piece of paper and went to Łódź, where she bought more fabric—as much as she could get for the points that she had managed to collect.

Fridays were market days in our town. Her elder son, Zenek, said to me: 'Janek, come to me every Wednesday and help me stick on these points.' As I was helping him, he would slip 100 or so points into my pocket. At first I said to him: 'Zenek what are you doing? Your mother needs these points to buy more material!' He said: 'Don't worry about my mother. You know my mother—she will take half a pig and go to Łódź and buy the material. You take the points, come to my mother, buy some fabric, make some pants for a farmer and you'll get some food. You look after your mother; don't worry about mine.'

MINA & JACOB

Not long after my return I found a job in another village working for a Polish tailor. I worked and lived with him on his family's farm the whole week and just came home to Wieruszów for Shabbat. This was a big help, since I could earn marks and buy food for the family. I lived and worked on that farm and the food was so good and plentiful that after the first couple of months when I went home for Shabbat, my mother thought I was ill, I was so swollen. I had put on weight.

The Polish tailor gave me Sundays off, saying: 'Jacob, if you want to sew trousers for the farmers, you can make money for yourself.' This was very cheap, fast work. I would make eight to ten pairs of these trousers every Sunday and the extra money I earned I would take home to my mother.

I worked for him from 1939 until the beginning of 1941. At one point he said to me: 'Jacob, don't go home. In the end they'll catch you and you'll end up somewhere in a camp. Stay here—and when it gets really bad, I'll try and get you some false papers and you can cross over the German border and find yourself a farm. You will go there as a Pole—and you'll see, you will survive. You will.' The village was only about eight kilometres from the border with Germany and this man knew every corner of it.

But I didn't listen. I couldn't leave my mother and my brother's wife and children. So I went home. Two weeks later I was grabbed by the Germans and taken to Poznań.

Max Procel described what happened to him:[21]

Every day we had to go to work for the Germans, cleaning. Whenever they needed some work, they could take us—they had Jews free of charge! They could take them to do any work they wanted. I was just over eighteen years old at that time.

I was also doing some business with leather which I had learned from my father, until I was send to the labour camp in Poznań.

As the spring of 1941 moved into summer, the Germans began to deport Jews to labour camps in the Poznań area, using the lists drawn up by the *Judenrat*. Among those taken were Jacob and Max.[22]

Top: Invading German forces crossing the Prosna River into Wieruszów.
Bottom: The burned-out Wieruszów synagogue.

Notes

1. United States Holocaust Memorial Museum (USHMM), *Encyclopedia of Camps and Ghettos, 1933-45* (Washington: 2012), Vol. 2, 115; Shmuel Spector, ed., *Encyclopedia of Jewish Life Before and During the Holocaust* (New York: New York University Press, 2001), 1,445
2. Jacob Widawski, transcripts of interviews conducted at the Consulate-General of the Federal Republic of Germany, 1974, 1975, Sydney; transcripts of testimony given at trial against Heinrich Niemeyer, 1978, 1982, 1989, Indictment StA Hannover 11 Js 5/73, Hannover; audio testimony for the *12th Hour Project of Oral Testimonies* (Sydney: Australian Institute for Holocaust Studies, 1990); video testimony (Sydney: USC Shoah Foundation Institute, 1995), code 2528
3. USHMM, *Encyclopedia of Camps and Ghettos*, 115; Guy Miron, ed., *The Yad Vashem Encyclopedia of the Ghettos during the Holocaust* (Jerusalem: Yad Vashem, 2009), 929; Beit Hatfutsot (Museum of the Jewish People) (Tel Aviv, Israel: 1996) Unit Id# 73076
4. Jacob Widawski, testimonies German Consulate-General Sydney; Hannover trial; *12th Hour Project* 1990; USC Shoah Foundation, code 2528
5. Max Procel, video testimony, 1997, Melbourne (USC Shoah Foundation Institute), code 30561
6. https://www.google.com.au/?gws_rd=ssl#q=distance+from+wieruszow+to+pabianice
7. Gwen Edelman, *The Train to Warsaw* (New York: Grove Press, 2014), 50
8. Martin Gilbert, *Never Again: A History of the Holocaust* (London: HarperCollins Illustrated, 2002), 52-53
9. Anna Ziółkowska, *Obozy pracy przymusowej dla Żydów w Wiekopolsce w latach okupacji hitlerowskiej (1941-45)* (Forced Labour Camps for Jews in Wielkopolska during the Years of Nazi Occupation (1941-45) (Poznań: Wydawnictwo Poznańskie (Poznań Publishing), 2005), 20
10. Tadeusz Wroński, *Kronika okupowanego Krakowa* (Chronicle of Occupied Kraków), (Kraków: Wydawnictwo Literackie, 1974), 34, 40; J. Abraham and Hershel Edelheit, eds, *History of the Holocaust: A Handbook and Dictionary* (Boulder: Westview Press, 1994), 241
11. Lucy S. Dawidowicz, *The War against the Jews* (New York: Bantam Books, 1986), 199-200; Jacob Apenszlak, ed., *The Black Book of Polish Jewry: An Account of the Martyrdom of Polish Jewry under the Nazi Occupation* (New York: American Federation for Polish Jews, 1943), 4; Gilbert, *Never Again*, 54-55
12. Apenszlak, *The Black Book*, 4; Gilbert, *Never Again*, 54-55
13. Zenon Szacfajer (Association of Friends of Wieruszów), *70-Rocznica Likwidacji*

Ghetta (70-year Anniversary of the Liquidation of the Ghetto), *Łacznik*, August 2012
14 Gilbert, *Never Again*, 53; Yosef Eisen, *Miraculous Journey: A Complete History of the Jewish People from Creation to the Present* (Jerusalem: Targum Press, 2004), 429
15 Beit Hatfutsot, Unit Id# 73076; USHMM, *Encyclopedia of Camps and Ghettos*, 116
16 Miron, *The Yad Vashem Encyclopedia of the Ghettos*, 929; USHMM, *Encyclopedia of Camps and Ghettos*, 116
17 Beit Hatfutsot, Unit Id# 73076
18 Isaiah Trunk, *Judenrät: The Jewish Councils in Eastern Europe under Nazi Occupation* (New York: Macmillan, 1972), 58-59
19 USHMM, *Encyclopedia of Camps and Ghettos*, 115-16
20 Jacob Widawski, testimonies, German Consulate-General; transcripts, Hannover trial; *12th Hour Project* 1990; USC Shoah Foundation, code 2528
21 Max Procel, testimony, USC Shoah Foundation, code 30561
22 Miron, *The Yad Vashem Encyclopedia of the Ghettos*, 929-30

4
Galicia Invaded

On the eve of World War II, Mina and her immediate family were living in Kraków and her eldest brother, Mechel, in Tarnów with his wife and son. The Sand and Laub families had many relatives in the Galician towns of Tarnów, Dynów and Kańczuga. The occupation of Galicia occurred swiftly, just days after the invasion, and shortly after the occupation of towns in the west of Poland, such as Jacob's Wieruszów. Kraków was occupied on 6 September 1939; Tarnów on the 8th and Dynów and Kańczuga in mid-September. These towns became part of the newly-created *Generalgouvernement*, with their citizens subject to German law.[1]

When the Germans bombed Tarnów on 3 September 1939 Mechel, like many others, fled further east across the Bug River towards Soviet-held territory.[2]

At that time, Tarnów was one of the largest Jewish centres in Poland. Its Jewish community numbered 25,000, or 45 percent of the total population. Immediately following occupation, the Germans confiscated Jewish property, forced Jewish men into slave labour and burned the town's synagogues and prayer houses.[3]

By 24 June 1941, Tarnów's Jews had been forced into a ghetto whose population rose to 40,000 with the inclusion of people from the surrounding area.

The first bloody *Aktion* (or raid) was carried out on 11 June

1942. Those who could prove that they were employed in essential work had their papers stamped accordingly. The others were marked 'for deportation'. Those unable to travel were killed in the Jewish Cemetery. On the 15th, around 6,000 Jews, mostly women, children and the elderly, were shot in the nearby forest and buried in communal graves, while another 10,000 were deported to Bełżec.[4]

Between September and November 1942, a further 6,000 Jews were transported from the ghetto to Bełżec. The liquidation of the Tarnów Ghetto under the command of Amon Göth, commenced on 2 September 1943, with around 3,000 sent to the Płaszów labour camp and 7,000 deported to Auschwitz. The last transport of Jews sent to Auschwitz was on 9 February 1944, after which Tarnów was proclaimed *Juden-rein* (free of Jews).[5]

This is when Mina's family members began to disappear. There are no records of the fate of her brother Mechel and his family, nor of the extended Sand family.

At the beginning of the War, Dynów had a Jewish population of some 1,200. Following Occupation in the second week of September, German soldiers rounded up some 300 Jewish men, marched them out of town and shot them on the edge of the forest.[6]

A favourite SS 'sport' was to lock Jews in a synagogue and set the building on fire, shooting anyone who tried to get out.[7] This was applied in Dynów, where on the second day of Rosh Hashanah, the remaining Jewish men were herded into the Great Synagogue, which was set alight. The men were burned alive, together with all the records—births, deaths and marriages of the Jewish community of Dynów.[8]

In mid-October, the Germans ordered the rest of the Jewish population, mainly women and children, to gather in the main street. From there they were forced across the San River into Soviet-held territory.[9]

After the murder and expulsion of the Jews of Dynów, only a few survived, hidden in surrounding villages. It is not known what happened to members of the extended Laub family, but it may be assumed that they were murdered along with the other Jews of Dynów.[10]

When it was occupied, there were 810 Jews living in Kańczuga.[11] On 18 December 1941, an order was issued forbidding them from leaving their homes and restricting their freedom of movement. In effect, an open ghetto was established, bounded by the town's limits.[12]

Deportations commenced in July 1942, with only those Jews who had been issued with special identity stamps permitted to stay.[13]

The liquidation of Kańczuga's Jewish community took place in a week: between 1-8 August 1942. Most were sent to a transit camp in Pełkinie for 'selection'. Children, the old and the weak were murdered in the forest and 150 able-bodied young were sent to labour camps, with the rest deported to Bełżec. A further 246 Jews were murdered around 12 August at the community cemetery in Siedliczka and buried in a mass grave on the site.[14]

It must be assumed that members of the extended Sand family were killed along with their friends and neighbours from Kańczuga.

Notes

1. David Crowe, *Oskar Schindler* (Boulder: Westview Press, 2004), 95
2. Voice recording, Galician Museum, 2010, Kraków
3. Voice recording, Galician Museum; Kazimierz Bańburski et al., *Żydzi w Tarnowie: Świat którego nie ma* (The Jews of Tarnów: A World which no longer Exists), (Tarnów: Muzeum Okręgowe w Tarnowie (Museum in the Round in Tarnów, 2003), 41-42
4. Miriam and Mordechai Peleg, *Witnesses: Life in Occupied Kraków* (London; New York: Routledge, 1991), 47-48; Bańburski, *Żydzi w Tarnowie*, 55
5. Bańburski, *Żydzi w Tarnowie*, 56-58
6. Mieczysław Krasnopoloski and Grzegorz Szajnik, *Dynów w okresie drugiej wojny światowej* (Dynów during World War II), (Kraków: CLICO, 2006), 23-24
7. Jacob Apenszlak, ed. *The Black book of Polish Jewry: An Account of the Martyrdom of Polish Jewry under the Nazi Occupation* (New York: Roy Publishers, 1943 and 1982), 4; Martin Gilbert, *Never Again: A History of the Holocaust* (London; HarperCollins Illustrated, 2002), 54-55
8. Ministerstwo Sprawidliwości Główna Komisja Badania Zbrodni Hitlerowskich w Polsce (Ministry of Justice Main Commission for the Investigation of German Crimes in Poland), *Rejestr miejsc i factów zbrodni popełnionych przez okópanta Hitlerowskiego na ziemiach Polskich w latach 1939-45: wojewodztwo Przemyskie* (Register of Places and Facts of Crimes committed by Hitler's Occupiers on Polish Soil in the Years 1939-45: Przemyśl district) (Warsaw: 1983), 25; Shmuel Spector, ed., *The Encyclopedia of Jewish Life Before and During the Holocaust* (New York: New York University Press, 2001), 349
9. Krasnopoloski and Szajnik, *Dynów w okresie drugiej wojny światowej*, 29-30
10. Spector, *The Encyclopedia of Jewish Life*, 349; Krasnopoloski and Szajnik, *Dynów w okresie drugiej wojny światowej*, 29-30; 43-44
11. The United States Holocaust Memorial Museum *Encyclopedia of Camps and Ghettos* 1933-45 (Washington: 2012), 521; Spector, *The Encyclopedia of Jewish Life*, 594
12. USHMM, *Encyclopedia of Camps and Ghettos*, 521
13. USHMM, *Encyclopedia of Camps and Ghettos*, 522
14. Spector, *The Encyclopedia of Jewish Life*, 594; USHMM, *Encyclopedia of Camps and Ghettos*, 522

5
Occupied Kraków

Kraków, as one of the major Polish cities with a Jewish population of some 60,000, was targeted at the beginning of the War.[1] By 5 September 1939, the Fourteenth Army was on its outskirts and by the following day German units had entered the city. First to arrive were motorized units which blocked the exits of major streets. Around midday, from the west came columns of the Wehrmacht. Immediately, armed foot patrols began moving through the streets. In the afternoon the first proclamations appeared on the walls of the city: immediate surrender of all arms and ammunition; any actions against German troops or sabotage punishable by death; a curfew running from 6.30pm to 5am.[2]

Mina recalled:[3]

> When the Germans invaded Kraków on 6 September 1939, the Poles themselves did not know that the invasion would move so quickly, so I don't think they were prepared. We had a pact with Great Britain and France, but they all stood by. Nobody came to help us. When the Germans invaded it was a tremendous shock for everybody. And with the invasion, everything stopped: our social life, studies—everything.

On 8 September, General Gerd von Rundstedt was given the title of Military Governor and Hans Frank installed as the General Governeur of Occupied Poland, charged by Hitler to 'exploit the Occupied land without mercy'. The *Generalgouvernement* had been established.[4]

Within the first few months of occupation, Germans introduced laws affecting all aspects of Jewish life. Jewish businesses had to display the Star of David and by November 1939, all Jews had to wear an armband with this distinctive symbol. Jews were forbidden to sell or move their assets; accounts held in financial institutions were frozen; schools closed; ritual slaughter prohibited; and Jewish places of worship ransacked and ultimately destroyed.[5]

The Kraków *Judenrat* was established, with Dr Marek Bieberstein appointed its head. In addition to administrative responsibilities, it worked with the Ordungsdienst (OD) (Jewish police) to keep order in Jewish neighbourhoods. On 10 October new registration cards were introduced, marked with a yellow stripe. Between 8-21 of November 1939, all Jews aged 18-55 were required to register with the *Judenrat*, and 68,482 Jews did so. The purpose of this was to have a comprehensive list of those available for forced labour, in line with Hans Frank's decree of 26 October that a pool of forced labourers be instantly available.[6]

On 6 November 1939, the same day that the *Krakauer Zeitung* (*Kraków Newspaper*) began publication, 183 university professors were arrested, including a number of Jews. They were loaded on to trucks and transported to Germany.[7]

Meanwhile German soldiers harassed and humiliated religious Jews, shaving their beards and yanking out their hair with their hands, often to the amusement of passers-by.[8]

Mina recalled:[9]

One day I went with my father to visit a cousin, and while crossing the bridge on our way back from Podgórze to Kraków, we witnessed German soldiers cutting the beards off Jewish men they had caught.

Another bad day was when they burned the Great Synagogue in Kraków. It was an ordinary morning and many people were inside, praying. The Germans brought with them another group of Jews from the neighbourhood, swelling the numbers. The SS opened the Ark of the Covenant, the Torah and ordered the rabbi to 'spit on the scrolls of the Ark. Spit on this.' When he refused, they beat him up. One secular man also refused to spit. So they shot him first. In the massacre which followed, everyone else was shot.

By 6 December 1939, German soldiers had sealed off the entire Jewish area of Kazimierz. Valuables were pillaged house to house. Numerous people were killed, most shot in the street. By 1 January 1940, Jews were forbidden, on penalty of death, to change or move out of their places of residence. In effect this made it impossible for them to leave the city.[10]

From 24 January 1940, Jews were forbidden to travel by rail in the *Generalgouvernement*. Trams were segregated, and Jews could ride only in the section clearly marked 'Für Juden' (For Jews).[11]

Miriam Peleg-Mariańska wrote:[12]

> Kraków in the winter of 1939-40. The children of my cousin had been expelled from their Polish school. Certain streets and places were 'forbidden' to us—for example, the Market Square, the Planty Gardens, and Sukienice (the Clothiers' Hall). The Jews had to leave the pavement and step into the road when a German approached.

Mina recalled:[13]

> From September 1939 until the beginning of 1941, we still lived in our flat on Jasna Street, in Stradom. It was a very hard time; we lived in fear and uncertainty. My brothers had stopped studying and everybody was working, trying to earn a living. We managed to save a little bit of money and bought a few gold coins for our future needs, in case the Germans changed the currency. During this time my sister Freüda and I were working as dressmakers, learning the trade as we went, earning a little. I was eighteen years old.
>
> There was a lot of hoarding and panic buying, with people stocking up on basic provisions. Luckily for us, my father worked as an accountant in the flour mill, so we had an ample supply of flour. If there was a shortage of bread, we could bake it ourselves. My mother even took a small container of flour around our neighbours, because shortages of basic food items were starting to bite. People couldn't work, private enterprises were few, and shops started to close down. The hardships had begun.
>
> During that first year of the War, I didn't personally experience antisemitism.
>
> Everybody was preoccupied with their own lives, with how to make ends meet.
>
> They sold valuables and tried to prepare for the uncertain future.

Between late August and early September 1939, many Jews left the city. Weighed down with whatever they could carry, they rode or walked east, towards Lwów and Lublin. Some of them crossed the San River into the Soviet Union, while others went to Romania and

Hungary. But around 80 percent returned to Kraków in the first week.[14]

Mina recalled:[15]

> During that first year of the War, my two youngest brothers, Wolf and Izaak, ran away from Kraków. They were part of a group of young men, fellow students, one of whom had a car—which was a great luxury at that time. The group packed into the car like sardines, but only got about twenty kilometres from Kraków before they were stopped by the Germans and the car confiscated. So they came back home.
>
> At the same time my oldest brother, Mechel, who was working as the accountant in a Tarnów mill, ran away with his boss towards the Bug River. Somebody denounced them as rich, so they were caught by the Russians. All communication with them stopped. We did not know where they were or what had happened to them. They must have been murdered.
>
> My middle brother, Israel, also ran away. He wrote us a letter saying that the Germans had caught him and put him in a labour camp. 'My dear parents, my legs are swollen, my hands are swollen and I am suffering from hunger and lack of water.' Then his letters stopped. That was the last we heard from him.
>
> So my two brothers, Mechel and Israel, were lost in the early months of the Occupation.

From 6 March 1940, Jewish physicians, dentists, dental technicians and midwives were limited to treating only Jewish patients. At around the same time, from March to July, registration of men for work was undertaken, and 73 percent of the Jewish male population of Kraków was registered.[16]

By mid-1940, Kraków's Jewish community had been stripped of most of its legal, employment and property rights.[17]

Although shops had reopened, there were great shortages and a black market flourished, with inflated prices for basic goods. Some assistance was provided by the Towarzystwo Ochrony Zdrowia or TOZ (Society for the Protection of Health), funded by the American Jewish Joint Distribution Committee (JDC or Joint), as well as the *Judenrat*. Together they operated a number of medical facilities, cared for orphans, and set up soup kitchens for the thousands of refugees who flooded into Kraków. By the end of May, basic food items such as sugar, eggs, potatoes and meat were rationed and could only be purchased using coupons. A distinction was made between the amount allocated to Poles and Jews: for example, 200 grams of meat was allowed for Poles, compared with 100 grams for Jews.[18]

On April 1940, Hans Frank stated:[19]

> The Jews don't interest me at all. Whether they have anything to eat or not is for me the last priority. The Poles are a different category, as I may need them. The Poles interest me only in so far as I see in them a reservoir of labour.

Alexander Bieberstein wrote:[20]

> The pauperisation of Kraków Jews escalated, particularly amongst pensioners, the infirm, the unemployed. The Jewish Council applied a special tax on the residents, to support the kitchens and shelters. In October 1939 there were only a handful of soup kitchens; by the spring of 1940, their number reached fifty.

An atmosphere of fear pervaded Kraków. Karolina Lanckorońska wrote:[21]

> On 3 May 1940, Kraków was severely shaken by a wave of arrests. A large number of young men were seized on the streets, in pubs, cafes and the railway station. I heard for the first time a word that came to figure so largely in everyone's vocabulary: *Łapanka* (roundup).

Jews from the surrounding areas flooded into Kraków, swelling the numbers to some 68,000. On 18 May 1940, Hans Frank ordered the 'voluntary departure' of all Jews by 15 August. Some 15,000, deemed to have essential skills, would be allowed to stay. Those who left voluntarily were told they could choose their new place of settlement and take their personal possessions with them. Those who did not leave would be expelled. The *Judenrat* was to make sure that all Kraków Jews complied with this order.[22]

A notice signed by Dr Bieberstein as head of the *Judenrat* appeared in the first issue of the new Jewish newspaper *Gazeta Żydowska* (*Jewish Newspaper*), published in July 1940:[23]

> **We ask all Jews of Kraków to change their place of residence voluntarily. The permits to travel by train, identity documents and all sorts of information concerning possible reductions can be obtained from the Migration Committee of the Jewish Community.**

By 5 June 1940, the Jewish population of Kraków had dropped to just over 54,000. However, deeming the 'voluntary' exodus inadequate, the Germans began enforced expulsion. On just one day they expelled some 30,000 Jews.[24]

On 15 August 1940, an ID card was introduced for those Jews permitted to stay in the city. A person could remain there only if they were employed and could include the names of their whole family with their application.[25]

Dr Bieberstein tried unsuccessfully to bribe the Germans to allow additional Jews to remain in Kraków. Consequently, he was arrested in September 1940 and sent to Auschwitz.[26]

Mina recalled:[27]

> Then came a deportation order from Hans Frank to clear Kraków and the whole district of Jews. We had received the order to leave and were desperate. We didn't know where to go. But my father had a friend who lived outside the city and he decided we would move there. We took with us only small packages. Towards the end of 1940, we moved to a flat in Górka Narodowa, on the outskirts of Kraków. We stayed there about six months, until March 1941, when the order came to move to the Ghetto.

On 7 January 1941 a decree was issued requiring all Jews aged over sixteen to spend twelve days clearing the streets of snow. The ID card was to be stamped by the *Judenrat* as proof of people having fulfilled this requirement. Without the required twelve stamps, it could be confiscated and the holder deported from Kraków. On 4 February, the card was replaced with the *Kennkarte*, which was only issued to those whose previous document showed they had fulfilled this work quota.[28]

From 27 February 1941, the only Jews allowed to remain in Kraków were those with the *Kennkarte*. To ensure compliance, street raids were common. Homes were also ransacked and Jews without the correct documentation were taken away.[29]

On 3 March 1941 a thirteen-point ordinance appeared in the *Krakauer Zeitung* (*Kraków Newspaper*) announcing the creation of the Jüdischer Wohnbezirk (Kraków Jewish Residential District or Ghetto), in the suburb of Podgórze.[30]

By 20 March 1941, when all the remaining Jews of Kraków, between 12-15,000, had to move into the Ghetto, more than 41,000 had left the city, either voluntarily or forcibly expelled.[31]

MINA & JACOB

JÜDISCHE GEMEINDE
KRAKAU — SKAWINERGASSE Nr. 2

PROTOKOLL

ŻYDOWSKI INSTYTUT HISTORYCZNY w POLSCE
ARCHIWUM
00-090 Warszawa, ul. Tłomackie ... aufgenommen am _15/VIII_ _____ 1940.

In der Kanzlei der jüdischen Gemeinde in Krakau erscheinen: _____
Laub Mina aus _Kraków_
derzeit wohnhaft in Krakau _Krasickiego 26_ und die Zeugen:

a) _Laub Frenda_ _____ von Beruf _____
wohnhaft in Krakau _Krasickiego 6_ ausgewiesen durch
Personalausweis, Kraków
_Nr 64/L/39_
und
b) _Finger Jetty_ _____ von Beruf _____
wohnhaft in Krakau _Garbarska 4_ ausgewiesen durch
Personalausweis, Kraków
_Nr 6636/38_

Beruf _Schneiderin_ aus _Kraków_
derzeit wohnhaft in Krakau _Krasickiego 26_
zuständig nach _____ ist uns persönlich bekannt.
Wir Bestätigen die Personengleichheit obiger Person mit untenstehendem Lichtbilde.
Obiges erklären wir, zwecks Erteilung eines Personalausweises von seiten der Jüdischen Gemeinde in Krakau in An... des (der) Genannten von Krakau nach _____
Die Richtigke... wir durch unsere eigenhändigen Unterschriften:

Laub. Frenda
Als Zeuge

Finger Jetty
Als Zeuge

Mina Laub
Antragsteller

Mina's ID card, as well as those for her siblings Izaak Mayer, Wolf and Freüda, show that the family was living in Kraków on 15 August 1940.[32]

MINA & JACOB

> Su
> 20775
>
> 133.
>
> An den
> **Beauftragten des Distriktschefs für die Stadt Krakau**
>
> Krakau
>
> Ich bitte um Ausstellung einer Kennkarte für Juden und um Einweisung in den Judenwohnbezirk Krakau
>
> Name: *Laub*
> (bei Ehefrauen Geburtsname):
> Vorname: *Mina*
> Staatsbürgerschaft: *Polnische*
> Erlernter Beruf: *Damenschneiderin*
> Derzeit ausgeübter Beruf: *Damenschneiderin*
> selbständig — ~~unselbständig~~
> Ledig — ~~verheiratet~~ — ~~verwitwet~~ — ~~geschieden~~
> Wohnhaft in: *Górka Narodowa* ←
> Strasse: Nr. *16*
>
> Kinder unter 14 Jahren (nur vom Haushaltsvorstand auszufüllen)
>
> | Name | Vorname | Geboren am |
> |---|---|---|
> | | | |
>
> *Laub Mina*
> (Eigenhändige Unterschrift)
>
> *) Nichtzutreffendes durchstreichen.
> Druck: ZKW., Krakau, VIII. 1941. 2889. 10 000
> Archiwum Państwowe w Krakowie

Mina's 1941 application for a Kennkarte gives her place of residence as Górka Narodowa 16. Application forms for her parents and three siblings (Izaak Mayer, Wolf and Freüda), list the same address.[33]

Notes

1. Aleksander Bieberstein, *Zagłada Żydow w Krakowie* (The Extermination of Jews in Kraków), (Kraków: Wydawnictwo Literackie, 1985), 18; Malvina Graf, *The Kraków Ghetto and the Płaszów Camp Remembered* (Tallahassee: Florida State University Press, 1989), 12-13
2. David Crowe, *Oskar Schindler* (Boulder: Westview Press, 2004), 69, 72; Bieberstein, *Zagłada Żydow w Krakowie*, 16; Tadeusz Wroński, *Kronika okupowanego Krakowa* (Chronicle of Occupied Kraków), (Kraków: Wydawnictwo Literackie, 1974), 13
3. Mina Widawski nee Laub, audio testimony for the *12th Hour Project of Oral Testimonies* (Sydney: Australian Institute for Holocaust Studies, 1990); video testimony (Sydney: USC Shoah Foundation Institute, 1995), code 2526
4. Wroński, *Kronika okupowanego Krakowa*, 15, 21
5. Bieberstein, *Zagłada Żydow w Krakowie*, 16-20; Wroński, *Kronika okupowanego Krakowa*, 26-27; Graf, *Kraków Ghetto Remembered*, 9-11
6. Bieberstein, *Zagłada Żydow w Krakowie*, 14, 20; Graf, *Kraków Ghetto Remembered*, 11; Wroński, *Kronika okupowanego Krakowa*, 26, 29, 37
7. Bieberstein, *Zagłada Żydow w Krakowie*, 20-21; Graf, *Kraków Ghetto Remembered*, 17-18
8. Graf, *Kraków Ghetto Remembered*, 12-13
9. Mina Widawski, *12th Hour Project of Oral Testimonies*; USC Shoah Foundation, code 2526
10. Graf, *Kraków Ghetto Remembered*, 16; Bieberstein, *Zagłada Żydow w Krakowie*, 22, 24, 25; Wroński, *Kronika okupowanego Krakowa*, 61, 63
11. Wroński, *Kronika okupowanego Krakowa*, 73, 75; Bieberstein, *Zagłada Żydow w Krakowie*, 28
12. Miriam and Mordechai Peleg, *Witnesses: Life in Occupied Kraków* (London; New York: Routledge, 1991), 5
13. Mina Widawski, *12th Hour Project of Oral Testimonies*; USC Shoah Foundation, code 2526
14. Bieberstein, *Zagłada Żydow w Krakowie*, 11-12
15. Mina Widawski, *12th Hour Project of Oral Testimonies*; USC Shoah Foundation, code 2526
16. Isaiah Trunk, *Judenrat: The Jewish Councils in Eastern Europe under Nazi Occupation* (New York: Macmillan, 1972), 71; Bieberstein, *Zagłada Żydow w Krakowie*, 25
17. Crowe, *Oskar Schindler*, 140
18. Wroński, *Kronika okupowanego Krakowa*, 100-11
19. Wroński, *Kronika okupowanego Krakowa*, 93

20 Bieberstein, *Zagłada Żydow w Krakowie*, 29
21 Karolina Lanckorońska, *Those Who Trespass Against Us: One Woman's War Against the Nazis*, (London: Pimlico, 2005), 41, 44-45
22 Crowe, *Oskar Schindler*, 143; Bieberstein, *Zagłada Żydow w Krakowie*, 32
23 Crowe, *Oskar Schindler*, 143
24 Wroński, *Kronika okupowanego Krakowa*, 101; Crowe, *Oskar Schindler*, 143; Bieberstein, *Zagłada Żydow w Krakowie*, 32
25 Crowe, *Oskar Schindler*, 143-44; Bieberstein, *Zagłada Żydow w Krakowie*, 32-33, 38
26 Bieberstein, *Zagłada Żydow w Krakowie*, 33
27 Mina Widawski, *12th Hour Project of Oral Testimonies*; USC Shoah Foundation, code 2526
28 Crowe, *Oskar Schindler*, 144; Bieberstein, *Zagłada Żydow w Krakowie*, 39
29 Crowe, *Oskar Schindler*, 144; Bieberstein, *Zagłada Żydow w Krakowie*, 40
30 Crowe, *Oskar Schindler*, 144-45
31 Wroński, *Kronika okupowanego Krakowa*, 141; Tadeusz Pankiewicz, *Apteka w Getcie Krakowskim* (Cracow Ghetto Pharmacy), (1st Edition published in Poland, 1947; English translation by Henry Tilles, New York: Holocaust Library, 1987), 1; Bieberstein, *Zagłada Żydow w Krakowie*, 40
32 Archives Poland: Kraków II, StGKr 921
33 Archives Poland: Kraków II Starosta Miasta Krakowa 1939-45 (District Head for Kraków), Microfilm Nr. J-13764; SMKr589; Strona (page) 127 for Eidla Laüb nee Sand; Strona 129 Freüda Laüb; Strona 131 Isaak Mayer Laüb; Strona 133 Mina Laüb; Strona 135 Moses Laüb; Strona 147 Wolf Laüb

1941

The Ghettos

On 23 November 1939, two months after Germany occupied Poland, Hans Frank issued a decree that all Jews twelve years or over must wear a white armband with a blue Jewish star. Then, from the spring of 1940 onwards, a series of ordinances was issued whose purpose was to isolate the Jews from Poles and subject them to special treatment. Thus began the systematic ghettoization of Polish Jewry.[1]

The identification system facilitated the enforcement of residence and restricted movement, enabling the police to pick up any Jew, anywhere, anytime. It also terrified the victims: wearers of the star were exposed, feeling that all eyes were fixed upon them.[2]

District by district, town by town, village by village, all citizens were obliged to register with the Nazi authorities. They were classified as either:

1. Reichsdeutsche, Germans born within the old frontiers of the

Reich
2. Volksdeutsche, ethnic Germans
3. Nichtdeutsche, non-Germans who could prove they had no Jewish ancestry
4. Juden (Jews)

Once classification was complete, segregation could begin. Initially ghettos were established in every town and village. Later Jews were concentrated in regional towns, and at the end were gathered into five major ghettos in the territory of the *Generalgouvernement*.

The first ghetto was established as early as 28 October 1939 in Piotrków Trybunalski, a town about twenty-six kilometres south of Łódź, and the last in 1943.[3]

The formation of ghettos was largely the same everywhere:[4]
1. Selection of an area as the ghetto site, usually set apart from the town in the poorest, most tightly-packed and least-developed slums.
2. Removal of all non-Jews from the area.
3. Moving Jews who had lived in other parts of the city, its suburbs and outlying villages, into the ghetto. No Jew was permitted to remain outside its boundaries.
4. Once the movement was completed, the area was sealed off and traffic diverted.

The day people were moved into a ghetto was everywhere a day of lamentation, a nightmare. Long processions of weary men and women, babies in their arms, children at their sides, carrying bags and sacks, with bedrolls on their backs or around their necks were the victims. The miserable remnants of their belongings were loaded on carts, wheelbarrows or other makeshift conveyances. They were pushed and shoved, screaming and groaning, into the ghettos.[5]

A council of Jewish elders, the *Judenrat*, was established in each ghetto. It was responsible for the registration of the Jewish population and its property; the supply of forced labour, registration for work camps and deportation; and administration of the ghetto: food supplies, housing, industry, health and police.[6]

A person was selected as *der Juden-Alteste* or Eldest of the Jews. His task was to receive German orders and ensure that they were carried out to the letter. His authority replaced all other Jewish institutions, which were deemed illegal.[7]

Most ghettos were guarded from the outside by the Schutzpolizei (regular uniformed police), who reported to the Gestapo, while the Jewish Police were used to maintain order within the walls. They were also responsible for rounding up those listed for deportation.[8]

Many Jews refused to serve in the Jewish Police. Some enrolled, however, hoping this would protect them and their families from persecution. In the end, along with the *Judenrat*, they met the same fate as their fellow Jews. When, in line with Heinrich Himmler's decree of 19 July 1942, ghettos started to be liquidated and their inmates sent to death or slave labour camps, they were included.[9]

Although initially envisaged as no more than temporary holding places until their inhabitants could be deported, some of the larger ghettos, such as Łódź and Warsaw, offered such great opportunities for profit and corruption that their Nazi administrators did not want to dissolve them. Accordingly, they were liquidated much later: Kraków on 13 March 1943; Warsaw on 16 May 1943; and Łódź on 7 August 1944.[10]

The smaller ghettos were liquidated in 1942, with some of their residents sent to larger ghettos, but most being executed on the spot or transported to extermination camps.[11]

Notes

1. Raul Hilberg, *The Destruction of the European Jews* (New York: Holmes and Meier, 1985), 58
2. Hilberg, *The Destruction*, 58-59
3. Ian Kershaw, *Fateful Choices: Ten Decisions that changed the World* (London: Allen Lane, 2007), 446; Aleksander Bieberstein, *Zagłada Żydów w Krakowie* (The Extermination of Jews in Kraków) (Kraków: Wydawnictwo Literackie, 1985), 43
4. Hilberg, *The Destruction*, 83-84; Lucy S. Dawidowicz, *The War against the Jews* (New York: Bantam Books, 1986), 206
5. Dawidowicz, *The War against the Jews*, 206
6. Hilberg, *The Destruction*, 87; Isaiah Trunk, *Judenrät: The Jewish Councils in Eastern Europe under Nazi Occupation* (New York: Macmillan, 1972), 44
7. David J. Landau, *Caged: A Story of Jewish Resistance* (Sydney: Pan Macmillan, 1999), 75
8. Lily Brett, *Just Like That* (Chippendale, NSW: Macmillan Australia, 1994), 88-89
9. Kershaw, *Fateful Choices*, 446; Bieberstein, *Zagłada Żydów w Krakowie*, 43; Lawrence L. Langer, ed., *Art from the Ashes* (New York: Oxford University Press, 1995), 155
10. Crowe, *Oskar Schindler*, 193, 195; Eugen Kogon, *The Theory and Practice of Hell: the German Concentration Camps and the System behind Them* (New York, Farrar, Straus & Giroux, 1950), 175; http://www.deathcamps.org/occupation/kielce%20ghetto.html; http://en.wikipedia.org/wiki/Lw%C3%B3w_Ghetto#The_Ghetto
11. Yitzhak Arad, *Bełżec, Sobibor, Treblinka: the Operation Reinhard Death Camps* (Bloomington and Indianapolis, Indiana University Press, 1987), 58

6
The Kraków Ghetto

The site chosen for the Kraków Ghetto was Podgórze, a working class industrial district situated on the southern bank of the Wisła River, across the bridge from the city centre and Kazimierz. A major rail line ran through it, connecting central Kraków with the suburb of Płaszów.[1]

Some 3,500 Polish residents living in Podgórze were relocated to Kazimierz, after it had been emptied of Jews. Excluded from the transfer were major factories and businesses producing goods for the Wehrmacht. The Germans also permitted one other non-Jewish business to remain in Podgórze, Tadeusz Pankiewicz's pharmacy, Pod Orłem (Under the Eagle).[2]

Jews were given a maximum of ten days to move to the Ghetto from other parts of the city, such as Górga Narodowa where Mina and her family had moved in late 1940. If they did not have *Kennkarten*, they had to leave Kraków. German guards were everywhere, constantly checking and rechecking these identity cards.[3]

The forced move into the Ghetto came just before Passover. The Germans often chose Jewish religious holidays to carry out major roundups or deportations, using the period of strict religious observance to catch victims when they were together and unguarded.[4]

MINA & JACOB

Mina recalled of the move to the Ghetto:[5]

> The six of us, my parents, two brothers, my sister and I, were living on the outskirts of Kraków when the order came to return. We entered the Ghetto in March 1941. It was very hard because they concentrated so many people together in such a small area. Kraków was a big city, but the part that they allocated for the Ghetto was small. We moved to Płac Zgody. The name means 'a place or square of agreement', which was ironic, since it was a place where they persecuted and killed people. We were living at Number 4, in the heart of this square. From my windows I could see everything that was going on there.
>
> The day that we entered the Ghetto, people transported whatever they had, on their bikes or in small vehicles—naturally not heavy furniture, just small items and personal belongings. Whatever we could, we took. We were still dressed well, because my father and brothers were still able to earn a living. I carried only my personal garments and some things of my parents', to help them. I sewed for myself a little bag and put inside it scissors, needles and a little bit of cotton. Later these 'tools' helped me a lot. Around my neck I wore a tiny container which I also made by hand, in which I put a couple of gold coins and photos of my whole family. The greatest tragedy for me later was when I was forced to throw away these pictures.

Stella Müller-Madej was a child of eleven when she was taken into the Kraków Ghetto, and one of Schindler's survivors. She wrote about her family's move there:[6]

A lot of people were heading for the Ghetto. Daddy was pushing an ordinary wagon that he had borrowed from the janitor. It was a beautiful sunny day, but no one was smiling about the splendid weather. The whole crowd around us was grey, gloomy and sad.

After Passover, bricklayers began to construct a three-metre high brick wall around the Ghetto. The walls erected were in the form of Jewish tombstones, terrifying symbols.[7]
Roman Polanski recalled:[8]

I saw some men at work on something right across the street. It looked like a barricade. Suddenly it dawned on me: they were walling us in. A main road cut our new metropolis in two. There was a barbed wire fence on either side of this busy thoroughfare. Residents of the Ghetto could watch the traffic go by, just as they themselves could be seen by those who used the road, but the road itself was out of bounds to us, off-limits and inaccessible.

There were three entrances to the Ghetto, guarded by Polish police in navy blue uniforms. The main entrance was from the side of the Podgórze Market Square. Above it was a huge six-pointed Star of David with the inscription Jüdischer Wohnbezirk (Kraków Jewish Residential District or Ghetto). Also located at the main gate was the central post of the German police and the seat of the *Judenrat*. The second gate was at the southeast rear of the ghetto, and the third was at the northeast entrance to Płac Zgody, just before you crossed the Wisła. This entrance was used primarily by Jewish workers fortunate enough to have been issued with permits to work outside the Ghetto.[9]

Kazimierz, the district where Jews had lived in for centuries, was destroyed. Stores closed and the restaurants and synagogues were empty and silent. Podgórze, on the other hand, became a crowded Jewish slum, with disease and hunger constant threats to human life. The Ghetto covered an enclosed area which measured approximately twenty hectares or a quarter of a square kilometre, and consisted of thirty streets and 320 buildings. By the end of 1941, an area which had previously been occupied by some 3,500 Poles housed 18,000 Jews.[10]

The Kraków Ghetto, like most of those located in large centres, was cut off from normal municipal services, which meant the creation of internal administrative machinery to serve the needs of its people and carry out the directives of the German authorities. Departments sprang up for Economic Affairs, the Budget, Labour, Health, Social Welfare and Burial. In all, nineteen departments were established.[11]

The heads of these Departments wielded a great deal of power. For example, the Chiefs of Labour Departments determined who was allocated easier tasks or better paid jobs or, vitally, jobs 'on the outside' where they had opportunities to buy a little food.[12]

The *Judenrat* in Kraków was made up of twenty-four prominent members of the Jewish community, initially headed by Dr Marek Bieberstein. He was replaced by Dr Artur Rosenzweig once the Ghetto was established.[13]

SS officers in charge of the Ghetto included Wilhelm Kunde, Hermann Heinrich and Horst Pilarzik. All of them were experts in the murder of Jews. Pilarzik often singled out Jews for petty reasons and shot them on the spot.[14]

On 5 July 1940, on orders from the Gestapo, the Kraków *Judenrat* organised the Jüdischer Ordnungsdienst (OD), or Jewish Police. Members were nominated by the *Judenrat*, and some of the people attracted to the OD were of dubious character. There were numbers of young men who categorically refused the offer. Mina was always proud of the fact that her brothers refused to join, despite the prospect of benefits to the family.[15]

The OD, headed by Symcha Spira, was responsible for carrying out the orders of the Gestapo, maintaining law and order in the Ghetto; discovering and disclosing any criminal or subversive activities; and accompanying SS men when the need arose. Spira took an active part in every deportation action.[16]

SS-Hauptscharführer Wilhelm Kunde explained why Spira was approved as Head of the OD:[17]

> **The selection was made for psychological reasons. If this position was filled by an intelligent, well-educated man, coming from a different social stratum, he would be lost and completely out of place. He would only make our job more difficult, as was the case with Dr Rosenzweig. Spira could be bought with a new fancy uniform which made him feel superior to the others.**

The OD office also included a jail were Jews were held, in unsanitary conditions, for alleged crimes. From here, they were sent either to the Kraków prison in ul. Montelupich or to Auschwitz.[18]

The Kraków *Judenrat* inherited from the pre-war Jewish community a hospital, two orphanages and an old-age home. Funding for these institutions came from private donations within the community.

A complex network of *Judenrat* organizations and facilities was created. Among the most important were:
1. Jüdische Soziale Selbsthilfe or JSS (Jewish Self-Help Society)
2. Jüdische Unterstützungsstelle or JUS (Jewish Aid Centre) which channelled aid from abroad to Jews in labour camps. It

continued to operate even after the Kraków Ghetto was closed.[19]

3. CENTOS (Federation of Associations for the Care of Orphans).[20]

The orphanage housed some 150 children who had been moved from an attractive sunny environment into cramped quarters. The ever-increasing number of orphaned children and lack of supplies made it increasingly difficult to run this refuge. Despite these difficulties, traditional Friday evenings and entertainments for the children were organized.[21]

Children often arrived on their own in the Ghetto, asking for help. There were also instances of Jewish children from the surrounding towns and villages, being brought in by Poles who had looked after them during the deportations.

Alexander Bieberstein wrote:[22]

I remember that one day they brought a girl to the orphanage who spoke only German. She was the daughter of an SS man and a Jewess, both of whom had died. The girl wore on her coat a swastika, claiming that it was the insignia of every German. She sang German Army songs. It is not surprising that she was unable to connect with the other children, turning away from them, deeming herself to be better.

Overcrowding in the Kraków Ghetto was endemic and getting a family apartment was almost impossible. Yehiel Dinoor wrote: 'The room was bare. The cupboard, the beds—everything had been sold for bread.'[23] Usually two or three families were forced to move into one apartment. Often a room with larger proportions was divided between more than one family, with each person allocated a living area of two square metres. Being constantly together, sharing a kitchen and bathroom with strangers, led to tensions and conflict.[24]

Joseph Bau was a Kraków-born graphic artist, who described the living conditions in the Ghetto:[25]

> **One kitchen served all families so its use had to be scheduled by the hour. A line of impatient people, some unable to contain themselves, always waited outside the toilet.**

Jewish enterprises still functioning in Kraków after 1939 were rapidly liquidated. Markets for the remaining factories and artisans' shops in the Ghetto were cut off by the wall, so that middlemen such as rag pickers had no customers. Jobs outside the Ghetto boundaries were largely lost, and inhabitants were out of work. Some people still had money and could live fairly decently in spite of the constantly rising prices of basic products now available only on the black market. Those who were not as fortunate were forced to sell or exchange jewellery or other possessions just to live day by day.[26]

At the Labour Office set up by the Kraków *Judenrat*, German, Polish and Jewish clerks prepared files on potential workers and assigned people to work outside the Ghetto as required by the German authorities, for example in the armoury. They were supervised by the Wehrmacht.[27]

These workers had their IDs stamped as proof that they were employed. However, frequent changes to the colour of the document meant that even employees of the most important factory were never really safe from deportation.[28]

The average daily food ration provided by the Germans was about 1,100 calories per person. But a working person needs at least 2,000 calories a day. Bread and potatoes were the staples, with potato peelings often substituted. Horsemeat was sometimes available, and fish on occasion. Root vegetables were usually in poor condition. Hunger obsessed everyone.[29]

Joseph Bau wrote:[30]

> Sometimes it was possible to obtain, for a price, a kind of stony loaf we called 'bread'. One winter's morning, at 4am, there was a long line of hungry customers. Hundreds had come and the line kept growing. At last they opened the store, and the first ones in line burst in. There were pitiful cries from people being crushed in the forward surge. The lucky ones clutched loaves of bread. Then the storekeeper pierced the air with a cry: 'That's it—there's no more!' He started to push us outside the store, towards the solid wall of disappointed customers still trying to press ahead.

Jews exercised their ingenuity: producing and preparing food, manufacturing goods for sale, marketing them inside the Ghetto, smuggling them outside. They made something out of nothing. The workers in labour brigades employed outside the Ghetto brought in food obtained by bartering clothing and household goods.[31]

In order to develop a level of economic independence and bring something like normal life to the Ghetto, in the spring of 1941, several bakeries, dairies, cafes, restaurants and other small businesses were allowed to open.[32] In addition, a small number of factories were operating within the Ghetto, owned by Poles and Germans. Optima housed a number of workshops where Jewish craftsmen were employed making shoes and clothing for the Germans.[33]

Mina recalled:[34]

> As soon as we entered the Ghetto, my father ceased to be employed. So we all did what we could to survive. Everybody

had to work. Naturally we were afraid that they would put us to road work or some other hard labour. Whoever could do a bit of embroidery or sewing, even if you weren't a dressmaker or tailor, when you registered for work and they asked: 'What is your profession?' you said 'I'm a dressmaker.' That is what I and my sister told them.

We went to work in a clothing factory which had been built on the site where previously a large chocolate factory called Optima had been located. We were sewing German military uniforms. My brothers worked part-time at whatever they could.

Another well-known factory which employed Jews from the Ghetto was owned by Viennese businessman Julius Madritsch, who had come to Kraków in 1940. He served as a purchasing agent for the Wehrmacht, and at the end of that year opened a sewing factory employing Jewish and Polish workers.[35]

He subsequently managed to get an order for uniforms from the Wehrmacht that qualified his firm as an 'armaments factory'. Because he wanted to create work opportunities for the Ghetto, Madritsch employed several Jews per sewing machine. Two shifts of Jewish workers marched daily from the Ghetto to their workplace in the Madritsch factory.

Jewish women worked there the whole day, with a half-hour break, for which they received tepid soup as 'payment'. Polish women were also employed by Madritsch, working in separate rooms and receiving money payment. This enabled trading between the two groups, the Jewish women bartering goods for a pittance. This meant that food reached the Ghetto.[36]

The main entrance to the Madritsch factory was outside the Ghetto walls and was guarded with special vigilance. Most of the time it was locked, opening only on special occasions. Jewish workers entered by way of an improvised path running through courtyards within the compound.³⁷

Overcrowding and insufficient food, coal and soap in the Ghetto led to the spread of diseases such as typhus, tuberculosis, dysentery and influenza. As far as possible, these were concealed from the Germans. Hospital cases of typhus were recorded as 'elevated fever' or pneumonia. The stricken were treated in their homes in a massive clandestine operation.³⁸

The Ghetto housed the Central Hospital and Hospital for Contagious Diseases, with a couple of smaller centres. In addition to resident Jewish doctors, non-Jewish surgeons came from outside to perform or assist in operations.³⁹

The single pharmacy, Tadeusz Pankiewicz's Pod Orłem, was open even at night. Pankiewicz practically lived in the Ghetto for two-and-a-half years. Located at pl. Zgody 18, directly opposite the Ghetto gate, the pharmacy was an ideal observation point for all deportation actions. Germans and the Jewish police visited it and often shared information with Mr Pankiewicz, which he then used to warn those in danger. The pharmacy also became a meeting place for the Jewish intelligentsia.⁴⁰

Mina recalled:⁴¹

> **We were living very close to the centre of the Ghetto. From our window, I could see everything that was going on. Opposite us was a pharmacy owned by Mr Pankiewicz, who was allowed to keep it open for the benefit of the Germans. But he was also a great friend to the Jews. The pharmacy was open day and night. Injured resistance fighters would come there at night and he would help them. Later he was recognized by Yad Vashem as a 'Righteous Among the Nations', because his actions were unique.**

Despite the ban on education, newspapers and public religious practices, cultural and spiritual life continued within the Ghetto walls. Libraries were established, writers continued to write, painters to paint and orchestras played.[42]

There was even some entertainment in the restaurants, with dancing and performances by local artists. Jews provided the entertainment, but they could never enjoy the performances, for few could afford such luxuries.[43]

Religious life went underground. Three synagogues were secretly established in the Ghetto.[44] Jews in ghettos throughout Poland came to pray in groups in internal rooms facing the courtyard, blinds drawn across the windows. The Kraków community managed to save religious objects from destroyed synagogues, moving 150 copies of the Torah and valuable religious artefacts to a building in ul. Limanowska.

Jews continued to observe Shabbat and the Jewish holidays, although at times they were forced to work during festivals such as Yom Kippur, under threat of severe punishment. In the Ghetto there was also a group of Orthodox youths, named Gerer Chasidim, who studied the Talmud (doctrine), in attics and basements and lived a communal life, helping one another and other people.[45]

Secret schools were opened, with children gathering in private homes for instruction. In many ghettos, kitchens were used as classrooms, the teachers being paid in bread.

Poet, writer and diplomat Czesław Miłosz wrote:[46]

> **I was earning my living in the Ghetto by giving lessons. All the young people were studying. I've never seen people study so much: English, French, Spanish, Hebrew—even Latin and Greek. Many vocabularies and much grammar went up in smoke. But it did help one to remain alive in the Ghetto.**

How can a person memorizing grammar admit to himself that there's no hope?

Mina described her daily life:[47]

> A daily struggle: beatings, humiliation, hunger. It was so crowded that walking in the street you were almost touching one another. The most tragic thing was the suffering of boys and girls—the youth. They were begging for a piece of bread. I couldn't give them any because we didn't have much. We received rations: a bit of bread, veggies—something. But children up to fourteen years old were deprived of any rations; they didn't get anything.
>
> The Ghetto was secured at the top by barbed wire and inside, between the bricks, they inserted pieces of glass, to prevent people from climbing over. But the hunger of the youth was stronger than the danger, and they did it often. Some of them were found dead and there were beatings by the Jewish Police, because they had orders to guard the Ghetto, to keep order. Even if they managed to get through, when they came back, what did they bring? A few potatoes hidden in their pockets or a piece of bread.

Day-to-day brutality continued, with SS men attacking and kicking Jews at random. More and more Jews were beaten at work; often bands of SS men lay in wait at the bridge to torment unsuspecting people returning to the Ghetto.[48]

Later the death penalty became the sole punishment for non-compliance with the Germans' regulations. For example, following the order of 27 December 1941 to give up furs, a thorough search of the Ghetto was undertaken. Whoever did not give up their furs was immediately put to death.[49]

Clandestine anti-German political activity was organized by various youth groups such as the Bund, Poalei Zion, Hashomer Hatzair and Akiva.[50]

A Polish language Jewish newspaper, *Gazeta Żydowska*, was delivered two or three times a week with the permission of the German authorities. Later the Underground published its own gazette.[51]

As the hardship continued, there was the ever-present threat of a sudden raid and selection of people for transport. Germans could enter the apartment of any Jew at any time. Sometimes they would come to steal whatever they saw that struck their fancy; sometimes they came solely for the sake of inflicting pain. Every knock on the door struck a note of terror in the inhabitants.[52]

Outside the Ghetto, normal life went on as usual.

Roman Polanski recalled:[53]

> Some stretches of the Ghetto perimeter were enclosed by a barbed wire fence, not a wall. From one particular position near the fence we could watch the weekly open-air film shows staged by the Germans in Podgórze Square for the inhabitants of Kraków. These included newsreels and anti-Jewish propaganda films. The part of the Ghetto that had no wall, only a fence, was where I now began sneaking out. It was like walking through a mirror and emerging on the other side, entering a different world complete with street-cars and people leading normal lives. Everything seemed sunnier, brighter, brisker, more prosperous. Two other boys came with me and we headed for a shop that sold stamps. The women behind the counter eyed us curiously. 'You boys are from the Ghetto, right? Aren't you taking a bit of a risk?' Being on

the outside was a great adventure, but my experience in the stamp shop showed it to be dangerous as well. It wasn't until I was back inside the Ghetto that I felt entirely safe.

The solidarity of families was the basis of preservation of life in the Ghetto and the Jewish continuity. The extended family was a stronghold, the source of comfort and moral strength, with the young and able-bodied supporting the old and feeble.[54]

Despite all the evidence to the contrary, there were still some Jews who held on to the belief that Britain or the United States would come to their rescue. Others didn't think the War would end soon.[55]

Ultimately, adapting to debilitating, unfamiliar physical conditions, to the habits of strangers and to extensive food shortages and poor sanitation, focused people's energies entirely on minute-to-minute survival.[56]

As a result of persistent under-nourishment, heart, kidneys, liver and spleen shrank in size. Weight dropped and skin withered. Active, busy, energetic people changed into apathetic, sleepy beings. Many fell asleep in bed or collapsed on the street and were dead by the following morning.

The Jewish community of Kraków and throughout Poland was dying.[57]

Top: Mina in front of 4 Płac Zgody, where the family lived in the Kraków Ghetto. Photo 1994.
Bottom: The building that housed the Optima factory. Photo 2010.

Notes

1. Malvina Graf, *The Kraków Ghetto and the Płaszów Camp Remembered* (Tallahassee: Florida State University Press, 1989), 35-36; David Crowe, *Oskar Schindler* (Boulder: Westview Press, 2004), 112
2. Crowe, *Oskar Schindler*, 146; Aleksander Bieberstein, *Zagłada Żydow w Krakowie* (The Extermination of Jews in Kraków) (Kraków: Wydawnictwo Literackie, 1985), 42; Isaiah Trunk, *Judenrät: The Jewish Councils in Eastern Europe under Nazi Occupation* (New York: Macmillan, 1972), 72
3. Graf, The *Kraków Ghetto Remembered*, 35-36
4. Crowe, *Oskar Schindler*, 147
5. Mina Widawski nee Laub, audio testimony for the *12th Hour Project of Oral Testimonies* (Sydney: Australian Institute for Holocaust Studies, 1990); video testimony (Sydney: USC Shoah Foundation Institute, 1995), code 2526
6. Stella Müller-Madej, *A Girl from Schindler's List*, extract contained in Crowe, *Oskar Schindler*, 147
7. Lucy S. Dawidowicz, *The War against the Jews* (New York: Bantam Books, 1986), 206
8. Roman Polanski, *Roman* (New York: William Morrow and Company, 1984), 13-15
9. Tadeusz Pankiewicz, *Apteka w Getcie Krakowskim* (Cracow Ghetto Pharmacy), first edition published in Poland, 1947, English translation by Henry Tilles (New York: Holocaust Library, 1987), 4; Crowe, *Oskar Schindler*, 148
10. Graf, The *Kraków Ghetto Remembered*, 36; Israel Gutman, ed., *Encyclopedia of the Holocaust* (New York: Macmillan, 1990), 831; James M. Glass, *Jewish Resistance during the Holocaust: Moral Uses of Violence and Will* (New York: Palgrave Macmillan, 2004), 125; Crowe, *Oskar Schindler*, 146; ARC main page Kraków Ghetto; www.deathcamps.org; https://www.google.com.au/?gws_rd=ssl#q=convert+20+hectares+to+kilometers
11. Rafael F. Scharf, *Poland what have I to do with thee?* (London; Portland: Vallentine Mitchell, 1998), 135; Abraham Lewin, *A Cup of Tears: A Diary of the Warsaw Ghetto* (London: Fontana/Collins, 1990), 16; Trunk, *Judenrät*, 44-45, 49, 51-52, 506
12. Trunk, *Judenrät*, 58-59
13. Trunk, *Judenrät*, 440
14. Graf, *The Kraków Ghetto Remembered*, 12; Pankiewicz, *Apteka*, 69
15. Bieberstein, *Zagłada Żydow*, 164-66
16. Graf, *The Kraków Ghetto Remembered*, 39; Crowe, *Oskar Schindler*, 149; Bieberstein, *Zagłada Żydow*, 166-67
17. Pankiewicz, *Apteka*, 136

18 Bieberstein, *Zagłada Żydow*, 165
19 Crowe, *Oskar Schindler*, 149-50
20 Gutman, *Encyclopedia of the Holocaust*, 831
21 Bieberstein, *Zagłada Żydow*, 212
22 Bieberstein, *Zagłada Żydow*, 214-15
23 Katzetnik 135633 (real name Yehiel Dinoor), *House of Dolls* (London: Frederick Muller, 1956), 61
24 Bieberstein, *Zagłada Żydow*, 42
25 Joseph Bau, *Dear God, have you ever gone hungry?* (New York: Arcade Publishing, 1996; English language translation; in Hebrew 1990), 178-80
26 Raul Hilberg, *The Destruction of the European Jews* (New York: Holmes and Meier, 1985), 92; Yehuda Bauer, *A History of the Holocaust* (New York: Franklin Watts, 1982), 170; Graf, The *Kraków Ghetto Remembered*, 57-58
27 Pankiewicz, *Apteka*, 9; Graf, The *Kraków Ghetto Remembered*, 56; Crowe, *Oskar Schindler*, 178
28 J. Abraham and Hershel Edelheit, eds., *History of the Holocaust: A Handbook and Dictionary* (Boulder: Westview Press, 1994), 193
29 Dawidowicz, *The War against the Jews*, 209-12; Martin Gilbert, *Never Again: A History of the Holocaust* (London: HarperCollins Illustrated, 2002), 57, 61
30 Bau, *Dear God, have you ever gone hungry?*, 178-80
31 Dawidowicz, *The War against the Jews*, 209-212; Gilbert, *Never Again*, 57, 61
32 Graf, *The Kraków Ghetto Remembered*, 39-40; Crowe, *Oskar Schindler*, 151-53
33 Graf, *The Kraków Ghetto Remembered*, 56; Crowe, *Oskar Schindler*, 184
34 Mina Widawski, *12th Hour Project of Oral Testimonies*; USC Shoah Foundation, code 2526
35 Crowe, *Oskar Schindler*, 155-156; Bau, *Dear God, have you ever gone hungry?*, 52; http://www.jewishgen.org/yizkor/schindler/sch010.html
36 Ryszard Kotarba, *Niemiecki Obóz w Płaszowie, 1942-1945* (A German Camp in Płaszów 1942-1945) (Warsaw-Kraków: Instytut Pamięci Narodowey [Institute of National Rememberance], 2009), 17
37 Bau, *Dear God, have you ever gone hungry?*, 43
38 Hilberg, *The Destruction of the European Jews*, 94; Bauer, *A History of the Holocaust*, 186; Dawidowicz, *The War against the Jews*, 214-15
39 Pankiewicz, *Apteka*, 63; Graf, *The Kraków Ghetto Remembered*, 49; Trunk, *Judenrät*, 157
40 Bieberstein, *Zagłada Żydow*, 95-96, 98
41 Mina Widawski, *12th Hour Project of Oral Testimonies*; USC Shoah Foundation, code 2526
42 Bauer, *A History of the Holocaust*, 186-94
43 Graf, *The Kraków Ghetto Remembered*, 39-40; Crowe, *Oskar Schindler*, 151-53

44 Bieberstein, *Zagłada Żydow*, 226
45 Elie Wiesel, *Twilight* (New York: Summit Books, English translation 1988), 46; Bieberstein, *Zagłada Żydow*, 222, 224, 226; Trunk, *Judenrät*, 187-88
46 Czesław Miłosz, *The Seizure of Power* (London: Faber & Faber, 1955), 24
47 Mina Widawski, *12th Hour Project of Oral Testimonies*; USC Shoah Foundation, code 2526
48 Graf, *The Kraków Ghetto Remembered*, 39-40; Crowe, *Oskar Schindler*, 151-53; Pankiewicz, *Apteka*, 10-11
49 Graf, *The Kraków Ghetto Remembered*, 42; Pankiewicz, *Apteka*, 13
50 Trunk, *Judenrät*, 536
51 Abraham Lewin, *Diary of the Great Deportation*, contained in Lawrence L. Langer, ed, *Art from the Ashes* (New York: Oxford University Press, 1995), 163
52 Graf, *The Kraków Ghetto Remembered*, 57-58
53 Polanski, *Roman*, 18-19
54 Dawidowicz, *The War against the Jews*, 220
55 Bieberstein, *Zagłada Żydow*, 51-52
56 Glass, *Jewish Resistance*, 125
57 Hilberg, *The Destruction of the European Jews*, 94; Bauer, *A History of the Holocaust*, 186; Dawidowicz, *The War against the Jews*, 214-15

7

The Wieruszów Ghetto

On 13 October 1941, two months after Jacob had been transported and forced into slave labour around Poznań, and six months after Mina had moved into the Kraków Ghetto, the Wieruszów Ghetto was set up. The Jewish population, 2,400 at the start of the War, was within a year reduced to 1,740. A year after that, between 1,200-1,400 Jews were forced into the sealed and severely cramped Ghetto.[1]

Among them were Jacob's mother, Brucha, his younger brother Abram, his sister-in-law Hindy, his nephews and other extended family and close friends. One of these, Issac Pankowski, recalled the move:[2]

> In September 1941 came another proclamation: that all the Jews would have to go to a certain enclosed area, by such and such a date. They had to bring all their belongings. When we went into the square, the Jewish Committee started allocating rooms where you could go. Poles who had lived in this area were moved out, and their empty homes given over, room by room, to the Jews. After we moved in, they fenced off the area.

Sigmund Józefowski recalled:[3]

> I was a child during the War. At that time, we used to fish the Prosna River. We used to pass the Ghetto area when we came up from the riverbank so I saw how the people lived there.
>
> The territory of the Ghetto stretched from ul. Dąbrowskiego, Kilinskiego, Zamkowej and Nadrzeczna through the Rynek (square) then on to ul. Wrocławska, which ran along the bank of the Prosna.
>
> There were two Ghetto gates, one at ul. Kilinskiego and the other one on the other side of the Rynek, at ul. Wrocławska. In that building there was a kosher butcher. There was also a mikva, the Jewish bathhouse. You went down the stairs, and it seemed that the bathhouse water was at the river's level. That area was divided into two chambers. In one chamber the men bathed; in the other the women. We used to look inside, because we were curious about it.

Harry Ezer described life in the Ghetto:[4]

> A typical day living in the Ghetto was very very miserable. It was *gehenem*! (hell). All day long, every day, the Germans searched our homes to see if there was still something left to rob. Then the forced labour. During winter there was not enough clothing, not enough wood, not enough food. It was terrible. The only good thing in this miserable time was that we were still with the family.

The Ghetto was congested, with three to four families living in a space adequate for one. The dwellings were dilapidated, the air fetid and the streets filthy. Toilets, running water, plumbing and sewage facilities, were stretched beyond capacity or repair. In the long, bitterly cold Polish winters, the water in the pipes froze. Staying warm took priority over cleanliness. Fuel was as scarce as disinfectant—and more expensive.[5]

Issac Pankowski recalled:[6]

> From the Ghetto we went out every morning to work. We lived in a tiny room—my parents, sister, little brother and I. My big brother was already in a Poznań camp. From this room there was a passage that led to a second room, where another family lived. The toilets were outside and there was no running water. We took water from the river or hand pump.
>
> I had a friend who worked in a bakery. Every day he took bread from there to a shop where it was sold. He told me that I should go to a place on the way to the shop at a certain time and 'if you steal a loaf of bread, you steal a loaf of bread. If you get caught, you get caught.' And that's what I would do.
>
> The *Judenrat* provided us with coupons. They would also give you kerosene on coupons. There was no electricity in the Ghetto, just kerosene lamps.

All Jews aged between six and sixty, men, women, and children, were ordered to report daily, at 6am, for forced labour. Some worked for German Army units stationed in the area, carrying water, cleaning shoes and boots and sweeping streets. Others were assigned the task of cleaning up the rubble of buildings that had been destroyed. The salvaged bricks were carefully cleaned, sorted, and packed for shipping to Germany.[7]

By the end of 1941 the Jews left in Wieruszów were primarily the sick, the elderly or the very young. Only a few workers whose skills were deemed essential by the local authorities remained.[8]

In line with Himmler's decree that all ghettos be eliminated by the end of 1942, the Wieruszów Ghetto was liquidated between 21-23 August 1942. The *Aktion* was carried out by German police and an SS unit, aided by local German and Latvian collaborators. At the beginning of the operation, healthy males, among them Issac Pankowski, were seized and sent to labour camps in the Poznań area. Issac recalled:[9]

> I stayed in the Ghetto until 1942. After the selection we were taken to the Wieruszów Station and put on a passenger train. We travelled to Wieluń. They didn't tell us where we were going, just that we were going to work. When we got to Wieluń they put us on another train. One German, not a soldier, came and said: 'You are going to work in Poznań.'

The remaining inhabitants of the Ghetto were marched some 200 metres to the grounds of the local Monastery and Church of the Paulites. The evening before, a squad of Germans had entered the Ghetto and murdered eighty-six old, sick people who were unlikely to make it to the Monastery.[10]

Zenon Szacfajer described that day:[11]

> Three truckloads of German soldiers arrived in Wieruszów. They surrounded the whole Ghetto area and undertook a selection. The Jews were told that those who were sick, wounded, or physically impaired in any way should report to the Church and Monastery of the Paulites, so that they could be medically examined. From there they would be sent to Germany for treatment. The mikva was where the eighty-six elderly or sick Jews were executed. They were buried in the grounds of the Jewish Cemetery.

MINA & JACOB

Sigmund Józefowski recalled:[12]

> My sister remembered that on that day all the Poles who lived outside the Ghetto were locked in their houses. They weren't even allowed to look out of their windows.
>
> When the Germans completed their executions, they loaded the dead on to wagons and drove them out of town to the Jewish Cemetery, where they buried them in a mass grave. They loaded them on to simple wagons, the type that you use to carry hay. My cousin remembers that he saw the Germans transport the dead bodies out of town.

In a conversation with Freda in February 1989 at the Jewish Cemetery, Józio Frankowski, Jakob's childhood friend, also described how he saw dead bodies being transported to the cemetery in open wagons. He saw that 'the blood was dripping down'. In fact, he recalled his mother recognizing a familiar dress on one of the victims. Was the victim in fact her close friend and neighbour, Brucha?

From the assembly at the Monastery, 104 men were selected and sent to the Łódź Ghetto for forced labour. The remaining 800-900 people were taken by train to the extermination camp at Chełmno.[13]

A work crew of Jews from Łódź was sent to collect whatever possessions were left in the Wieruszów Ghetto and deliver them to the Germans. The income received from the sale of these items was credited to the Ghetto administration in Łódź. Then the Germans ordered local Poles to give up their own homes and move into the empty Jewish houses.[14]

Jacob's mother, Brucha and his brother Abram, are believed to have been among the eighty-six people killed during the liquidation of the Wieruszów Ghetto. It is likely that his two young nephews

(Berek's sons) and their mother, Hindy, were also killed on that day.

Berek had been taken by the Germans in Wieruszów for forced labour, but he managed to escape, making his way to the Soviet Union, where he lived out the War years.

The fate of Jacob's other brother, Majer, remains unknown. He disappeared from Wieruszów after the invasion. Jacob believed that, like Berek, he was taken for forced labour and died somewhere in or around Częstochowa, where many young men from the Poznań region had been transported.[15]

With the liquidation of the Ghetto, the Jewish community of Wieruszów, which had been part of the town since the fifteenth century, ceased to exist.

One of the streets which formed the Wieruszów Ghetto. Photo 2010.

Notes

1. Zenon Szacfajer, (Association of Friends of Wieruszów), *70-Rocznica Likwidacji Ghetta* (Seventy-Year Anniversary of the Liquidation of the Ghetto), *Łacznik* (Wieruszów: August 2012); The United States Holocaust Memorial Museum, *Encyclopedia of Camps and Ghettos 1933-45* (Washington: 2012) Vol. 3, Pt A, 115; Shmuel Spector, ed., *The Encyclopedia of Jewish Life: Before and During the Holocaust* (New York: New York University Press, 2001), Vol. 3, 1,445; Beit Hatfutsot (Museum of the Jewish People) (Tel Aviv, Israel: 1996) Unit Id# 73076
2. Issac (Yitzah) Pankowski, transcript of oral testimony, 1993 (Jerusalem: Yad Vashem Archives), code 03-7202, V-D 242
3. Sigmund Józefowski, interview with Freda Widawski, Wrocław, 2010
4. Harry Ezer, oral testimony (USHMM, Washington: USC Shoah Foundation Institute, 1997), code 3693-3
5. Lucy S. Dawidowicz, *The War against the Jews* (New York: Bantam Books, 1986), 208-09
6. Pankowski, oral testimony, code 03-7202, V-D 242
7. USHMM, *Encyclopedia of Camps and Ghettos*, 117
8. Ibid.
9. Simon Wiesenthal, *Every Day Remembrance Day* (New York: H. Holt, 1987), 187; Pankowski, oral testimony, code 03-7202, V-D 242
10. Wiesenthal, *Every Day Remembrance Day*, 187
11. Szacfajer, *70-Rocznica Likwidacji Getta*
12. Sigmund Józefowski, interview with Freda Widawski
13. USHMM, *Encyclopedia of Camps and Ghettos*, 117
14. Guy Miron, ed., *The Encyclopedia of the Ghettos during the Holocaust* (Jerusalem: Yad Vashem, 2009), Vol. 2, 930
15. http://en.wikipedia.org/wiki/Cz%C4%99stochowa_massacre

The Camps

The camp system set up by the Nazis consisted of three types: forced labour, concentration and extermination camps. Concentration camps were established in Germany shortly after Hitler's rise to power (for example, Dachau, on 23 March 1933). Their main purpose was the elimination of every trace of opposition to Nazi rule, and also exploitation of prisoners' labour. Up to the outbreak of War, such camps held several types of prisoner: political or religious; 'anti-social' (habitual criminals and homosexuals); and those viewed as racially inferior, primarily Jews and Gypsies.[1]

As Hitler's Army advanced through Europe, the need for armaments as well as reliable roads and railways for the transportation of troops and equipment, escalated. At the same time, Germany's manpower was being diverted to the War effort, resulting in labour shortages. The solution was to use forced labour. In the first half of 1940, open work camps sprang up in Poland, created by the Wehrmacht, police or SS units, construction and road building companies and private firms.[2]

Germany's defeats in Africa and the Soviet Union further depleted its manpower, particularly skilled workers and engineers from armaments factories who had been diverted into the German Army. To fill the gap, Hitler demanded the deployment of concentration camp inmates: prisoners of war and Jewish forced labourers.[3]

These slave labourers were used for the production of armaments, including associated industries such as steel and coal mining; other goods, such as German Army uniforms; in the building and reconstruction of roads and railways; and to maintain agricultural production.[4]

Tens of thousands of camp prisoners were transferred to the armaments industry and to private firms producing components for it.[5] Camp inmates were hired out by the SS, at minimum cost, to military authorities and industrial companies. Private companies such as Krupp, Siemens, I.G. Farbenindustrie, HASAG and Thyssen became the largest exploiters of concentration camp prisoners.[6]

This escalating demand for Jewish labour ran parallel to the decision formulated at the Wannsee Conference of 20 January 1942 for the total destruction of European Jewry.

Those unable to work, the sick, the elderly, children and pregnant women, would be killed *en masse*. Those able to work would be exploited as slave labour, at a minimum cost to the Reich, until they were no longer of use. Physically demanding work for nine, ten and later eleven hours every day and appalling living conditions in the camps including a starvation diet, meant that a prisoner usually survived for only three months.

Concentration and labour camps became places of slow extermination. Selections were not carried out within minutes of arrival, but over days and weeks as prisoners laboured. Those who were incapable of enduring the effort were murdered on the spot or evacuated from the camp to others that absorbed these walking dead.[7]

There were some twenty main concentration camps scattered throughout Europe and six major facilities for the extermination of the Jews, all on Polish territory. The increase in the use of camp labour led to the growth of hundreds of sub-camps, in order to avoid a long trek to work. The growth of satellite camps served as an indicator of the degree to which prisoner labour was used. In 1942, only a small number of such camps existed, but at their peak in 1944 and early 1945, the number of large satellite camps exceeded 500. Some concentration camps operated up to a100 sub-camps, covering large areas where thousands of prisoners were housed and worked.[8]

Of the six extermination camps, those that directly impacted on Jacob's and Mina's families were:

- Chełmno (Kulmhof), the first place in Poland to use gas for mass murder, in mobile vans. Some 40,000 Jews were exterminated there, mostly from the Wartheland and including Wieruszów.[9]
- Bełżec, the first site where static gas chambers were used for extermination of an estimated 600,000 Jews from the Kraków, Galician and Lublin districts.[10]
- Auschwitz, the place that was to become synonymous with the destruction of the Jews. Auschwitz II-Birkenau became the main centre for their extermination. It is estimated that 1.1 million were murdered there.[11]

All the camps were sites of persecution, torture and terror. It is estimated that the total number of prisoners who died from weakness, starvation and disease in the camps during the War was half a million.

Exact numbers of those sent to the camps are not known. However, including the dead in Auschwitz and similar camps, it is reasonable to say that eight to ten million people passed through them during the twelve years of Nazi rule.[12]

MINA & JACOB

Notes

1. Eugen Kogon, *The Theory and Practice of Hell: the German Concentration Camps and the System behind Them* (New York, Farrar, Straus and Giroux, 1950), 20, 22; Raul Hilberg, *The Destruction of the European Jews* (New York: Holmes and Meier, 1985), 222-23; Helmut Krausnick et al., *Anatomy of the SS State* (English translation, London: William Collins, 1968), 450
2. Felicja Karay, *Death Comes in Yellow: Skarżysko-Kamienna Slave Labor Camp* (Amsterdam: Arwood Academic Publishers, 1995), 20
3. Guido Knopp and Peter Hurth, *Hitler's Henchmen* (ZDF 1996, English version SBS TV), disc 1, Albert Speer; Martin Gilbert, *Never Again: A History of the Holocaust* (London: HarperCollins Illustrated, 2002), 78
4. Karay, *Death Comes in Yellow*, 20
5. Daniel Blatman, *The Death Marches: The Final Phase of Nazi Genocide* (Cambridge: Harvard University Press, 2011), 38-39; Daniel Jonah Goldhagen, *Hitler's Willing Executioners: Ordinary Germans and the Holocaust* (London: Little, Brown and Company, 1996), 288
6. Kogon, *The Theory and Practice of Hell*, 96; Robert Gellately, *Backing Hitler: Consent and Coercion in Nazi Germany* (New York: Oxford University Press, 2001), 213; Felicja Karay, *HASAG-Leipzig Slave Labour Camp: the Struggle for Survival told by the Women and their Poetry* (London, Portland: Vallentine Mitchell, 2002), 19; Israel Gutman et al., *Anatomy of the Auschwitz Death Camp* (Bloomington: Indiana University Press, 1994), 45
7. Blatman, *The Death Marches*, 49
8. Gutman et al., *Anatomy of the Auschwitz Death Camp*, 41; Kogon, *The Theory and Practice of Hell*, 94
9. Claude Lanzman, *Shoah: The Complete Text of the Film* (New York: Pantheon Books, 1985), 3; Hilberg, *The Destruction of the European Jews*, 189
10. Rudolf Reder, *Bełżec* (Kraków: Fundacja Judaica (Judaica Foundation), (Auschwitz-Birkenau State Museum, 1999), 81
11. Janusz Nel Siedlecki, Krystyn Olszewski and Tadeusz Borowski, *We were in Auschwitz* (English translation, New York: Welcome Rain Publishers, 2000; first published in Polish in 1946), 3-4; Krausnick et al., *Anatomy of the SS State*, 475; Hilberg, *The Destruction of the European Jews*, 189; Marilyn Harran et al., *The Holocaust Chronicle* (Lincolnwood, Ill.: Publications International, 2000), 394
12. Krausnick et al., *Anatomy of the SS State*, 504

8
The Poznań Camps

Following the invasion of Poland in September 1939, plans had been made to connect the vast network of Germany's highways to Poland. The route was to run from Berlin to Warsaw, via Poznań.[1]

Fritz Todd, who was put in charge of building the highways, was informed that Jews from the Wartheland could be used for their construction. But they needed to be housed and employed separately from other 'free' workers. Based on an estimated ratio of 100-120 people to build one kilometre of highway, that meant that 15-18,000 young men, capable of undertaking hard physical work, would be needed.[2]

At first Jewish prisoners were taken from the Łódź Ghetto, and later from regional towns. During the years 1941-43, until the camps' liquidation in October 1943, it is estimated that at least 10,000-15,000 people were transported to some 140 camps.

These prisoners were exploited not only for the building of the highway, but also in extending railway networks from Germany into Poland, with the possibility of further extension to Moscow. The railways were also to be used for sending to the Reich wealth plundered from Poland, as well as Polish workers, and for transporting Poles and Jews to the *Generalgouvernement*.

The Autobahn (highway) and railway camps which held these forced labourers, like all others in occupied Poland, served also a second purpose: Vernichtung durd Arbeit (extermination through labour).³

The private firms which undertook the various construction projects paid the Reich for the use of Jewish labour. From 13 August 1941, the set rate for prisoner labour was 0.30 Reich Marks (RM) per hour, less than half the usual rate for unskilled labour at that time in Germany. From this, tax was deducted, plus two RM per day for upkeep: accommodation, food and maintaining the camp. The use of Jewish labour clearly offered huge profits for private firms, which they maximized by reducing upkeep expenses to a bare minimum.⁴

The prisoners were generally housed in wooden barracks, assembled on the spot from ready-made wooden pieces and surrounded with double rows of barbed wire. The barracks were divided into several rooms, with far too many prisoners allocated to each, resulting in severe overcrowding. They were fitted with bunks and some were provided with straw mattresses, others not. For covering, each bunk was allocated one blanket (very rarely two), usually flea-invested and torn, which were practically useless in protecting prisoners from the cold, particularly as there was no heating and often the roofs leaked. There was inadequate sanitation and access to water for washing.

The amount and quality of the food given to Jewish workers depended completely on each camp's Commandant. It was generally set at how much was necessary to enable them to continue working. Officially the weekly ration was to consist of 250 grams of horsemeat, 100 grams of fat and two-and-a-quarter kilos of bread. In reality, the prisoners were fed the worst produce, with little or no nutritional value.⁵

The starvation diet and unsanitary conditions led in a short time to infestations of lice, typhus epidemics, tuberculosis and other illnesses. Unless the disease was contagious, nothing was done to protect the prisoners from it. Nor was there attention to work-related injuries. There was little medical care or medicine. Some of the smaller camps shared a doctor, or a paramedic when no doctor was available. These conditions, coupled with the physically exhausting work, meant that it did not take long for most Jewish slave labourers to become not only too weak to work, but even to survive.[6]

On 10 December 1940, the first transport of 638 Jewish prisoners was sent to the Autobahn construction site from the Łódź Ghetto. By 1941 Jews from provincial ghettos and towns in the Wartheland were starting to be deported to the ever-increasing labour camps.[7]

In mid-1941, the *Judenrat* in Wieluń was forced to choose 400 young, strong men, to work on highway building. This transport was sent to the RAB Poggenburg in Żabikowo, close to Poznań. Jacob's prisoner records show that he was part of the transport from Weruschau (Wieruszów), arriving in Poznań in August 1941. From there he was sent to the transit camp of Poggenburg and put to work as a forced labourer in two camps: Kahlfelde (in Gołuski), followed by Guttenbrunn (Kobylepole).[8]

Jacob recalled:[9]

> The Germans gave an order to Wieruszów's Jewish Committee that skilled workers had to assemble at the local high school. Those who did not come would be shot! So we went there, maybe 500 young people. At around 11am we were surrounded by the Gestapo and taken to Wieluń. There we passed a so-called medical inspection 'to see if we were healthy'. There was a Polish doctor who only checked our eyes. If somebody knew him and put a few marks in his pocket, he just screamed out to the Germans 'trachoma' (a contagious eye disease), so the Germans yelled out 'Raus hier.' But I didn't have anybody to pay for me, so I had to go with the transport.

In the evening they loaded us on to regular passenger trains, and we set off. My mother, brother Abram, Berek's wife and children were left behind in Wieruszów. We didn't know our destination, and our families did not know where we were. Around midnight we arrived in Poznań.

The Jews being transported were escorted by a unit of the Security Police who behaved in a brutal way towards the deportees. Transportation was accompanied by beatings and harassment. Most of the deportees were young: Jacob was twenty. Separation from their families and associated fear placed huge psychological strain on them.

Jack Fogel, an inmate of the Poznań Camps, described that fear:[10]

That first night in the camp, when I was fifteen years old, sleeping on the bunk with all those people, I was crying the whole night. I had never been away from home for one night. I never went out on my own; I was always with my parents. And suddenly I was lying there alone. I knew that my family would be worried. Did they know what had happened to me? I didn't say goodbye! That was the most horrible night that I ever had in my life.

Max Procel recalled:[11]

I knew when we were going to leave, because my cousin, who was the president of the Jewish Community at the time, got the instructions from the Gestapo about the transport. Everybody was crying in the family. Nobody talked much—just crying. That was the last time that I saw my family. I never saw them again.

Poggenburg had been established in 1941 as one of the RAB forced labour camps for Jews building the Autobahn. It consisted of specially-constructed wooden barracks housing around 500 prisoners.[12]

Jacob recalled:[13]

> We were transported to Poznań by train and the first camp we were taken to was Poggenburg. This was a transit camp where they brought people from the whole area around Poznań and Łódź even before they started to establish ghettos in 1941. All the camps around Poznań were labour camps. Poggenburg had a German Commandant, but all the guards were Poles, not Germans. We arrived there at night and because it was dark, we did not realize that Poles were guarding our camp. We thought they were the Gestapo because they wore black uniforms. And we were given a big beating there, straight away that night. Straight away!
>
> They said to us: 'You are rats. We will kill you here; you'll not live long here.'

Camp commandants were always German. The link between them and the prisoners was the Head of the *Judenrat*. Guard, and work detail duties were performed primarily by Poles, who were sent to the camp by the local labour office. In addition, the camps were controlled by the local police and Gestapo units. As they worked, Jewish prisoners were supervised by German civilians, who controlled output.[14]

In addition to the guards, the camps had administrative personnel: storemen, clerks and cooks, whose duties included separate preparation of food for the staff and the Polish workers, who were quartered in a different part of the camp. The number of functionaries depended on the size of the camp, with some jobs,

particularly in the smaller camps, performed by the prisoners.[15]
Jacob recalled:[16]

> They built wooden barracks in these camps. There were already people in the camp when we arrived. We stayed there that night, a day and then the next day we all had to assemble in the *Appellplatz* (parade ground). The Commandant of this camp arrived with some 'buyers' who had come to buy 'horses' for work. From the 500 that accompanied me on the transport, they picked out around 300. With me were two of my cousins and some other friends from my town. They marched us out of Żabikowo under armed guard and we walked about six kilometres to another camp, Kahlfelde.
>
> At Kahlfelde we had to build an Autobahn. The highway was planned to go from Berlin through Poznań to Warsaw. There were Jewish people working there and, separated from us, there were free Polish workers, who were paid. When we started to build the highway, we only had to walk about one kilometre, but the further we progressed, the further we had to walk to work. We ended up walking ten kilometres. Working there eight or nine hours, then another two-hour/ten-kilometre march back!
>
> We woke up at 6am, got a cup of black coffee and 250 grams of bread, and with this we marched out to work. We worked with nothing else to eat during the day. After we walked back home to the camp in the evening, we got soup.
>
> The camp had wooden barracks, twenty-six people in each barrack, with two-tiered wooden bunks.
>
> When they took us from Wieruszów, they didn't tell us where we were going. So I was dressed in a little short-sleeved summer shirt, a pair of pants and shoes. Luckily, I had one

little jacket. That's all I had. They didn't give us any clothes. We had to provide our own. So we worked and lived in the clothes that we had arrived in. What could we do? We had to repair them constantly, because if you worked in them, they got torn.

Unlike the concentration camps, there were no uniforms in forced labour camps. Like Jacob, other prisoners had arrived in their own clothes, which were invariably inadequate for this type of work and for seasonal changes. The relentless cold, which the prisoners suffered not only at work but also in their barracks, often led to illness or death.[17]

Clothing worn by Jews was marked on the chest and back with a yellow Star of David. Generally, this was a badge made out of fabric and sewn on to the clothing. The Łódź Ghetto was responsible for distributing these badges, which were manufactured in their workshops. In some cases, the Star of David was provided to the camps by the Poznań Gestapo. Prisoners had to pay 0.10RM for each badge.[18]

Prisoners in the RAB camps were allowed to receive parcels from home. Clothing, food and other items sent by relatives helped many of them to survive, since they traded some of these items for food. To stop this 'illegal' trading, camp authorities often undertook inspections of the barracks, confiscating any items found.[19]

Max Procel recalled:[20]

> The only contact that I had with my family was through my sister, who sent a letter or postcard every day or second day. Once a week she would send me a kilo of food from home to the camp—but no money. Once my mother sent me a parcel and told me in a letter which arrived first: 'I am sending you

a challah (braided bread). Chew it properly.' So I knew that she had hidden something in there, and sure enough I found something hard in my mouth. It was a stone, a diamond, my mother's diamond. That diamond came in very handy later on.

For a while, Jacob also received parcels 'from home'. They were sent anonymously and it wasn't until after the War that he learned that they had been sent by his Polish neighbour and good friend, Zenek Frankowski. Using his contacts in the Polish police, he had been able to locate Jacob.

Jacob recalled:[21]

These Poznań camps, they were the worst that you could imagine. All of them, not only Kahlfelde, but all of them! Here people were suffering, dying from hard work and hunger, beaten every day at work. We had German overseers and Polish meisters, who were called the Vorarbeiter (foremen).

The firm that we were working for was Holzmann. The work was impossible to do in eight hours; that's why people were beaten. Say the width of the highway was seventy metres. We had to clear eight metres a day, at seventy metres in width, digging the grass up to the depth of a shovel: about a metre. Then we had to load that dug-up soil on to trolleys that were run on small-gauge railway lines, and carted away further up the line, where they were emptied on to a large hilltop. The Poles had to clear six metres a day; the Jews eight. This was impossible to do. And in addition, as the work progressed, we had to walk further from the camp.

A week before Yom Kippur, some religious boys from my town went to the German overseer with a request: 'Herr Meister, we have a very important Jewish holiday coming.

Can you let us have the day off, and we'll do an extra metre each day?' He readily agreed. So we did extra every day. It was hard enough to do the eight metres; we did nine. On Yom Kippur as we came out to the fields, the boys started to pray. The overseer came out and said, '*Verdammt Juden!*' (bloody Jews). Take your shovels and start work!' And from that day on we had to make nine metres a day, not eight. This was a killer. We got weaker and weaker and some prisoners couldn't keep up. If the Germans thought that you were trying to shirk work, you wouldn't survive, because you were beaten every day.

I was in Kahlfelde approximately a year-and-a-half. From there, I went on to a few other camps for brief periods, to dismantle the camps which had been liquidated. This was towards the end of 1942. By early 1943, I was already in Guttenbrunn.

Notes

1. *Obozy pracy przymusowej dla Żydów* (Forced Labour Camps for Jews), https://www.zabikowo.eu/historia/obozy-pracy-przymusowej-dla-zydow
2. Anna Ziółkowska, *Obozy pracy przymusowej dla Żydów w Wiekopolsce w latach okupacji hitlerowskiej (1941-45)* (Forced Labour Camps for Jews in Wielkopolska during the Years of Nazi Occupation), (Poznań: Poznań Publishing, Wydawnictwo Poznańskie, 2005), 36-37, 71, 73
3. Ziółkowska, *Obozy pracy*, 7
4. Ziółkowska, *Obozy pracy*, 39
5. Ziółkowska, *Obozy pracy*, 111-12
6. Ziółkowska, *Obozy pracy*, 103
7. Ziółkowska, *Obozy pracy*, 81-82, 86
8. Ziółkowska, *Obozy pracy*, 91

9   Jacob Widawski, transcripts of interviews conducted at the Consulate-General of the Federal Republic of Germany, 1974, 1975, Sydney; transcripts of testimony given at trial against Heinrich Niemeyer, 1978, 1982, 1989, Indictment StA Hannover 11 Js 5/73, Hannover; audio testimony for the *12th Hour Project of Oral Testimonies* (Sydney: Australian Institute for Holocaust Studies, 1990); video testimony, 1995 (Sydney: USC Shoah Foundation Institute), code 2528
10 Jack Fogel, interview with Freda Widawski, Melbourne: 2011
11 Max Procel, video testimony, 1997 (Melbourne: USC Shoah Foundation Institute), code 30561
12 *Obozy pracy przymusowej dla Żydów*, https://www.zabikowo.eu/historia/obozy-pracy-przymusowej-dla-zydow
13 Jacob Widawski, testimonies, German Consulate-General; transcripts, Hannover trial; *12th Hour Project* 1990; USC Shoah Foundation, code 2528
14 Ziółkowska, *Obozy pracy*, 56, 200
15 Ziółkowska, *Obozy pracy*, 33-35, 39
16 Jacob Widawski, testimonies, German Consulate-General; transcripts, Hannover trial; *12th Hour Project*; USC Shoah Foundation, code 2528
17 Ziółkowska, *Obozy pracy*, 134, 139
18 Ziółkowska, *Obozy pracy*, 138
19 Ziółkowska, *Obozy pracy*, 137
20 Max Procel, video testimony, USC Shoah Foundation, code 30561
21 Jacob Widawski, testimonies, German Consulate-General; transcripts, Hannover trial; *12th Hour Project* 1990; USC Shoah Foundation, code 2528

1942

9
The Kraków Ghetto Liquidated

Krystyna Chiger, a child survivor of the Lublin Ghetto, wrote:[1]

> Every day, they were killing Jews, taking Jews, punishing Jews. But when it was a big effort, they gave it a name. They called it *Aktion*.

Selections for slave labour or extermination were carried out intermittently during the life of a ghetto, particularly the larger ones. An *Aktion* consisted of rounding up the ghetto inmates, and dividing them up into:
- *Arbeitsfähig*, those fit for work;
- *Lebensfähig*, those able to survive;
- *Transportunfähig*, those not fit to be transported, who were often killed on the spot.[2]

As early as October 1941, the Germans undertook a number of selections in the Kraków Ghetto, 'in order to reduce the overcrowding'. Its population during the first year of its existence fluctuated between 16,000 and 18,000. Such fluctuations were caused, on the one hand, by the influx of Jews from the surrounding areas as Jewish towns were liquidated, while at the same time people were dying from starvation, being killed inside or transported out of the Ghetto.[3]

During the first raid, in October 1941, 1,000 were deported. Then in November and December of that year, streets and homes were raided, searching for people without *Kennkarten*, for transportation. The roundups and deportations were planned and executed by the Germans with the help of the Jewish Police.[4]

These 1941 deportations were followed by further raids over a number of days in June 1942, during which between 5,000 to 7,000 Jews were deported.[5]

The first roundup occurred on 2 June. The order regarding deportation sounded innocent enough: to ease overcrowding and prevent epidemics, the authorities were 'compelled' to resettle part of the Jewish population. Everyone could take along all they could carry. In the second round, the Germans made searches on the spot, seizing whatever they could. Larger bundles and luggage were generally appropriated at Płac Zgody, and what was left in the houses was pilfered by workmen brought in to clean up. During the third deportation, which took place on June 8, the Ghetto population was subjected to a new selection procedure: new registration papers, the so-called *Blauscheine* (blue cards) were issued. People without these were detained on the spot for deportation. Patients in hospital who could not get up were killed in their beds.[6]

Jews marked for deportation in this third selection gathered in the Optima yard, from where they were taken to the freight train station at Prokocim. After the deportees were marched away, the corpses of those who had been shot in Płac Zgody were piled up. Among the murdered was the famous poet and Yiddish folk-singer, known as 'the bard of the Jewish street', Mordechai Gebirtig. His best-known song *Dos shtetl brent* (*Our town burns*), was written in

1936 after a pogrom in Przytyk, and it called for action. In later years it became the anthem of the ghettos. In another of his poems, as he was forced to leave his home, he said prophetically: 'Farewell, Kraków, farewell.'[7]

Mina recalled:[8]

> In June 1942 came a number of selections. There came an order for all those aged fifty years and above to assemble in Płac Zgody. They were told that they would be relocated to a place in the country, where the work would be easier and they would have good living conditions. My father was at that time aged sixty-four and my mother sixty-two, so they went! There were huge numbers of people over fifty gathered in the square.
>
> The day was extremely hot and these people were made to stand out in the sun for hours and hours until everyone had been counted. The soldiers came out and had a good drink and a laugh. The silence was so depressing: to see how afraid everyone was. We were living on the ground floor, with windows facing on to the square. So as soon as I opened our window curtains, my sister Freüda yelled at me: 'Go away from the window—you'll draw attention to us. The soldiers will come and they'll beat us up if you look out.' I said 'I have to see where our parents are.'
>
> Then Freüda took a bucket of cold water and went out to give them something to drink. A soldier grabbed her. 'Where are you going, dummy, dummy—do you want to join them?' He hit her so hard that blood poured from her nose. She came back crying. She had not been able to reach our parents; she only saw them from afar. This was the first selection in June. The first transport, we later learned, went to Bełżec, the place they sent those 'chosen' for death.

Tadeusz Pankiewicz, the pharmacist, witnessed the scene:[9]

> Płac Zgody filled up slowly with people and their packages, bundles, valises. The searing sun burned; the heat was unbearable. Water was unavailable, and even if it were, it was forbidden to the sufferers. Fear, terror and madness could be seen in their eyes. Spira, with his entire personal staff, ran around like a madman. More new Gestapo men appeared in the Ghetto. Representatives of different military and police divisions and officials of various departments of the city authority appeared. At first the people stood. After a while they sat on the ground on their bundles.
>
> The SS men looked at the turmoil with jeering smiles. Two young fellows, about twenty-six years old, entered the pharmacy. They asked how they could get to the balcony. From the balcony they took photographs to show the world the 'humane' treatment of the deportees by the Germans.
>
> At first slowly, then faster, finally running, constantly being pushed, beaten and driven by Germans howling inarticulately, the crowd left Płac Zgody. In the square, which had been filled with people a short while ago, there remained only packages and bundles, and here and there prayer books wrapped in velvet.

Eyewitness Malvina Graf wrote:[10]

> The transport moved towards Płaszów Station, where trains were already waiting for their human cargo. Each train was made up of an engine car and a long string of freight cars; the people were loaded into the freight cars as if they were cattle. All were crying for water because the day was very hot

and the cars were without windows, making it difficult to breathe. The trains finally moved off, headed for an unknown destination.

Tadeusz Pankiewicz wrote:[11]

Those who remained could not believe that everything they saw had really happened. A terrible night fell, during which few could close their eyes. No one slept. Everyone waited.

The actual destination of the transports was only learned later. Making the rounds initially was the rumour that the deportees were being sent to the Ukraine to work on farms there. After a few months news began to trickle back to the Ghetto regarding the fate of the deportees. For the first-time, names were mentioned: Bełżec, Majdanek, Treblinka. But in spite of everything, the thought of mass murders, gas chambers and crematoria was still inconceivable.[12]

Following the June deportations, the Germans reduced the Ghetto area, even though it still housed a population of 12,000, thus exacerbating the overcrowding. The walls in this portion of the old Ghetto were torn down, and posts with barbed wire installed along its boundaries. Those who had been living in the area which was now outside the Ghetto walls were given until June 25 to resettle within the new boundaries. Individual passes to go outside the Ghetto were no longer available. Jews whose workplaces were outside were taken to and from work in groups, under escort.[13]

After the resettlement, contact between the Ghetto and the Aryan part of Kraków was severed, cutting off any assistance from the Poles, however desperately needed. As a result, food prices rose dramatically. They were at least ten times higher than outside, and life became more difficult. Disease and suicide were rampant.[14]

From 27-28 October 1942, the Germans launched another round of deportations. At 9pm on October 27, units of the German Order Police surrounded the Ghetto. These units were made up of Latvians, Lithuanians and Ukrainians who had volunteered for service with the Nazis. At the same time, the *Judenrat* ordered all Ghetto workers to gather at the main entrance.[15]

The following *Aktion*, with its barbarism, cruelty and bestiality, surpassed everything that Jews had previously endured in the Kraków Ghetto. The selection was done randomly, based on the whims of the German officers. Among the ones who had been rejected were people of all ages: old, middle-aged and young, men and women. Those so designated were then gathered together in Płac Zgody to await transportation. Everyone was crying. There was enormous chaos and confusion.[16]

The SS and the Sonderdienst (German auxiliary or 'special services' police) searched throughout the Ghetto for hidden Jews. Those found hiding were shot on the spot or beaten as they were driven to the collection point.[17]

At noon on 28 October, the Germans went into the Jewish Hospital and shot all the bedridden patients, dragging others outside to be finished off by a 'clean-up crew'. Other patients were shot as they tried to flee. By 5pm, the Germans had completed the roundup and were moving the new deportees to Płaszów Station. They murdered 600 Jews during these two days and sent some 7,000 to Bełżec.[18]

Mina recalled:[19]

> **Now started a very sad time. Because of hunger and malnutrition, an epidemic of typhus spread throughout the Ghetto. A commission of doctors went around inspecting and those found with a high fever were put on the list for the hospital.**

MINA & JACOB

> My two brothers Wolf and Izaak got typhoid. As my sister had to go to work, I stayed at home and nursed them as best as I could, with the little medication that we had. I put cold compresses on their heads and looked after them, because they were afraid to go to the hospital. We knew that the Germans shot sick people on the spot instead of going to the trouble of healing them. They were no longer useful for work, so they were killed. Despite my efforts, eventually they took my brothers to the hospital. I lost them during the October 1942 round of selections—or 'executions'.

Mina never saw her brothers again after they were taken to hospital. It is unclear how they died, since no records exist. Most likely they were shot in the hospital; if not, they were probably transported to Bełżec.

Included in the October 1942 roundup were the children of the Orphanage. They were marched into Płac Zgody for deportation. The Kraków Orphanage, which for eighty years had brought up thousands of worthwhile people, ceased to exist.[20]

The residents of the aged-care home were massacred on the spot. Some were killed in their beds and others dragged out into the courtyard and shot there. The bodies, with some who were simply wounded, were thrown on to platforms and transported to the cemetery in Płaszów.[21]

The October *Aktionen* affected every Jewish family, even those who did not experience loss. The cruelty seemed limitless as did the sorrow. And yet the Ghetto continued to survive: people went to work, shopped, cooked, hoped and prayed.[22]

The first indication of the fate of those transported came when, in November 1942, a letter was received in the Ghetto written by an eye-witness who had travelled from Lwów, passing Bełżec. She described seeing smoke above the treetops, in thick, black, billowing clouds. It was accompanied by a foul stench, the kind of odour that comes from burning flesh. She ended her letter with an appeal to Ghetto residents to run away, before it was too late. But it was already too late. Gone was the illusion of a peaceful life in the east. Now everyone knew what had happened to their families and friends who had been forced on to the transports.[23]

Mina recalled life in the Ghetto after the October deportations:[24]

> My sister and I were working in the Optima factory. After they had taken my brothers to the hospital, I also contracted typhus. I was absolutely terrified. We had learned a brutal lesson from our brothers and I was afraid to go to the hospital. During this typhoid epidemic, the health commission came to our flat. Among them was a Dr Liebeskind who knew and respected my parents very much. He approached my sister and asked her: 'Where are your parents? Where is your big family? You were a big family?' My sister started to cry. 'I lost them all! My parents were taken in the first transport and my brothers have just been killed. The only person left, the only close relative that I have with me, is my younger sister. But she has a fever.' He said: 'I will let her stay home—but remember, don't say a word to anyone. Tell everybody that your sister does not have typhus; she has pneumonia. But if they find out the truth, I will hang.' And he let me stay. He saved my life!
>
> I stayed on with my sister. Freüda was a very brave girl and what she did for me is hard to describe. In the factory, there were Jewish foremen, and she told them the truth. She said: 'I want to save my sister.' They saw that I was on their work list. She carried two *Kennkarten*, hers and mine. When you

came to work, to prove you were there, you checked one. She did that when she came to work and then, going out, she left the second to show that I was working the next shift. This continued for about five or six weeks. Everybody was amazed and wondered how she managed it.

During the day, soldiers patrolled the Ghetto. No one who hasn't been in a ghetto can appreciate the deathly pervading silence, the fear. Every midday, Freüda left the factory with a Jewish policeman who escorted her to our flat. When she unlocked the door, I would be lying there waiting for her, feverish, hungry, afraid. 'Mina, I am here.' She brought me bread, made me tea, bathed me and helped me as much as she could. She would then lock the door again and run back to the factory. She was in grave danger, but somehow, she did it—every day, for six weeks.

Afterwards I had complications. I went out too soon and developed an infection of the bone marrow in my left leg. This was very dangerous for I could not walk properly. We still had a few gold coins which we had purchased before coming to the Ghetto. My sister dug them out and somehow managed to bring in a very prominent doctor from outside. He brought a heating lamp with him which healed my leg a lot. This saved me.

Other news circulating after the October deportations was about the establishment of a camp in the area of the former Jewish cemetery. In November 1942, it was confirmed that a camp was being built in Płaszów for the Jews of Kraków and that the days of the Ghetto were numbered.[25]

People left daily to work constructing the Płaszów Camp. The future Commandant of the camp, Amon Göth, pushed the men to work faster, constantly threatening to shoot those who slowed down. He harassed the *Judenrat*, threatening severe penalties for negligence in executing orders. Workers who left each day frequently did not return at night, but were billeted in the camp.[26]

In December 1942, the *Kennkarte* was replaced with the *Judenkarte*. Each Jewish worker leaving the Ghetto also had to wear a large triangular patch on their outer clothing, indicating where they were assigned—for example 'W' for Wehrmacht.[27]

The Ghetto was subdivided into two sections: Ghetto A for the employed, while the unemployed and elderly were to occupy Ghetto B. The SS also used Ghetto B as a dumping place for another 2,000 Jews displaced from surrounding areas.[28]

Each section of the Ghetto was sealed off. All that remained of the former Kraków Ghetto was an area of four square blocks, in all less than half its original size.[29]

In Ghetto A, a day care centre, the Tagesheim, was set up for children whose parents left the Ghetto to go to work. They were of various ages and some were homeless, with unknown names and backgrounds. To protect them from being deported, Tagesheim children worked: they sealed envelopes or wove baskets. A Kinderheim (children's home) was also organized in Ghetto B.[30]

Then came the terrible winter of 1942-43. In the Ghetto there was a pervasive sense of sadness and hopelessness, as people realized that they, too, would soon have to leave.[31]

In Płaszów, people worked feverishly to finish building the barracks. Workers had already been living there since November 1942, housed in temporary barracks. Day by day the Ghetto population shrank, as transports of people were relocated to Płaszów.[32]

Mina recalled:³³

> Towards the end of 1942 I was on the list to go to the labour camp in Płaszów, to work in Madrisch factory, which was being moved from the Ghetto. My sister was not on the list. The march from Kraków to Płaszów was eight kilometres and, although my leg was a lot better, she knew I could not possibly go with this transport. So she exchanged our names and went instead of me. I stayed with other friends in the flat and continued to work at Optima.

By early 1943, the Ghetto had been closed off, concealed from the view of the people outside. A notice was posted ordering all Jews into the barracks in Płaszów.³⁴

Life in the Ghetto became more nerve-wracking as everyone sensed its imminent liquidation. Jews sold whatever they could, realizing that they would need money. Almost every day someone tried to escape. Stores gradually disappeared. No one replenished missing stock any longer and merchandise rapidly diminished.³⁵

Then the final day arrived. On Saturday 13 March 1943 at 11am, the *Judenrat* announced that by 3pm, the inhabitants of Ghetto A would be sent to the camp in Płaszów. The following day the Jews from Ghetto B were escorted to the station. The only ones who remained in Ghetto B were the unemployed, the sick, the elderly and small children. To forestall panic, the Germans promised that the children would be brought to Płaszów, once special barracks had been constructed to house them.³⁶

Tadeusz Pankiewicz remembered:³⁷

> The general mood was sombre. The street traffic was impossible to describe: shouts, people running loaded down

with possessions, looking for their proper places and for their relatives. The Germans encircled the streets. They were led by Amon Göth—tall, handsome, heavy-set, with thin legs, eyes of blue, about forty years old. He was dressed in a black leather coat, held a riding crop in one hand and a short automatic rifle in the other. Always with him were two huge dogs. He and his staff, together with the ever-present dogs, intensified our anxiety.

Jews from Ghetto A were ordered to line up in rows. Many were frantic with worry about the fate of their children, friends and relatives in Ghetto B. Everyone feared for the old and the infirm. Gunshots were then heard from Ghetto B. They came from the hospital. The Gestapo were shooting the sick.

Aleksander Bieberstein, director of the Kraków Ghetto Orphanage, wrote:[38]

> At three in the afternoon, the gate on ul. Węgierskiej was opened. First groups formed into rows, laden down with backpacks and other bundles, started to leave the Ghetto. Many Jews were gripped by the hope that Płaszów would be the last station, that they would survive.
>
> Right side stay.
> Left side…
> Trains[39]

Mina recalled:[40]

> 13 March 1943: the final liquidation of the Ghetto. There was no place to hide; I had to go! The Jewish Police dragged

us out of our houses. I can't blame anybody. They were doing what the Germans had ordered them to do.

The liquidation of the Ghetto was very cruel. People gathered under banners with the name of their factory were formed into columns of four or five. At the exit stood two big soldiers—they looked like butchers—and they were selecting: 'Right, left, right.'

What I saw is hard to describe. In front of my group a column of women with children in their arms went through the selection. They were ordered to hand over their children. What mother would willingly give away her child? Up until then, they had hidden their kids somewhere in the Ghetto: under the beds, under their skirts, afraid that they would be killed. But leaving the Ghetto, they carried their children in their arms and they had to give them away! If a mother did not want to give up her child, she was beaten until she handed the child over. It was unimaginable. The crying, the screaming, the wailing. I said to myself: 'My God, do you exist? Do you see what is going on here?' And I was thankful that I didn't have any children.

I was very afraid. I looked like a skeleton. Because of the typhoid, my hair had fallen out at the front, and I was afraid that I wouldn't be able to go through the gate without limping. I didn't believe that in this condition I would be selected 'for life'. But my girlfriends, with whom I had been at school until the War, gave me courage. They told me: 'Now you have to stand. You have no choice; there is no place to hide.' I said: 'If I have to pass through the gate where those butchers are standing, they won't let me through. They will select me for death.' But my friends said: 'You're still young. We will stand with you, and together we'll pass.' They tied a scarf around my head to cover my missing hair, put a bit of colour on my face, grabbed me under my arms—and together we marched through!

We marched eight kilometres, to another hell: Płaszów. The march was very hard for me. But I was always optimistic and held on to the hope that the War wouldn't last forever and that I would survive. The local population watching us march by did not help us—but what could they do? They had their own problems, their own struggles. A few called out 'God be with you'—but most did not care.

By 5pm Ghetto A had been emptied. Only members of the OD and a few members of the *Judenrat* remained. They had been ordered to stay behind until the liquidation was finished. German patrols shot anyone found on the street or hidden. Every home and apartment was searched: attics, basements.[41]

Malvina Graf wrote:[42]

> Ghetto A was empty and eerily silent. Not long before, there had been a great deal of movement and all kinds of noises could be heard, mostly the sound of those screaming, and people had been walking and running about. But now all was still. The buildings were empty; the windows and doors were flung wide open. Not a soul to be seen.

Tadeusz Pankiewicz recalled:[43]

> During the evacuation of Ghetto A, many people tried to escape through the sewers under the streets of Podgórze. Reports about the escapes reached the police. Sewer outlets were surrounded and the escapees captured and shot on the spot.

Fear prevailed in Ghetto B, where the jobless, women, children, the elderly and the infirm remained. In the morning, they gathered at Plac Zgody, each person carrying bundles containing clothing, bedding and even food. SS men marched into the Ghetto fully armed and Nazi dignitaries in large official cars drove in. Anxious to put on a show to impress the dignitaries, soldiers began shooting at random.[44]

The Kinderheim in Ghetto B and the Tagesheim in Ghetto A were liquidated, with most of the children killed.[45]

In preparation for the final transport, men and women were separated and more children taken. Jews from Ghetto B were selected by organizing a race of death in the square. Groups of people chosen at random were ordered to run, the outcome determining whether they would live or die. Amid jeering and laughter, they ran. Those who did not run fast enough were shot on the spot; while those who were reasonably good runners were separated from the others, since the Germans considered them strong enough to be sent to Płaszów. In all, 150 men were selected in this manner, but this was deemed too many by SS-Sturmbannführer Haase, Head of the SS and Police in Kraków. Accordingly, seventy-five were sent to Plaszów and seventy-five shot where they stood.[46]

After the German units had left the Ghetto, the remaining Jews were ordered to strip the murdered ones and deposit the corpses in the doorways of buildings. As trucks entered the Ghetto, nude bodies were thrown on, one on top of another. Often the wounded were thrown on the trucks with the dead. These trucks, loaded to the limit, were covered with blankets before entering the narrow streets of Płaszów. In all, the corpses of some 2,000 Jews who had been murdered in the streets of the Ghetto were brought to Płaszów and interred in a mass grave.[47]

Each subsequent morning, groups of Jews from Płaszów entered the Ghetto to empty it of everything left behind. Outside the Ghetto walls, the SS established two huge warehouses for furniture and medical and dental equipment. Material stolen from other localities in the Kraków district were also brought to these storage places, to be taken away in heavy trucks, principally to the Reich. The clean-up continued until December 1943.[48]

Two weeks after the liquidation of the Ghetto, Göth ordered all members of the *Judenrat* and the OD, including Spira, to Płaszów, where they were executed. Of the 2,600 OD men, some 300 who had been spared to keep order were deported together with their families, during the nights of 14 and 15 December 1943. On arrival in Płaszów they were also shot and burned. All of them possessed passports and believed the assurance of the occupiers: that they would be able to leave for overseas.[49]

Several days after the liquidation of the OD men, all workshops were transferred from the Ghetto to Płaszów.[50]

The barbed wire around the Ghetto was torn down and, some weeks later, the demolition of the surrounding walls began. With the exception of two small sections, all traces of the existence of the Ghetto were removed. A curtain was drawn over two years of suffering and pain.[51]

The Kraków Ghetto existed from March 1941 to March 1943. When first set up, it had held 20,000. Around 15,000 Jews were sent from it to extermination camps, most to Bełżec but others to Auschwitz-Birkenau. The rest were transferred to Płaszów.[52]

When the Laub family entered the Kraków Ghetto, it had consisted of six people. By March 1943, only two members, Mina and her beloved sister Freüda remained.

Malvina Graf wrote:[53]

Entire families had been destroyed, and with them a tradition of Jewish life that had survived even the worst times for Jews

in the history of Poland. Their contributions had been vast in the realms of education, science, literature, music, painting and philosophy. Their progeny lay lifeless in the gutters of the city that had housed one of the world's largest single concentration of Jews since the thirteenth century.

Deportation from the Ghetto. Photo: Yad Vashem Photo Archives. https://photos.yadvashem.org/photo-details.html?language=en&item_id=10155&ind=0

MINA & JACOB

Notes

1. Krystyna Chiger, *The Girl in the Green Sweater* (New York: St Martin's Press, 2008), 49
2. Yitzhak Arad, *Bełżec, Sobibor, Treblinka: the Operation Reinhard Death Camps* (Bloomington and Indianapolis, Indiana University Press, 1987), 59; Abraham Lewin, *Diary of the Great Deportation*, contained in Lawrence L. Langer, ed., *Art from the Ashes*, (New York: Oxford University Press, 1995), 168, 190
3. David Crowe, *Oskar Schindler* (Boulder: Westview Press, 2004), 149
4. Aleksander Bieberstein, *Zagłada Żydow w Krakowie* (The Extermination of Jews in Kraków), (Kraków: Wydawnictwo Literackie, 1985), 53-54; Malvina Graf, *The Kraków Ghetto and the Płaszów Camp Remembered* (Tallahassee: Florida State University Press, 1989), 41-42
5. Graf, *The Kraków Ghetto Remembered*, 48; Tom Keneally, *Searching for Schindler* (Sydney: Knopf/Random House Australia, 2007), Ryszard Kotarba, *Niemiecki Obóz w Płaszowie, 1942-45* (A German Camp in Płaszów 1942-45) (Warsaw-Kraków: Instytut Pamięci Narodowey (Institute of National Remembrance), 2009), 19
6. Crowe, *Oskar Schindler*, 106, 184; Graf, *The Kraków Ghetto Remembered*, 48; Tadeusz Pankiewicz, *Apteka w Getcie Krakowskim* (Cracow Ghetto Pharmacy), (1st edition published in Poland 1947; English translation by Henry Tilles, New York: Holocaust Library, 1987), 60-61; Bieberstein, *Zagłada Żydow*, 66
7. Bieberstein, *Zagłada Żydow*, 60, 65; Simon Wiesenthal, *Every Day Remembrance Day* (New York: Henry Holt, 1987), 125; Rafael F. Scharf, *Kraków—Blessed its Memory*, in Stanisław Markowski, *Krakowski Kazimierz: Dzielnica Żydowska 1870-1988* (Kraków's Kazimierz: Jewish Suburb 1870-1988), (Kraków: Wydawnicwo ARKA, 1992), 11
8. Mina Widawski nee Laub, audio testimony for the *12th Hour Project of Oral Testimonies* (Sydney: Australian Institute for Holocaust Studies, 1990); video testimony (Sydney: USC Shoah Foundation Institute, 1995), code 2526
9. Pankiewicz, *Apteka w Getcie Krakowskim*, 40-43
10. Graf, *The Kraków Ghetto Remembered*, 48
11. Pankiewicz, *Apteka*, 40-43
12. Pankiewicz, *Apteka*, 58-60
13. Crowe, *Oskar Schindler*, 187; Bieberstein, *Zagłada Żydow*, 67; Israel Gutman, ed., *Encyclopedia of the Holocaust* (New York: Macmillan, 1990), 831
14. Crowe, *Oskar Schindler*, 187; Bieberstein, *Zagłada Żydow*, 69; Pankiewicz, *Apteka*, 62-63
15. Gutman, *Encyclopedia of the Holocaust*, 831; Crowe, *Oskar Schindler*, 188
16. Graf, *The Kraków Ghetto Remembered*, 59-61

17 Crowe, *Oskar Schindler*, 189
18 Graf, *The Kraków Ghetto Remembered*, 63; Crowe, *Oskar Schindler*, 190
19 Mina Widawski, *12th Hour Project of Oral Testimonies*; USC Shoah Foundation, code 2526
20 Bieberstein, *Zagłada Żydów*, 196-97
21 Ibid.
22 Graf, *The Kraków Ghetto Remembered*, 64
23 Graf, *The Kraków Ghetto Remembered*, 69-70
24 Mina Widawski, *12th Hour Project of Oral Testimonies*; USC Shoah Foundation, code 2526
25 Pankiewicz, *Apteka*, 87; Graf, *The Kraków Ghetto Remembered*, 67-68
26 Graf, *The Kraków Ghetto Remembered*, 70-71; Crowe, *Oskar Schindler*, 190-91; Bieberstein, *Zagłada Żydów*, 80; Pankiewicz, *Apteka*, 90
27 Graf, *The Kraków Ghetto Remembered*, 56; Crowe, *Oskar Schindler*, 178
28 Pankiewicz, *Apteka*, 96-97
29 Graf, *The Kraków Ghetto Remembered*, 70-71; Crowe, *Oskar Schindler*, 190-91; Bieberstein, *Zagłada Żydów*, 80; Pankiewicz, *Apteka*, 80
30 Bieberstein, *Zagłada Żydów*, 219 Pankiewicz, *Apteka*, 103
31 Graf, *The Kraków Ghetto Remembered*, 70-71; Crowe, *Oskar Schindler*, 190-91
32 Graf, *The Kraków Ghetto Remembered*, 71-72; Pankiewicz, *Apteka*, 105-06
33 Mina Widawski, *12th Hour Project of Oral Testimonies*; USC Shoah Foundation, code 2526
34 Pankiewicz, *Apteka*, 102-03
35 Graf, *The Kraków Ghetto Remembered*, 72-73; Pankiewicz, *Apteka*, 106
36 Pankiewicz, *Apteka*, 106-07; Graf, *The Kraków Ghetto Remembered*, 72-73
37 Pankiewicz, *Apteka*, 107-08
38 Bieberstein, *Zagłada Żydów*, 84-85; Gutman, *Encyclopedia of the Holocaust*, 832
39 Jennifer Roy, *Yellow Star* (New York: Marshall Cavendish, 2006), 119
40 Mina Widawski, *12th Hour Project of Oral Testimonies*; USC Shoah Foundation, code 2526
41 Bieberstein, *Zagłada Żydów*, 86; Pankiewicz, *Apteka*, 111
42 Graf, *The Kraków Ghetto Remembered*, 73-74
43 Pankiewicz, *Apteka*, 113
44 Graf, *The Kraków Ghetto Remembered*, 74-76; Bieberstein, *Zagłada Żydów*, 220
45 Ibid.
46 Graf, *The Kraków Ghetto Remembered*, 76-77; Pankiewicz, *Apteka*, 118; https://www.tracesofwar.com/persons/69555/Haase-Willi.htm
47 Pankiewicz, *Apteka*, 120-21
48 Graf, *The Kraków Ghetto Remembered*, 78-80; Bieberstein, *Zagłada Żydów*, 90
49 Graf, *The Kraków Ghetto Remembered*, 79; Pankiewicz, *Apteka*, 131; Isaiah

Trunk, *Judenrät: The Jewish Councils in Eastern Europe under Nazi Occupation* (New York: Macmillan, 1972), 509; Bieberstein, *Zagłada Żydow*, 143, 167

50 Martin Gilbert, *Never Again: A History of the Holocaust*, (London: HarperCollins Illustrated, 2002), 136; Keneally, *Searching for Schindler*, 106, 111; Graf, *The Kraków Ghetto Remembered*, 60

51 Graf, *The Kraków Ghetto Remembered*, 84; Pankiewicz, *Apteka*, 149

52 Gutman, *Encyclopedia of the Holocaust*, 1140; United States Holocaust Memorial Museum (USHMM), *Encyclopedia of Camps and Ghettos 1933-45*, (Washington: 2012), Vol. 2, 864

53 Graf, *The Kraków Ghetto Remembered*, 77

10
Kraków's Amidah

In many ghettos of the *Generalgouvernement*, members of Jewish youth movements carried out Amidah (in Hebrew to stand up) against the Nazi oppressors. Resistance was an act of despair, inspired by the suicidal stand of the Zealots at Masada against Rome's Imperial legions.

The way the Kraków Ghetto had been set up created many barriers to resistance, limiting what could be done. It was compact and its thirty streets were constantly patrolled. A mere glance could reveal forbidden activity. While the Warsaw Ghetto Uprising is recognized as a symbol of Jewish resistance, the Kraków Uprising, which took place in December 1942, preceded Warsaw's actions, by some four months.[1]

By mid-1942, there were two main resistance organizations in the Kraków Ghetto. The first was led by Aharon 'Dolek' Liebeskind, the leader of the Akiva group and a skilled organizer who brought together Zionist youth organizations as part of the Underground.

The second band of fighters was headed by Heshek Bauminger. A former soldier in the Polish and Soviet Armies, he escaped captivity and returned to Kraków where he created a resistance group largely composed of young people from the Hashomer Hatzair movement. It established close ties with the local Communist resistance.[2]

In August 1942, the two groups joined to form the Żydowska

Organizacja Bojowa or ŻOB (Jewish Fighting Organization). The brutal roundup in the Kraków Ghetto on 28 October 1942 triggered a reaction from ŻOB. In the months that followed, ŻOB, with some support from the Polish underground group Armja Ludowa (People's Army), operated both in and outside the Ghetto: sabotaging railway lines; raiding German warehouses; and attacking and assassinating German soldiers, security police and Jewish informers. Members of ŻOB set fire to several trucks, truck-trailers and gasoline tanks located in the military barracks on ul. Grzegorzecka. On 2 November 1942, an attempt to assassinate the Gestapo informer, Marcel Gruner, with his wife, occurred. ŻOB executed an official of the Department of Press and Propaganda of the *Generalgouvernement*. They also stole German uniforms from the Optima factory in the Ghetto where Mina and her sister worked.[3]

In addition, they published an Underground newspaper, *HeHalutz HaLochem* (*The Fighting Pioneer*). About 250 copies were issued every Friday. The paper, written in Polish, called for help, and for military intervention in the War by free nations against the Nazis and their collaborators.[4]

Adele, Mina's daughter, recalls:

> It was December 1979. My husband and I were staying with family on Moshav (settlement) Regba, North Israel. A cousin highly recommended that I visit a museum nearby devoted to the Jewish ghettos in Poland during World War II: the Lohamei Ha Getaot, in Nahariya. It is part of the kibbutz founded in 1949 by Warsaw Ghetto survivors.[5]
>
> It was a modest building (greatly expanded in recent years), and as I wandered through, I came across an exhibition devoted to the Kraków Ghetto. Suddenly I was standing in front of a photo of Dolek Liebeskind. The accompanying

caption said: 'Leader of the Kraków Jewish Underground or ŻOB'. It told of his deeds and the group's courage.

I recalled a number of conversations with Mum of her experiences in the Kraków Ghetto. Among my favourite topics was the heroism of the Underground fighters. She spoke of their bravery during the actions carried out against the Germans. The Kraków Ghetto Uprising, perhaps less well known than the Warsaw Ghetto's fighters' brave stand, became a symbol of resistance not just to Kraków's Jewish community but to the wider Polish community, and had an immense impact on the Germans.

Mum knew Dolek, and his sister Mina (aka Mira) well. Together, they were members of the Akiva youth group in pre-war Kraków. Dolek, a few years older than the girls, was one of the leaders of Akiva. He was a man who had already earned the respect and admiration of the Jewish community. The girls, closer in age, became close friends.

Aharon Liebeskind (aka 'Dolek', 'Jan Ropa' or 'Adolf'), the General Secretary of Kraków ŻOB, was a law student and intellectual who was very well liked. Decisive and unrelenting, he held human life sacred and intervened many times to prevent hotheads. However, he was also prepared to sacrifice not only himself but those he held dearest.

In addition to Dolek, other key members of the Kraków ŻOB included Gusta Dawidson Draenger (aka 'Justyna'); Gusta's husband, Shimson Draenger (aka 'Szymek', 'Witek' or 'Marek Borowski'); Dolek's wife Rivka Spiner Liebeskind (aka 'Eva' or 'Wushka'); Dolek's sister Miriam Liebeskind (aka 'Mira' or 'Mirka'); Hela Szüpper-Rufeisen (aka 'Rufeisen-Szieper'); Leopold Wasserman (aka 'Poldek', aka Leopold Wodzinski); Juda Tannenbaum (aka 'Idek or 'Czesiek'); Joseph Bau; and Szymon Listgarten (aka 'Simek'), owner of the apartment at 13 Jozefinska, which became ŻOB's headquarters within the Ghetto.[6]

While incarcerated in 1943 in Montelupich Prison, Gusta wrote about the Kraków resistance on scraps of toilet paper. She recalled Dolek telling her:[7]

> 'Justyna, there is so much anger pent up in me. Sometimes I wish I had no responsibility for anyone else. I would just throw myself into the struggle. I would sow devastation around me until I perished, and I would die satisfied.'

This was not the tender Dolek to whom people came running when they needed someone to ease their pain. This was Dolek the fighter, who put armed struggle above all else.

Dolek took it upon himself to procure weapons, provide military training, and send groups into the forest. The first group he sent out to the forest, on 20 September 1942, was charged with making contact with the Polish Underground to obtain weapons. However, they were betrayed by informers and the mission failed. Of the group of six, only one fighter survived the ambush. The main reason for the failure of this mission was the lack of weapons. The entire group had only two guns!

Miriam Liebeskind, Dolek's sister and Mina's close friend, operated in Tomaszów, where she organized a large group of fighters and carried documents and money for the purchase of weapons.

Gusta recalled:[8]

> Mirka was constantly at risk because it wasn't easy for her to disguise herself as a non-Jew. She was small, with quick but

dignified movements. But what was most difficult to conceal were her raven tresses and her jet-black eyes. If anyone looked at her suspiciously, she would disarm suspicion with her cheerful, untroubled face.

Hela Szüpper-Rufeisen and Leopold Wasserman worked as couriers for ŻOB. Hela recalled:[9]

> They said: 'We have a very important job for you. You will go to Warsaw and come back with weapons.' Smuggling a person was also important, but smuggling weapons was the most important mission. I carried the guns in a belt around my stomach. I put a package of explosives in my handbag.
>
> Travelling back, I had to be happy. Not too happy, but not sad, because someone might say: 'Why are you so sad? Are you Jewish?'

Gusta wrote that the Germans viewed the possession of weapons as the gravest of transgressions. Hela's mission as a courier placed her in extreme danger, and it was truly a miracle that she had managed to acquire this contraband.[10]

Szymek Draenger, 'Marek', was an amateur typesetter experienced in etching and engraving. He was assigned to put these skills to use. Together with Joseph Bau, an accomplished artist, they forged train tickets, passes allowing entry into the Ghetto, foreign papers and *Kennkarten*. These enabled members of the Jewish resistance to move in and out of the Ghetto.

Gusta described their movements:[11]

> At first, Marek carried the whole 'office' in his coat pockets. Later he started carrying a briefcase, stopping in various

apartments whose occupants were out. He could work out of his briefcase until the occupant returned. After a while, his supplies had increased so much that Marek was walking around with a train of assistants behind him, carrying briefcases, boxes, a typewriter and a variety of packages.

The incessant moving around put Marek at serious risk and made it harder and harder to work. It became essential to find a permanent and well-hidden place where someone could always be on the premises. To this end I set up an apartment in a beautiful villa outside the Jewish Quarter, in Rabka, playing the role of an ailing wife spending the autumn in the resort region of Podhale with her 'nephew'.

Juda Tannenbaum supplied the blank forms. He was well liked and enjoyed access to all sorts of people, among them many workers in government offices, and even the police. He would casually walk into a government office and shake hands with the Wachtmeister (sergeant) with one hand, while the other was unobtrusively removing government forms, schedules and even official stamps from his desk.[12]

Adele recalls:

> The exhibit at Lohamei Ha Getaot confirms many details and provides confirmation of events Mum and I had discussed over the years, including the number of actions carried out by the Jewish fighters. As I stood that day transfixed, I was reduced to tears. Mum's experiences, so unbelievable at times, were made true to me by these photographs, these cold historical facts and statistics. Those young lives lost!

Dolek was only thirty when he took the responsibility for leading the Jewish fighters, for the group's actions and its destiny. The group's members ranged in age from seventeen to the late twenties. Most were former students, or white collar workers, with little or no combat experience. They were outnumbered and short of weapons. Material published since the War confirms that Dolek and his group fully realized that their desperate efforts would ultimately lead to their deaths. In fact, records show that only a handful of these fighters survived the War.

Towards the last months of 1942, following a number of selections and transportations, and as plans for the final liquidation of the Ghetto went ahead, the Jewish fighters carried out a number of actions. Mina recalled rumours flying around the Ghetto, that the Jewish group was responsible for these acts carried out against the Germans, both inside and on the streets outside.

The most daring of these took place in December 1942. Mina and other Ghetto inmates heard that, on 24 December, operating in squads of three, ŻOB teams struck simultaneously at three cafes in Kraków favoured by the SS and other Germans: the Cyganeria, the Esplanade, and the Zakopinaka Officers' Club, as well as the Officers' Casino housed in the National Museum and the Scala, one of Kraków's best-known movie theatres. The most successful raid was on Cyganeria, which was full of Nazi officers at the time of the attack. Eleven Germans died and many others were injured.[13]

Rivka Liebeskind recalled:[14]

> The Underground feared that any action by the resistance would endanger Ghetto inhabitants. They therefore decided to throw the bomb in the Polish part of Kraków, outside the Ghetto. We waved Polish flags and called upon the Polish people to revolt against the Occupation. The fact that we threw grenades was incredible. We wanted to motivate the Polish Underground into action. It was such a fantastic

operation that the Poles did not believe that Jews had carried it out. They were sure that Russian paratroopers organized it.

It had been customary for members of Akiva in post-World War I Poland, to assemble on Friday nights to celebrate Shabbat. In 1942, these gatherings were taking place inside the Kraków Ghetto where Akiva fighters were engaged in life-threatening anti-Nazi activities. Gusta Dawidson Draenger wrote:[15]

> The soul of the movement was concentrated in the apartment on Jozefinska 13. Anyone in the movement who came to Kraków would try to get into the Ghetto at any price, just to get a look at the place. Dolek often dropped in, and whenever he showed up, a group gathered around him. Then the evening grew both more festive and more pensive.
> On the Friday night of 20 November 1942, Aharon Liebeskind expressed a premonition: that this would be the last time they would greet the Shabbat together. Amidst the warm holiday spirit someone uttered the words 'This is the Last Supper.'

Rivka Liebeskind recalled that evening:[16]

> Celebrations were planned for the Kabbalat Shabbat. They waited for the lighting of the candles. The girls wore white blouses and the boys white shirts with collars open at the throat. Deeply moved, they sat around a table covered with a white cloth. First a moment of silence, and then rose from their souls a swelling hymn of praise to Shabbat. This particular evening, they greeted it as a group for the last time. They felt no fear for the future.

Dolek was seated at the head of the table, surrounded by those faces so dear to him, so filled with radiance and warmth. People crowded together. New arrivals kept coming—and somehow space had to be found. Dolek told us: 'This is the last evening we will be meeting together. We're condemned to die. But we must fight for three lines in Jewish history.'

Listening to Dolek, who always generated optimism, uttering strong words that encouraged you to believe in life and love it, I felt that today his words conveyed that the end was near: 'We are going on the road to death—remember that. Whoever wants to keep on living should not search for life here among us. We are at the end.'[17]

The German response to the December 1942 attacks was swift and brutal. They quickly surrounded ŻOB's hiding place at ul. 24 Skawinska and arrested many of the operation's leaders. At a bar on ul.3 Żuławeskiego, Dolek Liebeskind had a shootout with the Gestapo as they tried to arrest him. He killed two Germans and wounded two more, before committing suicide.[18]

Rivka Liebeskind recalled:[19]

As hideouts of the others who participated in the operation were discovered, and they were all caught, Dolek's hideout was also found. It was the headquarters' hideaway, containing weapons and money. Dolek and Yehuda Tannenbaum were hiding there when they were attacked. They were surrounded but defended themselves. After exchanging fire and shooting several Germans, they committed suicide. They weren't killed or caught. They committed suicide with their last bullets.

A telegram sent to Hitler's headquarters, describing the defeat of the Jewish Fighting Organization in Kraków, put a different spin on events:

> **Berlin, 25.12.42**
>
> **In searching a terrorist hiding place in Kraków the Jews who were found there, Adolf (aka 'Dolek') Liebeskind and Juda Tannenbaum, were shot after heavy fire exchange.**
>
> **The hiding place was located in the cellar of a building, occupied only by German railway officials. The Jews, possessing forged identity cards, appeared as Poles, and were smuggled into the building by the concierge, in exchange for large sums of money. In the hiding place were confiscated: 45 bullets, 4 pistols, 1 radio, 1 typewriter, 1 duplicating machine, 1 small printing press, 200 dollars, 1,540 zlotys, 2 uniforms; a Polish policeman and a German railway official. The Polish concierge and his wife were arrested.**
>
> **Reichs-Security Main Office (signed)**
> **Müller, Chief of Gestapo**

Yitzhak Zuckerman, who had been visiting that day from the Warsaw Ghetto, managed to return to Warsaw. The other members of ŻOB were tracked down by the Germans. Out of 150-60 Underground fighters in Kraków, only about twenty survived, hidden in the forests.[20]

Miriam Liebeskind was shot in Radom in January 1943.[21]

Gusta Dawidson Draenger escaped from Montelupich Prison but was killed fighting the Germans in the forests east of Kraków.[22]

In March 1943, the German police closed in on Heshek Bauminger, one of the original leaders, and in a hail of gunfire he perished, perhaps by his own hand.[23]

Rivka Liebeskind was deported to Birkenau on 19 January 1943. She survived, and settled in Israel until her death in 2007, as did Hela Szüpper-Rufeisen, Joseph Bau and Leopold Wasserman.

During their recent trip to Israel, Freda and Adele were amazed to discover that Leopold Wasserman was still alive and well. They describe their emotional meeting:[24]

> On 10 June 2019, we met with Mr Wasserman in Ramat Gan, Israel. He is now known as Yehuda Maimon.
>
> Born in Kraków in 1924, he is ninety-five years young. Despite the passage of seventy years, we communicated in Polish, a language he has rarely used since settling in Israel in 1946. He is quick-witted, his memory of his activities during the Kraków Uprising still sharp and clear.
>
> Aged fifteen when war broke out, he was still a teenager when he joined ŻOB in 1942, as a courier. He and a group of others lived outside the Ghetto, using forged papers and identities; he was Leopold Wodzinski. They risked their lives every day. Their strategy was twofold, he told us: to ensure that the Ghetto population was protected from reprisals, and to inspire the Polish community to rise up against the Nazis. His tasks included distributing leaflets; posting anti-German proclamations; raising Polish flags; and communicating with other members of the group.
>
> Yehuda confirmed that Dolek Liebeskind committed suicide, rather than being captured or killed by the enemy.
>
> He survived the War by joining the Polish Underground, and later was active in helping survivors make their way to Palestine via Romania. He became a member of the Palmach, and after Independence, a career officer in the Israeli Navy.[25]

Of his dead heroic colleagues, Gusta Dawidson Draenger wrote:[26]

> Other Underground fighters had to conceal their resistance activities but the Jewish fighters had to mask every part of themselves. Will anyone ever be able to comprehend how this group of idealistic dreamers took up arms, in spite of being deprived of the right to live as human beings and as Jews, denied even the right to eat? None of them feared death itself, but all dreaded the possibility of falling into the hands of the authorities.

Adele recalls:

> News of Dolek's death reached Mina in the Ghetto. She also learned later that her dear friend Miriam, involved with the group, had been captured and was believed to have been killed in Radom.
>
> Mum always remembered the Liebeskind family with a mixture of pride and a great deal of sadness. To her they represented the best of the pre-war Jewish community and became symbols of supreme human courage.
>
> On my return from that earlier visit to Israel, I shared my impressions of the museum I had visited with Mum. She was overcome, moved to tears of gratitude that her friends have been so remembered and honoured. A few years later, Mum and Dad paid their own homage to these brave and heroic young people while on a visit to Israel.

Let us finish with an extract from the Akiva Pledge:[27]

> I swear by everything most dear to me, and above all by the memory and honour of dying Polish Jewry, that I will fight with all the weapons available to me until the last moment of my life to resist the Germans, the National Socialists, and those in league with them, the mighty enemies of the Jewish people and of all humanity.

Top: (l-r) Rivka, Dolek and Miriam Liebeskind.
Photo: Yad Vashem Photo Archives.
Bottom: Adele, Michelle and Freda with Yehuda (Poldek) Maimon, Israel 2019.

MINA & JACOB

Notes

1. Tadeusz Pankiewicz, *Apteka w Getcie Krakowskim* (Cracow Ghetto Pharmacy), (1st edition published in Poland 1947; English translation by Henry Tilles, New York: Holocaust Library, 1987), 83, 114-15
2. Centre for Advanced Holocaust Studies, http://www.ushmm.org/research/center/erman/medal_award
3. http://en.wikipedia.org/wiki/Krak%C3%B3w_Ghetto; David Crowe, *Oskar Schindler* (Boulder: Westview Press, 2004), 191; Isaiah Trunk, *Judenrät: The Jewish Councils in Eastern Europe under Nazi Occupation* (New York: Macmillan, 1972), 539; Pankiewicz, *Apteka*, 84
4. JewishGen, *Jewish Resistance*, http://www.jewishgen.org/yizkor/schindler/sch015.html
5. https://en.wikipedia.org/wiki/Lohamei_HaGeta%27ot
6. Gusta Davidson Draenger, *Pamiętnik Justyny*, (Justyna's Diary), (Kraków: Centralna Żydowska Komisja Historyczna (Central Jewish Historical Commission), 1946) Note 53, 116; Joseph Bau, *Dear God, have you ever gone hungry?* (New York: Arcade Publishing, 1996) (English-language translation from Hebrew, 1990), 55
7. Draenger, *Pamiętnik Justyny*, 24-25, 100-01
8. Draenger, *Pamiętnik Justyny*, note 27, p 71; Aleksander Bieberstein, *Zagłada Żydow w Krakowie* (The Extermination of Jews in Kraków), (Kraków: Wydawnictwo Literackie, 1985), 244
9. http://jwa.org/encyclopedia/article/schupper-hella-rufeisen; Draenger, *Pamiętnik Justyny*, ix; Voice recording, Yad Vashem, 2009, Jerusalem
10. Draenger, *Pamiętnik Justyny*, 70-71
11. Bau, *Dear God*, 55; Draenger, *Pamiętnik Justyny*, 24-26; 64-68; 98, 101-03; Note 46, 1,032
12. Draenger, *Pamiętnik Justyny*, 24-26; 64-68; 98, 101-03; Note 46, 1032
13. http://en.wikipedia.org/wiki/Krak%C3%B3w_Ghetto; Crowe, *Oskar Schindler*, 191; Trunk, *Judenrät*, 539; Tadeusz Wroński, *Kronika okupowanego Krakowa* (Chronicle of Occupied Kraków), (Kraków: Wydawnictwo Literackie, 1974), 241
14. http://jwa.org/encyclopedia/article/liebeskind-rivka-kuper; Voice recording, Yad Vashem, 2009, Jerusalem
15. Draenger, *Pamiętnik Justyny*, 118-119
16. Voice recording, Yad Vashem, 2009, Jerusalem
17. Lucy S. Dawidowicz, *The War Against the Jews* (New York: Bantam Books, 1986), 311, 313

18 http://en.wikipedia.org/wiki/Krak%C3%B3w_Ghetto; Crowe, *Oskar Schindler*, 191
19 Voice recording, Yad Vashem, 2009, Jerusalem
20 Martin Gilbert, *Never Again: A History of the Holocaust* (London: HarperCollins Illustrated, 2002), 95
21 Draenger, *Pamiętnik Justyny*, note 27, 71; Bieberstein, *Zagłada Żydow w Krakowie*, 244
22 Draenger, *Pamiętnik Justyny*, 24-26; 95, 100-01
23 Gilbert, *Never Again*, 6
24 Yehuda Maimon, interview with Adele Abraham, Michelle Abraham and Freda Widawski, 2019, Ramat Gan
25 Ibid.
26 Draenger, *Pamiętnik Justyny*, 24-26; 64-68; 98, 101-03; Note 46, 1,032
27 Draenger, *Pamiętnik Justyny*, 141

11

Bełżec

Bełżec extermination camp operated from 17 March to early December 1942. It was the first killing site where stationary gas chambers and carbon monoxide were used. It is estimated that some 600,000 Jews from the Kraków, Galician and Lublin districts, as well as people from Germany, Austria and Czechoslovakia, were murdered there.[1] From mid-May 1942, transports consisting on average of 5,000 to 6,000 Jews arrived in Bełżec from the Kraków district and other areas of Galicia.

The camp was located half a kilometre from the Bełżec Station, along a railway spur. It occupied a relatively small area and was surrounded by a high fence of wire netting, topped by barbed wire and camouflaged with branches. Young trees were also planted around it to prevent observation from the outside.[2]

Bełżec was divided into two sub-camps. Camp I was the reception and administration area, and included the railway ramp and two barracks, one for undressing and the second to store clothes and goods the victims had brought with them. The second sub-camp was the extermination area. It included the gas chambers and the burial ditches. A narrow passageway, two metres wide and a few dozen metres long, called 'der Schlauch' (the tube), connected the undressing barracks in Camp I to the gas chambers.[3]

The camp garrison consisted of fifteen to twenty *T4 Aktion* SS men, already 'trained' in Germany in the extermination of the handicapped. In addition, a company of 100 returned Soviet POWs, mainly Ukrainians, plus 500 selected Jewish prisoners (the so-called Sonderkommando), were used to bury the bodies in mass graves and sort the victims' possessions.[4]

From Mina's testimony, it is assumed that her parents were among the 7,000 transported to Bełżec from the Kraków Ghetto between 2-8 June 1942.[5]

On 28 October 1942, a further 7,000 were transported to Bełżec.[6] As noted, Mina's two brothers, Wolf and Izaak, were in the Kraków Ghetto hospital on that day and since they were never seen again, it is likely that they were either shot on the spot (like most hospital patients) or also sent to Bełżec.

Rudolf Reder, one of only three people known to have survived the Camp, described the process. This is what Eidela and Moses would have faced after an onerous journey of some 250 kilometres from Kraków, travelling in a cramped, sealed car without food or water:[7]

> About noon the train reached the small station in Bełżec. Little houses stood around it, in which the Gestapo lived. The German who had driven the train to the Camp got down and, shouting and lashing out, drove the people from the train.
>
> As soon as the victims were unloaded, they were assembled in the yard, and SS-Scharführer Fritz Jierman gave a speech: 'Now you are going for a bath, and afterwards you will be sent to work.' Everybody cheered up and they were happy that they were going to work after all. They applauded. It was a moment of hope and delusion. There was total calm. The whole crowd moved on in silence.
>
> The building containing the chambers was low, long and wide, grey concrete with a flat roof covered in tar paper, and

above that another roof of netting covered with foliage. From the yard, three steps a metre wide and without railings led up to this building. A big vase full of different coloured flowers stood in front of the building. On the wall was clearly and legibly written: 'Bade und Inhalationsräume' (Baths and Inhalation Rooms). The men went straight through the yard into this building.

The chambers were completely dark, with no windows, and totally empty. A round opening the size of an electrical socket could be seen in each chamber. The corridor and chambers were lower than a normal room, not more than two metres high. The chambers were a metre-and-a-half above the ground, and at the same level as the chambers was a ramp at the doors, from which the bodies were thrown to the ground after asphyxiation.

Outside the building was a small shed, where the machine was: a gasoline-driven motor. It ran for twenty minutes. Right after the machine was shut down, the doors of the chambers leading to the ramp were opened from the outside and the corpses were thrown on the ground, making a huge mound several metres high. Eighty to one hunded litres of gasoline were used each day. On either side of the building with the gas chamber were graves.

Several dozen SS men used whips and sharp bayonets to drive the women to the building with the chambers and up the three steps to the gangway. Into each chamber 750 people were crammed. I heard the doors closing and the moans and screams which lasted ten to fifteen minutes, horribly loud, in different languages. Later the groans got quieter, and at the end everything became silent.

I belonged to a permanent death crew, the Sonderkommando. We dug the pits, the enormous mass graves, and dragged the bodies there. They were buried in tight layers placed one atop another, mountains of corpses of healthy people. They ordered us to put corpses a metre above a grave that was already full and dump more sand. Thick black blood seeped out of the graves and flooded the surface like the sea, and the orchestra played. It played from morning to evening!

In December 1942, the killing operations at Bełżec ended.

From October 1942 to April 1943, work detachments of Jewish forced labourers excavated mass graves and burned the bodies to remove all evidence of the crime. When the work was completed, the last prisoners were taken to the Sobibór Camp and murdered there.

Throughout the spring of 1943 and until the summer of 1944, every attempt was made to conceal evidence of the killing centre of Bełżec. The camp was ploughed over, new trees planted and a manor house built nearby.

For a long time after the War, the area of the former death camp was left abandoned. The first monument commemorating the victims was erected on its territory in December 1963. A memorial was dedicated on 3 June 2004.[8]

Dan Pagis recorded, 'written in pencil in the sealed freight car':[9]

Here in this carload
I, Eve
with my son Abel,
If you see my older boy,
Cain, the son of man,
tell him that I…

An anonymous poem carved into a plaque at the Bełżec Museum, states:

Mamusiu	Mummy, haven't
Ja przecież byłem Grzeczny!	I been good?
Ciemno! Ciemno	It's dark! It's dark

Notes

1. Raul Hilberg, *The Destruction of the European Jews* (New York: Holmes & Meier, 1985), 227-28; Malvina Graf, *The Kraków Ghetto and the Płaszów Camp Remembered* (Tallahassee: Florida State University Press, 1989), Note 20, 34
2. Yitzak Arad, *Bełżec, Sobibor, Treblinka: The Operation Reinhard Death Camps* (Bloomington and Indianapolis: Indiana University Press, 1987), 127
3. Arad, *Bełżec, Sobibor, Treblinka*, 24, 27
4. Rudolf Reder, *Bełżec* (Kraków: Fundacja Judaica (Judaica Foundation, Auschwitz-Birkenau State Museum, 1999), 81
5. Arad, *Bełżec*, 81; Christopher R. Browning, *Ordinary Men: Reserve Police Battalion 101 and the Final Solution in Poland* (New York: HarperCollins, 1992), 53; Arad, *Bełżec, Sobibor, Treblinka*, 74, 119, 126, 287
6. Arad, *Bełżec, Sobibor, Treblinka*, 387
7. Reder, *Bełżec*, 81, 90, 118-24, 126-27, 130
8. *Majdanek Bełżec: The German Death Camps, The Polish Memory Sites* (Państwowe Muzeum na Majdanku (State Museum of Majdanek), 2009), back page; Robert Kuwalek and Dariusz Libionka, *Bełżec Death Camp* (Museum/Memorial Site, Bełżec)
9. Transcript from exhibition at Museum/Memorial Site, Bełżec, 2010

1943

Death in the Camps

By the beginning of 1943, into the fourth year of the War, according to an official SS report, two and a half million Jews had been deported and were no longer alive.[1] Included in that horrific statistic were Mina's parents and four brothers; as well as Jacob's mother, his brother Abram, sister-in-law and nephews.

When in March 1943, Mina and her sister Freüda were transported from the Kraków Ghetto to Płaszów, Jacob was already in the Guttenbrunn labour camp, having been transferred there from Kahlfelde at the beginning of the year. He was unaware of the murder of his family in the Wieruszów Ghetto. Nor did he know anything of the fate of his brothers, Berek and Majer.

Notes

1   Walter Laqueur, *The Terrible Secret* (London: Weidenfeld and Nicolson, 1980), 14-15

12
Guttenbrunn (Kobylepole)

The Guttenbrunn forced labour camp was established at the end of 1940. Of approximately 1,140 Jews sent to the various Poznań camps, 734 were sent there. They were used as forced labour, working on the railway line from Kobylnica to Kobylepole. Their employers were private firms such as Philipp Holzmann, Heino Hecht AG, Grün and Bilfinger, Mannheim AG and a number of others.[1]

Evidence in the form of a hand written list shows that a number of people from Wieruszów were transported to Guttenbrunn. As Dr Anna Ziółkowska explained to Freda:[2]

> Next to some of the names is the symbol which denotes Philipp Holzmann—that is, as having been assigned to work for that firm. On the list are a number of people named Widawski from Wieruszów.

In addition to Jacob's testimony about Guttenbrunn, we will include in this chapter testimonies from other Wieruszów survivors of the camp: his friends, such as Issac Pankowski and Max Procel, plus other inmates including Morris Shell, Leon Jolson and Jack Fogel. When reading their testimonies, we should keep in mind that most of them were very young (aged from fifteen to their mid-twenties);

had come from close-knit families and small communities; and were frightened and alone.

Jacob recalled his first sight of Guttenbrunn:[3]

> **Early 1943 I came to Guttenbrunn and this was the first time that I saw this. They had put up gallows in the *Appellplatz*, with EIGHT hooks—EIGHT OF THEM!**

This image of the hooks came to symbolize for Jacob the brutality of the Nazi occupation. It remained with him for the rest of his life.

Like the other Poznań labour camps, Guttenbrunn was overcrowded, had poor sanitation, lack of basic medical care, inhuman working conditions, inadequate clothing and starvation food rations. What marked it, however, according to independent eye-witness reports, was its sheer brutality: hangings and beatings were common for minor infringements.

Jacob recalled:[4]

> **Guttenbrunn was run by the firm Holzmann. We belonged to the firm. If any other companies wanted slave labour from the camp, they had to come every morning to Holzmann and request the number of people they wanted.**
>
> **This Guttenbrunn was a very big camp. Any small group of survivors that were left from the various little camps around the region were brought here.**
>
> **It was located on a large country estate, with huge stables, in which they created the camp. They put electric wire around them and built inside the stables single-tiered wooden benches on each side, which ran the length of the building, around twenty-five to thirty metres. And on those benches, we slept. They gave us nothing: no straw to make mattresses**

like in the other camps. Nothing. Just the bare wooden bench and one blanket each. We slept in the clothes that we wore to work.

I had survived a couple of camps, but I said to myself that from here I would probably not get out. It was horrible—a horrible, horrible place. First of all, we were all covered with lice. All of us, because it was so dirty. We were going out to work, carrying cement, coming back and sleeping in the same clothes. The cement got wet and dirty and from the dirt bred lice. They deloused us every Sunday, but this did not help, because no matter how clean you tried to be, you were lying next to one another and each of us got lice from the other.

Jack Fogel described the layout of the camp:[5]

In the camp next to the hall where we slept there were also some buildings which housed a kitchen, offices, quarters for the overseers and people working in the kitchen who were Jews. There were no showers, but we had a washroom with a long trough and cold water taps. We washed there and washed our underwear and clothes there as well.

Jacob recalled:[6]

This was also a labour lager but here, instead of a highway, we were building railway lines. The railway lines were around twelve metres long. The Polish workers had special pliers that they used to grab the line from both sides. The Jews had to carry these lines on their shoulders. They were so heavy! Twelve Poles would carry a line using pliers, while nine Jews had to carry one line, on their shoulders.

Jack Fogel described the working conditions:[7]

> In Guttenbrunn, I was with Morris Shell and Leon Jolson. We were working on the railway, building new tracks. It was very hard, pick-and-shovel work. In the other camps we dug the earth out by hand. Here we had huge excavators. It was hard and dangerous work. One day one of the prisoners was accidentally caught in the jaws of the excavator and strangled to death. So we were digging up the earth, preparing it for the excavators; and also carrying the big steel girders, the lines. We were working very hard. We worked approximately twelve hours a day, six days a week.

Leon Jolson recalled:[8]

> Sometimes, half an hour after we came back from work, trucks came that needed unloading. So they took us out of the barracks and we worked half the night unloading them. It was slavery.

Morris Shell explained:[9]

> We were building a railway junction, and then we started to build all the lines. Before that we had to unload wagons of blue metal, for the railway lines and for the sleepers to be laid. First of all, the rafters were two wagon lengths, which two people had to unload, one on each end. I was once unloading these rafters, and my second happened to be a very tall man. When we pushed down, you both had to push simultaneously, but apparently he didn't push at the same time as me, and it jammed under my chin. I immediately

spat out a couple of teeth. I was badly cut under the chin, but there was no medical treatment. I just put a bit of water on it and a rag. Anyway, these were minor things. We just kept on working.

Once the buildings and the railways were completed, we had to build accommodation for the German railway staff. For them we built proper barracks, each one with separate rooms, about twelve in each building. They were built properly, from red bricks. We were supposed to go home at six in the evening, but a particular foreman, by the name of Franek, was such a vicious man that he used to keep us back to unload the bricks until ten o'clock in the evening. This was already in winter, January. It was cold and we were laying the canals for water pipes, sewage. The pipes were big, made from ceramic. In winter time without gloves, they were cold to handle.

When we came home from work, we got our portion of bread. At lunchtime they used to bring us soup. When I looked in the bowl I could see how much dirt was left behind. Sometimes, if we were lucky, they used to give us peelings from potatoes, but they weren't washed properly and still contained dirt. The first few weeks I couldn't stomach it. But the people who were already there, who had already been hungry for a year or so, for them this was the biggest luxury. Slowly I also got used to it and I wanted to go home and show my mother that I could eat soup now—since I was never a soup eater. But unfortunately, this did not happen.

Jacob recalled:[10]

Because the camp was so big, they gave you coupons, like a ticket for the cinema, for meals: one for breakfast, one for lunch, and one for dinner. A long queue would form outside the kitchen.

Fear of punishment and executions was all-pervasive. Whipping was the primary method of punishment, applied for infringement of camp rules. Jacob recalled[11]:

> In Guttenbrunn, on the other side from the Jewish camp was the Polish camp, for Polish workers brought from all over the country. They couldn't travel a few hundred kilometres each day to and from work, so they built them a camp. A gate separated us. We had electric wire around our camp; they didn't. We had Polish guards, all civilians; they wore those black uniforms, but they weren't Germans. For the first time we also had Jewish police, headed by Grün, a Jew from Leipzig.
>
> Standing in the food queue I met two boys from Hashomer Hatzair, from my organization. Their elderly father, Kiak, was a shoemaker and a very nice man. One of the Jewish policemen, Menashe Brutman, a real sadist, liked to box, so he would look for some poor guy from the camp to box with. He was twenty-four years old and one day he came up to that old man and punched him. I was standing close to them and said in Yiddish: 'Menashe, aren't you ashamed? You know that this elderly gentleman has children older than you? Why did you hit him?' He hit me so hard, with a chair leg, that I saw stars. Afterwards I met a couple of fellows who said: 'You're lucky that he didn't kill you.'

Death by hanging was the punishment for crimes such as escaping from the camp; going outside the borders to forage for food; or possession of an 'illegally' acquired parcel of food, clothing or other items. The executions had to be witnessed by all prisoners, including groups of Jewish prisoners brought in from other camps. Camp inmates were ordered to walk around the gallows with their faces turned to those who had been hanged. The aim was to terrify and demoralize.[12]

Despite the threat of death by hanging, prisoners did attempt to escape. They ran alone or in a group. Constant fear and the threat of capture accompanied escapees.

Dr Anna Ziółkowska reflected:[13]

> You can imagine what it would have been like for an escapee. Every escape is an act of desperation. But imagine a Jew who escapes from a camp in Poznań. Most likely he may not even be sure where he is—but he escapes. He looks dreadful: he smells and his clothes are rags. He may not even speak Polish, only Yiddish. But he escapes. He may be killed and any Pole willing to help him is risking his life too. An escapee caught by local police was handed over to the Gestapo and after interrogation was returned to the camp from which he escaped, where he was publicly executed.[14]

In May 1942, three prisoners attempted to escape: Hersz Leiserowicz, Chaskiel Leiserowicz and Aron Rosiecki. All three were caught a few days later.[15]

Poles from the town of Antonin were forced to play music during these executions.

One of the musicians described the scene:[16]

> It was a Sunday in autumn. I was then in the camp and played for the Germans. Around four in the afternoon, the Commandant ordered that the Jews be assembled in the

Appellplatz and told them to dance. At the same time, he ordered the hanging of a Jew who had escaped from the camp, for which the orchestra had to play marches.

Jacob recalled:[17]

As soon as they were ready for a hanging everybody, regardless of where we were working, had to march back to the camp. If they took us back to the camp in the middle of the day we knew at once that something was going to happen: a selection or a hanging.

And I will never forget this. It was in early 1943 when two fourteen-year-old Jewish brothers, twins from Wieluń, were brought into the camp. They were working for one of the commandants and had decided to run away. They simply wanted to go home to their parents. They had got about 100 kilometres away from the camp when they were caught by the Gestapo and taken to Poznań. When they brought them back to the camp after eight days, we could not recognize them after the beatings they had received. They then hanged them in our camp. On that day they hanged seven boys: these two and some others for having stolen something from the fields—raw potatoes or carrots or something, or for having stood up to the master, or some other 'crime'.

In the sick bay/hospital was a doctor from Berlin, Dr Hartstein. Once a prisoner was badly hurt in an accident. He lost half his face and broke his legs, so naturally the doctor tried as best he could to save him. The Commandant then told the doctor to kill him. The doctor refused, so they called the Gestapo in Poznań, who took him away. We did not see him for four weeks. When they brought him back, they hanged him on the same gallows as the boys. This was Guttenbrunn. Every couple of weeks they hanged four, five, six people.

Morris Shell recalled:[18]

Whenever there was a hanging, we were all brought in to watch. For me one day it was already the second episode of hanging, so I watched, but said to myself: 'At least it's not me.' We were already a little bit immune to it. This was our life: going on without knowing what tomorrow would bring, that maybe you would be the next one.

Once some boys got caught stealing potatoes from a field. One fellow was about six feet tall, and there was a little fifteen-year-old who wasn't even five feet. Can you imagine what a six-foot-tall fellow and a five-foot-short boy hanging look like? These are happenings that you can never forget.

Selections were also a common occurrence in the camp. Instructions from the Work Ministry of 25 September 1941 decreed that Jews no longer able to work were to be listed for the 'return transport', without stipulating their final destination. Subsequent transports from the forced labour camps indicate that Chełmno became the 'final destination' for physically wrecked prisoners, not only from the camps in Wielkopolska, but from all over the Wartheland.[19]

Leon Jolson recalled:[20]

Throughout the time that we were in Guttenbrunn, there were selections. We had to stand in lines. They realized that if we knew beforehand of the selection, we would get up in the middle of the night and pinch our cheeks to 'get colour', to still look healthy. So they would come in without telling us anything and mingle with us after we came back from work. We had numbers on our clothing, a white piece of cloth which was sewn on the chest and the leg. So they just wrote down the number.

Jacob recalled:[21]

> In the middle of 1943, there was a big selection and 750 people were chosen for extermination. At that time, I had been in hospital for about three weeks with a very bad case of diarrhoea; I probably weighed forty-five kilos. I thought this was the end for me. Twenty or more Gestapo men came from Poznań: the Commandant was there, the Jewish police, everyone. All the people from the hospital were selected for the transport, about ninety of us.
>
> I guess it was my destiny to survive! Before going to hospital, I had been working on the construction of a huge hall to house machinery. We had a foreman, a Pole, and his name was Franciszek or Franek. He was such a bandit, such a sadist—you could not imagine. He beat people up every day, but for some reason he liked me, maybe because I had once repaired some trousers for him. He came into the camp's hospital the afternoon of the transport, saw me there and said to me: 'Krawiec'—which means tailor in Polish—'what are you doing here? Do you want to die?' I said to him: 'Franciszek, what can I do? They put me here.' He said: 'Wait. I'll get you out. Don't worry.'
>
> First he went to the German Commandant and said: 'I want that boy out. He's one of my best workers.' So they said: 'Take him.' But I was not able to walk to the gate, I was

so weak. So he said to the other boys: 'Take him under your arms and walk him out so that the Germans don't see that he is weak or that he can't walk.' So they took me out and hid me in a storage shed. Franciszek told me: 'You know those going on the transport are all going to be killed. So hide here until tomorrow morning and then you go back to the camp with the boys, as though you had just finished the night shift. By then, the transport will be gone.' That's how I was saved. It was a miracle!

Those selected were loaded into cattle trains with tiny windows covered with mesh. They wrote on the wagons 'contagious transport'; you couldn't go near it. And they kept these people there for a night and two days, in the summer heat, without a drop of water. Half of them died in that train! Among them were two of my cousins, two young boys. The Germans had announced: 'Whoever is sick and is not able to work anymore, come voluntarily and we will send you back to Łódź, to the Ghetto.' So the boys volunteered, because their parents were in that Ghetto. Afterwards I started getting letters from my uncle asking what had happened to his sons, because they used to write to him sometimes. We didn't know what had happened to them. We only found out later that they had been taken to Chełmno and killed there.

Later I returned from work and the Block Leader called out to me: 'Widawski, Grün (head of the Jewish Police) wants you.' I thought: 'Oh my God, now I'm in trouble.' The Polish boys working in the camp were allowed to go home for a few days' 'leave' and they would bring food back to the camp. I knew some of them from Wieruszów. They had offered to share some of this food with me if I could get into their camp. So I took the risk and snuck off from work when I could. I wanted to live. That day, Franek was looking for me and couldn't find me since I was in the Polish camp organizing food to bring back to our camp. I would bribe the Block Leader with some food, and he would hide the rest for me. When I came back, Franek said: 'Where have you been?' and I told him that I had been to the Polish camp to see some boys from my town, from around Poznań. He was from Poznań too. 'I needed to eat, so the boys gave me some food.' He said: 'I could kill you'—but he didn't touch me. He didn't touch me.

Often the Poles who went on leave didn't come back on time. To discourage this, they would lock them up in the police station for a few days. One day the police asked for a couple of boys to work at the station. Grün chose me and another boy to go there. That's why he was looking for me, not as punishment because of my absence from work, as I feared. Grün then took us to the German Commandant and told him: 'These are the two best boys. I've chosen them to work at the police station.' So I began working there. We cleaned the station and the policemen's boots and took care of a little garden and a couple of ducks. This meant that I didn't have to work on the roads any more!

At the police station there were four officers: a policeman named Hanker from Germany, plus two Volksdeutsche. The police chief was an old German whose name was Glück, and he was probably sixty-five years old at the time, so they couldn't send him to the front. A very nice man. His wife, maybe twenty years younger, was a real beast, a real Nazi.

One of my jobs at the police station was to pick up food for the policemen from the kitchen in the Polish camp, where it was prepared for the Polish workers and German staff. One of the chief cooks, a Pole by the name of Edward, was a nice man. As soon as I came in, he said to me: 'Jacob, sit down behind the barracks and I will bring you something good,' and he would bring me out a meal, some meat and so on. Afterwards, we would take the soup and the second course to the station. The second course was a single portion per person, but the soup was in a bucket. So he put in extra. I took the soup to the policemen, each of them took a full plate, and the rest was left for us. Working at the station, I started to get a little healthier.

One afternoon Glück gave me half a loaf of bread and said: 'Take this with you to the camp.' I said: 'Herr Kommandant, I can't take this. If I take this bread into the camp, the Polish guards will kill me.' He replied: 'Tomorrow you will take a whole loaf—and just let them try to do something to you.' The Poles didn't touch me because they knew that I worked in that police station. After that I was no longer afraid of the Jewish policemen or the Polish guards.

I worked there for a few months and everything was going well. At that time, the Commandant was living in Poznań, which was six or eight kilometres away. Then he decided that he wanted to live closer to the police station. They threw out a Polish family that was living in Guttenbrunn in a beautiful villa, and he and his wife moved in. He then came to the officers and said: 'I am taking Jacob with me to work in my villa.'

So then I was working for him and his wife. And the difference between these two people! On Sunday mornings we would go out hunting. He had a big dog and a motorbike. In the morning I would clean his boots and make them shine beautifully. He would come into the kitchen, take a schnapps and give me a schnapps and a piece of strudel. But he would say: 'Go outside the house to eat it so that my wife doesn't see you.' He was afraid of her.

In that villa, I had a garden and two pigs and again I had to go to the kitchen in the Polish camp to take food and scraps for the pigs. As before, I had my meal in the kitchen. Sometimes when I was cooking the potatoes for the pigs, the Commandant's wife would say to me—very formally, never using the familiar 'you' address—'Herr Jacob, could you cook half a dozen potatoes for me?' When I cooked them, what she didn't finish she threw in the garbage. She wouldn't offer any to me!

On 9 August 1943, the order was given by Nazi authorities at the highest level to close the labour camps in Wielkopolska. The liquidation of the RAB camps, including Guttenbrunn, was in line with Heinrich Himmler's directive that all Jews in the occupied area were to be deported to concentration camps.[22]

Jacob recalled:[23]

In August 1943, we heard that our camp was going to be liquidated. Glück said to me: 'I will try and get permission for you to say here' and went to the Gestapo in Poznań. He came back the next day and said to me: 'Jacob, I can't do anything about it. You have to go.' I asked him where we were going. He said: 'You're going to a big concentration camp—but I don't know where.' I believed that he didn't know where. But before we left, he packed a rucksack for me with two loaves of bread, maybe half a dozen packets of cigarettes and two packets of butter. He said: 'Youngster, you will have this for a while.' But I didn't get even a bite of this, because as soon as we arrived in Auschwitz we had to throw everything away. Everything was confiscated.

A couple of weeks after this conversation with the Commandant, they transported us to Auschwitz.

On 26 August 1943, 315 prisoners were transported out of Guttenbrunn, emptying it. Jacob, Issac Pankowski, Max Procel, Morris Shell and others were on that transport.[24]

At the beginning of 1943 there were still some 11,000 prisoners working in 100 or so camps in the Poznań area; these were progressively liquidated. This was the consequence of the Third Reich's political agenda for the Jewish people. The decision to liquidate demonstrated that the use of Jewish labour was only a passing phase, flowing from economic need. Jews had created huge profits for German industrialists. But isolation in forced labour camps and destruction through their physical labour were only early stages of extermination. They were nevertheless an effective instrument in carrying out the Nazi's ultimate aim to destroy the Jewish people.[25]

Notes

1 Anna Ziółkowska, *Obozy pracy przymusowej dla Żydów w Wiekopolsce w latach okupacji hitlerowskiej (1941-45)* (Forced Labour Camps for Jews in Wielkopolska during the Years of Nazi Occupation (1941-45), (Poznań: Wydawnictwo Poznańskie, (Poznań Publishing: 2005), 95
2 Anna Ziółkowska, interview with Freda Widawski, Luboń (Żabikowo): 2010
3 Jacob Widawski, transcripts of interviews conducted at the Consulate-General of the Federal Republic of Germany, 1974, 1975, Sydney; transcripts of testimony given at trial against Heinrich Niemeyer, 1978, 1982, 1989, Indictment StA Hannover 11 Js 5/73, Hannover; audio testimony for the *12th Hour Project of Oral Testimonies* (Sydney: Australian Institute for Holocaust Studies, 1990); video testimony, 1995, (Sydney: USC Shoah Foundation Institute), code 2528
4 Ibid.

5   Jack Fogel, interview with Freda Widawski, Melbourne, 2011
6   Jacob Widawski, testimonies, German Consulate-General; transcripts, Hannover trial; *12th Hour Project*; USC Shoah Foundation, code 2528
7   Jack Fogel, interview with Freda Widawski
8   Leon Jolson (aka Liabiz Działowski), video testimony, 1996 (Sydney: USC Shoah Foundation Institute), code 17462
9   Morris Shell (aka Moshe David 'Dudek' Skorupa), video testimony, 1995 (Sydney: USC Shoah Foundation Institute), code 5117
10 Jacob Widawski, testimonies, German Consulate-General; transcripts, Hannover trial; *12th Hour Project*; USC Shoah Foundation, code 2528
11 Ibid.
12 Ziółkowska, *Obozy pracy*, 65, 201
13 Ziółkowska, *Obozy pracy*, 203; Anna Ziółkowska, interview with Freda Widawski
14 Ziółkowska, *Obozy pracy*, 202
15 Ziółkowska, *Obozy pracy*, 204-05
16 Ziółkowska, *Obozy pracy*, 211
17 Jacob Widawski, testimonies, German Consulate-General; transcripts, Hannover trial; *12th Hour Project*; USC Shoah Foundation, code 2528
18 Morris Shell, video testimony, USC Shoah Foundation, code 5117
19 Ziółkowska, *Obozy pracy*, 178-79, 181; 185-86
20 Leon Jolson, video testimony, USC Shoah Foundation Institute, code 17462
21 Jacob Widawski, testimonies, German Consulate-General; transcripts, Hannover trial; *12th Hour Project*; USC Shoah Foundation, code 2528
22 Ziółkowska, *Obozy pracy*, 228
23 Jacob Widawski, testimonies, German Consulate-General; transcripts, Hannover trial; *12th Hour Project*; USC Shoah Foundation, code 2528
24 Ziółkowska, *Obozy pracy*, 237-38
25 Ziółkowska, *Obozy pracy*, 239

ND# 13
Auschwitz

Oświęcim (in Polish), Oshpitzin (in Yiddish), a shtetl which the Germans renamed Auschwitz, gives cause for it to be one of the most sinister sounds in any language.[1]

Jacob recalled:[2]

> From Guttenbrunn to Auschwitz: the distance was not so great, about 400 kilometres. But they didn't want to bring the train in during daylight, so they loaded us up in the afternoon, around two or three o'clock. We travelled late into the night. Around midnight we stopped in a field where there were trees and nothing else. We didn't know where we had arrived. We couldn't see anything.

Prisoners were deported to Auschwitz in cattle cars or passenger trains. Like Jacob, they did not know their destination. Many died during the journey due to the appalling conditions. The deportations were executed according to plans prepared by the Poznań Gestapo and carried out by the Gendarmerie and Schutzpolizei.[3]

Issac Pankowski recalled:[4]

> They didn't tell us anything. A Pole who worked with me urged me to run away. But where could I run? So the day

before we left, he brought me an extra half a loaf of bread. There were rumours of a place not far from Kattowitz (Katowice), a place where they turned people into soap. I saw a sign that said 'to Kattowitz'. So I thought: 'It's really true; that's where they're taking us.' As we travelled, we didn't get any water, nothing. We arrived in Auschwitz at night.

Morris Shell described the transport:[5]

When we came to the railway, for the first time we were surrounded by the SS. There were already a few wagons loaded with inmates from other camps, and we joined them. They shoved us in into these big cattle wagons with barbed wire windows. I couldn't tell you how many people were in each wagon, but there was no room to sit or lie down: just standing up. Months before, when we had been working on the railway lines, the very same trains had stopped in front of me and I had looked in through these little barbed wire windows. It never dawned on me that these could be Jews. It never dawned on me that I was going to suffer the same fate a few months later.

Auschwitz was the invention of Reichsführer-SS Heinrich Himmler. On 27 April 1940, he ordered the establishment of a large new concentration camp near the Polish town of Oświęcim, sixty kilometres west of Kraków, and thirty-five-and-a-half kilometres south of Katowice, in the rich coal basin of eastern Upper Silesia. The site was selected because it was located at a major railway junction, at the centre of three big industrial areas. It offered good building ground plus a bountiful supply of water. The coal to be extracted, of relatively low grade, was intended to serve as raw material for the chemical industry. This camp became known as the Konzentrationslager (KL) Auschwitz-Birkenau.[6]

KL Auschwitz became the largest concentration camp in the Third Reich. It covered almost sixty-five square kilometres and consisted of three camps:[7]

- Auschwitz I, established in June 1940, contained twenty-two brick buildings of two storeys each; a hospital; two bathhouses; a gas chamber and a crematorium. It was the main camp where the central administration, Gestapo Headquarters and various firms working for the German Army were located.
- Auschwitz II, Birkenau, was built in 1941 for the mass murder of prisoners in its four gas chambers and crematoria.
- Auschwitz III, Buna Monowitz, was built in 1942 and served as a labour camp for the construction of vast synthetic rubber and petrol works.

In May 1940, thirty German prisoners, criminals, had arrived in Auschwitz from the Sachsenhausen concentration camp; on 14 June, the first transport of 728 Polish inmates had arrived from Tarnów. By March 1941, the prison population was 10,900, most of them non-Jewish Poles. However, by the beginning of 1943, ninety to ninety-five percent of the prisoners in Auschwitz were Jewish. By 1944 the total population had risen to around 81,000.[8]

The Birkenau camp was extended with the opening of a whole new sector, BII, which was subdivided into several camps designated by the letters *a* to *f*. Sector BIIa became the quarantine sector for new male arrivals.

Auschwitz I, II and III were overseen by one Commandant, the first SS-Obersturmbannführer, Rudolf Höss, from May 1940 to November 1943. Directly under the Commandant was the Schutzhaftalgerführer, who was always an SS officer.

Under them were the functionaries with whom the prisoners

had contact. They were the Rapportführer (report writer, at times also known as Schreiber or scribe/secretary); the block supervisor or Blockführer; the head of the work detail or the Kommandoführer; the Lagerkapo and a large staff of subordinate *Kapos*; plus, the guards' commander or Postenführer.[9]

The *Kapos* were responsible for the organization of work and its results; the dividing up and formation of work crews; escorting the crews to the work site; supervising the performance of the work; accompanying back to camp those who had survived the day; and seeing that those who had not survived were also delivered back to camp. As such they held enormous power over the prisoners and were universally disliked and feared.[10]

Until 1944, trains full of prisoners arrived at a station which became known as the Alte Judenrampe (the old Jewish platform or unloading ramp), located between Auschwitz I and Birkenau, about one-and-a-half kilometres from Birkenau.[11]

It is likely that Jacob arrived at this station.

At the ramp, SS doctors with brown gloves, together with other SS men, separated a small number of those capable of working from the mass of the other arrivals. They were then registered as prisoners and sent to the camp.[12]

Shlomo Venezia wrote:[13]

> A cheerful little station, very much like any other provincial railway stop: a small square framed by tall chestnuts and paved with yellow gravel. Not far off, beside the road, squatted a tiny wooden shed. This is where they loaded freight for Birkenau; supplies for the construction of the camp, and people for the gas chambers. Trucks drove around, loaded up lumber, cement, people—a regular daily routine.
>
> The doors opened on to the ramp, just opposite the potato

shed. My first feeling was a sense of relief. I didn't know how much longer it would have been possible to survive on this train without anything to eat, without any space, air or toilet facilities. Before entering the main gate, I noticed a sign placed near the barbed wire fence: Vorsicht Hochspannung Lebensgefahr (Beware, high tension, danger of death).

Jacob recalled his arrival at Auschwitz:[14]

> When they brought us into Auschwitz, suddenly they opened the wagons and we saw people walking around in striped uniforms on the platforms. We didn't know who they were; we never saw that in the other camps. These were the people who worked in the Sonderkommando (prisoners who were forced to dispose of the dead victims). As soon as we arrived, hundreds of the SS 'greeted' us, each with a German shepherd dog and machine gun in hand. They started to yell: 'Out, out, out, you bandits! Throw out whatever you have.' So I threw out my sack with the food and then everything was gone!
>
> In the front stood the Commandant from Auschwitz, two doctors and a few other big-shots from the SS. We started to march: some left, some right; nobody knew what this meant. But we noticed all the older people or those who looked really weak were sent to the left. Left, right, left, right: then we were marching.
>
> The two jobs that I had at Guttenbrunn, for the Commandant and at the police station with the extra food rations saved me, because they meant that when I came to Auschwitz, I was not a total *Muselmann* (a walking corpse/skeleton). I was twenty-two years old, small in stature, but still reasonably strong and healthy looking.

We start to march in rows of five. This train station was maybe one-and-a-half or two kilometres from the camp. I thought to myself: how can I escape from here? I was looking around, but it was impossible. Every second row, there was an SS man with a dog.

Then I saw the gate with the sign ARBEIT MACHT FREI (Work sets you free).

Rudolf Vrba testified:[15]

The trains with the Jews were coming in day and night, one per day, at times five per day, from all corners of Europe. The door was opened and the first order given was 'Alle raus' (everybody out). They used sticks, clubs, cursing.

Sometimes, SS dealt with it ironically: 'Good morning, madam. Will you walk out please?' or 'How nice that you have arrived. We are so sorry that it wasn't too convenient, but now things will be different.' Whenever a new transport came, the ramp was cleaned absolutely to zero point. No trace from the previous transport was allowed to remain— not one trace.

Issac Pankowski recalled his arrival:[16]

The yelling 'Alle raus' started. Everyone was told to drop whatever they had with them. Each one of us had brought some sort of parcel. They told us we would get our things afterwards. We looked around. The place was full of searchlights. We didn't know what they were. People in striped uniforms. We asked: 'Is there a hospital here? What happens here?' Their answer was: 'Don't ask questions. Don't talk.'

Morris Shell described his reactions on arrival:[17]

> When they opened the doors of the train, you thought you were on another planet. The SS; the dogs; the spotlights. It was hell! And immediately they took aside a few older people and a few young ones who looked unhealthy.
>
> They marched the rest of us. On both sides the motorbikes and the searchlights, the dogs barking, the shouting and screaming. We marched and marched. On that march, I knew that I was going to be exterminated. I just didn't know what method they were going to use.

Jacob recalled:[18]

> So they brought us into the camp at night and led us into a block. Half of the prisoners in our block were Gypsies and half our transport. In the morning they took us out and brought us to the bath-house. We were stripped of all our belongings. I had hidden some photographs from home, but you had to take off your clothing, everything. That's why I had nothing left.
>
> In the bathhouse were barbers who shaved all our hair— our heads, under arms, everywhere. They disinfected us with Lysol, after which we went into the showers. After we had washed, they threw us a pair of underpants and a shirt. Nothing else. Barefoot. The next day they gave us a pair of trousers and a jacket. Later they gave us a pair of wooden shoes. This was done in such a way as to humiliate you: a tall fellow would get a pair of trousers that reached halfway up his thigh, a little guy trousers half a metre too long. But you couldn't say: 'Hey, this is too long or too short' or you immediately got a beating. You had to wear what you were given.

Max Procel recalled:[19]

> When we arrived at the platform, I saw a Jewish man from Łódź whose name was Janek. He was the hangman in one of the Poznań camps, so he knew me from there. He saw that I was wearing riding boots, still in good condition. He demanded: 'Give me your boots.' But in the heel of one I had hidden the diamond. So I said: 'Janek, I can't give you the boots; I need them.' He replied: 'You won't need them. You'll be given new clothes and everything you've brought with you will be taken away.' So I took the heel off, took out the diamond, and gave him the boots.
>
> They took us to the bath-house and told us that we were going to have a shower and that we would be given uniforms when we came out. Luckily, I had already given him the boots—because they would have found the diamond. I swallowed it before going into the shower and the next day I passed it through my system and hid it inside my clothing.

The block for 'disinfecting', which included the showers, was situated between Crematoria II and III. New arrivals either received civilian clothes with garish red stripes on the back and sides, or striped prison clothes. In each case the clothes had been worn before by many people. Everything was torn and dirty. Meanwhile the suits, dresses and underwear which the prisoners had brought into the camp were sent off to the Reich.[20]

The personal particulars of each new prisoner were entered on a form bearing many detailed questions. The interrogation and registration of a new arrival was carried out by a work squad consisting of prisoners known as 'political clerks'. These numbered about twenty in all, and between them they knew nearly all the languages of Europe. In this process the prisoner lost his identity and became just a number, which was tattooed on his left forearm. The system of tattooing prisoners was only applied in Auschwitz, and only those selected for life were so marked. Some 400,000 were given numbers. The group which had come from Guttenbrunn with Jacob was tattooed with numbers ranging from 140,000 to 142,000. Jacob became 141,687.[21]

Morris Shell recalled:[22]

> When we got the number, we were frightened again. We thought that maybe this meant that we had been chosen for death. But the other inmates told us: 'Now that you have the number, you are going to go to work.' We still didn't believe it, but that's what happened. If you were tattooed, they had picked you as being able to go to work.

Shlomo Venezia described the tattooing process:[23]

> They used a sort of ballpoint pen with a sharp point that pierced one's skin and made the ink go in under the skin. They had to make these little penetrations until the number appeared on one's arm. It was extremely painful. When the man tattooing me finally dropped my arm, I immediately rubbed the front of my arm to lessen the pain. When I looked to see what he'd done to me, I couldn't make anything out under the mixture of blood and ink. I was suddenly scared that I might have wiped the number out. With a bit of spit, I wiped my arm clean and I saw the number that had been 'injected': 182,727. My identity.

Primo Levi wrote:[24]

> The operation lasted no more than a minute, but it was traumatic. Its symbolic meaning was clear to everyone: this is an indelible mark; you will never leave here. This is the mark with which slaves are branded and cattle sent to the slaughter, and that is what you have become. You no longer have a name; this is your new name. It was also a return to barbarism, all the more perturbing for orthodox Jews, as the tattoo is forbidden by Jewish law.
>
> At a distance of forty years, my tattoo has become a part of my body. I don't glory in it, nor am I ashamed of it; I do not display and do not hide it. I show it unwillingly to those who ask out of pure curiosity; readily, and with anger, to those who say they are incredulous. Often young people ask me why I don't have it erased, and this surprises me. Why should I? There are not many of us in the world to bear this witness.

Freda recalls that Jacob's response to questions about his tattoo ranged from serious to facetious. Where the situation was too difficult to discuss, or too incomprehensible to explain, such as a query from a waiter in Thailand, he would joke (like many others) that 141,687 was his girlfriend's telephone number. Conversely, when the question was posed by someone who Jacob thought would understand, he would readily explain. For example:

> In early February 1989 we were at Bangkok Airport waiting for a Lufthansa flight to Frankfurt. Opposite us sat a young man who was fascinated by Jacob's tattoo. His eyes darted from Jacob's arm to his face and back again. Finally, he walked across to him and said: 'Excuse me—I hope you don't

mind—but I have heard of this' [pointing to the tattoo], but have never met anyone who has such a tattoo. Can I talk with you?' He was a young German, knowledgeable about his country's bleak history and enthralled by this living memorial. He spent most of the flight talking with Jacob about his War experiences and his own concerns regarding the rise of ultra-right political parties in West Germany.

Those prisoners not sent to the gas chambers, like Jacob, were sent to the quarantine block. The Nazis set up quarantine for all prisoners brought into the camp, supposedly to avoid introducing infectious diseases. However, the main purpose, as with other 'laws' of the camp, was to reduce prisoners to a state of abject fear, to break their spirit and their will to resist. There were drills and 'sport' lasting many hours in the roll-call area. This period was a test of physical endurance that only the healthiest survived.[25]

Men for the most part went to BIIa Quarantine sector for a period of two to four weeks. Up to 1,000 men were crowded into wooden barracks originally designed to house fifty-two horses. They were without windows, except for small ventilation shutters in the roof. Men were crammed into three-tier bunks or 'hutches', without straw or blankets, and a few overflowing buckets served as lavatories. The stench of bodies encrusted with faeces was a nightly assault on the senses. When the barracks were full to capacity, those left over were forced to sleep 'under the stars'. In addition, during quarantine the prisoners did not work, which meant that they received reduced food rations.[26]

Jacob described his time in quarantine:[27]

On arrival they put us into quarantine in Block IIa and kept us there for about two weeks. The worst part was going out

at night if you needed to go to the toilet. You couldn't—because you could get killed. First of all, the block was dark, and if you went into the wrong room because you couldn't see, people there thought you had come to steal something. So even those who had stomach cramps wouldn't go out until morning, since they were afraid that they wouldn't find their way back to their room.

Shlomo Venezia described his sense of foreboding:[28]

> While we were in quarantine, we constantly saw smoke emerging from the chimney and it was impossible to escape from the acrid smell of burnt flesh that drifted through the whole camp.

Between 1942 and1945, more than forty sub-camps or satellite camps were set up over a wide radius around Auschwitz, in the industrial area of Upper Silesia. They were built near mines, foundries and other enterprises, and served as a huge pool of prisoner labour for the German war effort.[29]

By 1944, more than 40,000 Auschwitz prisoners had been employed in these industries, with over 8,000 engaged in the mining sector.[30]

The Buna Monowitz camp was the largest labour camp at Auschwitz. Set up in 1942 in the village of Monowice, it occupied an area of around fifteen square kilometres. It is estimated 25,000 prisoners were engaged in the construction of the IG Farbenindustrie plant, to produce synthetic petrol from coal. Buna also included lesser camps for the coal mines: Fürstengrube (in Wesoła), Königshütte, Jawischowiz (in Jawiszowice), Jaworzno (in Bobrek) and Janinagrube (in Libiąż).[31]

On 25 November 1944, Auschwitz III was re-named Konzentrationslager Monowitz, with jurisdiction over all auxiliary camps. This is how the Birkenau camp disappeared from the list of Nazi concentration camps.[32]

The satellite camps formed peculiar city-states set apart by boundaries. Each was run by a Kommandoführer, who was unofficially called Lagerführer. The Kommandoführen were nominated by the Commandant of the Auschwitz main camp. He had a Deputy and a staff of SS officers and guard units.[33]

Max Procel described how he was 'selected' for one of the sub-camps:[34]

> They said they wanted people to send to another working camp, so I went voluntarily. I came to the office and said to the clerk, a Frenchman: 'Put me down on the list.' He said: 'Get lost. I have enough; the list is full.' I took out the diamond I had hidden and said: 'Here is a diamond. Put me on the list.' So because of that diamond, I was send to Jaworzno.

Jacob recalled his selection to work in a sub-camp:[35]

> I was in quarantine for about two weeks. By then, we already had all our clothing, the wooden shoes, everything. One day they put us all in the *Appellplatz* and along came the Commandant of the Janina coal mine, Unterscharführer Baumgartner and his report writer, a German Jew from Hamburg, by the name of Scharne. I knew him from Guttenbrunn. Before the selection he warned me: 'Jacob, in two hours a buyer will come to take people out of Auschwitz to work. I hear we are going to a coal mine. Don't tell him that you're a tailor, or you'll rot here in Auschwitz.' The

Germans' view was that big fellows are strong, while a little fellow, a tailor, was nothing. So I said: 'Scharne, what should I tell him?' 'Tell him that you're a road builder.'

They lined us all up. Everybody had to have their shirts off, and we were just in our pants. SS Unterscharführer Baumgartner and another couple of SS men went through the rows of prisoners, looking for strong fellows. He asked everybody: 'What was your profession?'. He came to me and I looked well—a little fellow, but I looked strong. He asked: 'What was your profession?' I said: 'Road builder, Unterscharführer.' He screamed out: 'What?' So I yelled louder: 'Yes, Unterscharführer a road builder.' 'Scharne, put him on the list.' Scharne said: 'Yes, Herr Unterscharführer, this is one of the boys from my camp, a very good worker.' He wrote down the number 141,687 tattooed on my left arm, and I was on the list! And that is how I came to Janina, to the coal mine.

They picked out some 500 people, including five doctors. Later in the camp, they chose *Kapos* from the prisoners. They loaded us into open trucks, under SS guard, and they brought us to the Janina coal mine.

When Jack Fogel heard Jacob's story, he commented to Freda: 'From a sznider (tailor) to a builder. Whatever: that's how people survived.'[36]

From their testimonies, we know that 'the Wieruszów boys' and others who came from Guttenbrunn to Auschwitz with Jacob were scattered to several sub-camps:[37]
- Leon Jolson and Jack Fogel to Fürstengrube, a coal mine
- Max Procel to Jaworzno, also a coal mine
- Issac Pankowski to Lagischa, a power station
- Morris Shell to Eintrachthütte, a labour camp attached to steelworks.

Top: The site of the Alte Judenrampe. Photo 2015.
Bottom: Quarantine blocks in Birkenau. Photo 2010.

Inside the barracks and the latrines. Photographed by Marc Pelta, Jacob's cousin, on 20 March 2011. Contained in his book *Ma journeé á AUSCHWITZ* (My day in AUSCHWITZ, Amazon).

MINA & JACOB

Konzentrationslager AUSCHWITZ Art der Haft: Sich.Jude Gef. Nr 141 687

Name und Vorname: **Widawski Jakub, Israel**
geb. 1.5.1921 zu Weruschau, Kr. Welungen
Wohnort: Weruschau, Ciasnastr:6, Kr:w.o. Warthegau.
Beruf: Schneider Rel.: mos.
Staatsangehörigkeit: ehem. Polen Stand: led.
Name der Eltern: Szmul u. Ruchla, geb. Jakubowicz Rasse: jüd.
Wohnort: V:gest.M:unbekannt
Name der Ehefrau: Rasse:
Wohnort:
Kinder: keine Alleiniger Ernährer der Familie oder der Eltern: nein
Vorbildung: keine
Militärdienstzeit: von — bis
Kriegsdienstzeit: von — bis
Grösse: 157 Nase: gradl Haare: braun Gestalt: stark
Mund: normal Bart: keinen Gesicht: oval Ohren: abst.
Sprache: polnisch, deutsch. Augen: braun Zähne: gut,4 fe
Ansteckende Krankheit oder Gebrechen: keine
Besondere Kennzeichen: keine
Rentenempfänger: nein
Verhaftet am: -.8.1941 in Weruschau
1. Mal eingeliefert: 26. Aug. 1943 RSHA 2. Mal eingeliefert:
Einweisende Dienststelle:
Grund:
Parteizugehörigkeit: keine von — bis
Welche Funktionen: keine
Mitglied v. Unterorganisationen: nein
Kriminelle Vorstrafen: ang. keine

Politische Vorstrafen: ang. keine

Ich bin darauf hingewiesen worden, dass meine Bestrafung wegen intellektueller Urkundenfälschung erfolgt, wenn sich die obigen Angaben als falsch erweisen sollten.

Der Lagerkommandant

Jacob's Auschwitz prisoner record.
Transported from Weruschau (Wieruszów), August 1941.
Shows date of arrival in Auschwitz, 26 August 1943.

Notes

1. Rafael F. Scharf, *Poland, what have I to do with thee?* (London; Portland: Vallentine Mitchell, 1980), 178
2. Jacob Widawski, transcripts of interviews conducted at the Consulate-General of the Federal Republic of Germany, 1974, 1975, Sydney; transcripts of testimony given at trial against Heinrich Niemeyer, 1978, 1982, 1989, Indictment StA Hannover 11 Js 5/73, Hannover; audio testimony for the *12th Hour Project of Oral Testimonies* (Sydney: Australian Institute for Holocaust Studies, 1990); video testimony, 1995 (Sydney: USC Shoah Foundation Institute), code 2528
3. Anna Ziółkowska, *Obozy pracy przymusowej dla Żydów w Wiekopolsce w latach okupacji hitlerowskiej (1941-45)* (Forced Labour Camps for Jews in Wielkopolska during the Years of Nazi Occupation (1941-45), (Poznań: Wydawnictwo Poznańskie, (Poznań Publishing), 2005) 234-35
4. Issac (Yitzah) Pankowski, transcript of oral testimony (Jerusalem: Yad Vashem Archives, 1993), code 03-7202, V-D 242
5. Morris Shell (aka Moshe David 'Dudek' Skorupa), video testimony, 1995 (Sydney: USC Shoah Foundation Institute), code 5117
6. Israel Gutman et al., *Anatomy of the Auschwitz Death Camp* (Bloomington: Indiana University Press, 1994), 7, 10, 109; Jean E. Brown et al., *Images from the Holocaust: A Literature Anthology* (Lincolnwood, Illinois: NTC Publishing Group, 1997), 206; Helmut Krausnick et al., *Anatomy of the SS State* (English translation, London: William Collins, 1968), 473, 568; Ruth Ellen Gruber, *Upon the Doorposts of Thy House* (New York: John Wiley, 1994), 255-61; Alan Furst, *The Spies of Warsaw* (London: Weidenfeld & Nicolson, 2008), 69
7. Ana Novac, *The Beautiful Days of My Youth* (New York: Henry Holt, 1997), 303; Ota Kraus and Erlich Kulka, *The Death Factory: Document on Auschwitz* (London: Pergamon Press, 1966), 8
8. Israel Gutman, ed., *Encyclopedia of the Holocaust* (New York: Macmillan, 1990), 107; Gutman et al., *Anatomy of the Auschwitz Death Camp*, 10, 17; www.auschwitz.org; Martin Gilbert, *Auschwitz and the Allies* (London: George Rainbird, 1981), 34, 175; Kraus and Kulka, *The Death Factory*, 6, 13
9. Gutman, ed., *Encyclopedia of the Holocaust*, 113; Franciszek Piper, *Auschwitz Prisoner Labour: The Organization and Exploitation of Auschwitz Concentration Camp Prisoners as Labourers* (Oświęcim: Auschwitz-Birkenau State Museum, 2002), 381, 383; *Obozy hitlerowskie na ziemiach polskich 1939-45* (Nazi Camps on Polish Soil 1939-45), (Warszawa: Państwowe Wydawnictwo Naukowe, 1979), 361-62
10. Anna Pawelczyńska, *Values and Violence in Auschwitz* (London: University of California Press, 1979), 45-47

11 William Karel, *The Two Faces of Auschwitz* (documentary screened on SBS, 3 August 2012)
12 Krausnick, et al., *Anatomy of the SS State*, 479, 484; Kraus and Kulka, *The Death Factory*, 271
13 Janusz Nel Siedlecki, Krystyn Olszewksi, and Tadeusz Borowski, *We were in Auschwitz* (English translation New York: Welcome Rain Publishers, 2000; first published in Polish in 1946), 86, 88-89
14 Jacob Widawski, testimonies, German Consulate-General; transcripts, Hannover trial; *12th Hour Project* 1990; USC Shoah Foundation, code 2528
15 Rudolf Vrba, in Claude Lanzmann, *Shoah: The Complete Text of the Film* (New York: Pantheon Books, 1985), 40-43, 46
16 Pankowski, testimony Yad Vashem, code 03-7202, V-D 242
17 Shell, video testimony, USC Shoah Foundation, code 5117
18 Jacob Widawski, testimonies, German Consulate-General; transcripts, Hannover trial; *12th Hour Project* 1990; USC Shoah Foundation, code 2528
19 Max Procel, video testimony, 1997 (Melbourne: USC Shoah Foundation Institute), code 30561
20 Kraus and Kulka, *The Death Factory*, 15-16, 25-26, 28, 78
21 Ibid.
22 Shell, video testimony, USC Shoah Foundation, code 5117
23 Shlomo Venezia, *Inside the Gas Chambers: Eight Months in the Sonderkommando of Auschwitz* (Cambridge: Polity Press, 2009), 41
24 Primo Levi, *The Drowned and the Saved* (New York: Summit Books, 1988), 94-95
25 Anna Pawelczyńska, *Values and Violence in Auschwitz*, 60, 147; Danuta Czech, *Auschwitz Chronicle: 1939-45* (New York: Henry Holt, 1989, 1997), 829
26 Michael Moran, *A Country in the Moon: Travels in Search of the Heart of Poland* (London, Granta Books, 2009), 84; *Obozy hitlerowskie*, 363; Venezia, *Inside the Gas Chambers*, 44
27 Jacob Widawski, testimonies, German Consulate-General; transcripts, Hannover trial; *12th Hour Project* 1990; USC Shoah Foundation, code 2528
28 Venezia, *Inside the Gas Chambers*, 41
29 Gutman et al., *Anatomy of the Auschwitz Death Camp*, 17, 41
30 *Obozy hitlerowskie*, 365; Gutman et al., *Anatomy of the Auschwitz Death Camp*, 43
31 Czech, *Auschwitz Chronicle*, 827; Kraus and Kulka, *The Death Factory*, 214; Primo Levi and Leonardo De Benedetti, *Auschwitz Report* (Minerva Medica 1946; English version, London, Verso, 2006), 35; http://www.whale.to/b/sub.html
32 *Obozy hitlerowskie*, 361

33 Gutman et al., *Anatomy of the Auschwitz Death Camp*, 53
34 Max Procel, video testimony, USC Shoah Foundation, code 30561
35 Jacob Widawski, testimonies, German Consulate-General; transcripts, Hannover trial; *12th Hour Project* 1990; USC Shoah Foundation, code 2528
36 Jack Fogel, interview with Freda Widawski, Melbourne, 2011
37 http://en.wikipedia.org/wiki/Central_Labour_Camp_Jaworzno; http://en.wikipedia.org/wiki/Monowitz_concentration_camp; http://en.wikipedia.org/wiki/List_of_subcamps_of_Auschwitz; http://www.edwardvictor.com/Holocaust/Eintrachtshutte.htm

14
Płaszów

Kraków-Płaszów was the second largest camp after Auschwitz in the Kraków region, and one of the few that was established in the suburbs of a major city. In early 1943, after the Kraków Ghetto had been liquidated, its factories, machinery, stores and institutions such as the hospital were transferred to the new camp.[1]

When questioned about her experiences in Płaszów, Mina commented that no film, not even *Schindler's List*, could adequately portray the real horror:[2]

> They couldn't show in the film Commandant Amon Göth's personality. We had this fear of him in our bones, in our bodies. And who can show this in a film? Never. Whoever will make films, whenever stories will appear about our lives, nobody will be able to portray the fear and the terrible struggle that we went through.

The writer Tom Keneally noted:[3]

> When pressed to comment on the film *Schindler's List*, the survivors told Spielberg, the director, that he couldn't reproduce the stench of the camp, of their starved bodies, and of the bodies smouldering close to the surface of the soil.

MINA & JACOB

Mina recalled:[4]

> When I came to Płaszów, I was thinking only how I would manage in this camp. My sister, who had arrived there on an earlier transport, was lined up ready to go to work. At that time, she was part of the Saüberungskommando, the unit working in the liquidated Ghetto, sorting clothing and valuables left behind, for shipment to Germany. She saw me from a distance and I could see that she was crying, now that I was there. I thought: 'I know what you're thinking. You're thinking: how will she survive here?' The rule was that before you were selected for other work, everybody had to spend four weeks in Barackenbau, building the barracks for the camp. Very hard labour! And I, in my condition, after typhus, without hospitalization, without medication, had to do this hard work. It was the hardest time of my life.

As early as June 1942, three Judenlager (labour camps for Jews) had already been established in Płaszów. Working for various German firms they were known as Julag I Płaszów; Julag II Prokocim; and Julag III Bieżanów.[5]

Following the October Ghetto deportations, in November 1942, the decision was made to build a larger camp in Płaszów. SS-Oberscharführer Horst Pilařik, the leader of the Julag camps, organized a unit of 300 Jews who were initially brought every day from the Ghetto to help construct the camp. Once temporary barracks were put up, they were housed in them so they could stay overnight. After that more people were moved in every day. By 11 February 1943, when Amon Göth took charge, it held 2,000 Jews.[6]

The camp was a vast field on the rural outskirts of the city, some four kilometres south-east of Kraków's Rynek Główny (Main

Square). On a hilly, rocky terrain, near two granite quarries, it stretched beyond the hills to an area full of malaria-ridden swamps. At one end was the encroaching city and at the other the notorious old Austro-Hungarian hill fort, nicknamed Hujowa Górka (Prick Hill).[7] The camp was built over two adjacent Jewish cemeteries: the new Krakowski and the old Podgórski.[8]

Joseph Bau, an eyewitness to its creation, wrote:[9]

> **To prepare the area for construction, a tractor worked there. It pushed all the soil of the cemetery, along with decomposed bodies wrapped in rotting prayer shawls.**

The hilly terrain required immense human effort for the building of barracks, roads, water pipes and sewage lines. Hills had to be demolished and swamps drained—all by Jewish prisoners. The remains of the dead were dug up by earth-moving equipment and the bones thrown into a mass grave. Gravestones were pulled down and carried by hand to be laid as pavers. Headstones, with the names of the dead faintly visible, were used as steps.[10]

Following the liquidation of the Ghetto on 13 March 1943, 8,000 inmates—Mina among them—were brought to Płaszów, increasing the prisoner population to 10,000. By 3 September 1943, with the arrival of around 2,000 residents from the Tarnów Ghetto, the prison population stood at around 12,000. By November, after the three Julags were liquidated, and their inmates transferred, it was close to 14,000.[11]

To accommodate the extra prisoners, the area was expanded by September 1943 to eight square kilometres.[12] Villages were taken over, their inhabitants evicted, and their houses assigned to SS officers working in the camp.[13]

On completion, Płaszów contained 200 barracks, housing

25,000 Jewish prisoners, making it one of the largest forced labour camps in occupied Poland. It was divided into five main parts: the watch block; the Jewish barracks; the administrative buildings; the industrial buildings; and the mass graves.[14]

The camp was encircled by a double-row barbed wire fence charged with high-voltage electricity. Between each row was a deep ditch filled with water. Thirteen watchtowers were strategically placed every few hundred metres around the perimeter. Nazi guards, armed with machine guns, were on watch twenty-four hours a day. In addition to powerful searchlights mounted on each watchtower, spotlights were hung every few tens of metres on internal fence poles, lighting up the entire area.[15]

Individual areas of the camp: the living quarters for Germans; the Polish camp; and separate camps for Jewish males and females, were also divided with electrified barbed wire. Each section had a gate guarded by the Jewish Police.[16]

When Mina was brought to the camp, 180 barracks had been already semi-completed. They lacked water, electricity, heating, washhouses and latrines.[17]

The barracks were prefabricated buildings which had been carried up the hill to the camp from Płaszów Station by female prisoners. Constructed from thin boards, they generally measured forty by ten metres and contained three-storey bunks, built in the form of shelves. They housed 700-800 people. To construct each of these barracks, a builder usually allowed four weeks. But in Płaszów, such a barrack was built in four days.[18]

They were divided into two sections by a long corridor. In the middle of the hut stood a small heater for winter use. There were no closets or shelves. The only private property that the prisoners had, small items such as a dish or a spoon, clogs, a blanket or some clothing, were rolled up and hidden in their bunks. Men wore striped uniforms with a cap of the same thin material. Women still wore their own clothes, but were issued white kerchiefs. Both wore wooden clogs without socks.[19]

Mina recalled:[20]

> **My sister and I had two bunks together. And we kept our few personal things, some 'treasures' that still remained with us, such as a few photographs of our parents and the family inside a little sack that I had made. We hid this in the bunk, under the mattress.**

They were taking a huge risk, since not long after Mina's arrival, on 27-28 March 1943, an inspection was carried out throughout the camp and money or items of value were confiscated.[21]

The latrines used by prisoners were housed in two huts, one for men, the other for women. On each side of the huts were rough boards with thirty holes, 'eyes'; there were no partitions. Physical needs were taken care of in front of others, with lines of impatient prisoners anxious to take any free places. At the centre of the room was a long trough over which was suspended a pipe with a series of spigots, for washing. At least two people used every tap, while others waited for them to finish. This enabled 400 people to wash at the same time—when the water was running.[22]

In Płaszów, privacy did not exist. The 'beds' were wooden boxes, connected in bunk-bed fashion, one above the other, close to the next one. Prisoners undressed, ate, washed, slept and conducted all bodily functions in public.[23]

The lack of privacy would have been one of the most difficult aspects of camp life for Mina and others to bear. Adele and Freda remember that even after fifty years of marriage, having given birth to two children, she vigilantly guarded her privacy.

She recalled:[24]

> At this time the only person left from my family was my sister, who was with me in Płaszów. She started protecting me like my second mother, risking her life to cook for me the food which she managed to smuggle in from 'outside'.

Food was smuggled in by delivery drivers, by those who came in to work from outside, and by inmates who worked outside the camp.[25] Mina recalled:[26]

> As in all camps, the food and nourishment that we received in Płaszów was only about ten per cent of what a human being needs to survive. The food was delivered in terrible condition: potatoes and beetroot were rotten and frozen. I couldn't eat them, couldn't swallow, because of the stench! I said to my girlfriends: 'Let them kill me—but I'm not going to eat this.' They said: 'So you'll starve and you'll die.'

Unappetizing soup, cabbage mixed with beetroot, or sago, a dish made from barley, were doled out from a barrel.[27]
Joseph Bau wrote:[28]

> The colour of the soup depended on the kind of salt used. In winter, the cooks used the greenish salt used to melt the snow on the road; in summer they changed to the blue-ish kind that cattle ate. When the herring factory supplied skins and entrails, our food was called 'fish'. If some horses died in the stables, we had meat soup. When we spied barrels of spoiled sauerkraut that stank to high heaven, we knew we'd be eating cabbage soup for weeks.

Every evening the daily food rations were distributed in the barracks: 200-250 grams of bread per person per day, and a rancid square of margarine between twelve. The bread was a kind of dried dough made from a mixture of brown flour and sawdust, often covered with a growth of mould.[29]

Those who were able to restrain themselves saved half a slice of bread for the morning, so they could have it with the litre of 'coffee' they received for breakfast. The 'coffee' was in fact water to which black colouring had been added. It was difficult to drink because it was so bitter.[30]

Mina tried to survive on the meagre rations by saving the piece of bread for the following morning. But most other girls wolfed it down as soon as they received it.

Following the liquidation of the Ghetto, all the hospital staff, including doctors, came to Płaszów. A hospital for 140 patients was established as well as an infirmary. In addition, there were a number of sick bays which expanded as the population of the camp grew.[31]

Two types of surgical procedure were allowed: the setting of leg fractures and the removal of appendixes, since these did not leave the patient significantly disabled. Overall, it was dangerous to remain in the hospital too long, as the Nazis often required Dr Gross, the chief physician, to list fifty or more of the most seriously ill people for extermination.[32]

Throughout the whole of Płaszów's existence, it never received the medications most hospitals would. There were cases of typhus and typhoid fever which the Jewish doctors kept secret. They knew that those with typhoid fever would be shot.[33]

Cold, hunger, disease, lack of sanitation and privacy were characteristics of camp life. What made Płaszów a stand-out was the extreme cruelty of the Commandant, Amon Göth, and his underlings. As soon as SS-Sturmbannführer Amon Leopold Göth had taken over on 11 February 1943, he had unleashed a time of terror.[34]

Göth had been born in Vienna, and at seventeen joined the Hitler Youth. In 1930 he became a member of the SS. He moved to Poland soon after its invasion and became responsible for the administrative and financial aspects of mass deportations. He then went to work under Odilio Globocnik, the SS and Police leader in the district of Lublin, where he gained first-hand knowledge of different ways of exterminating Jews. In early 1943, he was transferred to the Kraków Ghetto, and supervised its liquidation, during which some 4,000 people were killed. Six months later he oversaw the destruction of the Tarnów Ghetto; again, thousands of people were killed.[35]

Amon Göth was a tyrant and a sadist who took advantage of a situation that gave him the power to mistreat prisoners without having to account for himself. He was big, weighing more than 100 kilos and standing 1.98 metres tall. For the slightest infraction of his rules, he would pummel a hapless prisoner's face and watch with pleasure as the man or woman spat broken teeth and their face became swollen and blue. When administering a whipping, he would compel the victim to count the lashes and if, in his agony, he made a mistake, to start counting again from the beginning.

If anyone escaped from the camp, their group was lined up and told to count off by tens. Then Göth would personally execute every tenth man.

His reputation for such bestial behaviour terrified everyone; the mere sight of him was enough to evoke fear. To appear even more frightening, he was often accompanied by his two large, ferocious dogs, Ralph and Rolf, who had been trained to attack Jews on command. Herr Rolf (Mr Rolf), was especially fond of attacking Jewish women after they were forced to undress.[36]

Göth had his own gang of equally cruel assistants. One carried two large guns which he fired at random during his frequent, raging outbursts. Another always carried a bullwhip in his hand, often striking people in their faces and causing the loss of, or permanent damage to an eye.[37]

The SS female guards entered the women's barracks at any time of the day or night. The one best remembered by survivors was Orlowska, who also carried a whip with her at all times and used it forcefully, sometimes for trivial reasons, sometimes for no reason at all.[38]

As soon as Göth took over the leadership of the camp, he enforced his own set of rules and regulations. He selected Wilek Chilowicz as the Jewish Lagerältester (camp elder), and Finkelstein as his deputy.[39]

The camp Police, the Ordnungsdienst or OD, consisted of 150 Jewish men. They were the mediators between the prisoners and the camp leaders, overseeing barracks and work groups. They incessantly spewed curses and used whips to enforce obedience during work. They assisted the SS guards in rounding up prisoners for selections and guarding them during lockups. In return, they had separate quarters, and the privilege of sleeping with their wives in special rooms that could be closed from the inside. They also got a double portion of thicker soup and a loaf of bread with jam.[40]

Each work division had a *Kapo*. Above them was the *Oberkapo*, who answered to the SS.[41]

Every hut or block had a Blockälteste. They were responsible for the cleanliness of the barracks; for carrying out the orders given by the SS through the OD; and for dividing the food rations.[42]

The guards, primarily Germans and Ukrainians, were used to carry out punishments such as beatings and were described as the 'best' killers. One would occasionally stand by the garbage pile outside the camp's inmates' kitchen to shoot any desperately hungry Jew who would dig through the scraps of food looking for something to eat. Others, while on guard duty, would shoot prisoners 'just for sport', claiming that they had been illegally trading.

Aleksander Bieberstein, an eyewitness, wrote:[43]

> Göth and his underlings lived in luxury. The Jewish camp leaders delivered the best food to them, clothing made to order and valuables—even girls and other forms of entertainment. His dogs were fed meat from the camp kitchen. There were no laws to obey; everything and everybody was subject to Göth's whims. He was the absolute ruler and knew how to take advantage of this. He often threw parties at his home to which he invited friends, as well as highly-placed SS men.

Ruth Göth, Amon's widow, recalled:[44]

> The camp was a kingdom and its Kommandant was its king. It was a beautiful time; we enjoyed being together. My Göth was the king and I was his queen.
> Who wouldn't have traded places with us?

Mina described Göth:[45]

> Life was very hard in Płaszów, because everybody was afraid of Göth, and he had his deputies and his helpers who did the same as he did. In his shape, his build, he looked like a demon. Dressed in a long black coat, black hat, white scarf and white gloves, he could be at the other end of the camp and then suddenly appear in front of you.
> He had two big dogs which he trained, so that when he yelled 'Jude' they would run at you and attack you. He treated these dogs better than the prisoners. They were bathed and they were fed; they lived in luxury. He lived in a red house, which we called the Blood House. Whenever he chose a girl to

come into his house to clean and to serve the dogs, everybody prayed for her. If she broke something, or made a mistake, her life was in danger. At any moment he could shoot her for no reason.

When Mina arrived, her first job was in the Barackenbau. Work there was very difficult, carried out in all weathers and 'on the run', amidst shouts from the SS. Those who slipped or stumbled were often crushed by the rocks they were carrying. Random shootings were commonplace. It was one of the worst jobs in the camp.[46]
Mina recalled:[47]

> We were divided into groups, and there was a female *Kapo* called Musia in charge of ours. After the War many people accused *Kapos* of brutal treatment of the inmates—and there were bad ones. But there were also good *Kapo*. This woman saved my life.
> Our job was to split big boulders into smaller pieces, using hammers. We were sitting doing this job the whole day, about twelve hours. When you had a big pile of smaller stones, you had to put them into wheelbarrows and cart them away. The wheelbarrows were very heavy. After my sickness, I couldn't manage a full wheelbarrow. I was limping on one foot and I was hungry. I looked like a skeleton, I couldn't even *move* a wheelbarrow!
> Musia saw that I was not lazy, that I wanted to work, that I was trying—but that I was struggling, limping. She said: 'Sit and continue working,' took the wheelbarrow and carted off the rocks for me.
> Five minutes later Amon Göth appeared. He expected a *Kapo* to be there to report to him. If somebody didn't report

correctly, in perfect German, he would shoot them on the spot. This day he asked: 'Where is the *Kapo*?' When he saw her coming back with the empty wheelbarrow, he took out his revolver and shot her—with no discussion. I felt very, very guilty that this woman had died because of me.

Violence and death at Płaszów took on many forms. As well as random shootings there were individual and mass executions and hangings, gruesome events the whole camp, including visitors, had to attend. Göth believed that the most effective way of controlling prisoners was the on-the-spot murder: for smoking a cigarette or for failing to take off caps quickly enough. For an attempted escape, or for other violations such as the smuggling of food, there was collective punishment. For every person who escaped, fifty men and women were shot.[48]

Mina recalled:[49]

> One day we were sitting in the circle, working with our hammers to break up the stones. From one end of the row to the other you could hear 'Sachse, Sachse' (meaning from Saxony) being whispered, warning that Göth was coming. I didn't dare to turn my head. I was afraid to look at his face, or to fall under his gaze, so as not to provoke him. But we knew that he was there, and that somebody would be killed.
>
> Working next to me was a friend, Zofia, and her mother, who was about fifty. He stood behind us and I thought to myself: 'My God, whose turn will it be now?'
>
> Without saying a word, he looked at the mother and did not like the way she was working. So he took out his revolver and shot her! Just like that.
>
> Naturally, her daughter started to scream and cry. He said

to her: 'One single word and you will be lying next to your mother.' Then he disappeared like the devil.

Another time they caught a girl whom I knew, Zosia Goldman, when she was cooking a few potatoes. They shot her on the spot and buried her in Hujowa Górka. She was a beautiful young girl, eighteen years old. But what did beauty mean in the Ghetto or the camp?

When I went out to work in the morning, I used to say goodbye to the others. They would ask me: 'Why do you say goodbye, Mina?' I replied: 'With Amon Göth, you never know what will happen during the day. Even if you give your all and are working hard, if he's in the mood, he'll kill you.' Every day somebody was killed.

As well as in the Barackenbau, prisoners worked in the two stone quarries next to the camp; in various specialist workshops in the camp's industrial centre, the Neue Gelände; in factories outside to which they travelled every day; or in sub-camps such as Oscar Schindler's Deutsche Emailwarenfabrik in Zabłocie.[50]

Work in the two stone quarries was extremely hard and was often used as a form of punishment. Prisoners were ordered to split stones with special picks or heavy hammers, and to carry the large, heavy rocks for long distances. Women employed at the quarries either carted rocks in wheelbarrows which were then used to pave roads in the camp, or operated the Mannschaftszug an invention of Amon Göth. This ran day and night, hauling building materials from the quarry up a fairly steep incline.

Jacob Stending, an eyewitness, described this invention:[51]

> It seems that only the quarry at the Płaszów camp could pride itself on the Mannschaftszug, a train with human locomotives.

> Consisting of three carts, it was towed by seventy women in two columns. The rope, about 100 metres long, was attached to their arms in such a way that as they walked, they pressed it to their arms with both hands so they could use their entire bodies to pull the load.

This work was done in twelve-hour shifts, each required to turn the carts around thirteen to fifteen times. In camp jargon, this was 'Wołga Wołga'.

This went on in spite of the fact that, not far from the camp, stood an unused locomotive which could have easily been used to move the rocks.[52]

The main street in the Neue Gelände was the Industrie Strasse, where six barracks of Julius Madritsch's clothes manufacturing factory, the largest private concern, were located. There prisoners produced work clothing and army uniforms for the Wehrmacht. The firm's workshop in Podgórze, before it had been relocated, had 800 workers using 300 sewing machines. By August 1943, its workforce had increased to 2000.[53]

We believe that after her time in the Barackenbau unit for the required few weeks, Mina went to work for Madritsch. Although this is not mentioned in her taped testimonies, among her papers she lists Madritsch as the firm that employed her during her incarceration in Płaszów. Her sister Freüda, after working to clean up the Ghetto, in September 1943 joined Mina at Madritsch, since Jewish labour units then ceased work outside the camp.[54]

In addition to the Madritsch factory, the industrial complex included a number of other workshops with different specialities such as electrical manufacture, watch-making, carpentry and printing.[55]

All of these workshops came under the management of Deutsche Ausrüstungswerke (DAW), with the exception of Madritsch and

Baufhof der Bauleitung, building suppliers. DAW also operated two 'specialized' workshops for custom-made tailoring and shoemaking. There suits and boots were made for high SS officials. A special fitting room was located in the office of the SS officials, where twice weekly camp craftsmen did fittings.[56]

The workshops on the Neue Gelände had day and night shifts, and people worked there on an alternating basis. Work allocation was determined by the ODs. At the end of each day, the *Kapos* and directors of every workshop had to submit reports to the camp command on what had been completed that day.[57]

Inmates were woken up at 4am, gathered together for an *Appell* at 5 and marched out to work at 6. Work lasted twelve to fourteen hours, with an hour's break for lunch. On Sundays work ceased at midday. Then the prisoners could use the afternoon for doing their laundry, mending their clothing or simply resting.[58]

With the continual threat of death, prisoners were in such deep depression that only macabre humour could provide momentary relief. 'Sports' meant keeping scores. Göth's frequent on-the-spot killings were counted using betting jargon: 'today 1:0; 2:0 6:0, 20:0'. Murder at the pits in the old cemetery, where a tractor worked around the clock, was called 'going under the tractor'.[59]

Following the liquidation of the Ghetto a spate of executions commenced in Płaszów. Over several weeks it is estimated that between 3000-4000 prisoners were shot in the area surrounding the camp, which contained at least ten mass graves. Göth also planned to build a crematorium and gas chamber, but this never happened.[60]

Mina recalled:[61]

Göth put up gallows to hang people. While we were resting after our hard work, they dragged us out of the barracks and we had to go to the *Appellplatz* and witness the execution. For

what? If they found something in your barracks like a newspaper, or you bought bread and had hidden it in your bunk, they executed you. Usually they hung three to five people at the same time. Once eight people were hanged! And we had to witness this.

All the Jews in the camp had to gather in the *Appellplatz* whenever there were selections for shooting, beating or hanging. In the spring of 1943, a sixteen-year-old boy was sentenced to be hanged because a Nazi had heard him humming a Russian tune. The following day, everyone had to assemble on the *Appellplatz* to witness this.[62]

Erna Rubinstein, an eyewitness, recalled:[63]

> The voice of the Commandant shouted: 'These three tried to escape from work; they are charged with treason and sabotage! For this, they will hang!' We all had to watch. The guards were walking around our columns, making us look. Those who looked away were prodded with guns; those who fainted—and many did—were poked until they came to. We were slowly learning to live with horror, tragedy and cruelty.

As the War reached its endgame, in November 1943, following the massacre of Jews at Majdanek and other camps, the only surviving prisoners for forced labour in the vital Nazi armaments industry were the 20,000 in Płaszów. It had become an important pool of Jewish labour for armament sites in the *Generalgouvernement*.[64]

Malvina Graf, an eyewitness, wrote:[65]

> Finkelstein came into the sewing shop and told the head that he needed people to be sent to work in the Skarżysko factory. The people who were selected went, fearfully, to Częstochowa,

Pionki and Skarżysko-Kamienna. As had been promised, they were given work, but few survived the terrible conditions.

Mina recalled:[66]

> One day on our way back from work, we were taken to an empty Polish camp. They kept us there the whole night and day, without food or water. I thought that this would be our end, that they were going to kill us. But a Commandant came and said to us: 'You are going to another camp. Don't worry—nobody will be killed. If you work, work and work, that will help you to survive.'
>
> This second camp was still in Poland, around 150 kilometres from Kraków. It was called Skarżysko-Kamienna.

On 16 November 1943, a transport of 2,500 Jews left Płaszów and arrived the same day at Skarżysko-Kamienna, to take on munitions work for one of Germany's largest arms manufacturers, the Hugo Schneider Aktiengesellschaft Metallwarenfabrik (HASAG) of Leipzig.

Mina was among them. She did not have the chance to say goodbye to her beloved sister, since they worked different shifts.[67] Mina only learned after the War what had happened to Freüda:[68]

> When I was transported to Skarżysko, my sister remained behind in Płaszów. A couple of days later, there was another selection and it was rumoured that they were also sending the second group to Skarżysko. My sister had such courage that she approached the Germans and said: 'Whether I am selected or not, I want to join this group.' They said: 'Well, if you want to go, you are very brave. You don't know where you're going.' Of course, she was hoping that she would join me. Unfortunately,

as I found out later, they were sent to another camp, to Pionki. We never saw one another again!

Records indicate that on 18 November 1943, 1,500 prisoners were sent from Płaszów to armaments plants in Kielce, Częstochowa and Pionki.[69]

From November 1943, Mina was alone. She had gone, at her tender age, from the safety and security of a loving family to having to face the horrors of captivity without a loved one by her side. Years later as she recounted her War experiences, it was clear that this final separation from her sister was one of the most traumatic events of her life.

The liquidation of the Płaszów camp occurred in stages between May and September 1944. The first transport left for Auschwitz in May, followed by others in August and September to Auschwitz, Stutthof, Mauthausen and Flossenbürg.[70]

On 6 September 1944, Reichsführer SS Himmler was informed by the SS and Police leaders in Kraków that the camp at Płaszów would shortly be dismantled, and that its Commandant Amon Göth was under investigation for embezzlement. He was arrested on 13 September and imprisoned in Vienna.[71]

Towards the latter part of 1944, Germany was on the defensive, with the Soviet Army advancing from the East, and the Western Front moving towards the German border. It thus became necessary to move able-bodied prisoners deep into Germany, and destroy evidence of the horrendous crimes committed on Polish soil.

In the last months of the camps' existence, the Germans took steps to cover all traces of the mass murders they had committed. This work was carried out by special, very secret squads, known as Sonderkommando 1005. Their task was to exhume all bodies, burn them and collect the ashes for disposal. During the final phase of these operations, the remaining bones were crushed, and the ashes searched for any valuables not found in previous searches. When a 1005 unit had completed a particular operation, it cleared the site and murdered all the slave labourers involved in the exhumation and cremation work. This intensive digging and burning lasted for six weeks, until 12 October 1944.[72]

The largest transport left on 15 October 1944: 1,600 Jewish prisoners were transported to Groß-Rosen, of whom 700 were transferred to Schindler's factory in Brünnlitz. The rest were sent to Buchenwald. This marked the demobilization of the Płaszów camp. Only some 600 inmates were left behind to liquidate it. The offices on Neue Gelände were closed and work was carried out sorting clothes that remained from inmates who had either been killed or forced to leave behind their possessions.[73]

It was the end for the Kraków Ghetto and its successor, the brutal Kraków-Płaszów Forced Labour Camp.

In total, some 150,000 inmates were incarcerated there, with between 8000-12,000 killed. They came from Kraków and other Polish cities, as well as from Hungary, Czechoslovakia, France, Belgium and Romania. The Supreme National Tribunal of Poland, in its indictment and eventual judgement against Amon Göth, stated that he had caused the deaths of 8,000 inmates.[74]

Almost no trace of the camp has survived, except a few nondescript buildings such as the former villa of the Commandant which stands as a ruin at ul. Helmanta 22. Apart from the cemetery, all annexed lands were returned to their original owners.[75]

Top: Płaszów Camp as it looked when it was in operation. Photo: http://www.scrapbookpages.com/Poland/Plaszow/Plaszow02.html
Bottom: Women inmates marching off to work. Photo from http://www.yadvashem.org/yv/en/exhibitions/through-the-lens/schindlers-list

MINA & JACOB

Notes

1 Ryszard Kotarba, *Niemiecki Obóz w Płaszowie, 1942-1945* (A German Camp in Płaszów, 1942-45) (Warsaw-Kraków: Instytut Pamięci Narodowey (Institute of National Remembrance), 2009), 35
2 Mina Widawski nee Laub, audio testimony for the *12th Hour Project of Oral Testimonies* (Sydney: Australian Institute for Holocaust Studies, 1990); video testimony (Sydney: USC Shoah Foundation Institute, 1995), code 2526
3 Tom Keneally, *Searching for Schindler* (Sydney: Knopf/Random House Australia, 2007), 261
4 Mina Widawski, *12th Hour Project of Oral Testimonies*; USC Shoah Foundation, code 2526
5 Malvina Graf, *The Kraków Ghetto and the Płaszów Camp Remembered* (Tallahassee: Florida State University Press, 1989), 68-69; United States Holocaust Memorial Museum (USHMM), *Encyclopedia of Camps and Ghettos 1933-45* (Washington: 2012), Vol. 2, 862; Abraham J. Edelheit and Hershel Edelheit, eds, *History of the Holocaust: A Handbook and Dictionary* (Boulder: Westview Press, 1994), 282-83
6 Graf, *The Kraków Ghetto Remembered*, 68-69, 87-88, 91; USHMM, *Encyclopedia of Camps and Ghettos*, 862-63; Magdalena Kunicka-Wyrzykowska, *Kalendarium Obozu Płaszowskiego 1942-45* (Calendar of the Płaszów Camp 1942-45), (Warsaw: Biuletyn Głównej Komisji Badania Zbrodni Hitlerowskich w Polsce) (Bulletin of the Main Commission on Hitler's Crimes perpetrated in Poland, 1982), 57; Aleksander Bieberstein, *Zagłada Żydow w Krakowie* (The Extermination of Jews in Kraków), (Kraków: Wydawnictwo Literackie, 1985), 105-06, 123; Kotarba, *Niemiecki Obóz w Płaszowie* 24-25, 41
7 Keneally, *Searching for Schindler*, 109-10; http://www.krakow-info.com/plaszow.htm; Kunicka-Wyrzykowska, *Kalendarium Obozu Płaszowskiego*, 56; Ministerstwo Sprawidliwości Główna Komisja Badania Zbrodni Hitlerowskich w Polsce (Ministry of Justice Main Commission for the Investigation of German Crimes in Poland), *Obozy Hitlerowskie na ziemiach polskich 1939* (Hitler's Camps on Polish Soil 1939-45) (Warsaw: 1979), 390; http://www.scrapbookpages.com/Poland/Plaszow/Plaszow01.html
8 Ministerstwo Sprawidliwości, *Obozy Hitlerowskie na ziemiach polskich*, 390; Kunicka-Wyrzykowska, *Kalendarium Obozu Płaszowskiego*, 56-57
9 Joseph Bau, *Years of Murder*, http://www1.yadvashem.org/download/education/conf/Eldar.pdf
10 Graf, *The Kraków Ghetto Remembered*, 87-88, 91; Bieberstein, *Zagłada Żydow*, 105-06; Joseph Bau, *Dear God, have you ever gone hungry?* (New York: Arcade Publishing, 1996), 137

11 Kunicka-Wyrzykowska, *Kalendarium Obozu Płaszowskiego*, 64-65; Tadeusz Wroński, *Kronika okupowanego Krakowa* (Chronicle of Occupied Kraków), (Kraków: Wydawnictwo Literackie, 1974), 289; Ryszard Kotarba, *Niemiecki Obóz w Płaszowie*, 69; Felicja Karay, *Death Comes in Yellow: Skarżysko-Kamienna Slave Labor Camp* (Amsterdam: Arwood Academic Publishers, 1995), 61-62
12 Crowe, *Oskar Schindler* (Boulder: Westview Press, 2004), 239; USHMM, *Encyclopedia of Camps and Ghettos*, 862
13 Graf, *The Kraków Ghetto Remembered*, 87-88, 91; Bieberstein, *Zagłada Żydow*, 101
14 Crowe, *Oskar Schindler*, 240; Bieberstein, *Zagłada Żydow*, 102, 112-13; Bau, *Dear God, have you ever gone hungry?*, 121; Kunicka-Wyrzykowska, *Kalendarium Obozu Płaszowskiego*, 57; Bieberstein, *Zagłada Żydow*, 106; Israel Gutman, ed., *Encyclopedia of the Holocaust*, (New York: Macmillan, 1990), 1,140; USHMM, *Encyclopedia of Camps and Ghettos*, 862
15 Graf, *The Kraków Ghetto Remembered*, 87-88, 91; Bieberstein, *Zagłada Żydow*, 105-06; Ryszard Kotarba, *Niemiecki Obóz w Płaszowie*, 41
16 Bieberstein, *Zagłada Żydow*, 107-08; Bau, *Dear God, have you ever gone hungry?*, 129; Ryszard Kotarba, *Niemiecki Obóz w Płaszowie*, 47
17 Crowe, *Oskar Schindler*, 285; Bieberstein, *Zagłada Żydow*, 104-05
18 Wroński, *Kronika okupowanego Krakowa*, 285; Ministerstwo Sprawidliwości, *Obozy Hitlerowskie na ziemiach polskich*, 390; Kotarba, *Niemiecki Obóz w Płaszowie*, 93
19 Bau, *Dear God, have you ever gone hungry?*, 126, 128, 135, 151
20 Mina Widawski, *12th Hour Project of Oral Testimonies*; USC Shoah Foundation, code 2526
21 Kunicka-Wyrzykowska, *Kalendarium Obozu Płaszowskiego*, 62
22 Bieberstein, *Zagłada Żydow*, 116-17; Kotarba, *Niemiecki Obóz w Płaszowie*, 47; Bau, *Dear God, have you ever gone hungry?*, 139
23 Graf, *The Kraków Ghetto Remembered*, 90-91
24 Mina Widawski, *12th Hour Project of Oral Testimonies*; USC Shoah Foundation, code 2526
25 Bieberstein, *Zagłada Żydow*, 129; Kotarba, *Niemiecki Obóz w Płaszowie*, 100
26 Mina Widawski, *12th Hour Project of Oral Testimonies*; USC Shoah Foundation, code 2526
27 http://www1.yadvashem.org/download/education/conf/Eldar.pdf; Kotarba, *Niemiecki Obóz w Płaszowie*, 94
28 Bau, *Dear God, have you ever gone hungry?*, 100, 143
29 Bau, *Dear God, have you ever gone hungry?*, 126, 128
30 Ibid.
31 Bieberstein, *Zagłada Żydow*, 125; Graf, *The Kraków Ghetto Remembered*, 89-90; 124-25; Kotarba, *Niemiecki Obóz w Płaszowie*, 89

32 Graf, *The Kraków Ghetto Remembered*, 124-26
33 Graf, *The Kraków Ghetto Remembered*, 125
34 Ministerstwo Sprawidliwości, *Obozy Hitlerowskie na ziemiach polskich*, 390 USHMM, *Encyclopedia of Camps and Ghettos*, 863
35 Tom Segev, *Soldiers of Evil: The Commandants of the Nazi Concentration Camps*, (New York: Berkley Books, 1991), 151-53
36 Bau, *Dear God, have you ever gone hungry?*, 115; Graf, *The Kraków Ghetto Remembered*, 85, 90-94; Segev, *Soldiers of Evil*, 154; Abraham and Hershel Edelheit, eds, *History of the Holocaust: A Handbook and Dictionary* (Boulder: Westview Press, 1994), 256
37 Ibid.
38 Graf, *The Kraków Ghetto Remembered*, 113
39 Graf, *The Kraków Ghetto Remembered*, 94; Bau, *Dear God, have you ever gone hungry?*, 132
40 Bau, *Dear God, have you ever gone hungry?*, 132; Kotarba, *Niemiecki Obóz w Płaszowie*, 73
41 Kotarba, *Niemiecki Obóz w Płaszowie*, 72
42 Graf, *The Kraków Ghetto Remembered*, 89
43 Bieberstein, *Zagłada Żydow*, 128
44 Segev, *Soldiers of Evil*, 24, 155
45 Mina Widawski, *12th Hour Project of Oral Testimonies*; USC Shoah Foundation, code 2526
46 Graf, *The Kraków Ghetto Remembered*, 87-88, 91; Bieberstein, *Zagłada Żydow*, 105-06; Kotarba, *Niemiecki Obóz w Płaszowie*, 105, 107
47 Mina Widawski, *12th Hour Project of Oral Testimonies*; USC Shoah Foundation, code 2526
48 Kotarba, *Niemiecki Obóz w Płaszowie*, 137; Crowe, *Oskar Schindler*, 257-58, 264
49 Mina Widawski, *12th Hour Project of Oral Testimonies*; USC Shoah Foundation, code 2526
50 Kunicka-Wyrzykowska, *Kalendarium Obozu Płaszowskiego*, 58, 62; USHMM, *Encyclopedia of Camps and Ghettos*, 864
51 Jakub Stending, *Płaszów, the Last Stop for the Jews of Kraków*, http://www1.yadvashem.org/download/education/conf/Eldar.pdf
52 Ministerstwo Sprawidliwości, *Obozy Hitlerowskie na ziemiach polskich*, 390; Kunicka-Wyrzykowska, *Kalendarium Obozu Płaszowskiego*, 58; Crowe, *Oskar Schindler*, 257-58, 264; Graf, *The Kraków Ghetto Remembered*, 101-02; USHMM, *Encyclopedia of Camps and Ghettos*, 864
53 Kotarba, *Niemiecki Obóz w Płaszowie*, 112-13
54 Kotarba, *Niemiecki Obóz w Płaszowie*, 93-94, 112-15
55 Crowe, *Oskar Schindler*, 245; Bieberstein, *Zagłada Żydow*, 108; Kotarba,

Niemiecki Obóz w Płaszowie, 49

56 Bieberstein, *Zagłada Żydów* 108; Kunicka-Wyrzykowska, *Kalendarium Obozu Płaszowskiego*, 58, 62; USHMM, *Encyclopedia of Camps and Ghettos*, 864

57 Kotarba, *Niemiecki Obóz w Płaszowie*, 106

58 Ibid.

59 http://www1.yadvashem.org/download/education/conf/Eldar.pdf; Kotarba, *Niemiecki Obóz w Płaszowie*, 137

60 Keneally, *Searching for Schindler*, 109-10; Crowe, *Oskar Schindler*, 265-66; Kunicka-Wyrzykowska, *Kalendarium Obozu Płaszowskiego*, 66; Kotarba, *Niemiecki Obóz w Płaszowie*, 135; Bieberstein, *Zagłada Żydów*, 110; USHMM, *Encyclopedia of Camps and Ghettos*, 864

61 Mina Widawski, *12th Hour Project of Oral Testimonies*; USC Shoah Foundation, code 2526

62 Graf, *The Kraków Ghetto Remembered*, 97

63 Erna Rubinstein, *The Survivor in Us All, A Memoir of the Holocaust*, http://www.nizkor.org/ftp.py?camps//plaszow/plaszow.001

64 Karay, *Death Comes in Yellow*, 61-62

65 Graf, *The Kraków Ghetto Remembered*, 109

66 Mina Widawski, *12th Hour Project of Oral Testimonies*; USC Shoah Foundation, code 2526

67 Kotarba, *Niemiecki Obóz w Płaszowie*, 170; Karay, *Death Comes in Yellow*, 61-62; Crowe, *Oskar Schindler*, 324-26; Kunicka-Wyrzykowska, *Kalendarium Obozu Płaszowskiego*, 65-66, 70

68 Mina Widawski, *12th Hour Project of Oral Testimonies*; USC Shoah Foundation, code 2526

69 Kotarba, *Niemiecki Obóz w Płaszowie*, 170; Karay, *Death Comes in Yellow*, 61-62; Crowe, *Oskar Schindler*, 324-26; Kunicka-Wyrzykowska, *Kalendarium Obozu Płaszowskiego*, 65-66, 70

70 Gerald Reitlinger, *Chronology of the Final Solution, the Attempt to Exterminate the Jews of Europe, 1939-45*, (London: Vallentine Mitchell, 1953), 322; Kunicka-Wyrzykowska, *Kalendarium Obozu Płaszowskiego*, 59, 69

71 Kunicka-Wyrzykowska, *Kalendarium Obozu Płaszowskiego*, 70; Graf, *The Kraków Ghetto Remembered*, 130-32

72 Crowe, *Oskar Schindler*, 202; Graf, *The Kraków Ghetto Remembered*, 133

73 Kunicka-Wyrzykowska, *Kalendarium Obozu Płaszowskiego*, 71; Graf, *The Kraków Ghetto Remembered*, 136-39

74 http://www.krakow-info.com/plaszow.htm; Ministerstwo Sprawidliwości, *Obozy Hitlerowskie na ziemiach polskich*, 391; USHMM, *Encyclopedia of Camps and Ghettos*, 865; Kunicka-Wyrzykowska, *Kalendarium Obozu Płaszowskiego*, 53-54

75 http://www.krakow-info.com/plaszow.htm

15
Skarżysko-Kamienna

Freda recalls:

On 23 June 2010, I travelled in comfort on a first-class express train from Kraków to Skarżysko-Kamienna. Coffee was served.

Looking out of the window at the gently-rolling landscape, smelling the sweet air of summer, I thought of Mum. How different her journey would have been! She was cramped into a dark, putrid-smelling cattle wagon, without any knowledge of where they were heading. She was not able to see out nor inhale fresh air. She was thirsty, hungry, cold and, above all, afraid.

Mina recalled:[1]

In late 1943 I was sent to Skarżysko-Kamienna. We travelled to Skarżysko by cattle train, 80 to 100 people per wagon. We had no food or water on the journey and the sanitary conditions were terrible. There were also a few children in the wagons, and I thought: 'My God, how have these women hidden their children? How come the Germans didn't notice them?' They just appeared on the train. During a stop, when the guards went to the other side of the train, I and a few girlfriends jumped down, grabbed some snow, made it into balls—we were in danger because they would shoot us for this—jumped back on to the train and gave the children these snowballs, 'to drink'. But by the time we arrived at the camp, all the children were dead!

Mina arrived in Skarżysko on 16 November 1943 as part of a transport of 2,500 prisoners from Płaszów.[2]

The camp at Skarżysko-Kamienna, 150 kilometres from Kraków, was the first of some 1,750 forced labour camps in the *Generalgouvernement* and the largest and most important of the fourteen factory camps established in the Radom area.[3]

From the beginning of the War, arming the military was Germany's primary objective. Following the occupation of Skarżysko on 6 September 1939 and the appropriation of the Polish ammunition plant Zakłady Metalowe MESKO SA, the German Armaments Office had wanted immediately to begin ammunition production. Because the Wehrmacht lacked the necessary resources, production was handed over to private companies, in this case Hugo Schneider AG or HASAG, which had been producing armaments since World War I.[4]

Following Poland's occupation, HASAG had begun operating in the Radom district in 1940, acquiring in January 1943 the state-owned ammunition factories in Skarżysko-Kamienna, the grenade factory in Kielce and the Raków foundry in Częstochowa.[5]

By the summer of 1944, HASAG still maintained six company camps for 14,000 Jews, constituting approximately 30 percent of the entire 'official' Jewish population of the *Generalgouvernement*.[6]

Initially the recruitment of Jewish labour for the Skarżysko-Kamienna plants was of a seasonal nature, depending on the availability of Polish workers. During the winter of 1940, mass arrests of Polish labourers had led to a shortage of manpower. A group of Jews from Skarżysko-Kamienna was immediately recruited. When in December 1941 the ghettos in the Radom area started to be liquidated, a pool of workers became readily available to HASAG.[7]

The nucleus of the camp was established in early 1942, when 2,000 Jews were brought in as permanent workers. By the time it was officially established as a Betriebslager or company camp in August that year, HASAG had brought in around 5,500 Jews.[8]

The timing of Jewish transports to the camp reflected the needs at the front. The Radom transports, from August 1942 to late 1943, coincided with the Stalingrad campaign; Jews were brought from Majdanek in the summer of 1943, before the new offensive on the Eastern Front; and the prisoners from Płaszów, Mina among them, were transferred in November 1943, when it became imperative to hold back the advance of the Soviet Army.[9]

During its thirty-two months of existence, more than fifty transports were brought to Skarżysko, an estimated 23,000-30,000 Jews from Poland and other parts of Europe. Most of them did not survive. For example, 70 percent of the prisoners brought from the Płaszów camp and surrounding ghettos perished.[10]

Survival depended on age, health and occupation. All prisoners fought for survival on two fronts: in the plant and in the camp. In the plant the back-breaking labour, constantly-increasing quotas and beatings from their German and Polish masters drained their strength. In the camp they fought hunger, over-crowding, filth, disease and their terror of the guards.[11]

The camp covered an area of three-and-a-half square kilometres and consisted of three plants, Werk A, B and C. A Jewish camp was erected beside each factory, in which the Jewish prisoners laboured alongside free Polish workers:

1. Werk A, the largest, held 3000-4000 prisoners
2. Werk B was small, holding up to 700 prisoners and was considered the best of the three
3. Werk C was the worst: 1500-2000 prisoners were held here and hardly anyone who worked in the factory survived.[12]

In the forest bordering Werk C was the firing range, Schiess Platz, designed for ammunition testing. Here the worn-out prisoners from all three camps were shot.[13]

In addition to the Jews, the Germans also used Poles, Volksdeusche and Ukrainians, to labour in their Skarżysko-Kamienna plants. However, unlike the Jews, these people were not prisoners. The Poles continued to work in the factories as they had prior to the Occupation, were paid and, as residents of Skarżysko or surrounding towns, returned home at the end of the day. In comparison, the Jews were incarcerated in camps from where they were marched to and fro to work each day, escorted by Jewish police.[14]

Egon Dalski, the General Manager of the HASAG factory in Skarżysko-Kamienna, also had overall charge of the camp from 1939-43, when he was succeeded by Paul Geldmacher. Each of the three camps operated as a separate unit, governed by their own authorities: a German commander with Polish deputies; the Werkschutz or factory guard, manned by Volksdeutsche and Ukrainians who were responsible for security, administrative supervision of the Polish workers and policing the Jewish camps; plus the Jewish internal administration.

This consisted of the Lagerältesten (camp elders); the police, headed by a Commander and a second-in-command; the functionaries, the Blockältesten and Stubendienst, responsible for cleanliness in the barracks and food distribution; and the Vorarbeiter, who escorted workers to and from the plant.[15]

Unlike the camp at Płaszów, a huge complex with a neat appearance and iron discipline, Skarżysko was run-down. It was situated in a deep, gloomy forest. Newly-arrived prisoners, despite their previous experience of camp life, were shocked at the living conditions. It contained ramshackle barracks with peeling walls sinking into pools of mud; refuse was thrown about everywhere; the sewers overflowed in the communal latrines whose stench was overpowering; and filthy bath-houses offered only a trickle of freezing water.[16]

Mina recalled:[17]

> On arrival in Skarżysko I instantly formed a very bad impression. The camp was segregated, one part for the men, and one part for the women, separated by barbed wire. The first sight that I saw behind the fences and the barbed wire was a man who had climbed into a container, a big barrel, and was licking the inside. I said to my girlfriends: 'This will be even worse than Płaszów.' Because despite the fact that Amon Göth was a murderer and we lived in constant fear, compared with Skarżysko, his camp was luxurious. It was clean and we had toilets and showers—cold water, but still it was there. And although the food was meagre and very basic, it was provided to us in sanitary conditions.
>
> But this camp was a killer. My first thought was that here there must be extreme hunger if a man was forced to lick a barrel. My second was the very bad conditions in the barracks. We slept on bunks, at the beginning without any covering, without any blankets—and it was November, the middle of winter. Płaszów was the first camp that I went to, and compared to the ones that followed, it wasn't so bad in one respect: we still had some of our own personal things and

we at least had blankets. Here you covered yourself with your coat, if you had one, or your clothing, and you were sleeping on wooden bunks. There were two to three people to a bed, but in one row we were about thirty to forty people.

To survive here was going to be a very slim chance. Very slim!

The prisoners from Płaszów who arrived in November 1943 were predominantly middle class Jews from Kraków, with secondary or higher education. The veterans sarcastically termed them 'Krakower inteligenz' (Kraków intelligentsia). They were still in relatively good shape in terms of health and nutrition, at least in comparison with those who had arrived much earlier, from Radom or Majdanek. The veteran prisoners stared enviously at the clothes of the newcomers. A woman wrapped in rags mumbling in Yiddish touched one of the Płaszów girls with a mixture of awe and greed. 'They still have coats!'[18]

Mina recalled her first meeting with Guta Cwyrenbrucher who was to become a dear life-long friend. Guta had come from Majdanek and had already been in Skarżysko some time before Mina's arrival. She was drawn to the newcomer's relatively healthy appearance and her decent clothes.

On arrival, the entire transport was searched and the prisoners ordered to hand over all their money and valuables. The following day they underwent the first selection. The strongest individuals were taken to Werk A and B. The 'leftovers', the elderly and the sick, were sent to Werk C.[19]

Mina recalled:[20]

> We stood in the *Appellplatz* and a German came, elegantly dressed in uniform and white gloves. He started to select people. They were choosing people like animals, like you

choose horses for work. We were divided into columns, into fifths, and they were choosing for the different HASAG factories. I was standing with my girlfriends from Kraków. I knew them and their families; they knew mine. All of us had lost our relatives and were alone, so now we were like family. But as we were forming into big columns, somehow, I became separated from my group of friends and found myself alone. I started to cry!

Not far from us, standing among the Germans, was a couple, Mr and Mrs Eisenberg. He was the Head of the Jewish Police. For some reason Mrs Eisenberg noticed me, my consternation, how upset I was that I had been separated from my friends. She gestured to me: 'Are you stupid?' I didn't know what she meant so I just started to form the next column. It appeared that we had been chosen for lighter work. She probably knew that my girlfriends had been put to very hard and dangerous work in ammunitions, where they would produce heavy shells and grenades. Any accident, where part of the shell fell on your legs, meant broken bones. Then you were finished.

The group I was with were also put to work in ammunitions, but we only produced small screws using light machinery. In comparison this work was safer and easier. We worked twelve hours a day, but we had slightly better conditions. For example, we could have a bath at work, and I felt blessed.

Werk A operated four major departments: Granatenabteilung, which produced shells and grenades; Infantrieabteilung, for small ammunition; Automatenabteilung for automatic weapons; and Werkzeugbau, which produced instruments.[21]

Most women worked in the Infantrieabteilung, manufacturing light ammunition for the infantry. Mechanized work proceeded along an assembly line manned by two twelve-hour shifts, with quotas constantly being raised. Based on Mina's recollections, it is most likely that she worked in this department.[22]

Werk B contained two main plants, one producing anti-aircraft ammunition and the smaller one blanks for the training of Wehrmacht soldiers. Both jobs demanded back-breaking labour from the prisoners, and were managed by two German overseers famous for their cruelty. Werk B also operated a food plant which consisted of a potato mill and kitchen in the camp grounds. Nearby was a farm where fruit and vegetables were grown and cows, sheep and chickens raised, to supplement the diet of the Germans in the plant. It employed around 120 Jews and 80 Poles. This was the most sought-after work.[23]

Werk C was the most infamous site in the entire Radom district. It contained the Pikryna, where underwater mines were packed with yellow picric acid powder, which dyed the workers' hair green and their hands black. Next to it was a production floor for land-based mines, with two huge vats containing boiling TNT. Three ladlers used buckets to pour the liquid into shell casings which were placed on tables. In order to fill the daily quota, the workers had to run from the vat to the table with their buckets. Since no protection was provided, the TNT not only gave them reddish-pink skin and hair, but also damaged their hearts and lungs. Everything around the Pikryna became tainted, including the soup. The average mortality rate in the department was twenty-five prisoners a week. In total, around 35,000 prisoners were poisoned by fumes from picric acid, most of them dying within two months.[24]

Mina recalled:[25]

Sometime later, I don't know why, Mrs Eisenberg sent for me. Something about me had caught her eye—maybe my appearance on arrival. I was dressed neatly and clean. I couldn't explain how she knew where to find me, how she found out who I was or where I was working. She had two little girls and I became their baby-sitter. She was the reason that I survived Skarżysko. Several times a week a Jewish policeman came to my work and escorted me to her place. I looked after the children, played with them, made them toys. This job was a blessing, because it meant that a few days a week I ate better food and was safe from the brutality of the factory managers. The Eisenbergs enjoyed their life, as people at the top, the Prominenten, the elite. But they were also good to me. I don't know why. Maybe this was 'divine intervention'? I don't know. But it was a godsend. And I did this job until the end of my time in Skarżysko.

Mina always recalled with pride that, despite the most difficult conditions, she did her utmost to maintain her personal hygiene and keep her clothes clean, to maintain a semblance of dignity and pride in her appearance.

Initially the prisoners brought to the factory in Werk A in spring 1942 were housed in a large, empty production facility, where 1,000 men and women were packed together, without mattresses or blankets. Others were quartered in former stables.[26] The living conditions in the camps were determined above all by HASAG's wish to save on production costs, with food rations and barracks below the level prevalent in other concentration camps. The mortality rate was massive.

In 1943, when the camp was expanded, new barracks were built at the three sites, divided into three rooms with a furnace in the middle.

Felicja Karay wrote:[27]

> The furnace became a hub around which the women would gather: one in an attempt to heat her remaining soup in a can, another trying to dry her only set of underwear. Any lucky person who had obtained a potato cut it into thin slices, spread it with garlic and fried it.
> The prisoner's first concern after registration was to secure a pallet, which became their castle. Here they arranged their meagre possessions: a few clothes, perhaps a blanket, a dish or two; here they ate, slept, received visitors, conducted business and hid treasures.

The latrines and shower huts were inadequate. Hot water was unheard-of. Once a month, prisoners were taken to a public bath in Werk A for a hot shower and to disinfect their clothing.[28]

In Werk B there was hot water in the barracks attached to the kitchen, to which prisoners were taken in groups escorted by policemen. This kept the mortality rate in this particular camp relatively low.[29]

Mina described the food:[30]

> When we came into the so-called 'dining room' we saw potatoes mixed with beetroot, which were either frozen or rotten, or soup made from beetroot. Often when I started to eat, I thought that I would vomit. So later, when I started to work for Mrs Eisenberg, at least a few times during the week I had better food. I was able to bring some back for my girlfriends. She always packed me a little parcel: a bit of bread and sometimes even a piece of cake. These were like manna from heaven! As soon as I got back to the barracks,

my friends swooped down on me like pigeons: 'Mina, what have you got today?' We would sit down on my bunk and have a celebration: a piece of bread!

Officially the inmates in all three camps received food twice each day. They got three-quarters of a litre of watery soup with dried potato flakes; 200 grams of bread; ersatz coffee in the morning and evening; and occasionally a dollop of jam. Twice a week a spoonful of sugar was added to the soup. On Saturday, a two-day ration of bread was distributed. A person needed a will of iron not to eat it up at once. For those who couldn't resist temptation, Sunday became a time to fast.[31]

The bakery and the kitchen were situated in the plant, not the camp. Although dark rye flour was provided for baking bread for the Jews, most of it was stolen by the Polish and German bakery managers, who used it to bake loaves which the Poles then sold to Jewish prisoners. The official 'Jewish bread' was made from the remaining flour to which dried potato flakes, produced at the mill in Werk B, were added.[32]

HASAG's policy of 'Austauch der Juden' or 'Jew exchange'—the replacement of worn-out prisoners by healthy ones—worked as long as new transports continued to arrive at the camp. When in the spring of 1944 it became clear that there were no more 'fresh' Jews available, the HASAG management had no choice but to improve their current prisoners' living conditions and diet, in order to ensure continued production. Food rations were improved: 350 grams of bread instead of 200, and twenty-five grams of sausage once a week.[33]

On entering Skarżysko, prisoners were stripped of personal valuables, including extra clothing and shoes. When their only set of clothing wore out (or was sold for bread), it was replaced with rags and paper sacks. For shoes the prisoners received wooden clogs, 'sabots', which chafed and blistered their feet. They were not given utensils, soap or towels and had to eat out of empty cans.[34]

Eyewitness Ilona Karmel wrote:[35]

Week after week passed. By now many of the Kraków women wore sabots instead of shoes, blankets instead of coats. By now, no shoes were safe from thieves, not even the wooden sabots which were often stolen to be chopped for kindling wood.

A black market existed in the camp. Craftsmen, using makeshift tools, created from scraps of tin useful items such as knives, scissors, thimbles, combs, bowls and spoons. Shoemakers developed a whole industry on their pallets, fixing soles with bits of rubber and manufacturing new shoes from wooden clogs and leather scraps they got from the Poles. Tailors sewed for the Prominenten, the Poles and even the Germans.[36]

Women mended clothes, or made small items of apparel, using 'tools' they had managed to smuggle into the camp: sewing needles, thread, knitting needles and scissors, and raw materials they had pilfered from the factory, risking death. For example, women in the ammunition quality-inspection department of the Instrument Division unravelled the cotton gloves they were given for sorting bullets and used the yarn to knit lacy scarves, cuffs and muffs. There was also a 'cosmetics' market: red chalk used to mark shelves and machine oil was made into a special 'cream' that served as both lipstick and blusher. On several occasions this 'makeup' saved exhausted women from death during selections, giving them a rosy glow.[37]

Those prisoners without special skills sold small pieces of bread or a handful of cigarettes. Others obtained apple peels from the Poles, from which they made 'tea' that added flavour to a cup of boiling water. Women who lacked the small amount of money needed to start a 'business' would turn to services: washing and cooking for the Prominenten, mending clothes or cleaning the barracks.[38]

Felicja Karay wrote:[39]

> **When the prisoners returned from the plant the camp became one great marketplace. In certain barracks, the pallets were turned into stalls. There was shouting and hawking just like in the shtetl.**

In all three camps epidemics broke out. There was typhus and vicious dysentery called 'Hasagowa' by the prisoners. The typhus epidemic of the winter of 1943-44 claimed the lives of a large number of prisoners, sparing those who had already been exposed to the disease in Płaszów or, like Mina, in the Kraków Ghetto.[40]

The lack of underwear made women susceptible to urinary-tract infections. Further, many women stopped menstruating as a result of malnutrition and hard labour. This happened to Mina. She recalled that although at the time she was relieved, given the dreadful sanitary conditions, after the War she was worried that she might never be able to conceive. Creating a family was, of course, very important to her.[41]

Those who fell ill were taken to the 'hospital', known throughout the camp as 'the first stop to the other world'. There was no medication. The 'hospital' hut was crowded, filthy and lice-infected. The ill lay two to a pallet, covered in rags.[42]

In the camps, those in charge of HASAG management created what amounted to a madhouse. Bullying, abuse, murder, rape, theft and extortion went on continually, unpunished.[43]

Attempts at escape were punishable by death. In Werk A and C,

Jews caught stealing materials from the factory were hanged. They included five Jews who tried to steal leather belts.[44]

Regular selections where held in all three camps to 'weed out' sick or weak prisoners. The woods surrounding Werk C concealed executions. From 1943 onwards, Polish political prisoners were brought from Gestapo jails in the Radom district, taken by truck into the forest, forced into pre-dug trenches and shot.[45]

In April 1944 a large section of the forest was enclosed by a two-and-a-half metre fence. Signs warned that anyone approaching it would face immediate death. Hundreds of prisoners held in the Gestapo's jails were transported to Werk C in sealed trucks, into which the exhaust fumes were funnelled, killing them on the way. The trucks then pulled up in front of the canvas-covered fence behind which was a makeshift crematorium, known by the plant workers as patelnia (frying pan), where bodies were burnt and the ashes scattered in the woods.[46]

People remember 1943-44 as a time in the camp when prisoners reached beyond the day-to-day struggle to stay alive into acts of solidarity and resistance. A basic mutual-aid cell was composed of survivors of the same family: for example, Mrs Karmel and her two daughters, Henia and Ilona. For those left entirely alone, the Landsmanshaft, Jews from the same city, served as a substitute family. For example, the Płaszowites helped one another, forming 'bands' of girls, who lived and cooked together and shared their bread rations, money and clothes. Mina emphasized the importance of this mutual support from her 'camp family'; she was close friends with the Karmels.[47]

Ilona Karmel wrote:[48]

> **Friends shared a bunk, strolled arm-in-arm through the streets and were watched over anxiously, being replacements for**

those swept away. Each found with the usual camp speed, in the usual camp way, by glimpsing a free place on a bunk, by asking: 'Are you, too, alone?'

Despite a ban on religious observance, some elements of tradition were maintained, always at risk of death. At Werk A, Rabbi Yitzhak Finkler's barrack was known as the Rabiner Barak. It became a centre of congregation, prayer and study. Tefillin (phylacteries) and prayer books were smuggled into the camp and men gathered to pray together whenever possible, particularly on Friday evenings. As Friday twilight approached, women lit candle stubs, shouting and quarrelling ceased and peace descended. Each woman would be alone in her corner, communing with herself, weeping for those who had been lost.[49]

In Skarżysko, even festivals were celebrated. Felicja Karay recalled how:[50]

> As Passover 1944 neared, people were stricken by terrible longing for the home they no longer had and the family they had lost, longing for the holiday and the Jewish traditions. We baked matzos on the stove in the barracks and used coffee for wine, pouring it into tins. Potatoes and beets served in place of all the holiday dishes. We 'got hold of' a table and covered it with paper, seating thirty prisoners around it. We didn't have a Haggadah (the text that sets out the order of the Passover service). There was utter silence and then my son got up and began to sing: 'How is this night different from all other nights?' We never heard the rest. After those words, everyone burst out crying.

Many men and women, including secular Jews, fasted on Yom Kippur, which became for them a day of mourning for their murdered relatives.

For Mina, the high holidays were a time of mourning for her lost family. They underscored her solitude.

Songs and poems written by the prisoners, and the plays and poetry readings they organized, were a form of resistance to the authorities. They also provided a means of escape from reality and an outlet for the constant fear, providing a source of hope and strengthening the will to keep fighting to stay alive.[51]

In all the barracks, lamentations, hymns and ballads were composed and sung. Popular lyrics passed from person to person. Mixed troupes of men and women presented songs in Yiddish and Polish, poetry readings, and skits and couplets composed to familiar melodies depicting camp life. Songs expressed prisoners' hope for a better future.[52]

Eyewitness Lunka Kaufmann recalled:[53]

> **We spent many evenings curled up on our pallets listening breathlessly to recitations and songs, dreaming of the good life that would someday come, of delicacies to eat and elegant clothes to wear. Starving, freezing, we forgot our bitter fate for a brief moment.**

Akiva's Kraków prisoners included the musicologist and violinist Mosze Imber, who had somehow managed to smuggle his violin into the camp. Mina knew him, since before the War he had conducted the group's Kraków choir, in which she sang as a soprano.[54]

She recalled that whenever possible, despite her total state of exhaustion after a hard day's work, she would join in the singing and attend 'performances' in other barracks.

Shabbat celebrations were also organized by Akiva members, with recitations of stories and poems and communal singing of Polish songs, Hasidic melodies and the Hebrew songs of Israel. On the banks of the Kamienna River, they sang of the Sea of Galilee![55]

One of Henia Karmel's verses goes like this:[56]

> In Skarżysko woods
> The echo bears
> My tormented song.
> And they sway, the trees
> To its musical beat
> As they sing along.
> They sigh as they shake
> Their tears uncontained,
> For to them alone
> Branches heavy with snow
> Have I willed my pain.

In the summer of 1944, columns of smoke rising from the burning bodies that had started to be removed from mass graves struck terror into the hearts of prisoners. The Commandant of Werk C ordered the Jewish administration to arrange 'public concerts' for the whole camp. A special platform was erected in the forest, with rows of benches for the German managers and camp commanders invited. The prisoners from all three camps sat on the ground. A violin, harmonicas and a trumpet were found and, as if by magic, a small band came into being. The program was full and diverse: a dance troupe and chamber choir; 'life reporting' on camp life, loaded with satiric barbs; and a modern dance performed by one of the women to the music of Kol Nidrei (from the Yom Kippur liturgy). The highlight was the performance of a mixed choir led by Mosze Imber that sang songs by Mordechai Gebirtig and others in Yiddish,

Hebrew and Polish.

That night, the cannons of the approaching Soviet Army could already be heard.[57]

Those taking an active part in the performance wondered if they might be the last remnants of their cultural heritage.[58]

In late June 1944, it was announced that security and discipline in the camp were to be increased. There was a feeling in the air that the end was near. In July, Soviet troops reached the border of the Radom district. The evacuation of the factories was speeded up.

Mina recalled:[59]

In Płaszów we had received no news of what was happening in the outside world. When we came to Skarżysko, the men's camp, where non-Jewish free labourers worked, was next to us. So when they came to the factory, we would ask, from a distance: 'Hello, what's the news?' They replied: 'The Germans will break their necks soon!' Newspapers were not allowed: people were killed if the authorities found a newspaper on their bunk.

Rumours increased in the camp that the Soviet Army was advancing from the east. However, for most prisoners, what was happening outside was secondary to their preoccupation with survival inside. Here the killings continued.

Mass selections were carried out in all three Skarżysko camps on Saturday 29 July, the eve of Tisha B'av, the festival commemorating the destruction of the Holy Temples. The night shift was not sent out to work and the camp was surrounded by a cordon of SS and Werkschutz men. First the debilitated, the ill and the picric acid workers were selected: some 600 people were killed on the spot. On the following day, all patients were removed from the hospital.

Towards the end of the selection, German executives arrived from the plant. They passed along the rows indicating all those they wished to be rid of, some of them healthy young men and women.[60]

During the night of 30 July, 250 prisoners escaped from Werk C to the surrounding forest through openings cut in the camp fence. Among them were most of the Jewish officials and police.[61]

Mina recalled that night:[62]

> The Eisenbergs came to a bad end. The Germans tricked them: they cut an opening in the fence. Who went first? Mr Eisenberg and his wife, a lot of Jewish policemen—they were afraid for their own lives. They knew that to the Germans they were only servants, to execute the job that they ordered them to do. They were afraid, and they tried to save their own lives. In the middle of the night, they started to move out through this opening. But waiting for them on the other side were soldiers who shot them, one by one.
>
> Earlier my girlfriends from the other barracks had urged me: 'Mina what are you going to do? Let's go, let's go. We will be free.'
>
> Sometimes you can sense danger. There was such panic that night. So I said: 'I don't trust the Germans, and I'm not going. Up until then, 1944, I went where they sent me. I was persecuted, humiliated and beaten and saw death every day. I'm not going now. If you want to, you go.'
>
> So we stayed and, in the morning, we were the happy ones.

Felicja Karay wrote:[63]

> On 'the night of the great escape', as shots heard from the forest told the tragic tale, there was total confusion in the

camp. The despised internal officials had vanished and neither the Germans nor Werkschutz had yet made their appearance. The two storehouses holding bread and clothes were broken into, and frenzied prisoners grabbed whatever they could get their hands on. No one knew what fate the next day held for them. Before dawn, Schultze entered the camp and ordered a roll call.

Over the next two days some 6000-6700 prisoners were transported from Skarżysko to the various HASAG plants in Germany: to Colditz, Flossenbürg and Leipzig, all sub-camps of Buchenwald. Most of the women from Skarżysko were sent to the women's camp at Leipzig, along with most of the plant's machinery and equipment.[64]

Mina recalled:[65]

> In 1944 there was another hard selection. They chose us by making us run around in the middle of the camp. Whoever had a bad leg or could not keep up they selected: 'Out, out, out!' The youngest they gathered together. I was lucky again; they chose me to live. We did not know at the time, but found out later on the road that the train was taking us to Leipzig, Germany.

In the summer of 1944, the camp was liquidated. The special unit of Jewish prisoners, the Sonderkommando 1005, removed bodies from the mass grave in which they had been buried in the Werk C area, and cremated them. A few weeks later, the people of the work detail were themselves shot and burned.[66]

Freda visited present-day Zakłady Metalowe or MESKO SA, on the site of the previous HASAG camp, in June 2010. It produces ammunition for artillery, rifles and pistols, as well as aerial bombs and missiles.

The main entrance, administration buildings and museum are now housed where Werk A was located during the Occupation. After the War, the area which previously held Werk C, across the road from the main entrance, was responsible for the manufacture of heavy-duty weapons. Until recently it was a restricted area. Even in 2010, entering this area was scrutinized a lot more closely than going into the main building.

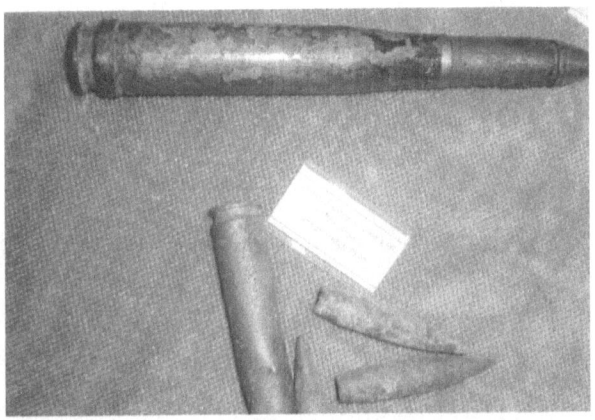

Ammunition manufactured in 1939-45, from the MESKO museum. Photo 2010.

The original museum, now abandoned because of lack of funds. Recently uncovered at the top of the building is a sign that reads 'HASAG Werk B'. Photo 2010.

MINA & JACOB

Notes

1. Mina Widawski nee Laub, audio testimony for the *12th Hour Project of Oral Testimonies* (Sydney: Australian Institute for Holocaust Studies, 1990); video testimony (Sydney: USC Shoah Foundation Institute, 1995), code 2526
2. Felicja Karay, *Death Comes in Yellow: Skarżysko-Kamienna Slave Labour Camp* (Amsterdam: Arwood Academic Publishers, 1995), 67-68
3. http://www.skarzysko.org/modules.php?name=Content&pa=showpage&pid=21; Martin Gilbert, *Never Again: A History of the Holocaust* (London: HarperCollins Illustrated, 2002), 78-79; Felicja Karay, *Women in Forced Labour Camps* (New Haven: Yale University Press, 1998), 285
4. Karay, *Death Comes in Yellow*, 9
5. United States Holocaust Memorial Museum (USHMM), *Encyclopedia of Camps and Ghettos* 1933-45, (Washington: 2012), Vol. 2, 310; Karay, *Death Comes in Yellow*, 9, 15; Israel Gutman, ed., *Encyclopedia of the Holocaust* (New York: Macmillan, 1990), 646
6. Karay, *Death Comes in Yellow*, xviii; Gilbert, *Never Again*, 1, 70-71; Felicja Karay, *HASAG-Leipzig Slave Labor Camp: the Struggle for Survival told by the Women and their Poetry* (London, Portland: Vallentine Mitchell, 2002), 234
7. Karay, *Death Comes in Yellow*, 22-23; 27
8. USHMM, *Encyclopedia of Camps and Ghettos*, Vol. 2, 310; Karay, *Death Comes in Yellow*, 29, 32
9. Karay, *Death Comes in Yellow*, 67-68; 235
10. Karay, *Death Comes in Yellow*, 73, 78-79, 244; Gutman, ed., *Encyclopedia of the Holocaust*, 1,360
11. Karay, *Women in Forced Labour Camps*, 286; Felicja Karay, *The Social and Cultural Life of the Prisoners in the Jewish Forced Labour Camp at Skarżysko-Kamienna*, in *Holocaust and Genocide Studies*, Vol. 8, (Oxford University Press in association with USHMM, 1994), 6; Karay, *Death Comes in Yellow*, 51, 186
12. Gutman, ed., *Encyclopedia of the Holocaust*, 1360; Karay, *The Social and Cultural Life*, 2, 4
13. Karay, *The Social and Cultural Life*, 4
14. Karay, *Death Comes in Yellow*, xvii, 49; Karay, *Women in Forced Labour Camps*, 286; Katarzyna Nazio, interview with Freda Widawski, MESKO Museum, Skarżysko-Kamienna, 2010
15. Gutman, ed., *Encyclopedia of the Holocaust*, 1,360; Karay, *Women in Forced Labour Camps*, 285-86; Karay, *Death Comes in Yellow*, 43, 83-85
16. Karay, *The Social and Cultural Life*, 15, 17; Felicja Karay, *Teaching the Holocaust through Music and Literature Written in the Camps*, (lecture delivered 13 October 1999), 2

17 Mina Widawski, *12th Hour Project of Oral Testimonies*; USC Shoah Foundation, code 2526
18 Karay, *Death Comes in Yellow*, 123; Karay, *Women in Forced Labour Camps*, 294
19 Karay, *Death Comes in Yellow*, 78-79
20 Mina Widawski, *12th Hour Project of Oral Testimonies*; USC Shoah Foundation, code 2526
21 Karay, *Death Comes in Yellow*, 89
22 Karay, *Women in Forced Labour Camps*, 287; Karay, *Death Comes in Yellow*, 90-92
23 Karay, *Women in Forced Labour Camps*, 287; Karay, *Death Comes in Yellow*, 143, 146, 150-53
24 Karay, *Women in Forced Labour Camps*, 288; Karay, *Death Comes in Yellow*, 168-69, 175-76; http://www.skarzysko.org/modules.php?name=Content&pa=showpage&pid=88
25 Mina Widawski, *12th Hour Project of Oral Testimonies*; USC Shoah Foundation, code 2526
26 Karay, *Death Comes in Yellow*, 75, 149-50
27 Karay, *Women in Forced Labour Camps*, 299; Karay, *Death Comes in Yellow*, 79
28 Karay, *Women in Forced Labour Camps*, 289
29 Karay, *Death Comes in Yellow*, 150
30 Mina Widawski, *12th Hour Project of Oral Testimonies*; USC Shoah Foundation, code 2526
31 Karay, *Women in Forced Labour Camps*, 286; Karay, *Death Comes in Yellow*, 170, 178
32 Karay, *Death Comes in Yellow*, 77
33 Karay, *Teaching the Holocaust*, 7-8; Karay, *Death Comes in Yellow*, 131, 238
34 Karay, *Women in Forced Labour Camps*, 289; Karay, *Death Comes in Yellow*, 78; Karay, *HASAG-Leipzig*, 62
35 Ilona Karmel, *An Estate of Memory* (London: Hodder and Stoughton, 1970), 141, 197
36 Karay, *Death Comes in Yellow*, 103
37 Karay, *Women in Forced Labour Camps*, 292; Karay, *Death Comes in Yellow*, 103
38 Karay, *Women in Forced Labour Camps*, 292-93
39 Karay, *Death Comes in Yellow*, 133
40 Gutman, ed., *Encyclopedia of the Holocaust*, 1,360-61; Karay, *Teaching the Holocaust*, 7; Karay, *The Social and Cultural Life*, 15, 17
41 Karay, *Women in Forced Labour Camps*, 289, 298
42 Karay, *Teaching the Holocaust*, 7; Karay, *The Social and Cultural Life*, 17-18
43 Karay, *Death Comes in Yellow*, 241, 247

44 Gutman, ed., *Encyclopedia of the Holocaust*, 1,361; Karay, *Teaching the Holocaust*, 7; Karay, *The Social and Cultural Life*, 8
45 Karay, *The Social and Cultural Life*, 3; Karay, *Death Comes in Yellow*, 244; Gutman, ed., *Encyclopedia of the Holocaust*, 1361; Karay, *Women in Forced Labour Camps*, 289
46 Gutman, ed., *Encyclopedia of the Holocaust*, 1362; Karay, *Death Comes in Yellow*, 63-64
47 Karay, *Women in Forced Labour Camps*, 295; Karay, *Death Comes in Yellow*, 125, 200, 212
48 Karmel, *An Estate of Memory*, 328-29
49 Karay, *Teaching the Holocaust*, 3; Karay, *Women in Forced Labour Camps*, 299-300; Karay, *Death Comes in Yellow*, 196-97
50 Karay, *Teaching the Holocaust*, 3; Karay, *Women in Forced Labour Camps*, 301
51 Karay, *Death Comes in Yellow*, 241, 247; Karay, *The Social and Cultural Life*, 1; Karay, *Teaching the Holocaust*, 9
52 Karay, *Women in Forced Labour Camps*, 301; Karay, *Death Comes in Yellow*, 135; Karay, *Teaching the Holocaust*, 5-6
53 Karay, *Death Comes in Yellow*, 219; Karay, *Teaching the Holocaust*, 6
54 Karay, *Teaching the Holocaust*, 6
55 Karay, *Teaching the Holocaust*, 7; Karay, *Death Comes in Yellow*, 212-18
56 Karay, *Women in Forced Labour Camps*, 301
57 Karay, *Teaching the Holocaust*, 8; Karay, *Women in Forced Labour Camps*, 303
58 Karay, *Death Comes in Yellow*, 223
59 Mina Widawski, *12th Hour Project of Oral Testimonies*; USC Shoah Foundation, code 2526
60 Karay, *Teaching the Holocaust*, 8-9; Karay, *Death Comes in Yellow*, 72, 224-25
61 Gutman, ed., *Encyclopedia of the Holocaust*, 1362; Karay, *Women in Forced Labour Camps*, 303
62 Mina Widawski, *12th Hour Project of Oral Testimonies*; USC Shoah Foundation, code 2526
63 Karay, *Death Comes in Yellow*, 227-28
64 Gutman, ed., *Encyclopedia of the Holocaust*, 1,362; Karay, *Death Comes in Yellow*, 72-73; 231
65 Mina Widawski, *12th Hour Project of Oral Testimonies*; USC Shoah Foundation, code 2526
66 Gutman, ed., *Encyclopedia of the Holocaust*, 1,362; Karay, *Death Comes in Yellow*, 63-64; Motek Striggler in David A. Hacket, *The Buchenwald Report* (Boulder, Colorado: Westview Press, 1995), 355-57

16
Freüda in Pionki

Mina's beloved sister Früda was probably transported to Pionki forced labour camp from Płaszów, on 18 November 1943. It is likely that she left in August 1944, bound for Sachsenhausen. Using the testimony of other prisoners, we will give a glimpse of what her life may have been like.

The Krusz-Pionki camp, 'the camp in the forest', was built next to a large explosives factory in the town of Pionki, some sixty-eight kilometres from Skarżysko and 220 from Kraków.[1]

In 1940, the Wehrmacht had taken over the gunpowder factory and a nearby power plant, forcing its pre-War Polish labourers to work there, and later using Pionki Jews. In 1942, when the Pionki Ghetto was liquidated, HASAG took over the plant and set up a camp. By 30 June 1943, the factory had a workforce of 3,500 Poles and 1,500 Jewish prisoners, half of them women.[2]

When the Soviet Army pushed into the Radom area in July 1944, it was decided to relocate the gunpowder factory to Germany. In August 1944, some 300 Jewish prisoners, including thirty women, were transported in four rail carriages via Częstochowa to the Sachsenhausen camp, to be used as labour to rebuild the factory in Glöwen. Once the Pionki factory had been closed, most of the Jewish prisoners were transferred to Auschwitz and Oranienburg.[3]

Eyewitness Gerszon Strykowski recalled:[4]

In 1943, I was sent to a camp in Pionki, the worst camp that I had experienced. Accommodation and food were not worse than in other camps, but the work was very hard and dangerous. I worked sixteen hours daily, four-hourly shifts in the ammunition and spirits' factories. We had to meet certain quotas per day. During an eight-hour shift in the spirits factory I had to move 128 bags, weighing sixty kilos, to the first floor. My teenage brother worked just as hard. With great difficulty we managed to do our work. Hundreds of our comrades died of exhaustion and starvation.

Eyewitness Salamon Reis recalled:[5]

Our food consisted of a slice of bread and watery soup. Alcohol was also used in the production of gunpowder, which the boys stole in small quantities, in order to barter it for a piece of bread. For this, they hanged my friend and ten others, carrying out the execution in front of us.

Eyewitness Rudolfina Laub [no relation to Mina], testified:[6]

Pionki was hell on earth. I had no clothing; I was starving. I had nothing to sleep on. At the beginning in the barrack in the forest, we had bare wooden planks. After the first horrific days, I finally received a mattress and a blanket. For one egg smuggled into the camp, for a few grams of butter, they murdered people.

When Soviet troops began to invade the area, aided by Polish partisans, the evacuation of Pionki's prisoners led to chaos. Prisoner Moszek Pantofel described the evacuation:[7]

> We were put into wagons. Travelling through Kielce, we were mistakenly attacked by Partisans, who took our transport for a German one. They exploded our train into the air. There were a few wounded and a few dead and others took the opportunity to flee into the forest.

After the War, a friend of the family, who had been with Freüda in Pionki described to Mina what had happened to her sister:[8]

> They stationed a train with German markings at the railway station in Pionki, and put the prisoners inside the wagons. The Soviet Air Force bombed the train because they thought it contained the enemy. Instead they were prisoners.
>
> I saw with my own eyes how a Russian soldier with tears streaming down his face, carried Freüda out from the train. Dead!

Notes

1. Ministerstwo Sprawidliwości Główna Komisja Badania Zbrodni Hitlerowskich w Polsce (Ministry of Justice Main Commission for the Investigation of German Crimes in Poland), *Obozy Hitlerowskie na ziemiach polskich 1939* (Hitler's Camps on Polish Soil 1939-45) (Warsaw: 1979), 386
2. United States Holocaust Memorial Museum (USHMM), *Encyclopedia of Camps and Ghettos* 1933-45, (Washington: 2012), Vol. 2, 278-79; Felicja Karay, *Death Comes in Yellow: Skarżysko-Kamienna Slave Labour Camp* (Amsterdam: Arwood Academic Publishers, 1995), 54
3. USHMM, *Encyclopedia of Camps and Ghettos*, 1,312
4. Gerszon Strykowski, oral testimony (Warsaw: Żydowski Instytut Historyczny (Jewish Historical Institute) Archives), code 301529
5. Salmon Reis, oral testimony (Warsaw: Żydowski Instytut Historyczny (Jewish Historical Institute) Archives), code 301791
6. Rudolfina Laub, oral testimony (Warsaw: Żydowski Instytut Historyczny (Jewish Historical Institute) Archives), code 301766
7. Moszek Pantofel, oral testimony (Warsaw: Żydowski Instytut Historyczny (Jewish Historical Institute) Archives), code 3012090
8. Mina Widawski nee Laub, audio testimony for the *12th Hour Project of Oral Testimonies* (Sydney: Australian Institute for Holocaust Studies, 1990); video testimony (Sydney: USC Shoah Foundation Institute, 1995), code 2526

1944

17

Janinagrube

Arbeitslager Janinagrube was established as a labour camp for men mining the Janina coal mine. Coal was of vital strategic importance as a resource used in the manufacture of German armaments. The camp was situated some thirteen kilometres from Auschwitz and operated from 4 September 1943 until 18 January 1945.[1]

Before the War, the mine had belonged to the French-Galician Joint Stock Coal Mine Society, and most of the miners came from Libiąż and the surrounding area. When the Germans occupied the town on 4 September 1939, Oskar Schade, a local resident of German descent, was appointed the mine's manager.[2]

In 1941, IG Farbenindustrie had started building Buna Werke in Monowice and had acquired the local Fürsten coal mine. On 1 January 1943, it also assumed control of Janina under a trust arrangement and the mine operated under the name Gute Hoffnung.[3]

From November 1939-January 1943, under German management, Janina was modernized. Output increased, but more was required. In 1942 additional labour of 150 prisoners-of-war (POWs) from Lamsdorf, were transferred to the new camp near Obieżowa, Kriegsgefangenen-Arbeitskommando E-562 Janinagrube, a branch of Stalag VIII B.[4]

However, these POWs were unwilling 'to assist the Reich, with whom England was at war, in their war effort'. Their output was low and did not yield the expected profits.⁵

On 16 July 1943, following inspection of the mine by Rudolf Höss and representatives of IG Farbenindustrie, the decision was made to replace the POWs with prisoner-labourers from Auschwitz. Concentration camp prisoners were not covered by the Geneva Convention and could be forced to achieve higher production levels and punished if they failed. In addition, 300 prisoners could be housed in barracks that had formerly been occupied by 150 British POWs, without incurring additional costs.⁶

It was also recommended that the camp be expanded immediately, so that by the end of the year it could hold 900 prisoners.⁷

On 26 August 1943 the POW camp began to be disbanded, and at the end of the month it was taken over by the management of KL Auschwitz.⁸

On 4 September 1943, the first transport of Auschwitz prisoners arrived in Janina, marking the establishment of the Auschwitz sub-camp Janinagrube.⁹

Of the 300 prisoners transported, around 250 were Polish Jews who had been brought from various forced labour camps in the Poznań district, tattooed with numbers in the series 140,000-142,000. That first transport also contained some Polish and Czech prisoners of German descent.¹⁰

Jacob's prisoner record number, 141,687, fell within that range. He recalled:¹¹

> I was part of the first transport to Janina. The camp director introduced himself following our selection. He said: 'I am your Unterscharführer Baumgartner. I will be your Camp Director in Janina.' They loaded us into open trucks under SS guard and they brought us to the Janina coal mine, about thirteen kilometres from Auschwitz.

The POWs were guarded by the Wehrmacht, but when we came, the SS were already there. They took the POWs away and they brought us—the slaves—from Auschwitz.

When we arrived, an old SS man came out of the kitchen and said: 'Boys, form a queue and you'll get some food I've cooked for you.' I remember this as if it happened yesterday. He cooked macaroni with milk for us: very thick, heavy soup! We hadn't seen such soup for years! They gave us half a loaf of bread and a piece of wurst made from horsemeat—maybe 300 grams. The boys started to hug and kiss one another. They said: '*Ich hob zay in dreat*' (Yiddish, meaning 'you can go to hell'). 'If they give us food like this, we will survive anything. We'll survive!'

Eyewitness Eugeniusz Ciećkiewicz recalled:[12]

At the end of my time in quarantine, I was called into the Politische Abteilung [the Political Department or camp Gestapo], where I was asked how much I knew about mining. I told them that I had been attending mining school. The next day, after the evening *Appell*, they read out a list of numbers, mine included. We were told that we were leaving the following day in a transport. This was the first transport to the sub-camp Janinagrube. I remember that in this transport there were mainly Jews and two Poles: me and Zygmunt Szwajc.

Until the end of 1944, small transports of prisoners continued to arrive at Janinagrube, mostly Jews from Poland, Czechoslovakia, Hungary, Greece and finally France. Records indicate that in November 1944, of 886 prisoners, 717 were Jews.[13]

When at the beginning of the twentieth century the mine had

begun to be developed, housing camps in groups of twelve brick buildings were constructed around Obieżowa and Leśniowa. Additional wooden barracks had been built in 1942 for the British POWs, some 400 metres from the mine.[14]

The 300 prisoners who arrived in September 1943 were initially housed in these wooden barracks. Then the camp was substantially expanded on land around Obieżowa. The new development, on sloping land with sandy soil, was rectangular in shape, measured 15,000 square metres and was surrounded by local villages.[15]

Eugeniusz Ciećkiewicz recalled:[16]

> **One day, Baumgartner called me to his office and asked whether I would be able to draw a sketch for extending the camp. I prepared a plan for the sewage in the extended area and for two barracks. A Lagerkommando (work unit) was formed, which I supervised.**

The construction unit was formed from a group of tradesmen who had arrived on the first transport: bricklayers, carpenters and metal-workers. The remaining 280 prisoners were sent to work in the mine.[17]

Jacob recalled:[18]

> When our transport reached the Janina mine there was no camp there: we were housed in barracks and empty apartment blocks while we built the camp.
>
> As soon as the first transport arrived, prisoners able to work were used in the coal mine. Those who were weaker or not healthy enough worked constructing the camp, more barracks, the kitchen building, the hospital, fencing and the guard towers.

Those of us sent to the mine had every second Sunday free. On these 'open' Sundays as well as after work, we were also used in the on-going construction of the camp. We worked during the day, at night, on Saturdays and Sundays. People became worn out.

After about six months, finally the barracks were finished. I was housed in Block 2, across from the hospital.

The camp also took over a two-storey brick building in the Obieżowa housing estate which had two ground-level extensions. In one of these was the administration office and in the other the storehouse for the miners' carbine lamps. Its cellar contained three standing 'punishment' rooms which were so small that anyone imprisoned there could stand, but not move.

Three ground-level barracks with windows, on brick foundations, measuring twenty-six by eight metres, were built, housing 150-200 prisoners. The smaller barracks with lower ceilings housed two-tiered bunks and the taller ones three-tiered.[19]

Each prisoner was assigned his own bunk. But with the arrival of additional transports and the subsequent overcrowding, it was necessary to squeeze in two prisoners per bed. They slept on pallets stuffed with straw, and covered themselves with a single blanket. The barracks also contained a table and one wardrobe.

The camp's kitchen was located in a separate wooden block. It contained a storeroom for provisions, a dining room and a canteen. At first meals were cooked in the kitchen for both prisoners and guards. Then a separate kitchen was built for the SS.

Jacob recalled:[20]

Initially, before the camp was completed, we washed after our shift with the civilian miners. The worst part was that the

SS guards didn't want to wait for us to bathe. They rushed us out of the bath-house while some of us were still wet. We didn't have towels to dry ourselves and we only had our camp uniform to put back on—nothing else. In winter, with temperatures of twenty-two to twenty-five degrees centigrade below zero, people fell sick, one after another. You didn't want to be beaten by the SS, so you ran out of the bath-house early and stood out there in the cold and the frost.

Up to the autumn of 1944, sanitary conditions were primitive. Then a washroom in a separate stone structure and a two-sided covered latrine were built, at the same time as the extra barracks. Initially there was only cold water: a metal trough with taps. Prisoners who worked down the dirty mine were most affected by the lack of hot water. At the end of 1944 hot water was connected to the camp by piping steam from the mine, and showers were added to the washroom.[21]

Prisoners wore the usual striped uniforms and those who worked in the mine were given a second set of work clothes into which they changed in the mine's bathroom, before going down to work. When hot water was connected to the camp, the prisoners were escorted straight from the mine shaft in their work clothes, which were always soaked, to the camp bath-house, where they washed and changed.[22]

Footwear consisted of boots with wooden soles nailed to uppers of leather or leatherette, or cloth and rubber, material taken from shoes left by prisoner convoys. They were completely unsuitable for marches and caused foot ulcers. Anyone given boots that were the right size or a matching pair could count himself lucky.[23]

The camp's hospital, the Häftingskrankenbau (HKB), occupied a separate wooden building. In addition to an outpatients' clinic, it contained a room with a number of beds, plus living quarters for the doctor and dentist, who were also prisoners.

Two small walls were erected between the clinic and the bathhouse, screening this area from the *Appellplatz* where roll calls were held and from where workers marched out to work in the mine.

The Blockführerstube, where the camp guards lived and the canteen for the SS was located, was outside the camp, near the gate and a sports' ground for the SS.

The POW camp had been half the size of the new one, and surrounded with a wire fence. After the new buildings were erected, the camp was enclosed by a double row of barbed wire with an electric current of 350 vaults running through it. Four watchtowers stood on each corner of the external fence. Electric lamps were hung on the surrounding posts and remained on all night long. Searchlights were mounted at windows facing the camp and guards on sentry duty were armed with hand-held machine-guns.

The camp's main gate, with the sign Arbeitslager Janinagrube, was located at the end of the extended main street, which ran through the Obieżowa settlement.

Jacob recalled:[24]

> After every shift we changed our dirty clothes and got fresh clothing from a warehouse looked after by a prisoner—Egon was his name. We had two uniforms, one that we wore to work in the mine and a clean one that, when you came home, you exchanged in the storeroom, with your Häftling (prisoner) number.
>
> We prisoners wore rubber boots, wooden clogs or leather shoes. I had to wear shoes since I worked with an electric machine, the Haspel-winch. I couldn't work in rubber boots.
>
> At first the food was not too bad because, as heavy

labourers, we received additional rations from the mine. For breakfast we received 400 grams of bread and during the day a bowl of cabbage soup, sometimes a piece of horse sausage or a little marmalade. When we came up from the mine in the evening, we also got soup, 250 grams of bread and sometimes a piece of sausage. Oh luxury! What could be better than their feeding us like this?

But as soon as we had finished building the camp, the Commandant and the SS became smarter. They wanted to get their hands on our rations, so they said to the directors of the mine: 'Give the prisoners' rations to us and we'll cook them.' So the SS took our extra food. After that we didn't see any extra bread or soup.

The daily allowance became 250 grams of bread and a few grams of margarine, sometimes supplemented with jam or sausage; a litre of Ersatz-Kaffee and a litre of soup, most often made with potatoes, carrots or turnips. Sometimes noodles or beans were added or a little bit of meat. Since most prisoners worked three shifts, by the time they came to eat, the food was cold. Those who worked the night shift did, however, receive an extra portion.[25]

The kitchen was run by an SS officer, helped by the prisoners.[26]

At the beginning of the War, a police unit had supervised the miners, but by the end of 1940 all managerial positions were in German hands. Poles performed more menial jobs, with the miners extracting the coal treated worst, as they did the dirtiest and hardest work.[27]

Franz Kröger, the mine's Director, was a Volksdeutsche whose only concern was to increase output. Eyewitness Dr Orlik, described him:[28]

Kröger was short and about forty years old. This man tortured prisoners to death. I did their autopsies and reported the cause of death to the manager of the mine. He didn't react, his main concern being increasing prisoners' output.

Kröger's technical staff were like him. They were generally young miners from Upper Silesia who had avoided being sent to the Front by working down the mine. They were Germans by birth, or wanted to pass as German; they belonged to the Nazi Party and they wore SS uniforms. They could speak Polish, but used German both at work and at home.

Civilian miners who worked underground alongside the prisoners remember the brutality with which they were treated. The Head Foremen, Nadsztygarzy, and the Pit Foremen, Sztygarzy, were notorious. Worse was Wilhelm Balzarek who beat prisoners who could not meet the required output until they fainted or died. He inspired universal fear. He also had the power to send prisoners to Auschwitz-Birkenau for extermination.[29]

In March 1944 Baumgartner was replaced by SS-Oberscharführer Hermann Kleimann. Baumgartner remained at Janinagrube as Kleimann's assistant. The reason for the change is not known, although Kleimann was crueller than Baumgartner. Prisoners and SS men alike were afraid of him. In September 1944 Kleimann was replaced by SS-Unterscharführer Rudolf Kamieniczny, who would remain the camp's Commandant until its liquidation.[30]

Jacob recalled those who ran the camp:[31]

The camp Commandant, SS-Unterscharführer Baumgartner, was big and about thirty years old. He had a younger Polish wife and I remember that Scharne told us one Sunday that Baumgartner had become a father. That happened about a year before liquidation.

After the first five or six months Baumgartner was no longer our camp Commandant but became the leader of the guard detail. Compared to other SS officers, Baumgartner behaved decently. I never saw him torture or kill prisoners. I can say with conviction that he was a good man. Not dangerous. Not one of the other SS guards was like Baumgartner.

He was replaced by an SS-Oberscharführer. Who knows why? One day he was no longer the Commandant. This Oberscharführer was a bit older and had the mentality of a criminal. He beat and tortured many prisoners.

Dr Orlik, Dr Levi and Dr Halpern had arrived on the 4 September transport. Dr Orlik was the main doctor.

The report writer was Scharne, from Hamburg. I believe his deputy was named Stein. The Lagerälteste or camp elder was a certain Willi, who was tall and slim. Before him there had been another camp elder with a green label [criminal prisoner]. I believe his name was Franz.

Of the *Kapo* I remember a Moszkowicz and a Levkowitcz. I also recall the *Oberkapo*, a Pole named Sigmund.

There was also a Blockältester or block leader named Laßmann, who was a Hungarian of about twenty-eight, a big slim man. The Blockfüren were SS officers. Three or four of them were always in the camp. The Blockältesten were prisoners. Our Blockältester was Franz; I don't know his family name. He was a German prisoner and he behaved decently towards me.

The kitchen *Kapo* came from Germany. He was a boxer and a big-time criminal. He had a green label. In the kitchen there was also an SS-Rottenführer, an old man.

During my entire time in Janina we were guarded by the

same SS men. I can recall a young man of about twenty-six, an officer who commanded the SS guards who marched us to and from the mine. He was an SS-Unterscharführer with two stars, and the youngest of the officers. He was big, about six feet tall, had dark hair, and was known as 'the Bandit'. He was exceptionally sadistic and tortured people. Every day he would pick someone out of the line-up—maybe a face he didn't like—and 'play' with him. He would ask him to lie down, get up, lie down, stand up—all day long! These guards were Reichsdeutsche or Volksdeutsche. I can't say that one group treated the prisoners differently from the others; that depended entirely on the individual. Mostly we didn't know their names. No prisoner knew the names of SS guards. They didn't introduce themselves!

They all wore the same uniform, greyish-blue. The Commandant wore a round cap. The others wore Schiffchen caps.

Eyewitness Arie Torner recalled:[32]

> I knew the *Kapo* Jozef Schwierzek from Auschwitz and from the Janina mine. He was known for his extreme brutality and bestiality. He beat prisoners until they fell down dead and then he trampled on them. Nobody surpassed his brutality. He caused many deaths in Auschwitz and Janina.

Sentry duty was performed by fifty SS men from the Third Company. Some of the SS guards who have been identified were: SS-Obersturmbannführer Herman Blumenau; SS-Rottenführer Heinrich Niemeyer [sometimes spelt Niemeier]; SS-Sturmmann Hans Jochum; SS-Schütze Ferdinand Kruckenberger and SS-Schütze Adam Nischt.[33]

From time to time, the SS undertook inspections of the camp, with visits by the Chief of Staff, SS-Sturmbannführer Hartjenstein and by the Commandant of KL Auschwitz I.[34]

While most prisoners laboured extracting coal, some were in the division that built the gangways or the galleries, or helped operating electrical and motorized machines. A few prisoners worked on the surface of the mine in what was called 'the yard', sorting and loading wood on to wagons for the mine galleries.[35]

Jacob described his work:[36]

> In the coal mine, they grouped us into three shifts: first, second and night shift. We marched every day from our camp to the coal mine, some two-and-a-half kilometres each way. We marched guarded by the SS and as we marched they made us sing.
>
> What was my job in the mine? When I was in Poznań, one of the jobs I had was helping an electrician, building electrical poles for the Polish camp. So when I came to the coal mine, I told them I was an electrician and was put to work operating an electrical winch machine, the Haspel-winch. These were large machines which pulled up wagons full of coal using an electrical cable. We had to turn the wagons around when they came up, unload them, put them back on the cables and send them down either loaded with materials or empty.

By August 1944, some 800 prisoners were employed at the mine, of whom 522 worked underground and 208 on the surface, in work shifts lasting between eight and nine hours.[37] The mine operated around the clock, prisoners working three shifts, with one above ground. Those working on night shifts carried carbide miners' lamps. The SS guards who escorted prisoners to and from work counted them before they went down in the lift and after they came up. Two SS men were on duty during each shift, checking every wagon filled with coal and wood which came up from the mine.[38]

On arrival at the extraction unit, the prisoners were divided into groups of ten and, under the direction of the Head Foreman made their way to where the Sztygars allocated individual tasks. Each miner was given two prisoners to help him, and they worked together every day for eight hours. The civilian miner was responsible for extracting the coal, while the prisoner's job was to load it. Since each miner had to fulfil a quota, it was important for him that he work with strong, healthy prisoners. Informal groups of miners and prisoners got to know one another as they worked side by side. Some miners quietly helped the prisoners by sharing their food. It was not uncommon for a miner to bring a double portion of bread or some other food from home. Often prisoners found food left for them at their work station. It was also sometimes possible to pass on political news or information about the progress of the War to prisoners.[39]

Officially, of course, contact between the prisoners and miners was forbidden and punished severely. Breaking the rules was punishable by being sent to a camp, imprisonment or even death. However, it was impossible for a miner to work with a prisoner for eight hours and not say a word, so contact was routine.[40]

Jacob recalled:[41]

> I worked in the first department, under the German Obersztygar Balzarek and the Pole Sztygar Wilschak. They weren't prisoners. Wilschak was a decent man who often gave me bread. Balzarek was known for his brutality. He often beat prisoners and civilian workers so badly that they needed to be treated in the hospital.
>
> My Foreman was Jan Kulas, about whom I cannot say

anything negative, despite the fact that he had a reputation for being a sadist. Once he even gave me a bonus of five marks for my good work and my service at the machine!

Eugeniusz Ciećkiewicz explained:[42]

> For good work the prisoners received vouchers for the camp canteen, with which they could 'purchase' cigarettes or mineral water.

Work in the mine was debilitating. Most prisoners were assigned to jobs that needed strength, not skill, such as loading coal or hauling trucks. Because such tasks were the most difficult, strenuous and physically exhausting, they often resulted in accidents. Many prisoners suffered fractures and internal injuries. The work was a little easier in the underground workshops, electrical or mechanical, but there were few jobs for prisoners there.[43]

Of the prisoners in Janina, the Polish Jews had the most rewarding contact with the miners. They spoke Polish and so understood instructions from the lower levels of management, who were Poles. They assigned them to work in transport and workshops, as 'professional' help. The Polish Jews were generally people under thirty, used to physical labour. They were poor people: shoemakers, tailors and small-time traders, used to hardship, and they formed a hard-working partnership with their miners.[44]

Workers who spoke German were given clerical and supervisory positions. Doctors and male nurses were, for example, mostly Czech. Those who spoke no German, Polish or Yiddish, such as the Greek prisoners, could neither understand German commands nor communicate with their fellow prisoners. They were badly treated by the guards and functionaries and shoved into the worst and hardest jobs. Most intellectuals found the physical work demanding and quickly weakened, unless they were able to use their skills to entertain those in charge. Artists painted portraits of the *Kapos* and guards, and actors and singers performed.[45]

Eugeniusz Ciećkiewicz recalled:[46]

> **In the underground mine I worked in Section IV. Accidents occurred often, as prisoners were given the most dangerous work. Not all of them knew German so they didn't understand the Sztygars' and *Kapos*' orders and their helplessness often caused accidents.**

From survivor testimonies it would appear that the mortality rate in Janinagrube due to the tough work conditions, malnutrition and brutal treatment was particularly high. Despite the strongest prisoners being sent there, their tolerance of work in the mine lasted a mere four to six weeks. Dr Orlik estimated that, on average, a healthy prisoner could work in the mine for a month. Jacob was resourceful and lucky. Having been assigned work in the electrical workshop meant that he managed to survive Janina for one-and-a-half years![47]

Apart from the criminals, most non-Jewish prisoners at Janinagrube were political dissidents. There were only about ten Polish prisoners, who performed various functions inside the camp or worked in groups heavily guarded by SS men.[48]

In September 1944, seventy prisoners were chosen for work relocating heavy ammunition to the nearby forest, where the Germans had begun stockpiling goods. Eugeniusz Ciećkiewicz recalled:[49]

> **I was transferred to the Bombenkommando, as the Vorbeiter, the only Pole among a group of seventy Jews. Wagons carrying torpedoes were shunted down a railway siding from**

the mine towards Leśniowa. We loaded heavy ammunition on to trucks which transported it to the forest close to Libiąż. We stacked it in the forest and camouflaged it. Unloading was done by hand, without any cranes, lifts or safety equipment. This was very hard and dangerous work, with prisoners subject to extensive bruising and accidents.

To maintain the highest possible output, sick or unproductive prisoners were transferred back to Auschwitz, where they were killed in the gas chamber. They were replaced by new prisoners. As early as 1942, IG Farbenindustrie had demanded quick transport to the 'mother camp' of prisoners who were unfit for work.[50]

Jacob recalled:[51]

Dr Fischer came to the camp every four weeks to select sick prisoners. Those who could not work any more were taken away. We knew that they were taken to the crematorium in Birkenau.

Dr Orlik was assisted by an SS orderly. The role of paramedic was performed by the German prisoner, Max Buchhalter. Because of frequent work-related accidents, in spring 1944 a surgeon was brought to the camp. Medicine was provided by the Monowice camp, and also by IG Farbenindustrie. However, there was never enough medicine, since the number of sick prisoners was constantly increasing.[52]

Four prisoners were allocated to assist the dentist at the hospital, a French prisoner, Ladislaus Broad. The most common operations were teeth extractions and healing 'mouth cavities'—most likely indicating scurvy.[53]

Once a week a special truck carted corpses back to Auschwitz, where they were burned in the crematorium.[54]

In addition to injuries caused by mistreatment and accidents, the most common illnesses were dystrophic diseases, hastened by malnutrition; gastrointestinal diseases due to low or high stomach acid or gastro-duodenal ulcers; starvation-induced diarrhoea caused by bad food and prolonged exposure to cold; bronchitis and pneumonia.[55]

Prisoners avoided being admitted to the hospital, since already meagre food rations were reduced by half for patients, meaning that there was no chance of being restored to health. Prisoners also feared the selections which were often carried out in the hospital.[56]

At Monowitz, major surgery, such as partial or full surgical removal of the stomach, for gastro-duodenal ulcers, was often performed.[57] The hospital was also a place where SS medical officers experimented. SS-Hauptsturmführer Dr Friedrich Entress, camp physician from 1941-43, performed stomach operations when there was the slightest complaint about stomach trouble. Dr Vilém Jurkovič recalled:[58]

> I was one of the first Czechoslovak doctors to work at the Auschwitz prisoners' hospital; I started there in May 1942. The physicians and hospital orderlies were often doctors with long years of specialist experience, so operations carried out by them were done in line with normal medical practice. But on occasion the SS doctor might take it into his head to operate, to keep his hand in or to practise a particular operation. In this event a serious stomach operation might be performed on a catarrh case, or a thyroid gland removed in the case of a simple swelling.

Jacob recalled:[59]

> After that bout of diarrhoea in Guttenbrunn, I had trouble with my stomach: stomach catarrh. I had a lot of acid made worse by inhaling gases in the coal mine. Sometimes I would lie on the floor writhing in pain. The head *Kapo* on my shift was Willie, a political prisoner and a Mischling [half-Jew, half-German]. Willie went to the doctors one day and said: 'You bastards, that boy is in great pain. Why don't you do something for him?' So they put me in the hospital. Dr Levi, a young Jewish doctor from France, heard that the surgeon wanted to operate on me. He warned: 'Don't let them operate. You don't have an ulcer; you just have mild catarrh. Once the War is over, you can live a normal life with this illness. If they operate on you, you won't survive. They're just experimenting.'
>
> I had only been in the hospital for a couple of days when they decided to put me to work outside, unloading trolleys. Who was working there? Only *Muselmanner*! They were already finished, just waiting for the selection to go to Birkenau. After working there for two days, I thought to myself: 'Oh no—I've been through so much, I'm not going to die now. This is not for me.' So I went to the report writer, Scharne, and said to him: 'I'm going back to the coal mine.'
>
> He reported this that evening to Commandant Baumgartner, who had a great deal of respect for the 141st because we were the prisoners who set up the camp. When Scharne told him: 'We have a 141st, whom we took out of the coal mine because he was ill. But he has volunteered to go back.' The Commandant called me forward and started shouting. 'You see this boy? He has already worked in the coal mine for one-and-a-half years. We took him out because of his health—but

he volunteered to go back. *Kapo*, two extra loaves for the boy!' And I went back to the mine.

Being made to stand while waiting for the roll to be called was one of the worst forms of punishment imposed on the prisoners. This occurred twice daily. The names of those who were to be punished for low output or some other 'crime' were read out. Usually the punishment was five to twenty lashes. A prisoner could be given twenty lashes for disagreeing with a Sztygar.[60]

In August 1944 a group of prisoners started digging a tunnel under the fence. At the same time, others were digging ditches for sewage pipes to remove waste from the camp. One day Kleimann came to see what progress was being made and, after removing some planks, found the tunnel. Five prisoners were arrested, accused of planning an escape and taken to Auschwitz I. After two months, one of them was brought back to Janinagrube and hanged in front of the assembled prisoners. Authorities came from Auschwitz to watch the execution, and prisoners from other sub-camps were also brought in and made to watch.[61]

Jacob recalled:[62]

> Every evening we had to stand in formation for the roll to be called. The SS kept us there for two or three hours and we had to do punishment exercises.
>
> I never saw killings in the camp, other than the hangings; I only heard about them. I know that there were staged boxing matches arranged by Heinrich Niemeyer. There was a certain Wassermann, a professional boxer, whom they brought from Auschwitz to Janina to fight prisoners. The boxing ring was set up near the front gate so that those living outside the camp could watch.

By the second half of 1944, it was obvious that the tide of the War was turning. The Front was moving closer to the German border. In May 1944 Himmler issued an order that not one concentration camp prisoner should fall into the hands of the Allies. Existing camps must be destroyed and their prisoners transported deep inside Germany.[63]

On 12 January 1945 an offensive was launched by the Soviet Army, and the nearby towns of Kielce and Częstochowa were liberated the next day. From 15 January 1945, the Germans began evacuating the Auschwitz camps, including the sub-camps located next to mines and factories, belonging to Auschwitz III-Monowitz.[64]

On the evening of 17 January 1945, the final roll call was held in Janinagrube. There were 857 prisoners, all Jews, non-Jews having been evacuated on 6 December 1944. On 18 January at seven in the morning, prisoners were marched out of the camp, heading towards KL Groß Rosen. They passed through forests on the road to Auschwitz.

But when they reached the main camp, they found no one in charge. The authorities had left Auschwitz the day before.[65]

Jacob recalled:[66]

On 18 January 1945, they started to evacuate our camp. On the 15th we were still working. I was on the first shift and as we came up from the mine, I was surprised that the second shift of workers, whom we usually met coming up, had not arrived. Nobody was there. I asked around and was told by the civilian miners: 'Don't you know? It's evacuation!' When we arrived back in the camp, we found out that we were being evacuated from Janina.

On 25 January 1945, Libiąż was liberated by the Soviet Army. Sixty prisoners, left behind in the Janinagrube camp because of poor health, were helped by local Polish residents. The gravely ill were moved to hospital and those who were healthier remained, slowly regaining their health.[67]

After liberation, some of the buildings that had been occupied by prisoners were dismantled, while others were occupied by civilian workers. In the 1960s any remaining barracks were dismantled, and the area was used for landfill by the residents of Obieżowa.

All that remains now is a memorial built where Janinagrube was located. It is intended to honour those who toiled and perished there.[68]

Freda remembers her visit to Janina in July 2010, where she met an eyewitness:

> **Pani Fredzia, now in her eighties, was ten years old during the War. She was born and lived in the area where Janinagrube was situated. During the War her family was moved out, but she continued to visit her grandmother, who lived near the camp. She remembered where the barracks had stood, and told me that she would watch people, shuffling along in their wooden clogs, being marched to the coal mine. She said that her father worked as a Sztygar there during the War and remembers that he used to take a second breakfast to the prisoners.**

Top: Janinagrube barracks, still standing in the 1960s.
Photo from http://libiaz.pl/index.php?option=18&action=articles_show&art_id=1017&lang=pl
Bottom: This monument, all that remains of the camp, was erected by the Libiąż community on 9 April 1965, in memory of Janinagrube.
The plaque reads:
NEVER AGAIN WAR—
NEVER AGAIN EXTERMINATION CAMPS
IN MEMORY OF VICTIMS DESTROYED DURING THE
YEARS OF NAZI OCCUPATION IN THE AUSCHWITZ SUB-CAMP
NEXT TO THE COAL MINE JANINA, Janinagrube.
ON THE 20TH ANNIVERSARY OF LIBERATION 25.1.1945-25.1.1965
COMMUNITY OF LIBIĄŻ

Notes

1 Franciszek Piper, *Auschwitz Prisoner Labour: The Organization and Exploitation of Auschwitz Concentration Camp Prisoners as Labourers* (Oświęcim: Auschwitz-Birkenau State Museum, 2002), 244-45; Ministerstwo Sprawidliwości Główna Komisja Badania Zbrodni Hitlerowskich w Polsce (Ministry of Justice Main Commission for the Investigation of German Crimes in Poland), *Obozy Hitlerowskie na ziemiach polskich 1939* (Hitler's Camps on Polish Soil 1939-45) (Warsaw: 1979), 371, para. 3299; United States Holocaust Memorial Museum, USHMM, *Encyclopedia of Camps and Ghettos 1933-45*, (Washington, 2012), Vol. 1, Pt A, 253

2 USHMM, *Encyclopedia of Camps and Ghettos*; Pawel Stanisław, *Z cyklu 'Dzieje Libiąża': Podobóz 'Janinagrube' w Libiążu w latach okupacji 1943-45* (From the series 'The History of Libiąż': Sub-camp 'Janinagrube' in 'Libiąż' during the Years of Occupation 1943-45') (Libiąż: Opracowania Regionalne, Stanisław Pawel Jaworzno: Biuro Turystyczne Pasja) (Libiąż: Regional Study of Stanisław Pawel, Jaworzno, Tourist Office Pasja, 1998), 3-4

3 Emeryka Iwaszko, *Podobóz 'Janinagrube': Zeszyty Oświęcimskie: 10* (Sub-camp 'Janinagrube': Auschwitz Notebooks: 10) (Oświęcim: Państwowe Muzeum w Oswiecimiu) (State Museum in Auschwitz, 1967): 59-60; *Obozy w Libiążu w latach II wojny światowej* (Camps in Libiąż during the Years of World War II) http://libiaz.pl/components/download/send.php?pos_id= 126, 2; Piper, *Auschwitz Prisoner Labour*, 378; Stanisław, *Dzieje Libiąża*, 7

4 Stanisław, *Dzieje Libiąża*, 5; *Obozy pracy w Libiążu*, (*Labour Camps in Libiąż*) (no publication details), 71; *Obozy w Libiążu*, 5

5 Stanisław, *Dzieje Libiąża*, 5-6; *Obozy pracy*, 71-72

6 Iwaszko, *Podobóz 'Janinagrube'*, 60-61; Stanisław, *Dzieje Libiąża*, 5

7 Ibid.

8 *Obozy pracy*, 72

9 Stanisław, *Dzieje Libiąża*, 7; *Obozy pracy*, 72-73; Iwaszko, *Podobóz 'Janinagrube'*, 69

10 Iwaszko, *Podobóz 'Janinagrube'*, 69; Stanisław, *Dzieje Libiąża*, 10

11 Jacob Widawski, transcripts of interviews conducted at the Consulate-General of the Federal Republic of Germany, 1974, 1975, Sydney; transcripts of testimony given at trial against Heinrich Niemeyer, 1978, 1982, 1989, Indictment StA Hannover 11 Js 5/73, Hannover; audio testimony for the *12th Hour Project of Oral Testimonies* (Sydney: Australian Institute for Holocaust Studies, 1990); video testimony, 1995 (Sydney: USC Shoah Foundation Institute), code 2528

12 Eugeniusz Ciećkiewicz, recorded testimony in Stanisław, *Dzieje Libiąża*, 36-38

13 Stanisław, *Dzieje Libiąża*, 10; *Obozy w Libiążu*, 18
14 Stanisław, *Dzieje Libiąża*, 1-2; 4-5
15 Iwaszko, *Podobóz 'Janinagrube'*, 59, 66
16 Stanisław, *Dzieje Libiąża*, 36-38
17 Iwaszko, *Podobóz 'Janinagrube'*, 74-75; USHMM, *Encyclopedia of Camps and Ghettos*, Vol. 1, Pt A, 254
18 Jacob Widawski, testimonies, German Consulate-General; transcripts, Hannover trial; *12th Hour Project* 1990; USC Shoah Foundation, code 2528
19 Iwaszko, *Podobóz 'Janinagrube'*, 66, 68; *Obozy pracy*, 74; Stanisław, *Dzieje Libiąża*, 36-38
20 Jacob Widawski, testimonies, German Consulate-General; transcripts, Hannover trial; *12th Hour Project* 1990; USC Shoah Foundation, code 2528
21 Iwaszko, *Podobóz 'Janinagrube'*, 72
22 Iwaszko, *Podobóz 'Janinagrube'*, 72-75; Stanisław, *Dzieje Libiąża*, 14
23 Primo Levi and Leonardo De Benedetti, *Auschwitz Report* (Minerva Medica 1946; English version, London: Verso, 2006), 38
24 Jacob Widawski, testimonies, German Consulate-General; transcripts, Hannover trial; *12th Hour Project* 1990; USC Shoah Foundation, code 2528
25 Iwaszko, *Podobóz 'Janinagrube'*, 72; Stanisław, *Dzieje Libiąża*, 12
26 Iwaszko, *Podobóz 'Janinagrube'*, 72-73
27 Stanisław, *Dzieje Libiąża*, 1; 3-4
28 Iwaszko, *Podobóz 'Janinagrube'*, 80; Maria Leś-Runicka, *Historia kopalni węgla kamiennego Janina w Libiążu* (The History of the Coal Mine Janina in Libiąż), (Libiąż: Południowy Koncern Węglowy ZG Janina (the Northern Coal Concern ZG Janina, 2008), 48-49
29 Leś-Runicka, *Historia kopalni węgla*, 48-49
30 Iwaszko, *Podobóz 'Janinagrube'*, 68; http://tiergartenstrasse4.org/Janinagrube.html; USHMM, *Encyclopedia of Camps and Ghettos*, Vol. 1, Pt A, 255
31 Jacob Widawski, testimonies, German Consulate-General; transcripts, Hannover trial; *12th Hour Project* 1990; USC Shoah Foundation, code 2528
32 *Obozy w Libiążu*, 25
33 *Obozy w Libiążu*, 15
34 Iwaszko, *Podobóz 'Janinagrube'*, 69
35 Iwaszko, *Podobóz 'Janinagrube'*, 75; USHMM, *Encyclopedia of Camps and Ghettos*, Vol. 1, Pt A 254; *Obozy w Libiążu*, 24
36 Jacob Widawski, testimonies, German Consulate-General; transcripts, Hannover trial; *12th Hour Project* 1990; USC Shoah Foundation, code 2528
37 *Obozy w Libiążu*, 30
38 Iwaszko, *Podobóz 'Janinagrube'*, 75; Stanisław, *Dzieje Libiąża*, 14
39 Stanisław, *Dzieje Libiąża*, 15

40 Iwaszko, *Podobóz 'Janinagrube'*, 80; Stanisław, *Dzieje Libiąża*, 18-19
41 Jacob Widawski, testimonies, German Consulate-General; transcripts, Hannover trial; *12th Hour Project* 1990; USC Shoah Foundation, code 2528
42 Stanisław, *Dzieje Libiąża*, 36-38
43 Stanisław, *Dzieje Libiąża*, 16
44 Stanisław, *Dzieje Libiąża*, 21
45 Stanisław, *Dzieje Libiąża*, 22-24
46 Stanisław, *Dzieje Libiąża*, 38-40
47 Iwaszko, *Podobóz 'Janinagrube'*, 76; *Obozy w Libiążu*, 17
48 Iwaszko, *Podobóz 'Janinagrube'*, 71; Stanisław, *Dzieje Libiąża*, 20
49 Stanisław, *Dzieje Libiąża*, 38-40
50 *Obozy w Libiążu*, 18-20
51 Jacob Widawski, testimonies, German Consulate-General; transcripts, Hannover trial; *12th Hour Project* 1990; USC Shoah Foundation, code 2528
52 Iwaszko, *Podobóz 'Janinagrube'*, 73; USHMM, *Encyclopedia of Camps and Ghettos*, Vol. 1, Pt A 254
53 Iwaszko, *Podobóz 'Janinagrube'*, 73
54 Iwaszko, *Podobóz 'Janinagrube'*, 80
55 Levi and De Benedetti, *Auschwitz Report*, 48-52
56 Iwaszko, *Podobóz 'Janinagrube'*, 73, 76
57 Levi and De Benedetti, *Auschwitz Report*, 56-57
58 Ota Kraus, and Erlich Kulka, *The Death Factory: Document on Auschwitz* (London: Pergamon Press, 1966), 74-77
59 Jacob Widawski, testimonies, German Consulate-General; transcripts, Hannover trial; *12th Hour Project* 1990; USC Shoah Foundation, code 2528
60 Iwaszko, *Podobóz 'Janinagrube'*, 74; Eugen Kogon, *The Theory and Practice of Hell: The German Concentration Camps and the System Behind Them* (New York, Farrar, Straus and Giroux, 1950), 104-06
61 Iwaszko, *Podobóz 'Janinagrube'*, 74; *Obozy w Libiążu*, 26-27; 38-39
62 Jacob Widawski, testimonies, German Consulate-General; transcripts, Hannover trial; *12th Hour Project* 1990; USC Shoah Foundation, code 2528
63 Stanisław, *Dzieje Libiąża*, 27; *Obozy w Libiążu*, 75
64 *Obozy w Libiążu*, 75
65 http://tiergartenstrasse4.org/Janinagrube.html; Iwaszko, *Podobóz 'Janinagrube'*, 82; Stanisław, *Dzieje Libiąża*, 29
66 Jacob Widawski, testimonies, German Consulate-General; transcripts, Hannover trial; *12th Hour Project* 1990; USC Shoah Foundation, code 2528
67 Iwaszko, *Podobóz 'Janinagrube'*, 82; Danuta Czech, *Auschwitz Chronicle: 1939-45* (New York: Henry Holt and Co, 1997), 800
68 Stanisław, *Dzieje Libiąża*, 30

18
Mina in Leipzig

In August 1944, Mina was transported from Skarżysko-Kamienna to Leipzig, Germany, a distance of some 700 kilometres.[1] She was now completely on her own. Six months had passed since she had been separated from her sister Freüda. She described her journey:[2]

> Our transport left Skarżysko in the summer of 1944. We travelled in cattle cars, sixty or seventy per wagon. There were no sanitary facilities, no food and no water. We travelled like this for three days and three nights, stopping and starting. We didn't know where we were going until we arrived in Leipzig. When they opened the wagons, hundreds of people were dead. It was a horrendous journey.
>
> After this trip, we said: 'We won't survive any more. Finished!' We were like skeletons. Young women who were eighteen, twenty, twenty-two years old—my friends—looked like seventy-year-old women.

Fela Schechter, who was also part of the transport, recalled:[3]

> On this journey to Leipzig, the unbelievable heat exasperated our thirst and longing for unavailable water. The stench of our naked bodies, lying on top of one another, poisoned

every drop of fresh air which managed to squeeze through a thin slit in the door. Women were fainting from hunger, the heat and lack of air. During the whole trip, fear gripped our hearts, whether or not they were transporting us to death, despite the assurances of the SS.

During the War, Leipzig was one of Germany's most important centres for manufacturing arms. The demand for labour could not be met by German workers alone, and while some foreign workers came voluntarily, the vast majority were slave labourers forcefully deported to Germany. Most were either Jews or Roma (Gypsies), and came from Eastern European countries.[4]

In 1944, HASAG was one of the five biggest armament companies operating in Leipzig. It had been instructed by Albert Speer, the Minister of Armaments and War Production, to increase the production of anti-tank shoulder missiles, as a priority. This required many more workers. From July 1944 until early 1945, HASAG transferred to its German factories able-bodied Polish and Jewish workers, plus most of the equipment and raw materials from its facilities in the *Generalgouvernement*. To accommodate the prisoners, camps were established next to the factories.[5]

The HASAG camp in Leipzig-Schönefeld opened on 9 June 1944, and became a sub-camp of KL Buchenwald. Over time, it held around 5,300 prisoners, of whom 230 were men and 5,070 women. The reason for the disproportionate number of female slave labourers was that HASAG paid the SS less for them. Further, women had demonstrated greater adaptability and resilience, plus a much lower mortality rate than men.[6]

In the spring of 1944, SS-Unterscharführer Wolfgang Plaul, Leipzig's Commandant, selected the first group of some 800 women from Majdanek to be transported to Leipzig. These were followed by transports from Ravensbrück of more than 2000.[7]

On 4 August 1944, a transport of 1,273 arrived at the camp directly from Skarżysko-Kamienna. Mina was among them. On 3 December 1944, a final transport of Hungarian Jewish women arrived in the camp from Ravensbrück. With this transport Leipzig became the largest female sub-camp of Buchenwald, with prisoners from most of the European countries under Nazi occupation.[8]

On arrival, the women were greeted by a large detachment of SS officers and overseers. Prisoners were lined up five across and marched out, crossing the industrial zone. The few Germans they passed in the street stared at them wide-eyed: they'd never seen anything like this before! They came face to face with emaciated women with yellow, green, red or purple hair and yellow faces.

When the column reached the camp gate where Commandant Plaul was waiting, he delivered a speech, as he did whenever a new transport arrived:[9]

> **I am in charge of this prisoner camp. You will work in the HASAG-Werke Leipzig-Schönefeld munitions and ammunition factory. I am hoping for your co-operation. I now wish you pleasant work and am expecting you to help in the War effort of my fatherland, Germany.**

The new prisoners could hardly believe their eyes. This camp was a building with grass around it. Group by group they were directed to the cellar, where they were ordered by local prisoners, Polish and Russian women, to get undressed, hand over their property and line up in front of the showers. Panic immediately ran through the ranks. Showers? By now Jews knew very well what was behind the doors of the showers in Auschwitz. Finally, the first group entered and fearfully turned on the taps. Real hot water! What joy![10]

Mina recalled:[11]

> After we arrived, they put us into a big hall, ordered us to take off our clothes and told us: 'You will have a bath in the other one.' You had to undress and leave everything behind. They took it all away before giving us our striped uniforms.
>
> Leipzig was a harsh camp, only women. The head of the SS was also a woman. While we were having this bath in the second hall, she walked around between the naked women with a whip, beating everybody, to make us afraid of her. They thought that if they were cruel, we would have respect for them, we would be afraid of them. This is what she wanted to show us.

The women were then lined up and checked for lice. If any were found, all the hair on the affected woman's body was shaved. Then they were given thick cotton underwear and were ready to enter the camp.[12]

They were registered on 5 August 1944, assigned registration numbers 1-1,200. The new arrivals were recorded in the order that they stood in line and then a list compiled in alphabetical order. Mina was recorded as prisoner number 179. She must have been one of the first in line, one of the first off the train.[13]

Each woman was issued with a two-part Häftings-Personal-Karte (identification card). The upper half showed her number, name, date of birth, family status, religion, pre-war address, parents' names and father's occupation. Date of arrival in the camp was noted as 4 August 1944, and under 'supplied by' appeared RSHA (Reich Main Security Office). 'Reason for arrest' gave such information as 'Polit. Polin Jüdin' (Political. Polish Jewess). The bottom half of the card listed the prisoner's occupation and the articles of clothing that the inmate had given up on arrival in the camp. This section of the card was left empty for the women from Skarżysko.[14]

The camp was situated two kilometres from the factory and surrounded by a low, high-voltage barbed wire fence and SS guard watch-towers. The sign on the gate read Schutzhaftlager (Preventive Custody Camp).[15]

Female prisoners such as Mina were accommodated in a former factory building, several storeys high, with a number of balconies. This was the building surrounded by grass. It was divided by partitions that did not reach the ceiling into 'blocks': large halls with high ceilings. Several hundred women were housed there. The blocks were equipped with four-tiered wooden bunk beds, two women to a pallet. Unlike in Skarżysko, here each pallet had a mattress and a blanket, and everything was incredibly clean.

A cellar contained shelters and food stores, plus two large washrooms with hot and cold showers and flushing toilets—but without doors or toilet paper. On the ground floor was the kitchen, a huge dining hall, the canteen and the Schreibstube (administration office). A small infirmary was on the first floor.[16]

SS-Unterscharführer Wolfgang Plaul was the Commandant of all the HASAG camps for women. The general opinion was that he treated all of them equally, and that he was a 'good, kind Commandant'.[17]

The prisoner functionaries consisted of two groups of administrators: the SS overseers and the internal prisoner administration. The 'Oberka' (*Oberkapo*) or female overseer was directly responsible to the Commandant and it was her job to supervise the lower-ranking staff and ensure that they and the prisoners reported for work at the plant precisely on time at 6am.

Unlike the Commandant, the Oberka had a reputation for extreme brutality: she beat the inmates with her fists, particularly if she found any contraband during inspection. Her favourite collective punishment was a general roll-call in which all the women were ordered to assume a kneeling position. She was hated with a passion.

The overseers under the Oberka belonged to two work details: one which escorted the prisoners on the way to, from, and within the factory, and the other which guarded prisoners inside the camp. The latter conducted frequent searches of prisoners' pallets, turning over blankets and mattresses and disposing of anything that might ease their lot, such as sewing materials, a knife, an extra pair of underpants or some rag that served as a towel. Any forbidden articles of clothing or mementos were immediately confiscated.[18]

Joanna Szumańska, the Lagerälteste or camp elder, gained a reputation for brutality. She ordered night-time roll-calls even in the most freezing weather. Anyone who did not keep in line was punished by having her soup and bread taken away the following day.[19]

Mina recalled:[20]

> I saw so many things which are hard to describe: how frequently they killed somebody at work, for nothing, for instance. I was working at the ammunition factory doing twelve-hour shifts. During one night shift the machine was running smoothly so I took out a needle to darn a hole in my stocking. They were my last pair and I wanted to repair them. The forewoman, an SS supervisor, was walking around and she saw me. She approached and beat me up so badly, in a way I had never been beaten during the whole War. In fact, it was the first time in the camps that I had been beaten up. She hit me very hard as an example to the others. From that time on I was very afraid. I promised myself that I would never again do such a stupid thing.

Polish women held positions of Blockälteste or Blokowa in charge of each block, and controlled the camp office, food stores, canteen, infirmary and camp security.[21] On 31 January 1945, HASAG-Leipzig had a total of eighty-one SS guards, of whom fifty were female overseers.[22]

Unlike the HASAG factories in Poland, there were no middle level Polish overseers or prisoner *Kapos* in the Leipzig plant. This meant that there was direct contact between the prisoners and local staff, many of whom seemed to believe that the prisoners were whores. A short item in the local paper reported that Leipzig had been *Juden-rein* until the recent arrival of a group of Jewish women arrested for prostitution, whom the authorities were attempting to rehabilitate as 'productive elements'.

Henryka Karmel wrote:[23]

I, a whore no. 906, I write poems!
You don't believe me?
Well it's true
Trust me,
My father never stole,
I am a fine upstanding woman, and always was,
But to use the popular term,
Just not quite the right race…

Leipzig-Schönefeld was less terrifying than other camps. For example, escape attempts were not punished with death. However, there was an extensive regime of *Appells* to torment the prisoners. There were two types of assemblies. The first were 'routine' roll-calls conducted each morning and evening, when the supervisors counted the prisoners and reported the numbers to the SS. The second were punitive, collective punishment for all sorts of offences. If a prisoner escaped, the others would be made to stand or kneel for hours on end. An untidy block was also the cause for a general disciplinary muster. Individual punishments were more inventive: head-shaving; three days of solitary confinement in a bunker with no food; being made to stand in the courtyard for several hours. In addition, the SS constantly used dogs to intimidate the prisoners. The most severe penalty, twenty-five lashes, was administered in Buchenwald.[24]

The HASAG factory consisted of a row of large, mostly red brick buildings. Each housed several big factory floors surrounded by a number of smaller rooms. The women of Leipzig-Schönefeld worked mostly in the Nordwerk and in Factory Building F, where they assembled grenade parts, stamped the production dates on shell casings, inserted detonators or monitored the screwing of shell tips on to a range of different bombs. They worked in unhealthy conditions: hot, filled with metal dust and lacking in fresh air.[25]

Prisoners were woken at 4am when it was still dark and cold outside. They had to put their pallets in order as fast as possible, bolt down a slice of bread if they had any left from the day before and gulp their coffee. Hundreds of women from the blocks poured out as the supervisors shouted to hurry the stragglers. Then the first SS overseers would arrive, shoving and striking prisoners to straighten the lines. When they were lined up, the officials appeared: the Lagerälteste, the Oberka and the Commandant. Each Blokowa, took her place at the entrance to her block and made her report: how many in the work detail and the numbers who were ill, to remain in the camp.[26]

The women marched to the factory in rows of five, arranged according to their place of work, escorted by armed SS guards and the overseers. They were not permitted to talk or even turn their heads. Anyone who didn't keep up got shoved. The guards didn't strike them, since they were passing through streets where free civilians walked. Guard dogs ran between the rows ready to sink their teeth into anyone who stepped out of line.[27]

Felicja Karay recalled:[28]

> **Dawn breaks. The first pedestrians appear in the streets. They stare silently at the strange creatures in their striped dresses. Some gape in wonder, others in pity, others whistle and call out: 'Dirty Jews!' We were marched through the whole city. Everyone could see us.**

The work started precisely at 6am. There were only a few German foremen and the small number of German men at work were either elderly or crippled. There were more German women, either factory workers or assigned to supervise the prisoners. All the non-German men at the plant were slave labourers, some housed in several fenced-in barracks near the Leipzig camp. Others were 'free' labourers, Poles or Italians. They could leave the camps in which they were housed but had to report for work daily and were under constant supervision.[29]

The Jewish women who arrived in August 1944 were assigned to the production of S-Zü, which they interpreted as short for Zünder, various types of detonators. These were connected with the manufacture of shoulder missiles, shells of different sizes and parts for planes.[30]

The work was hard, laborious and exhausting. The night shift suffered severely from lack of sleep, since it was virtually impossible to get more than four or five hours rest during the day in the camps because of the noise: the food distribution and the constant reporting for assemblies. SS overseers were everywhere, keeping their eye on the prisoners and meting out punishment.[31]

Prisoners were responsible for the underclothes and uniforms that had been distributed to them on arrival, and had to wash these themselves. Identical camp uniforms had been issued: undershirts, underpants, socks, a single blue-and-grey-striped dress known as pasiak and a striped jacket. Periodically, the dresses were disinfected and underwear was replaced. 'Lucky' prisoners were given shoes, but most had to make do with wooden clogs. Bras were forbidden but the women got around this by sewing their own.[32]

Mina recalled:[33]

> I had a lot of ideas, which maybe helped me to survive. They were throwing out scraps of material used for cleaning the machines, so from time to time I pinched a piece. I took out a sleeve from a man's shirt or a small piece of cloth. Once I grabbed a piece of material and hid it down my front, smuggling it into the camp. I was afraid to tell even my girlfriend. I climbed up to the highest bunk and she asked me: 'Mina what are you doing up there?' They always promised us that they would give us extra underwear and socks, but they didn't. The days were severe and cold; temperature sometimes fell to minus twenty-five degrees. Snow and cold everywhere. Every day we were made to stand outside for hours, as they counted and counted. People often contracted pneumonia and other illnesses. This was what they were aiming at: to destroy as many of us as they could.
>
> I said to myself: 'They're not going to give us any underwear. But I can sew. I'm a dressmaker. I can make something.' So from these pieces of rag I cut a sort of bra—even if I had no idea how to make a bra—and pants. After an *Appell*, I said to my girlfriend: 'You know what? I don't feel so cold because I made these.' She pleaded: 'Mina, why don't you make some for me?' And I said: 'I can do that for one or two of us, but not for everybody. I can't risk my life.

You bring me the fabric and I'll do it.' So I made maybe a dozen sets of 'lingerie'. I was young and I didn't really know much about sewing, but they say 'necessity is the mother of invention.' I did what I could. We survived.

Each transport arriving at Leipzig enjoyed a 'honeymoon' period, courtesy of HASAG. Food rations were better, as Felicja Karay recalled:[34]

> **Wide-eyed and hungry, the new prisoners from Skarżysko gazed at the rations: half a loaf of delicious bread, a spoonful of salad, jam and even sweet coffee! What was going on? It was impossible; something must be wrong here. They couldn't be plying them with these delicacies just to kill them afterwards?**

The prisoners were issued with a bowl, a spoon and a cup. Such luxuries—there had been no bowls in Skarżysko. However, in the winter of 1944-45, hunger became the prisoners' most serious problem. In February 1945, the bread ration was reduced from half a loaf to one-fifth; potatoes cooked in their skins disappeared; and the soup ration doled out at the factory at noon became the main meal for the hungry prisoners. The 'sweet' soup containing groats and macaroni which had initially been served once a week was more and more often replaced with turnip soup which gave the prisoners severe diarrhoea.[35]

As in other camps, Leipzig prisoners used their skills to 'earn' extra bread, a bowl of soup or a piece of soap. Most of the raw materials were pilfered, or 'organized' from the plant. Some made belts from rubber straps, others fashioned comb cases from bits of plastic or barrettes from wire. One group set up a 'workshop' making slippers. For raw materials they used old blankets and the cartons in which food rations were brought to the blocks. The slippers were sold for bread, margarine or jam. Other industrious women washed dresses in exchange for bread, or did sewing jobs for a bowl of soup or a bread ration. Barter also helped them to maintain a degree of personal hygiene, with some Jewish prisoners even willing to trade their bread ration for a handful of soap powder.[36]

Prisoner Gela Meiserdorf wrote about the hunger:[37]

I'm hungry!—is what you hear everywhere
I'm hungry!—each woman cries in your ear.
So there's no choice—whoever can snatch
A little extra food, hides it in some cache.
Some sewing or laundry are willing to do
In exchange for a sausage or two…
Some for the price of a piece of bread
Will clean the lice from another's head…
In short, an interesting symptom, did you know?
That here the art of barter flourishes so!

The savage pressure in the factory got worse. HASAG tried to 'raise morale' by rewarding good work. Those who exceeded their work quota received vouchers for an extra soup ration or coupons, in exchange for which the women could purchase small items in the canteen such as a comb, a little mirror, a toothbrush or sometimes a bar of soap. On very rare occasions they could buy a pair of rubber shoes or fabric shoes with wooden soles, without which they could not expect to survive.[38]

HASAG provided reasonable sanitary conditions and medical care for its prisoners. This was in order to maintain its skilled workers as the pool of available slave labour shrank. Since the

Leipzig camp was located in the city, they also wanted to protect the local population from the spread of infectious diseases.[39]

The medical staff consisted of a doctor for the SS plus four doctors and thirteen nurses for prisoners; they were mostly Poles. The Leipzig Revier (hospital) offered prisoners basic health care, with HASAG providing some drugs and limited medical supplies.[40]

Cases of pneumonia, influenza or diarrhoea were generally cured. Especially in winter, prisoners suffered from arthritic and rheumatic pains, and the Jewish women, particularly the older ones, often suffered from ulcers on their legs and other skin infections. Work accidents were also very common.[41]

Despite the hunger, cold and hard labour, prisoners sought relief in cultural activities. They were introduced simultaneously by the four large national groups: the Poles, French, Jews and Russians. Most performances or gatherings were associated with religious or national holidays. Although in essence these were Underground activities, neither the internal administration nor the German commanders forbade them.[42]

On Friday nights the women gathered for the traditional Shabbat. The core of the Kraków group was made up of former members of Akiva. Songs made familiar by its choir, of which Mina had been a member, were sung within the walls of the Leipzig camp in honour of Rosh Hashanah. They shared memories of home and the longing the women felt for it.[43]

Felicja Karay recalled Yom Kippur 1944:[44]

> We all fasted, even the women who didn't observe the holy day in ordinary times. This time it was a sign of the solidarity of resistance. In the evening we embraced and wept. What could we possibly have wished for ourselves? That next year we would meet in freedom?

In one block the women greeted the holiday by singing songs in Yiddish and Hebrew. They all remembered their families gathered around the holiday table: grandparents, parents, brothers and sisters. In the camp almost everyone was alone. Heartfelt prayers rose from every corner. There were no memorial candles to light and not everyone knew the prayers, but their fellow prisoner Ilona was there to pray in all their names:[45]

> In my house no memorial candles will glow,
> For millions would have to burn,
> To mark all the days of mourning in the year,
> For the dead who will never return…
> It burns like a bonfire so great and so sad
> For me, for you, for the joy expired…

Prisoners did not usually work on Sundays, so there was a small amount of leisure time. This was used for many forms of recreation.[46]

Often people gathered in small groups of close friends in the corner of a block or on the bunks. They reminisced about their lives at home and at school. Familiar melodies sometimes punctuated the conversation. Serious literary evenings were organized by women from the Kraków group on Sundays and after work. One group might listen to recitations of works by Adam Mickiewicz, Poland's revered poet. Others preferred the poems of Jewish poet Julian Tuwim, a major figure in Polish literature. These gatherings invariably featured poems by the Karmel sisters. All the Jewish prisoners were familiar with the sisters and their mother, who had been through Płaszów and Skarżysko together, and were now in Leipzig.[47]

The groups composed and sang songs which satirized the camp. According to Mina's testimony, the following was a collaboration between Bella Flour, Maryla Goldberg, the Karmel sisters, Sala Reich and Mina herself. (Translated from the Polish by Sylwia Eckley and Vieslava Mataczynski). The first verse and chorus were:[48]

Hasag jest nasz Ojciec. Hasag jest nasz Tato.	HASAG is our Father, HASAG is our Dad.
Hasag chce zapewnić nam długie lata	HASAG wants to guarantee we have long lives
Daje nam 'Raj' tu w Lipsku całym,	So here in Leipzig, he gives us 'Paradise',
Daje nam masło i chleb biały	He gives us butter and white bread
Daje nam mieszkanie komfortowe,	He gives us a comfortable flat,
Daje nam prycze 4-ro piętrowe,	He gives us four-tiered bunks,
Kloset, salę i łazieńki i więzienne te sukienki	Loos, rooms, bathrooms and these prison dresses
Bo Kommandant pragnie by wszystko szło tu składnie,	Because the Commandant desires all to go smoothly
By uspokoic nerwy nim pójdziemy na konservy.	To calm our nerves, before we are turned into preserves.

In these leisure activities, the various nationalities competed. The French put on a 'hat parade', a collection of headwear made of rags and rubbish, and presented a program including extracts from a ballet, a choral performance and a play. The Poles celebrated Polish Independence Day with a concert of folk songs and dances. The Russians staged part of Chekhov's *The Cherry Orchard*.[49] In December, everyone excitedly anticipated Christmas and Hanukkah, for which the Kraków group decided to organize a public concert. At the end of the block, a table covered with white paper was positioned, and an improvised menorah with actual candles placed on it. Behind the table was a cardboard set depicting rocks and palm trees.

One of the women lit the first candle of Hanukkah and recited the traditional prayer. Then they sang the familiar, well-loved Hanukkah songs. When Ilona Karmel told the story of the Maccabees, Jewish rebel warriors who rose up and founded their own dynasty, the audience breathed a deep sigh. 'God! Could there be a miracle for us too? Could we ever find a place in the Land of Israel?' Although happiness and joy were in short supply in the camp, they sang another Hanukkah song celebrating them. It was better to sing together than to curl up in a corner and cry.[50]

The Kraków group put on a New Year's Eve show for the whole camp, titled Alexander Jazz Band, in honour of a famous group of pre-war Warsaw. The program included dance, song, recitation, sketches and a play. Materials for the costumes and sets were pilfered from the plant. Ilona Karmel wrote a play entitled *Die Abenteuer des Sokrates im Konzentrationslager* (The Adventures of Socrates in a Concentration Camp).

Hunger, cold and roll-calls were forgotten amid the feverish preparations. Commandant Plaul, the camp officers and the SS women were all invited. They sat in the front row of the hall with thousands of prisoners crammed in behind. The five girls of the Alexander Jazz Band were decked out in evening clothes, jacket, bow-tie and black top hat, made from the cardboard used to cover windows during the black-out.

When the chorus line started to dance to a song, the huge crowd began swaying to the rhythm. This performance brought the spirit of the world outside, the spirit of freedom, into the camp. Then came the play, and the adventures of poor unfortunate Socrates were greeted with laughter. Here not even his wisdom could help him![51]

The room went wild as the prisoners all rose, cheering, applauding thunderously, weeping and shouting. Anyone who attended that show will never forget New Year's Eve 1945.[52]

Amid the joy, the threat of a death transport was still ever-present. In late 1944, a selection had taken place after a visit by SS-Sturmbannführer Paul Budin, the General Manager of HASAG, who announced that he had no intention of paying for sick prisoners. The first to be moved, on 17 September 1944, had been a number of children aged four to thirteen, including those born in Leipzig, accompanied by their mothers.[53]

Those selected were told that they were going to Ravensbrück, but in fact were transported to Auschwitz.

Felicja Karay wrote:[54]

And so the days passed in work and rest, despair and hope, day following night, night following day. If they could only hold out! Not falter! Not be sent away with the transport!

From the time of the prisoners' departure from Poland to their arrival in Leipzig, there had been rumours that the Nazis were defeated. However, Mina and her fellow prisoners had no access to news or papers nor any contact with the local people. Prisoners in Leipzig were traumatized, terrorized, starving and focused on survival.

In late 1944, as the winter had become more severe, there were frequent air raids over the Leipzig factories. When these raids increased, the kitchen was closed and everyone went hungry.[55] However, the prisoners welcomed the thunder of each explosion as bombing became part of the camp routine, because they hoped that this meant that the Allies were gaining the upper hand and the end was near.

By the beginning of 1945, Germany was under siege on both the Eastern and the Western Fronts. In January 1945 Poland, including Warsaw, Kraków and Auschwitz, was liberated by the Soviets. In

February, Berlin and Dresden were subject to heavy bombing by the Allies, and by March, British and American Forces had crossed the Rhine. The Germans were in retreat all over the country.[56]

From mid-January 1945, the bombing of Leipzig occurred even in broad daylight, on some days as early as ten in the morning and then again at noon. The women were ordered to stop the machines and go down to the shelters. Sometimes leaflets were tossed from planes. One contained a list of the German cities that had already been destroyed and occupied by the Allies. Occasionally, words of encouragement reached them. When crates of Russian munitions, war booty, were delivered to be cleaned and readied for shipment to the front, the women found messages in Yiddish: 'Jews, hold on!'[57]

March 1945 passed slowly. Hunger became starvation and in the plant the Germans were edgy. The overseers took out their anxiety on the prisoners.

Felicja Karay recalled:[58]

We asked ourselves: 'If we live to see liberation, where will our home be?' All that was left were memories of our family homes, a carefree childhood, relatives, holidays.

On 2 April 1945, Hermann Pister, Buchenwald's Commandant, informed his senior staff that he had received instructions from Berlin that the camp would not be evacuated, but handed over to the Americans, who were nearby. Jewish prisoners, however, were to be separated out and prepared for departure.[59]

In early April 1945, the transfer of thousands of prisoners began from Buchenwald's sub-camps to the main one. The complex then consisted of some sixty camps for men and twenty-six for women, housing some 80,000 prisoners.[60]

At the same time, transports from other camps closer to the

Eastern Front began arriving in Leipzig. The women including Mina were still marched to the plant every day as the authorities pretended that work was proceeding as usual. But their labour no longer had any purpose. The women assigned to the sewing shop noticed that the overseers were at work on civilian clothes, in an air of frenzy. The only thing that mattered, it was understood, was to delay departure of the Volkssturm (People's Storm-National Militia) for the front, for as long as possible. It was rumoured that the Americans were twelve kilometres from Leipzig.[61]

In an air raid on Tuesday 10 April, a bomb fell on to the camp wall, damaging the water and electrical mains, killing one Russian, and injuring several Jewish women. The following day there was heavy shelling nearby. Preparations for evacuation were stepped up.[62]

On the 12th the HASAG factory was closed down. All its supplies, including shoes and soap, had been cleared out by the workers. Tension in the camp was high. Prisoners hadn't received bread for three days and were barely able to stand for lack of sleep and nourishment. That night, hordes of prisoners descended on the food stores, breaking down the doors, screaming and fighting among themselves. Each woman grabbed whatever she could find. Chaos reigned.[63]

Evacuation of the camp began on Friday 13 April 1945. An extra portion of food was distributed. Beginning with the Jewish women, around 4,000 inmates, including Mina, were sent on a march, a Death March. Another 800 were evacuated on 14 April.[64]

The sick, those who had just given birth, the Soviet POWs, several women from internal administration and a 200-strong Reinigungskommando (clean-up commando), including several dozen Jews, spent two further days clearing out whatever was left in the camp. They were evacuated on 15 April. A small number of women were left behind.

A few days later American troops reached the camp. They took the women by truck to a hotel in the centre of town. Sometime later, the former prisoners received the news that Paul Budin had ordered that the HASAG administration building should be blown up.[65] Archives and company documents were destroyed, and it is also believed that he and his wife perished in the explosion.[66]

Ramona Bräu from the Buchenwald Museum explained in 2010:[67]

> There is speculation that not all the documents were completely destroyed, and that the US Army recognized the importance of the information they contained, especially concerning the Panzerfaust and other weapons. The Panzerfaust was one of the major pieces of equipment built by HASAG at the end of the War. That is why HASAG was in a very good position to get raw materials and workers—because they were a vital industry to the end.

In June 1945 the HASAG plant changed over to peace-time production, making pots and lamps. Following the occupation of East Germany by the Soviet Union, three 'commissary trustees' were appointed by the new regime to manage the Leipzig property. Records indicate that by 1947, the plant had ceased to exist.[68]

MINA & JACOB

Extract from Mina's prisoner record provided by the International Tracing Service (ITS reference 7636516), Bad Arolsen.
These details were confirmed by Dr Andrea Lörz of the Leipzig Memorial of Forced Labour, which holds a New Arrivals list dated 4 August 1944, listing prisoner number 179 as Laub, Mina, from Krakau.

MINA & JACOB

Notes

1 https://www.driving-route-planner.com/route-planner
2 Mina Widawski nee Laub, audio testimony for the *12th Hour Project of Oral Testimonies* (Sydney: Australian Institute for Holocaust Studies, 1990); video testimony (Sydney: USC Shoah Foundation Institute, 1995), code 2526
3 Fela Schechter, *Ucieczka przed śmiercią* (Escape from Death) (Warsaw: Żydowski Instytut Historyczny (Jewish Historical Institute), 20
4 *Remember for the Future: A Memorial to the Forced Labourers in Leipzig during National Socialism* (Leipzig: The Leipzig Memorial of Forced Labour), 6, 8
5 Felicja Karay, *HASAG-Leipzig Slave Labour Camp: The Struggle for Survival told by the Women and their Poetry* (London, Portland: Vallentine Mitchell, 2002), 19, 21-22
6 Israel Gutman, ed., *Encyclopedia of the Holocaust* (New York: Macmillan, 1990), 646-47; David A. Hacket, ed., *The Buchenwald Report* (Boulder, Colorado: Westview Press, 1995), 190-91; Abraham J. and Hershel Edelheit, eds, *History of the Holocaust: A Handbook and Dictionary* (Boulder: Westview Press, 1994), 277; United States Holocaust Memorial Museum (USHMM), *Encyclopedia of Camps and Ghettos* 1933-45, (Washington: 2012), Vol. 2, 378; Karay, *HASAG-Leipzig*, 3
7 Karay, *HASAG-Leipzig*, 24; USHMM, *Encyclopedia of Camps and Ghettos*, 378-79
8 Karay, *HASAG-Leipzig*, 37-38, 122; USHMM, *Encyclopedia of Camps and Ghettos*, 379
9 Karay, *HASAG-Leipzig*, 58-59, 63
10 Karay, *HASAG-Leipzig*, 59
11 Mina Widawski, *12th Hour Project of Oral Testimonies*; USC Shoah Foundation, code 2526
12 Karay, *HASAG-Leipzig*, 59
13 Ramona Bräu interview with Freda Widawski, Buchenwald Museum, Weimer, 26 August 2010
14 Karay, *HASAG-Leipzig*, 61
15 Karay, *HASAG-Leipzig*, 45-46
16 USHMM, *Encyclopedia of Camps and Ghettos*, 379; Karay, *HASAG-Leipzig*, 46, 59
17 USHMM, *Encyclopedia of Camps and Ghettos*, 379; Karay, *HASAG-Leipzig*, 108
18 Hacket, ed., *The Buchenwald Report*, 190-91; Karay, *HASAG-Leipzig*, 109-10
19 USHMM, *Encyclopedia of Camps and Ghettos*, 379; Karay, *HASAG-Leipzig*, 107, 113
20 Mina Widawski, *12th Hour Project of Oral Testimonies*; USC Shoah Foundation, code 2526

21 USHMM, *Encyclopedia of Camps and Ghettos*, 379; Karay, *HASAG-Leipzig*, 51-52, 107, 113, 118, 141
22 USHMM, *Encyclopedia of Camps and Ghettos*, 379; Karay, *HASAG-Leipzig*, 42, 44
23 Karay, *HASAG-Leipzig*, 88
24 USHMM, *Encyclopedia of Camps and Ghettos*, 379; Karay, *HASAG-Leipzig*, 49
25 USHMM, *Encyclopedia of Camps and Ghettos*, 379
26 Karay, *HASAG-Leipzig*, 63
27 Karay, *HASAG-Leipzig*, 64
28 Karay, *HASAG-Leipzig*, 83-84
29 Karay, *HASAG-Leipzig*, 64-65
30 Karay, *HASAG-Leipzig*, 65
31 Karay, *HASAG-Leipzig*, 65-67, 69, 141
32 USHMM, *Encyclopedia of Camps and Ghettos*, 379; Karay, *HASAG-Leipzig*, 47, 62
33 Mina Widawski, *12th Hour Project of Oral Testimonies*; USC Shoah Foundation, code 2526
34 Karay, *HASAG-Leipzig*, 47-48, 59
35 Karay, *HASAG-Leipzig*, 47-49, 62, 97-98
36 Karay, *HASAG-Leipzig*, 146, 148-49
37 Karay, *HASAG-Leipzig*, 147-48
38 Eugen Kogon, *The Theory and Practice of Hell: The German Concentration Camps and the System behind Them* (New York, Farrar, Straus and Giroux, 1950), 114, 119; Karay, *HASAG-Leipzig*, 47, 96-97
39 USHMM, *Encyclopedia of Camps and Ghettos*, 379; Karay, *HASAG-Leipzig*, 48-49
40 Karay, *HASAG-Leipzig*, 48
41 Karay, *HASAG-Leipzig*, 48-49, 157
42 Kogon, *The Theory and Practice of Hell*, 132; Karay, *HASAG-Leipzig*, 170-71
43 Karay, *HASAG-Leipzig*, 171-72
44 Karay, *HASAG-Leipzig*, 173-74
45 Karay, *HASAG-Leipzig*, 174-75
46 Kogon, *The Theory and Practice of Hell*, 129
47 Karay, *HASAG-Leipzig*, 178-80
48 Mina Widawski, *12th Hour Project of Oral Testimonies*; USC Shoah Foundation, code 2526
49 Karay, *HASAG-Leipzig*, 185-87
50 USHMM, *Encyclopedia of Camps and Ghettos*, 379-80; Karay, *HASAG-Leipzig*, 99, 182-85

51 USHMM, *Encyclopedia of Camps and Ghettos*, 379-80; Karay, *HASAG-Leipzig*, 99, 189-91
52 Karay, *HASAG-Leipzig*, 198-99
53 Karay, *HASAG-Leipzig*, 154-56
54 Karay, *HASAG-Leipzig*, 103, 154
55 Karay, *HASAG-Leipzig*, 76, 152
56 https://en.wikipedia.org/wiki/Timeline_of_World_War_II_(1945%E2%80%931991)
57 Karay, *HASAG-Leipzig*, 98-99, 103, 154
58 Karay, *HASAG-Leipzig*, 210-13
59 Daniel Blatman, *The Death Marches: the Final Phase of Nazi Genocide* (Cambridge: Harvard University Press, 2011), 144
60 Blatman, *The Death Marches*, 143
61 USHMM, *Encyclopedia of Camps and Ghettos*, 380; Karay, *HASAG-Leipzig*, 213-14
62 Karay, *HASAG-Leipzig*, 215
63 Ibid.
64 USHMM, *Encyclopedia of Camps and Ghettos*, 380; Karay, *HASAG-Leipzig*, 216
65 USHMM, *Encyclopedia of Camps and Ghettos*; Karay, *HASAG-Leipzig*, 216-17
66 Gutman, ed., *Encyclopedia of the Holocaust*, 647
67 Bräu, Buchenwald Museum, 2010
68 http://www.petromax.nl/HASAG.html, 4; Karay, *HASAG-Leipzig*, 227-28

1945

Death Marches

In the spring of 1945, Hitler's order to evacuate the camps at the approach of the enemy and to transfer their inmates into existing camps further away, led to a chaotic finale for concentration camp prisoners. More than a third of the inmates lost their lives during the exhausting evacuation marches, and in the transport trains which took weeks to reach their destinations.[1]

The term Todesmärsche (Death Marches) refers to columns of prisoners marching under heavy guard over huge distances, under sub-human conditions. Hundreds of thousands of walking skeletons, dirty, hungry and thirsty, were marched from camp to camp. Anyone who could not keep up was shot. Of the estimated 714,000 prisoners in the concentration camp network in January 1945, at least 35 percent were dead four months later. The Death Marches were simply the continuation of the work of the concentration and extermination camps: that is, Jews were intended to die.[2]

Jewish survivors report German cruelties and killings until the very end. Among the murderers during the evacuations and Death Marches were concentration camp personnel, such as camp guards and members of the SS Death's Heads. Yet many were not SS men, but belonged to civil defence forces and to different kinds of military or police units. Operating under virtually no supervision, the guards were their own masters. The instructions that they received before setting out on the marches did not include more than a general directive to shoot any prisoner who tried to escape. In reality, the permission to murder escaping prisoners was expanded into a far-reaching licence to kill indiscriminately whoever they chose.[3]

The operation of evacuating the camps through Death Marches was the last massive organized crime of Nazi Germany.[4]

Notes

1   Helmut Krausnick et al., *Anatomy of the SS State* (English translation, London: William Collins, 1968), 504
2   Yehuda Bauer, *A History of the Holocaust* (New York: Franklin Watts, 1982) 357, 359; Robert Gellately, *Backing Hitler: Consent and Coercion in Nazi Germany* (New York: Oxford University Press, 2001), 243; Daniel Blatman, *The Death Marches: The Final Phase of Nazi Genocide* (Cambridge: Harvard University Press, 2011), 1-2, 5, 87; Martin Gilbert, *Never Again: A History of the Holocaust* (London: HarperCollins Illustrated, 2002), 144
3   Daniel Jonah Goldhagen, *Hitler's Willing Executioners: Ordinary Germans and the Holocaust* (London: Little, Brown and Company, 1996), 355, 360-65, 369; Blatman, *The Death Marches*, 368, 370, 376-78
4   Shmuel Krakowski, *The Death Marches in the Period of the Evacuation of the Camps*, in *The Nazi Concentration Camps* (Proceedings of the Fourth Yad Vashem International Historical Conference, 1980), 485, 487-89

19

Jacob's Death March

On 17 January 1945, with Soviet troops advancing from the east, the last roll-call was taken in Auschwitz. The final count was 31,894 in Auschwitz I and II (Birkenau), and 35,118 in Auschwitz III (Monowitz), including outlying satellite camps such as Jacob's Janinagrube. Over the next two days 58,000 prisoners were moved out, all but a few on foot, in freezing weather.

That January, conditions were harsh, with raging blizzards.[1] Jacob and his fellow Janina prisoners were sent on a march northwest towards Gliwice, fifty-five kilometres from Auschwitz.[2]

As they left the camp, the prisoners took with them a small portion of bread. They wore inadequate clothing, because it was anticipated that at Auschwitz, they would be loaded on to evacuation trains. They ate what they could along the way. During the nights they slept in barns or on the bare ground.[3]

On the marches, those who were too weak to continue were shot and their bodies thrown into the nearest roadside ditches. These difficult conditions were described in the documentary *The Long March to Freedom*:[4]

> The conditions in the winter of 1944 and into 1945 were one of the most severe and horrendous that Eastern Europe had faced in a generation. Thick snow on the ground and

temperatures plunging to minus twenty-five (below zero) were common at that time of the year.

Alongside the marches, the local population was running away from the advancing warfront, so roads were packed with vehicles and troops and getting through was difficult. In addition, they were under constant bombardment from the Soviet Air Force.[5]

Jacob recalled:[6]

> We were evacuated from Janina on the morning of 18 January 1945. We marched from the coal mine to Auschwitz, and from Auschwitz to Gliwice. We left about 10am and arrived in Auschwitz later that day. The SS did not have any transport —no autos or trucks, nothing—other than sleighs, which were about one-and-a-half metres long. They piled all their baggage, provisions and ammunition on the sleighs, and we prisoners had to pull them. They were marching with machine guns, and we had to pull these sleighs, all the way to Auschwitz.
>
> At the beginning of the march, they gave us half a loaf of bread each and a tiny piece of margarine. They probably knew that we would not get anything else after that.
>
> My biggest problem was that before we set out, I needed some decent winter shoes. In the middle of 1944, they had brought transports of Hungarian Jews into Auschwitz who had been told that they were going to a work camp. Everybody had brought the best that they had: fur coats, the best shoes. I went to the storeroom where a friend from Guttenbrunn worked, and he let me take a beautiful pair of winter shoes. I tried them on, and when you're young you're stupid. I thought that these would be perfect for marching in the snow, but I didn't realize that they were too small for me.

Marching the thirteen kilometres to Auschwitz was hell! The only choice was to take them off and walk barefoot, but it was winter, twenty-four degrees below zero, with snow one-and-a-half metres deep. I was carrying a rucksack for Egon, our *Kapo*. I said to him: 'Egon, I am in trouble. I can't walk. I took a pair of shoes this morning and they're too tight.' He said: 'Are you stupid? How could you take tight shoes? But luckily I have an extra pair of shoes in my rucksack.' These shoes were made of fabric, with a little bit of leather around and rubber soles. I put them on: relief! The only problem was that my feet got wet walking through the snow.

We arrived in Auschwitz in the evening. We didn't go into the camp, because it was already evacuated. Only a few sick people had been left behind. The whole of the IG Farben transport rested outside in the cold, with no shelter.

Then they distributed bread, a loaf of one-and-a-half kilos between two people, and half a packet of margarine. We rested for a couple of hours and then started to march again, towards Gliwice, some fifty-five kilometres.

In Auschwitz we were joined by prisoners from the Fürstengrube, Jawischowitz and Buna Werke camps. The entire group by then numbered about 6,000 people. You can imagine weak people marching in columns of five, surrounded by armed SS guards who carried rifles, pistols and hand grenades. The road from Auschwitz to Gliwice was covered with dead bodies. There were thousands of people killed on that march.

Our good fortune was that Baumgartner, the Commandant of our camp, was a smart guy. He could see what was happening, that they were shooting people like rats. So he gave the order that Janina's prisoners should separate from the other groups and march under their own SS guard. He marched with us, so nothing happened to our group; nobody got shot. I marched in about the tenth row of the Janina prisoners. Close to me were the brothers Malinowski who had worked with me at the mine, and the report writer Scharne was in front of me. There were also many *Kapos* on the march.

The march to Gliwice lasted two days and two nights. We slept and walked, slept and walked. The night before we came to Gliwice, we stopped in a field in which stood a burnt-out brick factory. But there were still some stables standing in which we rested that night.

The next morning, Baumgartner asked Dr Orlik: 'How many people do we have who are not able to march further, that are too weak?' Dr Orlik replied: 'Around twenty.' Baumgartner ordered that these prisoners should be left in that brick factory. He didn't want to be responsible for their deaths: 'What happens to them after we leave, I don't know—but I won't shoot them.'

The next morning, we marched out again. We walked for a whole day and then we entered Gliwice about 9pm.

Gliwice was located before the War just over on the German side of the frontier dividing German Lower Silesia from Polish Upper Silesia. Four camps were located there: Gleiwitz I–IV, all sub-camps of Auschwitz. Gleiwitz I and Gleiwitz II, were assembly points for thousands of evacuees. From there the prisoners were taken to camps inside Germany.[7]

Jacob recalled:[8]

We arrived in Gliwice on a harsh, cold winter's night, frosty with a full moon. They took us into the empty barracks—all the prisoners had been already evacuated—and kept us overnight there. Total confusion! There were many people and not enough barracks for everyone, so those who did not have enough strength to push in slept outside, in the snow. Many people died there.

On the morning of the third day, at about 8am, we marched out of the Gliwice camp and they took us to the railway station. Baumgartner had marched us into the camp and to the station, but when we reached the train, he disappeared. I didn't see him again. I don't know what happened to him. He was replaced by Heinrich Niemeyer.

Niemeyer's treatment of prisoners was completely different from Baumgartner's. The prosecutor at his trial stated:[9]

> During the evacuation, the transport Commandant, Heinrich Niemeyer, issued clear instructions to the guards to shoot to kill any prisoner who stumbled or fell during the march. Survivors estimated that one of the guards, Woland, murdered between twenty and fifty prisoners during the march. Woland and Niemeyer displayed particular devotion to duty in killing feeble Jewish prisoners.

On 21 January 1945, the prisoners who arrived in Gliwice were loaded on to open freight cars. The trains stopped often, so by the next day they had not moved far. Many prisoners died of hunger, exhaustion and exposure.[10]

Jacob recalled:[11]

> They loaded us on to a freight train with open carriages, twenty-four degrees below zero outside. They crammed sixty,

seventy people—as many as they could—into each wagon, and on every platform SS guards with machine guns were stationed. As soon as we were loaded into the trains, our group was no longer guarded exclusively by SS from Janina.

The train moved, then stopped and started, again and again. Something was happening! Maybe they thought that the Russians were closing in, or that partisans were nearby. They were afraid. They didn't know what to do.

Suddenly, about midday, we heard shooting and the train stopped. About twenty minutes later the SS started yelling: 'Everybody out!' During this unloading many people were killed, because the guards didn't even open the doors of the carriages. You had to jump down from the top. Anyone who took too long to jump, or couldn't jump, they shot! They shot people like birds. We left many dead and wounded people on that train.

Then they assembled the whole transport and we were again formed into columns and started to march. Where we were going, we didn't know. We were marching on a highway with snow up to our knees. After about five kilometres, we arrived at a fork in the road. The transport stopped and the SS called: 'All Germans step out.' We didn't know what was going on, but my *Kapo* nodded at me to also come forward. When I did that, out came a couple more Jewish boys. Three Jewish boys among the Germans! We were about twenty-five prisoners. Among us were the Lagerälteste, six or seven *Kapos*, a number of Blockältesten and six SS guards, of whom not one was German. They were Croatians and Hungarians.

Our group was marched back to where the train had stopped, back to the place of the massacre. We were ordered to unload the equipment: the arms, ammunition and baggage that the SS had left behind. The rest of the transport continued on ahead and we were supposed to re-join them later.

I spotted a small wooden military case lying next to the train and kicked it. It opened. Inside was an SS woollen jumper and a pair of high boots. I took the jumper, put it on under my camp uniform, threw away my wet shoes made from rags, and put those boots on. Now I was dry. I was warm!

Our work took about an hour, by which time the rest of the transport had moved further into the forest. Once we had picked up the ammunition, we started to walk in the same direction. Each of us was carrying a load of guns and grenades. I remember the scene clearly: a beautiful road, cutting through a little village and curving into a forest. We again came to the fork in the road, just outside the forest. Suddenly we heard fierce firing coming from the forest, as if the front was nearby.

One of our Blockältester, a German political prisoner, stopped and said: 'Boys, do you hear what is going on there? These bandits are killing our brothers. But they won't get us!'

He loaded up his machine gun and pointed it at the SS guards. The other *Kapos* did the same. The guards pleaded: 'Please don't shoot us.' He said: 'Nobody will shoot you. Just put your guns down'—and then he let them go. Some of the Blockältester and *Kapos* were already wearing civilian clothes underneath their camp uniforms, but we, the Jews, were not so prepared.

The Blockältester said to us: 'Listen boys, we cannot go as a group, because there are hundreds and hundreds of SS around in this area. If they catch us, they will kill us too. Everybody has to try and save themselves as far as possible.

We have to disappear!' As soon as he said this, the other two Jewish boys and the rest of the group, including the Lagerältester, took off. I looked around. I was alone with Egon, the Austrian *Kapo*. He said to me: 'Jacob, what do we do?' I said: 'We run away!' Franz, the Blockältester had told us we should take the rifles, which we did, but we didn't know what to do with them, so we threw them away and just kept on going.

It is reported that some 330 prisoners were shot and killed in the forest.

After eighteen days and nights on the road, of the 800 taken from Janina, 200 reached their destination, all in a weakened state. That was the real end of Janinagrube.[12]

No more than a quarter of the 60,000 evacuated from Auschwitz survived the march. Of the boys who had been transported with Jacob from Poznań to Auschwitz and selected for various sub-camps, Morris Shell had ended up in Mauthausen, Max Procel in Buchenwald and Issac Pankowski in Groß-Rosen.

Jacob recalled:[13]

It was not so easy, running away. We had already been walking a few days without food. The piece of bread that we got in Auschwitz we ate straight away that night. So Egon and I decided to go back to the little village we had passed. We were hungry, unshaven, cold and miserable. We had nothing. As we approached, in the distance we saw a house in a field, a little bit out of the village. Although we were afraid, we went up to that house and knocked on the door. A woman opened it. Luckily this was a Polish family, an elderly couple and their daughter. I said to her: 'Good evening', in Polish, and she answered me in Polish: 'Good evening; come in.' We told her what had happened to us and that we wanted some civilian clothing. She said: 'We have nothing to spare. The Germans took everything.' Then the young woman started to cry, telling us that her husband had been sent to Auschwitz and she had only got his ashes back. 'What I can do is make you some hot soup.' We said: 'We'd like to sleep for a few hours since we haven't slept for four or five nights.' She said: 'Go into the stable and sleep there.' If somebody had come into the stable, she could have pretended she knew nothing about us. We did that and lay down on the straw. This was the best sleep that I ever had! We were warm and our bellies were full of soup on this bright frosty winter's night!

After a few hours, the woman knocked on the door and said: 'My good people, you have to go. Our village is full of SS. They've put up posters on every house warning that if they find a prisoner hiding somewhere, they will burn down that house and shoot the whole family. You have to go.'

So we left the house and started walking along the highway towards the forest, when suddenly, who knows from where, we heard: 'Stop. Stand still and hands up.' Two Volksdeutsche, wearing armbands with swastikas and carrying machine guns, had found us. Egon told them that we had lost our transport and were looking for our people. 'That's good,' they said: 'You go straight down that road and about one-and-a-half kilometres from here is a station where you'll find the SS. They will take you back to your transport.' Luckily, they didn't go with us but went on looking for other escapees. Because Egon had spoken such good German, they trusted him. So they went one way and we went the other, in the direction they had told us we should go. We walked up the highway for maybe another kilometre and didn't see anybody—but we could hear yelling and shooting. I said to Egon: 'Stop. I won't give myself up. If they catch and shoot me, so be it. Let them kill me in a field—but I won't go on my own to be shot by them.' Egon said: 'So what shall we do?' I answered: 'We'll run!'

So we ran. Again, the snow was up to our thighs. We ran through the field, towards the forest: we were going, going, going. By the time we reached the forest we were tired and hungry. Because we hadn't shaved, we looked like wild animals. We continued moving on through that whole night.

At dawn we spotted a big farm with a huge barn about fifty metres long. This looked like a good place to hide. But when we quietly opened the door, I saw machinery standing there. I said to Egon: 'I think they're threshing wheat here.' He said: 'Are you crazy, in winter? Nobody does that in winter. Threshing is done at the beginning of autumn.' But I replied: 'I'm telling you, Egon, I can feel it, I can smell it.' He convinced me there was nothing to fear and we crawled up to where they stored the straw and fell asleep.

At around 11am when the sun was shining through the slats of the barn, I woke up. I heard the threshing machines going downstairs! These machines separated the wheat grain, which you eat, from the husks and the straw. They were packing them into square packs, and each would have weighed about seventy or eighty kilos. One worker was passing packs to another, then stacking them up. They would have been on top of us, so we had no choice: we had to come out. At that moment the hardest thing for me to accept was that we were defenceless. We had thrown away our rifles, too afraid to carry them. When the girls who were working saw us emerge from the straw, they ran out screaming. Immediately about ten workmen rushed into the barn. As we came down, each one was pointing a pitchfork at us.

Egon pleaded with them in German, since these were all Volksdeutsche. 'Let us go. We're from Auschwitz, from the camp and we've lost our transport. We're not murderers; we're not criminals.' But nothing helped us. They kept us under guard until two policemen came and took us away.

We were in a little village about five kilometres from Czerwionka. The two policemen took us to a shed and when they opened the door, we saw that there were already three Jewish boys there, dressed in civilian clothes. They had gone to the Poles for help, and they had given them food and clothes to change into. But then they too had called the police! Next morning, they brought in another two, so now we were seven. We stayed there that day and overnight. The next morning, the Commandant of this little police station came with two policemen and marched us out. I asked one of them where we were going. He said: 'You're going to a bigger police station, in Czerwionka.' I said: 'Don't talk nonsense. I know we're going to be killed.'

But they did take us to the police station in Czerwionka. It had its own Commandant and six policemen, four of whom were Volksdeutsche. When we arrived, I let Egon explain that we had been cut off from our group and were wondering around lost. The Commandant took off his hat, threw it on the floor and said: 'Lock up these bandits.' There were already fifteen others in the room, so our group made twenty-two. They were mostly Jewish boys who had run away from different places. Everybody was already in civilian clothing, except for Egon and me.

They kept us there for seven days, without food. The only facility we had in that room was a water tap. If you felt a little weak, you just put your head under the water. Some boys had already organized German marks, and they asked the policemen to buy them some bread. But they replied: 'You don't need anything to eat. You're all going to be shot.'

One of the policemen was a real beast and he picked on me. It was a case of mistaken identity: he mistook me for another prisoner whom he suspected of planning to escape. One day this man came in and said to me: 'You, shorty, come out.' He also took Egon. He had seen that I had good leather boots, while my Austrian mate had only wooden shoes. He said to me: 'Take off your boots' and he wanted Egon to take them from me. Egon tried them on, and tears streamed down his face. He said to the gendarme: 'I can't get them on—they're too small'—although to me they seemed big enough.

While we were outside, I could see that the policemen were packing up their station. But I thought: they'll always have time to finish us off! This was my most bitter time. I thought about how I had endured so much. Why in hell did I run away? Maybe if I had stayed with the transport I would be alive. Or maybe I would have been shot in the forest. Who knows? But you always wonder if you have made the right choice.

Early on the Friday evening we heard shots coming from the cemetery just across the street. We didn't know what was happening. In fact, that night the Volksdeutsche had gone on patrol with that policeman to the cemetery, shot him in the back and run away. On Saturday afternoon, we heard somebody call out in Polish: 'Boys, are you alive?' We said: 'Yes.' I got up on the table, looked out and saw the same four Volksdeutsche. They said: 'The police have run away. We'll come back this evening and let you out.' The other boys wanted to break down the door and get out straight away, but I said: 'I know the Germans. This could be a trick and they'll shoot us as soon as we get out. If it's true that the police have gone, we can stand it until tomorrow, can't we?' So we stayed.

After half an hour or so, two young girls brought us some food: potatoes cooked in their skins and a big bucket of hot milk. They passed these to us through the window, since the Volksdeutsche didn't want to open the main door in case the police returned. We hadn't eaten for eight days! But I didn't have more than half a potato and a glass of milk, because my stomach wouldn't have taken it. We hadn't eaten for so long.

Later in the afternoon, two of the Volksdeutsche came back with the Mayor of the village, who promised that he would let us out after dark. He asked how many we were, and how many of us were Jews. This question was impossible to answer. We were all Jews; they had already taken away the Austrians, including Egon. So we pretended that we were dumb and didn't answer. At about 7pm they brought us civilian clothing: a pair of pants, a little jacket and a hat, and let us out of the police station. The Mayor said: 'You can go wherever you want, but I don't want to see you in my village.' He thought that we were common criminals.

At the beginning of 1945, the highways, roads, and railway stations of western Poland, Eastern Prussia and Silesia were crammed with hundreds of thousands of men, women, and children, all making their way westward, fleeing the Soviet Army. Villages and towns became ghost settlements after the exodus of their German inhabitants. Cooking pots were abandoned on gas burners and plates on the table when householders fled their homes without even finishing a meal.[14]

Jacob recalled:[15]

> So we were free. We put our civilian clothes over the concentration camp uniforms, the pyjamas, and each of us went his own way. But we had no documents, nothing, and this town was full of Germans. They were pulling out, but any one of them could have stopped us and asked for papers. If you didn't have any documents, they shot you on the spot.
>
> I was left with an elderly Jewish gentleman, a man perhaps sixty-five or sixty-six years old, who was from my region, from Katowice in Silesia. I didn't know him; he must have been from another camp. We heard that the Russians were now some forty kilometres from Katowice. Luckily, he was from the area so he knew which direction we needed to go, and we started walking towards Katowice. We walked at night-time on the main road, although this was very dangerous because the Germans were retreating west. German tanks, the Wehrmacht and the SS passed us by. But we couldn't walk in the forest or across the fields, because the snow was chest-deep. On the road, because many vehicles were moving, they flattened the snow, so at least you could walk on it.
>
> We continued walking along for half the night, when suddenly we saw, some fifty metres away in the forest, an empty track with a house at the end. A house in the forest with a smoking chimney! My companion said to me: 'Let us go in and have a look.' I said: 'But you know who will be there: a Volksdeutsche or a German.' He said: 'What other choice do we have? We have to try.'
>
> We went up to the house and knocked on the door. Nobody

answered. We knocked again, but still nobody answered. Then we gingerly pushed open the door and quietly stepped into the kitchen. There was nobody there! Just the kitchen with a hot stove, and soup on it still cooking. Warm food on the stove, but nobody was there! They had run away. Later we found out they were Volksdeutsche. We worried that we were not safe—but we had no other choice, so we decided to stay and take our chances. We turned down the kerosene lamp that was burning to dim the light. We were warm, we ate the hot soup, and for the moment we were OK. Who cares what would come later, what would happen to us? For now we had food in our stomachs.

We stayed there for three nights and four days, like mice under a bush. We could hear many vehicles passing by: cars, trucks, tanks, all on their way to Germany. We were afraid to make a move, because at any time somebody could have spotted the house.

Notes

1   Novac, Ana, *The Beautiful Days of My Youth* (New York: Henry Holt, 1997), 238-42
2   Daniel Blatman, *The Death Marches: The Final Phase of Nazi Genocide* (Cambridge: Harvard University Press, 2011), 96-97
3   Pawel Stanisław, *Z cyklu 'Dzieje Libiąża': Podobóz 'Janinagrube' w Libiążu w latach okupacji 1943-45* (From the series 'The History of Libiąż': Sub-camp 'Janinagrube' in Libiąż during the Years of Occupation 1943-45') (Libiąż: Opracowania Regionalne, Stanisław Pawel Jaworzno: Biuro Turystyczne Pasja) (Libiąż: Regional Study of Stanisław Pawel, Jaworzno, Tourist Office Pasja, 1998), 29; Emeryka Iwaszko, *Podobóz 'Janinagrube': Zeszyty Oświęcimskie: 10* (Sub-camp 'Janinagrube': Auschwitz Notebooks), (Oświęcim: Państwowe Muzeum w Oswiecimiu) (State Museum in Auschwitz, 1967), 82

4   *The Long March to Freedom* was shown on SBS television, 4 May 2012
5   Stanisław, *Dzieje Libiąża*, 29; Iwaszko, *Podobóz 'Janinagrube'*, 82
6   Jacob Widawski, transcripts of interviews conducted at the Consulate-General of the Federal Republic of Germany, 1974, 1975, Sydney; transcripts of testimony given at trial against Heinrich Niemeyer, 1978, 1982, 1989; indictment StA Hannover 11 Js 5/73, Hannover; audio testimony for the *12th Hour Project of Oral Testimonies* (Sydney: Australian Institute for Holocaust Studies, 1990); video testimony, 1995 (Sydney: USC Shoah Foundation Institute), code 2528
7   Alan Furst, *The Spies of Warsaw* (London: Weidenfeld & Nicolson, 2008), 4; Blatman, *The Death Marches*, 88; http://www.whale.to/b/sub.html; Shmuel Krakowski, *The Death Marches in the Period of the Evacuation of the Camps*, in *The Nazi Concentration Camps* (Proceedings of the Fourth Yad Vashem International Historical Conference, 1980), 479
8   Jacob Widawski, testimonies, German Consulate-General; transcripts, Hannover trial; *12th Hour Project* 1990; USC Shoah Foundation, code 2528
9   Blatman, *The Death Marches*, 95, 453 (Note 113); Krakowski, *The Death Marches*, 479
10 Danuta Czech, *Auschwitz Chronicle: 1939-45* (New York: Henry Holt and Company, 1997), 788
11 Jacob Widawski, testimonies, German Consulate-General; transcripts, Hannover trial; *12th Hour Project* 1990; USC Shoah Foundation, code 2528
12 Primo Levi, *The Periodic Table* (New York: Schocken Books, 1984), 122; Iwaszko, *Podobóz 'Janinagrube'*, 82; http://tiergartenstrasse4.org/Janinagrube.html
13 Jacob Widawski, testimonies, German Consulate-General; transcripts, Hannover trial; *12th Hour Project* 1990; USC Shoah Foundation, code 2528
14 Blatman, *The Death Marches*, 75-76
15 Jacob Widawski, testimonies, German Consulate-General; transcripts, Hannover trial; *12th Hour Project* 1990; USC Shoah Foundation, code 2528

20

Jacob's Liberation

Jacob recalled:[1]

Around midnight of the fourth day we'd been in the house, the silence was suddenly broken by the sound of a motorbike arriving. We sat quietly as we heard them stop, then there was knocking on the door and a shout: 'Open up!'—in Russian. My elderly mate grabbed me and said: 'Jacob, we're free! They're Russians!' I didn't know Russian then, but he understood it.

Two soldiers armed with sub-machine guns came in. We immediately took off the civilian clothes so they could see our striped prison uniforms and we told them that we were prisoners from the camps. But they were still suspicious. They pointed their guns at us and we had to walk in front of them while they checked the kitchen. But they didn't find anything. They marched us up to the first floor. In the bedroom we saw a photograph of a couple, an officer of the Wehrmacht and his wife. The Russians shot at the photograph. Everybody wanted to shoot 'Gitler' (the Russians couldn't pronounce Hitler), so they shot at this picture instead.

We started to tell them our story. They said: 'We know. We freed Auschwitz and saw some sick people.' They had a flask with a little bit of alcohol, so they gave us a drink. Outside there were chickens, and they shot a couple and cooked them for us. They stayed with us for a few hours. As they left, they warned us: 'Don't move from here, because there are thousands of Germans in these forests. We are the advance guard. We're scouting for accommodation for our Colonel, and we think this house would be ideal. We have to go now, but tomorrow our Commandant will be here. You stay here and wait.'

The next day, three or four big trucks of Russian soldiers arrived with the Russian Colonel. He was a Jewish doctor from Kiev. He said to us: 'Don't rush off. There are still a lot of Germans around and they're shooting people. Wait until our Army secures this area and then I'll send you home.'

After six or seven days, the Colonel asked where we were from. The old man told him he was from Katowice. The Colonel told us that Soviet troops had already taken Katowice and established a transit camp there for survivors: 'Our soldiers are travelling backwards and forwards carrying supplies, so they'll take this old man back to Katowice.'

Then he asked me: 'Where are you going?' He passed me the map and I showed him where Wieruszów was. He said: 'That's good. We're going to Praszka and passing Wieluń.' I said: 'If you can get me to Wieluń, that's close enough. From there I can even walk home!' When the Red Army arrived, he stopped one of their trucks and they took me to Wieluń, about forty kilometres away.

I thought to myself that maybe I would find somebody alive from my family in Wieluń. I had cousins who lived there before the War. I arrived there about two in the afternoon and went straight to my cousin's house. There was nobody there.

I couldn't find anybody. Not one Jew was left in Wieluń! So I thought to myself: what will I do here? I didn't know any of the Poles. I didn't have anywhere to sleep and night was quickly approaching. And of course, it was winter. I reasoned that if I went to my hometown, at least I would find somebody there I knew, that I could go to for help.

It was the 5th or 6th of February 1945 when I started to walk home. But I did a stupid thing: instead of walking along the highway, I took a short-cut. Along the highway the distance was thirty-two kilometres from Wieluń to my town; the short-cut reduced that to twenty-four. But there was still a 5pm curfew in place, since the War had not yet finished. The Red Army was just passing through Poland. As I was walking home, night fell. At that time in Poland, nothing was organized. There was no order, no authority in place, just a lot of Polish gangs roaming around, right-wing bandits, antisemites, targeting and killing any Jews or Communists who had survived the War. They put on a uniform, a soldier's cap, an armband and became policemen!

Halfway to Wieruszów, about twelve or fourteen kilometres from my town, is a large village called Czastary. Before the War, six or eight Jewish families lived in that village, but during the War nobody did. Suddenly I was stopped by two of these 'policemen' and the first thing they said to me was: 'Show us your documents.' I said: 'I have no documents.' I opened my jacket and showed them my camp uniform; I rolled up my sleeve and showed them my tattooed number from Auschwitz. I told them: 'You want a document? Here is my document!'. So they knew that I am a Jew. They said: 'You can't move now because of the curfew. You have to stay here overnight. But in the morning, you can go.'

They took me to a farmer who also had a bakery in the village and they told him: 'Let him stay here till tomorrow morning.' The baker was a very nice man and his wife straight away brought me some hot food. The bakery's oven had a platform above it and in small towns in winter, people used to sleep there because it was very warm. That's where I fell asleep. The baker had overheard the men who brought me talking. They had said: 'Later, around midnight, we'll come back and take that bloody Jew out to the forest and shoot him.' So even though I was almost home I was still in danger.

But the farmer saved my life! He woke me up and said: 'My boy, you have to leave.' I said: 'But why? They told me to stay until morning.' He replied: 'Don't ask questions. My son has already prepared the horses. He'll take the sleigh, to keep things quiet, and take you home to Wieruszów. Otherwise those bastards will kill you.'

So that's what happened. The son brought the horses and he took me home. I was really back home!

At the end of the War, a few Jewish survivors such as Jacob, including some of those sent to the Łódź Ghetto or the Poznań camps, or who had fled to the Soviet Union returned to Wieruszów. But as word reached them about the murder of Jewish returnees by Polish bands, they sought refuge in larger cities, or left Poland altogether.[2]

Jacob recalled:[3]

It was around six o'clock in the morning as I came into my Wieruszów. The road from Wieluń to my town passes the church and people were going in.

I didn't have anyone I knew but the Frankowski family, our Catholic neighbours. I knew that I would be safe with them. I went to their house, knocked on the door and Mrs Frankowska answered. You can imagine her reaction when she saw me: she was really like a mother to me! She crossed herself maybe twenty times: 'Oh my God, Jacob—you're here.' I was of course tired and dirty. She drew me a bath and even though I was a grown-up man by then, twenty-four years old, while she was around fifty-seven, she bathed me like her baby.

Mrs Frankowska welcomed Jacob with warmth and loving care. He would later recall that seeing his emancipated body she cried and held him close, thanking her God for his survival. One of her own sons, Zenek, was missing and she was very worried about him. Jacob had long suspected that Zenek, his close childhood friend, was in fact working for the Polish Underground, and while he tried to reassure his mother, he privately suspected that he had been killed.

Jacob recalled:[4]

I started asking her questions about who was in the town, who had already come back. She said: 'For now I'm not going to tell you anything. Eat something and sleep for a few hours. Joseph [her younger son] is at work, but he'll be home around four. I'll wake you up then and we'll talk.'

I knew nothing of my own family. From the day that I had left home, I had no idea what had happened to them. At the beginning of the War, we didn't know about Auschwitz, concentration camps or crematoria.

When I woke up, she told me: 'Two Jewish boys have returned. One is Josef Szwartz.' Josel was his name and I had been with him in school and in Hashomer Hatzair, the Jewish youth group. He had been in the Wieruszów Ghetto, so I found out a lot from him about my mother's fate. He had been a lucky fellow. When they were liquidating the Ghetto, they took some people into the church which stands by the Prosna River. He managed to escape the church, jumped into the river and swam across to the other side. He wandered around for days until one day, when he couldn't bear the hunger any more, he went to a local farmer for help. They were Volksdeutsche, and they gave him food and then called the police. He was subsequently sent to a camp.

The other boy who returned back was Moshe Asher. They told me that he was now an officer working at Russian headquarters. I went there straight away and told him the whole story of what had happened to me in Czastary. He told the Commandant, who said: 'What, such bandits, such antisemites are still here?' The next day he asked me if I could recognize these two men. I said of course I would. So this Commandant, with six or seven soldiers, Moshe Asher and me, went to Czastary and talked to the baker, who told us their names. We found them and the Russian officer didn't take them to the police station. Instead he took them to that same forest and said: 'Here, where you wanted to shoot this Jew, you will die.' And he shot them both.

Now I was back living in my little town. Twelve kilometres away was another small place, Borysławiec. I was in Guttenbrunn with four Cohen brothers who came from there. Two of them had escaped from the Death March and come back home. The other two went on the Death March to Germany, where they were liberated and where they stayed. The brothers who were in Germany urged the others to leave Poland. But after the camps these boys were tired, and they had already met two sisters, so weren't eager to leave. There were already four Jews in Borysławiec. Then another two survivors came back from a camp in Częstochowa. I became a frequent visitor, seeking their company.

There were still many gangs roaming around Borysławiec, killing Jews and Communist leaders. Poland after the War was besmirched by a number of pogroms such as that in Borysławiec, the worst being in Kielce, where forty-two survivors were murdered.[5]

One of the Cohen brothers from Germany came to Poland to try and persuade his brothers to leave. He came on a Wednesday and on the Thursday, he and his whole family were killed by the Polish bandits. I had been in that town just the day before!

My friend Max Procel had also returned and was living in another town nearby. He had heard what had happened in Borysławiec and knew that three of us were back in Wieruszów. So he went to the local Polish police station and told them to get us out. The Commandant came to meet us, and said: 'Boys you have to run away from here. I have to hide myself as well'—because these bandits also killed local policemen. They killed anybody 'in authority'.

So although I was one of the first ones to return, I ran away to Brzeg, seventy-eight kilometres from Wieruszów.

The other two boys from Wieruszów, Max Procel and Issac Pankowski, had both been evacuated from the Auschwitz sub-camp of Jaworzno on 17 January 1945. Max was by then twenty-four and Issac twenty-six.

Max's journey had taken him on the Death March to Buchenwald, Germany and then on to Theresienstadt, Czechoslovakia, where he had been liberated by Soviet forces on 8 May 1945. He had procured a horse and buggy and made his way through Czechoslovakia back into Poland. He recalled:[6]

> I arrived in Wieruszów at the end of May 1945. Wieruszów after the War was pretty much unchanged. The main houses, like our house, were still standing. The Poles kept asking: 'Are you still alive? I thought the whole family was gone.' My cousin told me that my parents and three sisters had been taken to the Łódź Ghetto, from where they were transported for extermination. I didn't know what had happened to my brothers. All I knew was that they didn't survive. So I was alone and there was no reason for me to stay in my home town.
>
> There were already a few survivors back in Wieruszów, some who had returned three months earlier. Since it was difficult to make a living in this small town, the four of us decided to leave and try our luck in a larger town, Brzeg.

Issac had been evacuated from Jaworzno sub-camp, taken on a Death March to Blaeckhammer, then by truck to the Groß-Rosen camp, some 250 kilometres from Auschwitz, where he was liberated. Soon after he returned to his home town of Kępno, he recalled:[7]

> I got off the train in Kępno and walked into the city. A Gentile looked out his window and recognized me. He was someone that I'd known before the War, so he took me into his house. The next morning, I went to the City Hall and they assigned me a house that had belonged to a Volksdeutsche—not our house. Nobody knew anything about my family, because after they threw us out of Kępno, there was nobody left there.
>
> I met a couple more Jewish survivors and together we stayed for a while in Kępno, which appeared safe because

it had a Red Army presence. We started making and selling wooden shoes. It was still acceptable for farmers to go out into the fields wearing wooden clogs.

Then, one day Russian soldiers who were also Jewish, came to warn us that it wasn't safe to remain there, because there had already been an attack in Borysławiec. So we moved to Wrocław, a large regional town.

Later, I got married and had four children. I lived in Wrocław with my family until 1957, when we emigrated to Israel.

Pelagia Frankowska, Jacob's neighbour and 'second mother', born in 1888. This photo was provided by her son, Stefan Frankowski, in 2015.

Picture of the first survivors who returned to Wieruszów in 1945. Jacob is still wearing the boots that he had found during the Death March.
Photo from his album.
1. Jacob Widawski, 2. Moshe Asher, 3. Sruel Libszitz, 4. Dvora Baun,
5. Coppel Poncz, 6. Duwcze Szpira, 7. Frania Styczka, 8. Josel Szwartz

MINA & JACOB

Survivors at the mass grave in Wieruszów.
Photo from Wieruszów Yizkor (Memorial) Book, p.304.
1. Jacob Widawski, 2. Issac Pankowski, 3. Max Procel,
4. Mosze Kożuch, 5. Sala Pankowski, 6. Cesia Kożuch

The sign states:
Here rest the remains of 88 people of Jewish nationality, murdered in Wieruszów, amongst them the married couple Lewek Daniel and Regina Knopf. The above were murdered by the German Gestapo on 21-8-1942 during the final liquidation of the Wieruszów Ghetto
'Honour their memory'

Adele recalls:

Later this handful of survivors organized and laid a memorial stone in the Wieruszów Jewish Cemetery, and said Kaddish for the Jewish community annihilated by the Germans. Among the survivors pictured with Jacob at the cemetery are: Max Procel, Isaac Pankowski, Moshe Kożuch and Sruel Libszitz. They remained his close friends for the rest of their lives. Photo from Jacob's album.

1. Jacob Widawski
2. Max Procel
3. Issac Pankowski,
4. Mosze Kożuch
5. Sruel Libszitz

Jewish cemetery, Wieruszów

Of the more than 2,000 Jews who lived in Wieruszów prior to the War, around twenty, or 1 percent, survived. Today, Wieruszów has a population of nearly 15,000, with no Jews. The unmarked Jewish cemetery is situated along a road without a name, northeast of the town centre, behind the railroad. Built before 1822, the last known Orthodox or Progressive/Reform Jewish burial took place in 1945. The isolated suburban flatland has no sign or marker. Access is open to all with no wall, fence or gate. About 250 stones are visible. The oldest gravestone in the cemetery is from the first half of the nineteenth century. The municipality owns the property which is now 'not used'. Adjacent property is agricultural and residential. The cemetery was vandalized during and after the War, and has not been maintained since. Photo 2010.[8]

MINA & JACOB

Mina and Jacob at mass grave and memorial.
The monument to Holocaust victims and the marked mass grave were erected by Abram Majerowicz. They replaced the cardboard sign held by the group of survivors who returned to Wieruszów in 1945. It is believed that Jacob's mother, Brucha, his brother Abram and his sister-in-law and nephews (Berek's family), lie buried in this grave. Photo 1994.

Jacob's Journey

Notes

1. Jacob Widawski, transcripts of interviews conducted at the Consulate-General of the Federal Republic of Germany, 1974, 1975, Sydney; transcripts of testimony given at trial against Heinrich Niemeyer, 1978, 1982, 1989, Indictment StA Hannover 11 Js 5/73, Hannover; audio testimony for the *12th Hour Project of Oral Testimonies* (Sydney: Australian Institute for Holocaust Studies, 1990); video testimony, 1995, Sydney (USC Shoah Foundation Institute), code 2528
2. United States Holocaust Memorial Museum (USHMM), *Encyclopedia of Camps and Ghettos* 1933-45, (Washington: 2012), Vol. 2, 117
3. Jacob Widawski, testimonies, German Consulate-General; transcripts, Hannover trial; *12th Hour Project* 1990; USC Shoah Foundation, code 2528
4. Ibid.
5. http://en.wikipedia.org/wiki/Kielce_pogrom
6. Max Procel, video testimony, 1997, Melbourne (USC Shoah Foundation Institute), code 30561
7. Issac (Yitzah) Pankowski, transcript of oral testimony, 1993 (Jerusalem: Yad Vashem Archives), code 03-7202, V-D 242
8. Zenon Szacfajer, (Association of Friends of Wieruszów), *70-Rocznica Likwidacji Ghetta* (70-year Anniversary of the Liquidation of the Ghetto), *Łacznik* (August 2012); Wieruszów Commune publication, Wieruszów: 2010; http://www.iajgsjewishcemeteryproject.org/poland/wieruszow.html

21

Mina's Death March

At the beginning of 1945, Mina found herself in Leipzig, Germany, having been transported there from Skarżysko-Kamienna in August 1944.

During the final months of the War, from March to May 1945, as camps on German soil were evacuated, prisoners were shuffled aimlessly from place to place around Germany, until the final surrender.[1]

By 13 April 1945 when the first group of 400 Jewish women prisoners left Leipzig-Schönefeld, with Mina amongst them, Jacob had already been back home for two months.

Mina recalled:[2]

> The end of our captivity was horrible. We were weak; we were starved almost to death. One night they woke us: 'Get up!' We had to get dressed and go out on the road on what we later called the Death March. They took us out from the Leipzig camp some time in mid-April 1945. I think all the prisoners were evacuated then from all the camps because the Germans were expecting the Americans to arrive: 'Die Amerikaner are coming,' they said. They planned to march us from Leipzig towards Dresden, via Cavertitz. It was spring so the snow was melting. We marched almost barefoot through

the mud, because our shoes were in very bad condition.

All the concentration camps did the same. These marches were their last solution: to dispose of as many of us as possible. Anyone who fainted or was weak was shoved along with shouts of: 'Forward! You have to march.' People were falling down from cold, sickness and hunger. They killed those who were too weak and left the road black with bodies.

Prisoner Fela Schechter recalled:[3]

> On 13 April, with the Americans twenty kilometres from Leipzig, the camp was evacuated. Ten days and nights of marching, under the bayonets of SS men, feeding on grass and raw potatoes. We moved along never-ending roads and highways, sleeping in ditches or fields, in the rain and mud. I dreamed of the most miserable barrack, the dirtiest bunk, so that I could rest. We walked towards freedom, but the signposts which measured the distance travelled were the shrivelled-up corpses of female prisoners that we passed in the ditch every few steps. This was the final step of our captivity.

The prisoners made their way on foot towards the northeast, as the American forces advanced from the west and the Red Army advanced from the south. Group one marched from Leipzig to Cavertitz along the Elbe, as indicated:[4]

Leipzig → Wurzen (29km) → Oschatz (30km) → Riesa (13km) → Glaubitz (8km) → Strehla (13km) → Kreinitz (6km) → Cavertitz (15km)

The distance between Leipzig and Cavertitz is approximately fifty-seven kilometres. However, the circular route taken by Mina and her fellow prisoners totalled some 114 kilometres.

The streets were quiet and deserted. All around were ruins and destruction, with hardly one building left intact. Here and there fires were burning. Flanked by armed SS, the prisoners marched in rows of five, each person wrapped in a blanket. They were constantly prodded to go faster because their guards were afraid of air raids.[5]

The reaction of German civilians to the columns of walking skeletons going through their towns was largely indifference: they looked upon these 'sub-humans' with hostility and moral disgust.[6]

Olga Horak, a survivor of a Death March through Germany, wrote:[7]

> Along the icy roads we trudged, frozen in body with emotionless faces and glazed stares. Through villages and towns, we marched. Thousands of German evacuees were also fleeing in the wake of the Russian advance and they clogged the roads with us. I saw innumerable horse-drawn farm carts, wheelbarrows and old-fashioned carriages laden with luggage, household goods and food. Not one of those thousands ever attempted to throw even a scrap of bread or potato in our direction.

Felicja Karay recalled:[8]

> The German farmers would flee in horror when they saw us coming. In general, they were hostile to us. They were afraid to come out of their houses. At most, they would set buckets of water for us along the road, but the SS men with us would knock them over on purpose.

These civilians had been living for more than ten years in a political and social climate in which antisemitism, xenophobia and fear of the faceless Slav/Jewish/Communist/criminal rabble were dominant in the propaganda they were fed. That 'rabble' was now invading their German home towns.[9]

Mina recalled:[10]

> Our group of friends was joined by a woman from Kraków. Her husband had been a very famous solicitor and she was well-educated. She was not old, maybe forty-five to forty-eight years old. But to our group of girls, average age twenty, twenty-two, she was an older lady. She said: 'I hope if I join you, I will survive.' A short time later, this woman fainted and we were very much afraid that she would be killed. We had two choices: to help her or leave her on the ground. I was holding her up as we passed through a village, but its doors were closed to us. A girlfriend of mine summoned up her courage and went up and knocked on a door, saying: 'Will you help me, please?' She spoke German well and a German woman gave her a little bit of warm soup. As soon as she brought this soup, I poured it into the fainting woman's mouth—and she revived. She stood up and started walking together with us. She survived!
>
> While we were marching, hungry because there was no food, we saw that the farmers had brought out little green potatoes for planting. They said that such potatoes were harmful to eat, but we dug them out or tried to steal a few from a field when we could. We even ate grass—because we were so hungry. For ten days we had received no food!

Felicja Karay recalled:[11]

> As we marched, periodically the guards stopped to rest in a

building along the way, while the women lay down in the mud at the side of the road. Thousands of women in striped dresses, black with dirt and covered in lice, their faces as pale as ghosts and their eyes revealing their terror of death.

Mina recalled:[12]

> Once during the march, they gave us a rest. We were so tired, walking and sleeping on our feet. We sat down at once and slept, sitting up in water and snow. Two of my girlfriends and their mother, the Karmels, lay down. It was night time, dark. Then a passing German vehicle crushed Ilona's legs and killed her mother. This was a horrible, horrible sight, the memory of which still haunts me!

On 17 April 1945, the line halted in a field near a forest. The women grabbed at nettles and ran to the trees to gather wood for a fire. But there was a fence around the woods and the shooting started immediately.

Felicja Karay wrote:[13]

> We moved like sleepwalkers. We no longer noticed the corpses lining the road or the shots being fired. The Germans kept changing the direction we were walking in. They wanted to fall into British or American hands—because they were terrified of the Russians. From time to time, American planes circled overhead. The SS officers attempted to conceal themselves among us, even putting on prisoners' striped uniforms. Tired and hungry themselves, the guards often begged food from houses along the way, but refused to allow the local people to feed us. If they got any beets or potatoes, they did

not hand them to us, but threw them on the ground the way you feed dogs, just to enjoy watching us trample each other to get to them.

Towards the end of April, the women were divided into smaller groups and each sent in a different direction. In some instances, the Death March went on for more than two weeks. Towards the end, some SS officers thought it judicious to hide from the prisoners that they were going to run away. They locked the prisoners in a barn, changed into civilian clothes and took off.[14]

Mina described what happened to her group:[15]

> One day we marched into a small town called Cavertitz, close to the River Elbe. Our group of 500 survivors was divided between some barns and we were left there. In our barn there were maybe eighty to 100 women. It was a great relief that when we went inside we saw straw where we could lie down and relax our terribly swollen legs.
>
> Our guards wanted to get rid of us; we could feel this. They were already wearing civilian clothing underneath their uniforms. We stayed in the barn and it was eerily quiet. Nobody came.
>
> The next morning the SS returned. They were afraid they hadn't done their duty. They said: 'Get up! You have to keep going. We're moving on.' This was the first time that I said: 'No!' My girlfriends asked: 'Are you sure? What if they plan to kill us here?' I replied: 'Didn't you see how many they killed on the road? Why should I walk in such conditions? Here I have grass, straw and we can at least straighten our legs and lie down on something.' 'Yes, but we're hungry. What are we going to do?' 'Listen', I said. 'Do what you feel is best for you

and don't look at what I'm doing. Everybody is responsible for themselves.' Stubbornly, I decided to stay put—and so did most of the others.

Another group went with the SS and later a German farmer passed by and told us: 'In the next village there are twenty dead people lying in the road. They've killed them.' They had taken these women from the barn and shot them in the neck in the village, to get rid of as many as possible.

We stayed in this barn for three nights and three days, without food or water, too afraid to go out. In the end I said: 'We have to do something.' Some of the girls had blankets which were overlocked with cotton thread. I still had a needle and a small pair of scissors. I said: 'You know what we're going to do? I am a bit of a dressmaker. We are going to take these blankets and make dresses.'

You should have seen these dresses! I'm sorry I didn't take a picture! They were just to cover our bodies and to hide our striped uniforms. We were afraid to go out in our uniforms, because you couldn't trust the Germans. You didn't know what was going on in the street.

Eventually five of us opened the barn door. I said: 'What will be, will be' and we went out. You can imagine our fear—but we had to go and look for help. Terrified, we walked into the village. An elderly lady told us that the local Mayor hadn't run away from the advancing Red Army and showed us where he lived. So we walked on, propelled by our hunger. There was no other way to get help.

We found the Mayor and told him that we were a few hundred women: survivors, ex-prisoners. We had been without food and water for several days. He had to help us.

After a few hours, the villagers brought us some food:

> large baskets with cooked potatoes. Buckets of milk. Bread! We threw ourselves on this food like hungry wolves. I was standing away from it all, crying for joy and with terrible bitterness, watching what state, what condition, they, the German Nazis had brought us to!

How many died along the way? No one can say for sure. However, as noted, it is estimated that more than one-third were murdered or died in a period of three weeks on the Death Marches.[16]
Mina recalled:[17]

> I survived! I was alive! To my own eyes, I don't know *how* I survived. This delicate Mina—I was always slim and delicate—marched hungry for ten or twelve days, while all around me were corpses.
>
> On the Death March with me were four girlfriends. We were like sisters and helped and supported each other along the way. Their names were Guta Cwyrenbrucher, Dora Goldenberg, Dora Rosenthal (the two Doras), and Pola Blaszkowska.

The five friends all survived the War and remained close throughout their lives.

MINA & JACOB

Notes

1. Daniel Jonah Goldhagen, *Hitler's Willing Executioners: Ordinary Germans and the Holocaust* (London: Little, Brown and Company, 1996), 328-30; Daniel Blatman, *The Death Marches: The Final Phase of Nazi Genocide* (Cambridge: Harvard University Press, 2011), 53, 57
2. Mina Widawski nee Laub, audio testimony for the *12th Hour Project of Oral Testimonies* (Sydney: Australian Institute for Holocaust Studies, 1990); video testimony (Sydney: USC Shoah Foundation Institute, 1995), code 2526
3. Fela Schechter, *Ucieczka przed śmiercią* (Escape from Death) (Warsaw: Żydowski Instytut Historyczny (Jewish Historical Institute), 21
4. United States Holocaust Memorial Museum (USHMM), *Encyclopedia of Camps and Ghettos 1933-45*, (Washington: 2012), Vol. 1, 380
5. Felicja Karay, *HASAG-Leipzig Slave Labour Camp: The Struggle for Survival told by the Women and their Poetry* (London, Portland: Vallentine Mitchell, 2002), 217
6. Goldhagen, *Hitler's Willing Executioners*, 365
7. Olga Horak, *Auschwitz to Australia* (East Roseville: Kangaroo Press, 2000), 62
8. Karay, *HASAG-Leipzig*, 221
9. Blatman, *The Death Marches*, 404-05
10. Mina Widawski, *12th Hour Project of Oral Testimonies*; USC Shoah Foundation, code 2526
11. Karay, *HASAG-Leipzig*, 218-19
12. Mina Widawski, *12th Hour Project of Oral Testimonies*; USC Shoah Foundation, code 2526
13. Karay, *HASAG-Leipzig*, 220-21
14. Karay, *HASAG-Leipzig*, 223-24
15. Mina Widawski, *12th Hour Project of Oral Testimonies*; USC Shoah Foundation, code 2526
16. Blatman, *The Death Marches*, 152
17. Mina Widawski, *12th Hour Project of Oral Testimonies*; USC Shoah Foundation, code 2526

22

Mina's Liberation

Mina recalled:[1]

On 23 April 1945, the first Russian convoy arrived: three young boys about eighteen or nineteen years old. They knew about the camps and were looking for survivors. We all ran out—we were still in the barns in Cavertitz—and they threw us everything that they had in their pockets: cigarettes, chocolates, biscuits.

The Russian women among us were ready to leave immediately with the Red Army, but the soldiers told us to stay where we were until they could organize transport and an escort for us, because we were all very weak. Many among us were unable even to walk. It was still very dangerous since there were German snipers shooting from rooftops at survivors. But the Russian girls didn't listen. The soldiers were on horseback and the women formed into a group and marched behind them. Those of us from Poland, Germany and France were a bit more cautious. We were afraid. We stayed in the barns for another few days.

We were later taken to the Soviet command post and they helped us immediately with accommodation, food and clothing. In town, we were put into empty flats which the

Germans had left behind. We found jars of preserves: plums, peaches and apples. Some people opened all the jars and tasted everything. I said: 'You must be crazy! After not eating for so many days, you're now going to eat plums?' But many were tempted. Their bodies could not digest the food properly, so they got very ill and some died.

The most critical problem facing the freed prisoners was where to go and what to do next. The former Jewish prisoners from the Leipzig camp had one of two alternatives, as did other Jews. Some returned to Poland to search for family members and remained there. Thousands of others scattered to Displaced Persons' (DP) camps, to await their chance to emigrate to Palestine, the United States or other Western countries.[2]

Mina recalled:[3]

I wanted to return to Poland but there was a problem with transport, so I went to the Soviet command. They asked where I had been born and where I would like to return. I told them my whole story and what I had been through. I said that I wanted to go home. I knew that my parents and my brothers had been destroyed, were dead. But I hoped that if I had survived all this, then maybe my sister was alive. I told the Russians: 'I've lost my family, but maybe my sister or aunties or uncles are alive. So I want to go back.' I showed them on the map where Kraków was located. They said: 'We can take a few people across the border,' where they had some garrisons.

So they took me from Cavertitz, back into Western Poland as far as Brzeg on the River Odra, some 370 kilometres away.

On 18 January 1945, Kraków had been liberated by the Soviet Army.⁴ In the first post-war weeks, it was like an international city because of all the foreigners passing through. It became a transit station for concentration camp survivors. The Jewish Committee, which came into being immediately after the liberation of Kraków, compiled lists of survivors and those who had been killed. Its offices were on ul. Długa, close to where the Laub family had lived before the War.⁵

Simon Wiesenthal described the atmosphere:⁶

> At Kraków station somebody stole my wife's suitcase with everything she owned. That was her homecoming. To cheer her up, her friend suggested that they walk into town. Perhaps they would meet someone they had once known. The beautiful old city of the Polish kings looked deserted and ghost-like that morning.

Mina recalled:⁷

> From Brzeg I travelled with a friend back to Kraków, to register myself with all the offices that I possibly could, in the hope that I would find somebody from my family. This was the reason I had come back to Poland.
>
> I looked around and at the beginning nobody among the friends who had accompanied my sister Freüda knew what had happened to her—or at least wanted to tell me the truth. I went up and down ul. Długa, going through lists of survivors registered with the Red Cross and the Jewish Council. At the same time, I was searching people's faces, looking, looking for Freüda.
>
> A friend of the family, who had survived with her daughter, invited me to come and stay at their place, because

our apartment had been taken over by new tenants. So I stayed there, and one day I said to her: 'You know, somebody told me that in Warsaw there are a lot of people who were in Pionki. Maybe they can tell me about my sister. My next trip will be to Warsaw.' She said: 'You're killing yourself for nothing. I'll tell you the truth about what happened to your sister.' Then she told me that Freüda had been killed at the Pionki railway station by Russian bombs. She added: 'Give up this search. Don't even try and look for her. She's not alive!'

I didn't recover any of our belongings after the War. We had left valuables with our neighbours, a Polish Christian family, for safekeeping: our fur coats, photographs and many other possessions that meant something to us, heirlooms and mementoes. My mother had thought that after the War, we would get them back. Unfortunately, the keepers didn't give me back even a piece of cloth. Everything was lost! I was very distressed, because these people had been our neighbours for many, many years and we had trusted them. I knew for certain that we had left our belongings there, because I had helped my mother and father carry our things to them. When I came to collect them, at first, they denied that we had left anything with them. Then they maintained that the Germans had taken everything.

So there was nothing to keep me in Kraków. I returned to Brzeg.

Adele explains:

Mina was now really alone. Despite all her efforts, she was never able to find anyone from her immediate or extended family who had formerly lived in Kraków, Tarnów, Dynów or Kańczuka. She had no home because the family's apartment had been taken over by strangers. She wasn't even able to recover any possessions that linked her to her family.

Years later Mum told me that this was the point when she knew she would do everything in her power to leave Poland. She was heartsick at the inhumanity shown her. The families had been neighbours for years and the Laub family had trusted them to take care of their most precious possessions. Yet now they proved indifferent to Mina's pleas, so callous.

Joseph Bau, a pre-War resident of Kraków wrote:[8]

> Full of excitement, I ran towards the street where I was born, to the house where I grew up. Nothing had changed, but our former neighbours, whom I met in the corridor, whispered to me that our apartment was occupied by the janitor, who kept a knife handy by the door. He had moved in right after my father handed him the key when we were forced to move to the Ghetto. I asked no more questions.

Like Mina, most other survivors from the Kraków area returned there in the months after liberation to try and find their families. Rafael Scharf wrote about their loss:[9]

> There is a multitude of them—nowhere. That crowded, eternal absence is far more tangible here than anywhere else in the world. How is one to settle down to the normal business of living when one knows that all the people who one then knew—family, friends, neighbours, teachers, shopkeepers, beggars—have perished, from hunger, from a bullet,

from gas, in torment, and that oneself, just through some odd twist of fate, did not perish with them?

They had left behind empty houses, workshops, counters and small stalls. They had left behind their temples, houses of prayer and their schools. New tenants, mostly Poles, had taken over their empty houses. They themselves had lost their homes in the War or had been poor, with no place of their own.[10]

Around 4,000 survivors of ghettos and concentration camps, most of them former residents of Kraków and its surrounds, settled in the city for a short time. Some tried to re-establish their lives but ultimately were driven out by the rising tide of post-war antisemitism. For example, on 11 August 1945, several Jews were killed in a pogrom in Kraków instigated and carried out by Poles belonging to reactionary Polish organizations.[11]

In 1946, thousands of Jews who had fled to the Soviet Union at the beginning of the War returned to Poland and made their homes in Kraków. Several Jewish organizations were established, including a branch of the Jewish Historical Commission, the forerunner of ŻIH. Most Jews emigrated from Poland between 1947 and 1951, but the last Jew only left Kazimierz in 1968.

About 700 Jews lived in Kraków at the end of the 1960s.[12] Today the Jewish community is officially around 150, mostly Holocaust survivors, although it is estimated that an additional thousand or so are Jewish but do not present as Jews. A few thousand more are unaware of their Jewish ancestry.[13]

Despite the tiny population, however, interest in preserving Jewish history has in recent years been rekindled. A new Jewish research institute has been established at Jagiellonian University and a Jewish Cultural Centre set up in Kazimierz. Every year, Kazimierz hosts a Jewish cultural festival offering music, dance, film and theatre, which thousands attend. Religious services are held in the old Remuh Synagogue, and concerts staged in the beautifully restored Tempel. And yet Kraków remains a Jewish ghost town!

On liberation, Mina, as the only one of her family to have survived the War, had nothing to remember those who had perished: her parents, sister Freüda, brothers Mechel, Israel, Wolf (Wilhelm or Wilek) and Izaak Mayer (Izio), Mechel's wife and son, aunts, uncles and cousins. All that she had were memories of her beloved family and their peaceful life in pre-war Kraków.

The only person from her family later found to have survived the War was her beloved cousin, Henryk Sand, the violinist. She remembered him fondly. Among her papers was the photo of him shown, dated Tel Aviv, 1949. No correspondence between them exists and we don't know what happened to him. Searches conducted in recent years in Israel, proved fruitless.

In the late 1970s Mina managed to obtain a photo of her paternal grandfather from her cousins in the United States. But it wasn't until 2010 that photographs of her parents, sister Freüda, brothers Wolf and Izaak Mayer, were unearthed in the Kraków State Archives. Up until now, despite our extensive researches, no records have been found for her brother Israel, nor Mechel and his family.

Henryk Sand, Tel Aviv, 1949. Photograph from Mina's photo album.

MINA & JACOB

Mina's Journey

MINA & JACOB

Notes

1. Mina Widawski nee Laub, audio testimony for the *12th Hour Project of Oral Testimonies* (Sydney: Australian Institute for Holocaust Studies, 1990); video testimony (Sydney: USC Shoah Foundation Institute, 1995), code 2526
2. Felicja Karay, *HASAG-Leipzig Slave Labour Camp: The Struggle for Survival told by the Women and their Poetry* (London, Portland: Vallentine Mitchell, 2002), 226
3. Mina Widawski, *12th Hour Project of Oral Testimonies*; USC Shoah Foundation, code 2526
4. Mariusz Kluczewski, *Without Blackout: Everyday Life of Occupied Kraków*, in materials of the State Archive of Kraków (Kraków: Archiwum Państwowe w Krakowie (The National Archives of Kraków), 2009), 25
5. Miriam and Mordechai Peleg, *Witnesses: Life in Occupied Kraków* (London, New York: Routledge, 1991), 109, 141, 146
6. Simon Wiesenthal, *The Murderers Among Us* (London: Heinemann, 1967), 56
7. Mina Widawski, *12th Hour Project of Oral Testimonies*; USC Shoah Foundation, code 2526
8. Joseph Bau, *Dear God, have you ever gone hungry?* (New York: Arcade Publishing, 1996, English language translation; in Hebrew 1990), 162
9. Rafael Scharf, *Cracow–Blessed its Memory*, in Stanisław Markowski, ed., *Krakowski Kazimierz: Dzielnica Żydowska 1870-1988* (Kraków's Kazimierz: Jewish Suburb 1870-1988), (Kraków: Wydawnicwo ARKA, 1992), 15
10. Stanisław Markowski, *Krakowski Kazimierz*, 5
11. Simon Wiesenthal, *Every Day Remembrance Day* (New York: Henry Holt and Company, 1987), 181; David M. Crowe, *Oskar Schindler* (Boulder: Westview Press, 2004), 462-63
12. Israel Gutman ed. *Encyclopedia of the Holocaust* (New York: Macmillan, 1990), 833
13. Professor Johnathan Weber, from a lecture at the Sydney Jewish Museum, Sydney, 2011; http://polishgrammar.com/jewish-krakow/

PART 3

Together

Poland Post-World War II

Aftermath

On 30 April 1945, Adolf Hitler shot himself in his bunker in Berlin. His wife, Eva Braun, committed suicide by taking cyanide. Their remains were taken into the garden outside the bunker and set alight. The next day, on 1 May, General Hans Krebs met with General Vasily Chuikov, the commander of the Soviet forces in Berlin and requested a cease-fire. That evening Goebbels and his wife committed suicide, after having poisoned their six children with cyanide. On 7 May the Germans signed an unconditional surrender to take effect the next day: 8 May 1945, Victory in Europe, or V-E-Day.

During April and May 1945, Allied soldiers liberated the concentration camps in Germany. There they found as many dead prisoners as living ones. Those who had survived were starving and emaciated, many far too weak and sick to survive more than a day or two beyond their liberation. Adults on average weighed around thirty kilos.[1] When Mina was liberated on 23 April, she weighed thirty-five kilos!

In February 1945, while Jacob was making his way back to Wieruszów and Mina was still in Leipzig, the big three, Churchill,

Roosevelt and Stalin, met in Yalta to determine the future of Germany and the countries it had occupied. Poland was reduced in size by one-sixth, losing territory in the East, but gaining some land in the west. The new borders were drawn up at the Potsdam Conference of July-August 1945. The German cities of Danzig, Stettin and Breslau (renamed Gdańsk, Szczecin and Wrocław), plus all of Silesia (renamed Śląsk), were incorporated into Poland's territory.[2]

These border changes resulted in great population shifts and social upheaval in the immediate post-War years. More than a million Poles were repatriated from the border areas of Ukraine, Lithuania and Belorussia. These were now incorporated into the Soviet Union. At the same time, another quarter of a million returned from the Russian interior. In 1945-46, two million people settled in the new western provinces, its German population forcibly expelled.[3]

Of the 3.5 million Jews who had lived in Poland in 1939, 10 percent survived, the majority by escaping to the Soviet Union. Among the 160,000 repatriated by July 1946 was Jacob's eldest brother Berek. Some 50,000 had also survived hidden on the 'Aryan side' among non-Jews. Another 50,000, Jacob and Mina among them, had miraculously survived the ghettos and the camps.[4]

Newly-freed Jewish prisoners, or those repatriated from the Soviet Union, had no one to return to and nowhere to go. On reaching their home towns, they were often confronted with rejection, at times hate.[5]

Their family homes were in ruins or occupied by others, and finding a way to earn a living presented a real challenge. Jewish camp survivors who remained in Europe after the War were a tiny minority. They felt isolated to a degree rarely experienced before by any group of people. There were no graves to mark the burial places of their dead. All their loved ones, friends and acquaintances had disappeared without a trace.⁶

The Jewish population in post-War Poland was destitute, emaciated, ruined, sick, and traumatized.

Notes

1. Primo Levi and Leonardo De Benedetti, *Auschwitz Report* (Minerva Medica 1946; English version, London: Verso, 2006), 13-14; Gilbert, Martin, *Never Again: A History of the Holocaust* (London: HarperCollins Illustrated, 2002), 150; Ministerstwo Sprawidliwości Główna Komisja Badania Zbrodni Hitlerowskich w Polsce (Ministry of Justice Main Commission for the Investigation of German Crimes in Poland), *Obozy Hitlerowskie na ziemiach polskich 1939-45* (Hitler's Camps on Polish Soil 1939-45) (Warsaw: 1979), 364-65
2. http://en.wikipedia.org/wiki/Potsdam_Conference
3. Jan T. Gross, *Fear: Anti-Semitism in Poland after Auschwitz* (Princeton and Oxford: Princeton University Press, 2006), 22, 26; Anita Prażmowska, *Poland: A Modern History* (London: IB Tauris, 2010) 161, 164
4. Albert H. Friedländer, *Out of the Whirlwind* (Garden City, NY: Doubleday, 1968), 416-17
5. Gutman et al., *Anatomy of the Auschwitz Death Camp*, 477-80; Gilbert, *Never Again: A History of the Holocaust*, 150-51
6. Ibid.

23

Brzeg

The Meeting Place

By the end of May 1945, Jacob and Max started to share a vacant house in Brzeg with a couple of other Wieruszów survivors.

Following her liberation in Germany and return to Poland, Mina arrived in Brzeg towards the end of April 1945. She was with her 'camp family', Guta, Pola and the two Doras. They were joined by Jamina (Mina) Lippshütz, also a Leipzig survivor. The girls stayed in Brzeg while Mina travelled east to Kraków in search of her family.

In the months after the War ended, they also heard rumours of continuing danger throughout Poland for the remaining Jewish community. When she found no family members in Kraków, Mina decided to return to the west, hoping to find refuge in Brzeg. She knew that there was a strong Red Army presence there which, with the local police, offered some security. She and her friends joined the few hundred Jewish survivors who had gravitated to the area searching for a safe haven. She settled into an apartment with her friends.

Brzeg, on the banks of the River Odra, was named for the Polish word meaning shore. Between 1311 and 1675, it was the capital of Lower Silesia, much of which was part of the Kingdom of Bohemia.

MINA & JACOB

By the eighteenth century, Brzeg and most of Silesia had been annexed by Prussia and the city became part of Germany in 1871. Historical records show a Jewish presence in the town from the fourteenth century.

When the town was captured by Soviet troops on 6 February 1945, it became part of Poland under the provisions of the Potsdam Conference of August 1945.[1]

By mid-1945, Jacob and Mina, both torn from their lost families as teenagers or young adults, were now faced with creating their own community and support networks.

Mina recalled:[2]

> When we came to Brzeg, it was very hard to start living again! I wandered around crying while others were celebrating the liberation, dancing in the streets, singing songs. I said: 'What is there to celebrate? I've lost everybody. What's so good about this?'

So despite her life-saving ability to laugh and make the most of life, there was an underlying melancholy and sadness in Mina during these years.

Max Procel recalled:[3]

> I arrived in Wieruszów at the end of May 1945. There were already a few people at home, back from the camps. They often made a living by travelling into the countryside and bringing back a piece of butter, a few eggs. I said: 'This is not making a living.' So I and three others went by train to a place called Brzeg. It was an empty city, as the Germans had run away, scared of the Russians. We took a house: two storeys, with everything in it. The Soviet Army was stationed there

and they looked after the place. We started to do business with them. They controlled the shops and the warehouses and took whatever they could. We bought things from them and traded these goods in other parts of Poland. We were happy: we were making money, living.

Then one day one of my partners told me: 'I went into the city today and met some Jewish girls.' 'What, Jewish girls here?' I replied. I didn't know any still existed. They had come from Germany with the Soviet forces and were now staying in Brzeg. The Russian Commandant, a Jew, had given them permission to live in the Russian compound and they were working in the warehouses.

By then I had a motorbike, so we went there. We met six girls. I asked them: 'Where the hell did you come from?' They told us their story. They had been liberated near Leipzig in Germany. Now they were working for the Russians for a piece of bread, some onions and a bit of oil. I explained to them that I was in business and that we had money. They couldn't believe it. I also told them where the four of us lived. By this time we had some Germans working for us, cooking and cleaning. I went home and told the German woman who was working in the kitchen that tomorrow we would have some guests. She should make a special dinner.

When the girls came to our place, the table was laid in a way fit for a king or a queen, with porcelain and silver cutlery. All this had been left behind by the Germans. We sat there talking until early morning: four boys and six girls. The girls said to one of the girls, Guta: 'Go to Max and ask him if we can buy something.' They noticed that I already had eyes for her. So she came to me and asked if they could buy some provisions. I told her to take whatever she wanted. Two days later, she came again, and asked me if I could buy some more provisions for them on our next trip.

They started coming over regularly and I started talking seriously to Guta. Soon we were engaged. I was twenty-four and she was twenty. I went to Łódź, where I knew a few more people from my town, we made arrangements, and on 24 January 1946 we were married.

Freda explains:

According to Mina, it took Jacob almost a year to win her. He courted her earnestly, showering her with attention and gifts: a pair of beautifully-styled leather boots and a sewing machine. But she hesitated. They were from such different backgrounds and she really knew nothing about him. Physically he did not fit her image of a handsome man, since he was small and frail. But over time his kindness, gentleness, cheeky smile, warmth and inherent goodness convinced her. They were married in June 1946. Their wedding was held in one of the finest restaurants in Brzeg, with friends providing the music. Jacob managed to find some fine light grey fabric for Mina's wedding suit and a small piece of lace for her hair. Despite these modest beginnings, their happy union was to last for over fifty-eight years.

Mina recalled:[4]

Our wedding day was on 11 June 1946 in Brzeg. It was sad not having my family there. But there were about twenty-eight survivors, which was nice. I was pretty happy to at least have my friends with me, to help us celebrate.

> Our outfits were terrible. It was hard to get clothes or materials after the War. Later on, when one of my girlfriends also married, I gave her my outfit to wear.

Adele explains:

> From this group of young people, three other couples were to marry. Although they formed a close-knit extended family, they continually missed their loved ones and their lives before the War. These friendships were, however, to sustain them and last their whole lives.
>
> Following their marriage, Mina and Jacob established a home for themselves in a tiny apartment in Brzeg. Jacob began travelling the region, trading with the local farmers. He would buy valuables such as gold or silver and re-sell them in town.
>
> Then, in late 1946, Jacob learned that his eldest brother, Berek, had survived the War in the Soviet Union and had made his way back to Poland. There was a thirteen-year difference between the two brothers, with Berek the eldest and Jacob the youngest in the family. Jacob was overjoyed at this news and quickly made arrangements to travel to the north of the country to bring his brother, with his second wife, to Brzeg.
>
> But Jacob was also to learn that there were no other survivors from his immediate or extended families.

Bella Grill (nee Nejman) described Brzeg at that time:[5]

> When the War broke out, my parents and I escaped from Warsaw to the Soviet Union. My brothers, Michał and Jasiu, joined the Army as volunteers in what became the Armja

Wasilewska, a Polish division of the Red Army that was stationed close to the Afghan border.[6]

In 1946 we were allowed to return to Poland and settled in Wrocław. My two brothers were still in the Army and we didn't know where they were.

In Wrocław there were special offices where they had lists of people looking for their families and my father found Jasiu, still in the Army, stationed in Brzeg. So we packed our bags again and went to live there.

The city was not badly damaged. The destruction was largely of the area around the Odra River. It was a very lovely German city, full of greenery, parks and the river. It was peaceful! At that time, it had a population of some 40,000, with a small Jewish community that had mostly returned from the Soviet Union. The Air Force had a large base inside the city which had taken over the German barracks, while the Polish Army was stationed outside the city. We settled into an apartment and that's when I met Jacob Widawski, through my brother Jasiu. I was twelve years old at the time.

Max Procel recalled:[7]

> Then all of a sudden, we had to leave Brzeg. We had received a letter from the Armja Krajowa, that antisemitic group, which warned that if we didn't leave, one of us would be shot. So we left the city and settled in Wrocław.

In late 1946 or early 1947, Mina and Jacob also relocated from Brzeg to Wrocław. They hoped that the larger Jewish community already there would provide greater security.

Mina recalled:[8]

When I first returned to Poland, my dream was to live in Kraków. For everyone, the place that is naturally dear to your heart is where you grew up. But it was unbelievably hard: you couldn't get a flat there as not a lot of building was going on in the first few years after the War. After a short time in the small town of Brzeg, we decided that it would be safer in a larger city and moved to Wrocław. We got a flat there easily and I said to myself: 'If I have to learn to forget my family, I have also to forget Kraków.'

For Mina and Jacob, as for most Polish Jews, there was no going back to their towns and villages and fulfilling their desire to take up their pre-War lives. The country they knew had changed beyond recognition. They now had to establish and live new lives, without family or external support, under a new socio-political system.

During the Nazi occupation, an elaborate network of Underground institutions had been set up in Poland: the Armia Krajowa or AK (Home Army), plus clandestine versions of pre-war political parties. Once Poland was liberated, the Polish government-in-exile had no authority over the liberated areas and Soviet-sponsored organizations filled the power vacuum. The Polish Committee of National Liberation, PKWN, formed a provisional government on 31 December 1944. On 19 January 1945, a new government was established, with Edward Osóbka-Morawski, as Prime Minister and Władysław Gomułka as Deputy Prime Minister.[9]

'Free elections' were held on 19 January 1947, with the Polska Partia Robotnicza or PPR (Polish Workers Party), obtaining the majority vote. The consolidation of Soviet control of Poland was completed within a year of this election, with total power vested within the newly-formed Polska Zjednoczona Partia Robotnicza, PZPR (United Polish Workers' Party). Civil society, in the form of associations, self-help groups, producers' co-operatives and cultural clubs, all became subject to central control.[10]

With the onset of the Cold War, Polish territories were treated as a security zone and Soviet troops were stationed throughout the country, especially at the border with Germany. West European states limited all economic, social and cultural contacts with Poland, accepting its place within the Soviet bloc.[11]

Economically, Poland was in dire straits. The War had destroyed the country's infrastructure and production. Withdrawing German forces had either dismantled industries and moved production to the Third Reich, or had destroyed what they could not take with them.[12]

The border changes meant vital resources were lost, which delayed the country's recovery. The state took over control of industrial production and imposed pro-socialist socio-economic policies on agriculture, on small-scale factories and on retail outlets. The aim was to force a rapid pace of recovery prioritizing heavy and extractive industries. As a consequence, consumer and light industries were neglected and shortages of everyday goods became the norm. The black economy began to flourish.[13]

Writer Jerzy Kosinski described the situation:[14]

> I knew quiet lanes where young girls solicited men older than my father. I found places where men dressed in smart clothes with gold watches on their wrists traded in objects the very possession of which could get them years in prison. I saw the militia organize a manhunt and I saw armed civilians killing a soldier. In daytime the world was at peace. The War continued at night.

From 1945, the Polish government passed a series of decrees temporarily making the state the trustee of 'abandoned property', which applied primarily to former Jewish properties. Since Jews had made up one-third of Poland's urban population and the majority of them had been killed, these properties represented a sizeable body of real estate. In Wrocław, the local militia took over the synagogue building even though the Mayor had already assigned it to the Wrocław Jewish Committee.[15] Jewish cemeteries and synagogues continued to be ruined as local people carted away roofs, bricks, tombstones or anything of use to their own construction projects.[16]

The illicit and illegal theft of Jewish property during the War became one of the underlying reasons of subsequent conflict between Poles and Jews. Not only were returning survivors often greeted with hostility, but in some instances with violence.

Within a year of the end of the War, more than 1,000 Jews had been murdered on Polish soil, by Poles. They were attacked when they came to ask for the return of homes, workshops or belongings they had left with Poles.

Jan Kowalczyk, Kraków Voivodeship Commissar for Productization of the Jewish Population, wrote to the Presidium of the District Commission of the Labour Unions:[17]

> It is an undeniable fact that the living conditions of the Jewish population in country towns are extremely difficult. Because of the terror of reactionary elements, the Jewish population runs away from these locations in order to save their lives, and concentrates in larger towns.

MINA & JACOB

Photos from Brzeg found in a box belonging to Guta and Max Procel,
donated by their son, Harry, in 2011.
Top: Mina (left) and Dorota (Dora) Rosenthal, 1945.
Bottom: At a friend's wedding: 1. Guta and Max Procel and
2. Jacob, Brzeg, 1946.

MINA & JACOB

Top: Mina's and Jacob's wedding day, Brzeg, 11 June 1946.
Bottom: Mina recalled: 'This photo was taken in Brzeg not long after our wedding. We are with Dora, my closest friend from Leipzig. I am wearing the light grey suit which was my wedding outfit.'

11 June 1994, forty-eight years later! Mina and Jacob celebrating their anniversary at the Ratuszowa restaurant, Brzeg.

MINA & JACOB

Notes

1. https://brzeg.pl/miasto/rys-historyczny/; http://en.wikipedia.org/wiki/Brzeg; http://en.wikipedia.org/wiki/Potsdam_Conference
2. Mina Widawski nee Laub, audio testimony for the *12th Hour Project of Oral Testimonies* (Sydney: Australian Institute for Holocaust Studies, 1990); video testimony (Sydney: USC Shoah Foundation Institute, 1995), code 2526
3. Max Procel, video testimony (Melbourne: USC Shoah Foundation Institute, 1997), code 30561
4. Mina Widawski, *12th Hour Project of Oral Testimonies*; USC Shoah Foundation, code 2526
5. Bella Grill, interview with Freda Widawski, Sydney, 2011
6. http://en.wikipedia.org/wiki/Wanda_Wasilewska
7. Max Procel, video testimony, USC Shoah Foundation, code 30561
8. Mina Widawski, *12th Hour Project of Oral Testimonies*; USC Shoah Foundation, code 2526
9. Jan T. Gross, *Fear: Anti-Semitism in Poland after Auschwitz* (Princeton, New Jersey: Princeton University Press, 2006), 5-7, 12-14; 19; Anita Prażmowska, *Poland: A Modern History* (London: IB Tauris, 2010), 161-62
10. Grzegorz Berendta, ed., *Społeczność Żydowska w PRL przed kampanią antysemicką lat 1967-68 i po niej*, (The Jewish Community in PRL before the Anti-Semitic Campaign during the Years 1967-68, and After), (Warsaw: Instytut Pamięci Narodowej, IPN, Institute of National Remembrance, 2009), 42; Prażmowska, *Poland: A Modern History*, 168-70
11. Prażmowska, *Poland: A Modern History*, 179-80
12. Prażmowska, *Poland: A Modern History*, 171; Roman Polanski, *Roman* (New York: William Morrow and Company, 1984), 40
13. Prażmowska, *Poland: A Modern History*, 172-73, 175
14. Jerzy Kosinski, *The Painted Bird* (USA: Houghton Mifflin Harcourt, 1965), 280
15. Gross, *Fear: Anti-Semitism in Poland*, 47-48, 51
16. Jean E. Brown et al., *Images from the Holocaust: A Literature Anthology* (Lincolnwood, Illinois: NTC Publishing Group, 1997), 376; Gross, *Fear: Anti-Semitism in Poland*, 36, 39-40
17. In Gross, *Fear: Anti-Semitism in Poland*, 29, 134-37

24
Life in Wrocław

In early 1947, Mina and Jacob moved to Wrocław, some forty-five kilometres from Brzeg. They settled in an apartment at 30 ul. Niemcewicza. Their Książeczka Stanu Cywilnego (ID/resident's card) shows that they were still living there in December 1952.

Breslau, located on the Odra River, is an ancient settlement and capital of the region of Śląsk.[1] Before World War II, it was the largest and most important city of eastern Germany, with 620,000 inhabitants. It contained a university, several theatres, parks, an airport, railway stations and a zoo, and produced daily newspapers. There were large factories and markets.[2]

Breslau had a flourishing Jewish community of approximately 20,000, among them wealthy merchants, physicians, and scientists of national and international reputation. However, within six years of Hitler's ascent to power, their number had halved and by late 1941, only 8,000 were left.[3]

In January 1945, with the Soviet Army advancing, Hitler had ordered Festung-Breslau (Fortress Breslau) to be defended to the last man. When the survivors of the garrison finally surrendered to Soviet forces after the fall of Berlin, over 70 percent of this historic city had been demolished.[4]

The new Polish-German boundaries established at Potsdam in August 1945 included Breslau (now named Wrocław) within Polish territory. At that time, the city had a German population of close to 190,000, with a Polish population of just 17,000. However, during 1945-47, almost all of the German inhabitants fled or were forcibly expelled and resettled in Germany. The city was repopulated by Polish and Jewish refugees: camp survivors; Jews repatriated from the Soviet Union; and deportees from Polish lands annexed by the Russians. For example, much of the population and many of the institutions of Lwów, together with thousands of their employees and possessions were transported west and resettled in the rubble of the abandoned city.[5]

By the end of 1946, the Jews living in Wrocław had reached some 15,000.[6]

Leo Kantor, in his film *W Poszukiwaniu Utraconego Krajobrazu* (In Search of a Lost Land), observed:[7]

> **Wrocław became the largest enclave of Holocaust survivors. They all arrived almost broke. All their property had been confiscated, burned or looted. They lined up in queues for food packages and clothing which were sent by Jewish charitable agencies from the West.**

Hersz Friedman, a friend of ours, recalls:[8]

> **My family and I arrived in Wrocław from the Soviet Union towards the end of 1946. My father's sisters and their families were already living there, in an apartment block which stood on the corner of ul. Niemcewicza and Olbińska. We settled into the same building. Across the courtyard was a second block where Mina and Jacob lived.**

MINA & JACOB

Mina recalled:[9]

> And then our children were born: Adele and Freda. Adele is named after my mother, because in Jewish tradition we name our children after our ancestors. She was born on 7 December 1949. Freda was born on my birthday, 9 November 1951. We named her Freda Bronia (Brucha), after my sister and Jacob's mother.

Adele observes:

> I was born just four years after the War ended. It's remarkable, given that Mina was skeletal at the end of the War, weighing thirty-five kilos with her body starved of nutrients for six years, upsetting her biological rhythms. She had worried about not being able to conceive or bear children, so important to both her and Jacob. They very much wanted to have a family again, to recreate in some small measure what had been lost. Because they were young, with better nourishment, they slowly grew stronger and healthier. Jacob was always relatively healthy and strong, although plagued by chronic ulcers and stomach cramps.
>
> When she was pregnant, Mina glowed with happiness. Mum was to tell me later how thrilled she was that, while I was a relatively small baby, everything went well physically for mother and child. Emotionally, it was a difficult time for her, since she missed her own mother and sister very much and envied other new mothers who had family support. Happily, two years later another bouncy, healthy daughter completed their little family. Family legend indicates that I was very curious about my baby sister and sometimes poked

her to annoy her when she was a toddler. But overall, born only two years apart, we have been very close and enjoy a special relationship.

By this time many of our parents' friends were also expanding their families. They continued to give each other support.

In early 1953, the family relocated to 17B Kluczborska Street. Their apartment on Niemcewicza was taken over by Jacob's brother Berek and his growing family, who had also moved to Wrocław from Brzeg.

Adele remembers their life on Kluczborska Street:

> It is Friday night and our tiny apartment is very clean and the enticing aromas of food fill the air. Our apartment consists of one large open room divided into two spaces. One, a small alcove cordoned off with a curtain, Jacob and Mina use as their bedroom. The other part we use as our sitting and dining room; with a small area serving as our children's bedroom. Large windows look out over the building's courtyard. Between the two zones a huge floor-to-ceiling tiled stove provides warmth for the apartment. Dad fills it with coal which he has to bring up from the cellar, four flights of stairs below.
>
> We have a large kitchen which holds a big wooden table on which Mum does her sewing and cooking preparations. We do not have a bathroom, but instead share a toilet with our immediate neighbour. In winter, the water freezes over so we use buckets of warm water from the kitchen to flush. We have no bath and like most people use a local public bathhouse. Mum has to fill a large tub with water so that my sister and I can have a bath in the kitchen.

This is an old building, probably dating back to the eighteenth century, and it is very forbidding in its darkness. You enter from the street via a huge iron gate which opens onto a cobblestoned walkway which leads to a wide staircase on the left or straight to an outside courtyard, which then connects with a similar building at the back of the complex. We imagine horse-drawn carriages passing through the heavy iron gate.

Streetlights are still powered in the early 1950s by gaslight. These lights are beautiful in their design and decoration and hold a special fascination for me. We have regular visits from chimney sweeps. One spring I watch a stork busy building his new home atop one of the chimneys and am fascinated to hear that he has flown all the way from Africa.

Freda recalls:

As a child I remember spending hours sitting on the wide window ledge looking down into the courtyard and at the building opposite. We lived on the third floor, and I loved jumping down several stairs at a time, as if flying.

The main entrance to the building, which was often unlit and smelled of urine and alcohol, was a great source of fear for me as a child and to this day fills me with anxiety and foreboding.

Hersz Friedman recalls the public bath-house:[10]

The Rzymska Łaźnia or Roman Bath-house, was located on a little street off ul. Świdnicka. It was for both men and women, but they came on different days. You had hot and cold showers there and everything that you needed.

> I used to go to there on Saturdays after work to meet my friends. It became a social meeting place. We would bring a bottle of vodka, something to 'bite on': drink, talk and go into the water. We would spend a couple of hours there, relaxing together. [The Jewish bath-house, the mikva, was next to the synagogue.]

Life in socialist Poland during the 1950s was marked by food shortages, lack of commodities and infrastructure; political repression and arbitrary arrests. Poland was now under the Soviet sphere of influence both domestically and in foreign policy. This meant rejection of Western values; relentless anti-West propaganda; censorship of any information from the 'outside'; and a ban on personal communications with the West. Bigotry and antisemitism prevailed.

Because the state owned all forms of production, dual economies existed side by side: the official economy and the underground, illegal one. Officially, urban workers, including professionals, now classified as public servants, earned their meagre wages in government-operated offices, factories and co-operatives, or in a small number of privately-owned shops. Consumer goods were rationed and mostly available only after queuing for hours on end—sometimes 'just in case'. In the unofficial economy, everybody made 'a little something on the side', either by trading on the black market or by selling their services or access to goods, for some extra cash or those hard-to-buy items. Luxury items were available in specialty shops, where these scarce goods could only be bought with foreign currency (American dollars or Deutschmarks).[11]

Jacob used the organizing skills he had acquired in the camps to provide for his family: to *załatwić zprawy* (organize or wangle) within the underground economy. Officially he worked in a small clothing factory. Unofficially, he made a living 'na lewo' (on the side), trading in goods that he acquired from farmers or small-shop owners that he knew in Wieruszów. Often, he obtained lengths of fabric that they had been allocated as a consignment from the government. In addition, he and Mina made clothing for sale. He would trade these and the fabrics at the Hala Targowa (Market Hall) or on the black market, which in the early 1950s was located at Biskupa Nankiera Square, across the road from the Hall. He would also sell them to friends, tailors that he knew in Wrocław.[12]

Hersz Friedman recalls:[13]

> I worked for the tailoring factory Zgoda, but sometimes I did other work on the side, to make a bit more income. So I would go to the Hala Targowa and purchase some material from people there such as Jacob.

Adele explains:

> During the 1950s social services, health, schools, universities, transport and the arts were heavily subsidized by the government. This meant that most people had access to concerts, operas and the cinema.
>
> Food and clothes were scarce, poorly-made or unavailable. I recall Mum asking me to stand in line at the baker's or the local grocer's. She would come later to join me as the line snaked on for metres. I was also sent by my teacher to buy her two slices of cheese or ham for lunch.
>
> By 1956, some private farm holdings and small-scale private enterprises were permitted. Farmers were allowed to keep small plots, and those who met the government-set production quotas were permitted to keep any additional

produce, or resell it and keep the profit. This is how Jacob's friends, the Frankowski family, were able to on-sell some of their produce. Poland relied on the farming sector to supply necessary food and other produce, and the Soviet model of collectivization was less rigidly followed.

One of Jacob's illegal activities included the sale of gold watches on the black market for hard currency, especially American dollars. He undertook this on behalf of an old camp friend from Kahlfelde, David Hercygier, who was by then living in Berlin. David's girlfriend, Ewa Lemberg, smuggled the watches into Poland and brought them to Jacob for sale.

Unfortunately, unknown to Jacob, Ewa was at that time under investigation for espionage. When she was arrested, all her associates were caught in the net, including Jacob.

Adele recalls:

> One evening Dad didn't return home from the city. Mum was very worried: without a private phone, communication was difficult. She had no idea where he was, or where to look for him. While a neighbour took care of us, Mum, sick with worry, ran to look for him at the local shops that he frequented, some of which had Jewish managers. She searched for him in the city centre and among the Hala Targowa stands. There was no trace of her husband.
>
> When nothing had been heard for a couple of days, Mum ran for help to Joseph Frenkiel, a Jewish neighbour and a well-known and highly-respected criminal lawyer. Two generations of the Frenkiel family had survived the War in the Soviet Union and returned to Poland in 1945.
>
> They lived across the street from us, and while not close

friends, some contact had been established between the two families courtesy of Mum's dress-making skills. She created made-to-measure garments for Mr Frenkiel's wife, sister and mother. They also had a special soft spot for Mum, since members of their extended family came from the Kraków region.

Mr Frenkiel made enquiries and discovered that Dad had been arrested, accused of smuggling and 'speculation'; of dealing in foreign exchange; and of being a 'Western spy'. These were serious and politically-charged offences in Poland. There was no telling how long Dad would have to stay in prison before the case against him went to court, nor any indication of its possible outcome.

Jacob's arrest and interrogation records show that he was arrested on 16 April 1954 by the Ministerstwo Bezpieczeństwa Publicznego, MBP (Ministry of Public Security) or UB. He was charged with illegal trading in foreign currency and sentenced to three years' imprisonment. In court he was represented by Mr Frenkiel. Thankfully he was cleared of any involvement with Ewa's alleged espionage activities. No information is available about her fate.[14]

Freda recalls:

Dad coped with his imprisonment by using the skills that he had acquired in the camps: his ability to talk to anyone and his warmth and charm. In later life he described doing alterations to clothes and making a suit for the prison warden, who in turn 'looked after' him.

Mina was left alone to support herself and her two daughters, aged five and three. Without extended family to rely on, she used her ingenuity and skills to earn a little bit of income. She made cloth dolls on consignment and did alterations. She also relied on the assistance offered by her Jewish friends and neighbours. She would often leave me with our neighbours, the Kesler family, when going out to deliver her completed work, taking Adele, who was older and could walk further, with her. The Keslers lived across the corridor and were the only other Jewish family in our apartment block.

The Frenkiels were also a great source of moral and practical support, giving Mina sewing work whenever they could.

Mum was ashamed of Dad's imprisonment and frightened of what reprisals the authorities might take against her. She hid his true whereabouts, teaching us to tell those who asked that our father was 'away in the Army'.

Adele remembers:

Mum had to become the sole provider for her children. I recall watching her make the cloth dolls, her fingers nimble and quick as she completed each new creation. One morning I woke to see her still bending over her sewing and realized that she had not slept at all, working throughout the night. She was having great trouble making ends meet with no family to turn to for support or financial help.

Sometimes one of Dad's Wieruszów friends came to visit, bringing gifts of bags of potatoes or chicken or meat packages or other food. Dad's old friend and neighbour, Mrs Frankowska, frequently travelled to Wrocław to sell her farm produce at the city's market. She stayed with us for the night and shared items she had brought with her.

Our Jewish friends in Wrocław helped as much as they

could, although Mum was too proud to ask them for financial help. The Nejmans, a Jewish family my parents knew from Brzeg, tried to help her by coming to visit to provide her with some support. They often brought food or produce.

Sadly, the stress, poor diet and long hours affected Mum's health and the consequences were very serious. She developed rheumatic fever and had to be hospitalized for some weeks. Before she was admitted, she had to get a couple of her friends to take us in.

Freda and I were separated. She stayed with the Kożuch family while I was sent to the Lippshütz family. I found the separation from both my mother and Freda very difficult. The family tried to be kind to me, but their two sons were some years older than I was and both parents were distant and reserved. The loneliness and the separation from my loved ones caused nightly nightmares and embarrassing bed-wetting. One day, in a desperate effort to hide the offending sheets, I stuffed them into the bedroom cupboard. Mrs Lippshütz found them and became very cross with me for not telling her. I think I was about five years old at the time. She must have found the whole experience quite demanding and difficult.

Freda was younger, and overall had an easier time adjusting to our changed circumstances. The Kożuch family had two daughters and a son. Mrs Kożuch had a reputation for generosity of spirit, hospitality, great cooking and baking skills and for being very warm. I recall Mrs Lippshütz taking me for a visit to the Kożuch home, probably realizing that visiting my sister and the others would lift my spirits.

Thankfully, Mum recovered and after several weeks we were happily reunited.

Freda remembers:

Because of the time that I spent with them, the Keslers and the Kożuchs were always close to my heart. The Kesler family consisted of three generations: an elderly couple and their invalid bachelor son Hersz and their daughter, Annia, with her husband David Ringel and daughter Renia, who was a year older than me. Similarly, Cesia Kożuch was like a beloved aunty, someone who always represented warmth and safety.

Adele describes visiting Jacob:

I recall one very long, bleak train trip to visit Dad in prison. It was winter or autumn, cold and rainy, the grey sky underscoring our mood. Mr Nejman escorted us on this trip and I recall how grateful Mum was for his help. We had a very brief visit with Dad. I remember his hugging us close to him. Then there was the long trip back to Wrocław.

Freda recalls:

I have only one memory of going to visit Dad. I am in a long, dim tunnel, at the end of which stands my father. I run towards him and into his outstretched arms.

Although sentenced to three years, Dad was released from prison early, as part of the general amnesty of 1956. He had to adjust to civilian life again and Mina to having him back home. Mum made sure that Dad had time alone with us, to get reacquainted. She would send us out together to the cinema, to the park or to visit friends.

However, the consequences of his imprisonment remained with the family for a long time. I recall the police or the secret service coming into the apartment late one evening and conducting a search, including under our beds. This frightened me greatly, as Adele and I were alone with our elderly babysitter, Mum and Dad having gone out. The fear of police stayed with me for the rest of my childhood.

Adele remembers:

While Dad was in prison, Freda and I attended a day care centre, where I recall getting a disgusting porridge for lunch: it was cold and difficult to chew and digest. To this day, I cannot eat porridge or tofu.

In 1956, aged seven, I entered the local public primary school, on ul. Nowowiejska, a major road nearby. There were several children in our street who also attended the same school and, as we grew older, we walked to and from school on our own. I was a good student and my two best friends were also at the top of the class. We considered ourselves superior beings, privately making fun of our slower-witted classmates.

As I matured, I began to pepper my parents with questions about our small family and the missing grandparents, aunties, uncles and cousins. My Gentile friends talked about visits from family at Christmas, or how they were making plans to visit grandparents and other extended family during the annual school vacations.

My earliest memory, when I was no older than four or five, was being conscious of Mum's distress. She was lighting candles and tears were running down her cheeks. I saw her unhappiness and was confused. She was the one who usually gave comfort and wiped away the tears when I fell or hurt myself. I asked her why she was crying. She told me that she was feeling sad and missing her family. But she was quick to reassure me.

I also recall Mum's obvious distress on hearing some neighbours talk in German. In Wrocław during the early 1950s, there was still a sizeable population of ethnic Germans, or Poles of German descent who spoke German. If Mum heard them speaking while taking a walk, she would turn pale and become visibly distressed. When I asked about it, she explained that she did not like the sound of the language.

I was aware from an early age how much Mum missed her family and that something called the Wojna (War) had been a very, very bad thing. Overall, our parents tried to protect us from the horrors they had gone through, adjusting their explanations and recollections as we matured.

Aged nine, I began to study history and learned the bitter truth of the fate of Polish Jews, including our family's experiences. Troubling questions and later, real anger and resentment towards our fellow Poles were never far from the surface. Every day our teachers tried to convey socialist ideals of equality of opportunity and equal rights for all. I found it difficult to reconcile the friendly attitude they, fellow students and the Gentiles I was coming to know showed towards me with the stories I was hearing of betrayal, indifference and cruelty shown to the Jews during the War by their Polish friends and neighbours. 'Where were you when my people went to their slaughter?' I asked. 'Why did you not help or do more? It is acknowledged that association with Jews was strictly forbidden under the German Occupation, the penalty possible death. You did not have to be a friend, but did many of you have to betray your Jewish neighbours who were hiding from the Gestapo?' I remember feeling such anger. The idea that fear, greed or avarice could make people behave in such inhumane ways was shocking.

I learned that Jewish cemeteries, synagogues and places of religious significance had been destroyed or vandalized. People showed no respect for other religions and stole bricks and headstones to use as building materials. Where was the Church and the pious Christians? They showed themselves to be lacking in morality, humanity and compassion. 'You call yourselves Christians and claim to love your fellow man,' I thought. 'Why doesn't this include Jews? Why were my parents' families massacred?'

I was filled with anger and rage. My parents tried to explain the history of antisemitism in Poland, but I'd met the parents and grandparents of my classmates and they were kind to me. They did not seem to hold these antisemitic views. Or did they?

Jews returning from the Soviet Union told stories of poverty and famine there during the War, of the millions who perished in the bitter cold winters. But they also recalled the kindness shown them by the Russian people: 'We were starving, dying from hunger, but so were most Russians. At least we did not fear for our lives,' was often repeated. I heard this from Mr Frenkiel and his family and the Keslers, among many others.

I will always be grateful to my parents who, despite their own traumatic experiences and sadness, did not transfer their pain or hatred to us. They went to great lengths to stress that, despite their experiences, they believed that there were good and bad people among Poles and even Germans. Jacob's and

MINA & JACOB

Mina's experiences were different; each had different ways of coping with the horror they endured. But they were united in instilling a sense of balance to what I was discovering and my angry reaction to what I was learning.

MINA & JACOB

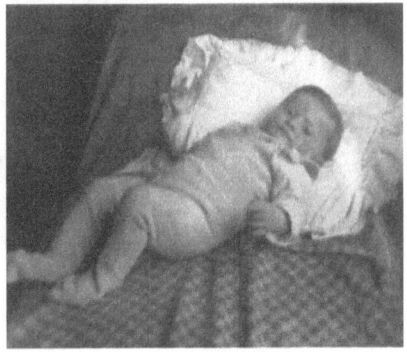

Top: (left) Mina in 1947. (right) Jacob, Mina and Max, Wrocław, 1947.
Bottom: (left) Adele (Adela), born 7 December 1949.
(left) Freda (Fredzia) Bronia, born 9 November 1951.

MINA & JACOB

Mina with Mosze Kożuch and his children and Adele, (front centre, in fur-trimmed coat and white stockings). Wrocław, 1950.

Top: Adele and Freda on a toboggan, 1953.
Bottom: Mina with Freda and Adele in our park, Wrocław 1956.
Adele is in her school uniform.

MINA & JACOB

The apartment block where the family lived
on ul. Kluczborska 17B, Wrocław. Photo 2008.

Adele and Freda in front of the apartment block. Photo 2008.

MINA & JACOB

Top: Adele on the right, and Braha (Berek's daughter), in the courtyard of no. 30 ul. Niemcewicza. Photo taken 2015.
Bottom: Mena (Berek's youngest son) in front of 30 ul. Niemcewicza, 2015.

Top: Hersz Friedman (right) in the tailors' co-operative Zgoda, Wrocław 1954. Jadwiga Feszter Konin wrote: 'In the uniform department of the Zgoda co-operative worked the foreman Hersz Frydman [this was the Polish spelling adopted by the authorities for Hersz's surname]. As long as the Jews ran the co-operative, we lived well, but after they left for Israel and the States, it struggled.'[15]
Bottom: Hala Targowa (Market Hall) where Jacob traded. Photo 2010.

MINA & JACOB

Notes

1. Adam Zamoyski, *Poland: A Traveller's Gazetteer* (London: John Murray in association with Azimuth Editions, 2001), 268
2. Ibid.
3. Walter Laqueur and Richard Brietman, *Breaking the Silence*, (London: The Bodley Head, 1986), 117-18
4. Michael Moran, *A Country in the Moon: Travels in Search of the Heart of Poland* (London: Granta Books, 2009), 315-16; Norman Davies, *God's Playground* (New York: Columbia University Press, 1981), 382
5. Norman Davies, *God's Playground*, 374-75, 382; Moran, *A Country in the Moon*, 315-16; http://en.wikipedia.org/wiki/Wroc%C5%82aw;
6. http://wroclaw.jewish.org.pl/gmina-i-centrum/historia-gminy/
7. Leo Kantor, *W poszukiwaniu utraconego krajobrazu* (In Search of a Lost Landscape), 2014 https://www.youtube.com/watch?v=dytss8MxKiw&feature=youtu.be
8. Hersz Friedman, interview with Freda Widawski, 2011, Sydney
9. Mina Widawski nee Laub, audio testimony for the *12th Hour Project of Oral Testimonies* (Sydney: Australian Institute for Holocaust Studies, 1990); video testimony (Sydney: USC Shoah Foundation Institute, 1995), code 2526
10. Hersz Friedman, interview with Freda Widawski
11. Anita Prażmowska, *Poland: A Modern History* (London: IB Tauris, 2010), 179
12. Marek Hłasko, *Piękni Dwudziestoletni* (Beautiful Twenty-year-olds), (Warszawa: Da Capo, 1995), 10
13. Hersz Friedman, interview with Freda Widawski
14. Instytut Pamięcia Narodowej/IPN (Institute of National Remembrance), Wrocław, 2010
15. Gołda Tencer, ed., *And I still see their faces: Images of Polish Jews* (Fundacja Shalom/Shalom Foundation), plate 45; http://motlc.wiesenthal.com/site/pp.asp?c=jmKYJeNVJrF&b=479021

25
Recreating Culture

The Jews who settled in Dolny (Lower) Śląsk felt more confident and united together, despite religious differences and divergent political views. (There were eleven political parties!) Wrocław's newly-formed Jewish community set about creating a cultural life, and this was to become a vehicle for their post-war identity.

In May 1945, the Jewish Committee Office was established on ul. Włodkowic. It took on the running of the White Stork Synagogue, three prayer houses, a canteen and youth dormitories. A number of Jewish organizations, schools and co-operatives were also set-up.[1] However, as the Communist Party gained more and more control in Poland, Jewish organizations came under its jurisdiction. Towarzystwo Społeczno-Kulturalne Żydów w Polsce, TSKŻ (the Jewish Social and Cultural Association in Poland) was founded and regional Jewish community bodies were forcibly merged into it.

Despite such external pressures, by the end of 1946 there were four Jewish schools in Wrocław: primary, music, ballet and high schools. The Jewish Academics Club, an active, vibrant Jewish student association, was also established. The first university degree attained by a Jew was celebrated by the entire community.[2]

In late 1946, a professional Yiddish Theatre of Dolny Śląsk was created in Wrocław. Shalom Aleichem's play *The Bloody Joke* was the first performance. On 2 April 1949 the theatre found a permanent home at 28 ul. Świdnicka. It was built by volunteer labour with donations collected by the Jewish community from all over Dolny Śląsk. The legendary Jewish star Ida Kamińska performed there and was also the theatre's Director. She convinced Jakub Rotbaum, one of the most celebrated Yiddish theatre directors of the time to return from abroad and take the position of Artistic Director.

The theatre was the most popular form of entertainment in the Jewish community, since it served as a window into a world of values and traditions that no longer existed. It provided free entertainment on Friday evenings, as well as concerts, assemblies and works commemorating the Warsaw Ghetto Uprising. Initially it functioned as an independent Jewish institution without government intervention. Despite the imposition of the socialist realist style, it managed to some extent to perform pieces with Jewish character.

Adolf Rudnicki noted:[3]

> These days when I want to breathe in the air of my fathers' world, the only place that I can find it is in Yiddish theatre. The theatre is the only relic of that life.

Adele recalls:

> Freda and I attended the Torah and Yiddish language classes and took part in concerts at the Jewish Theatre. I recall with pleasure my sister's star turn in front of the community, where she did a great job reciting an old and difficult poem in Yiddish. This reduced Mum to tears. In the same concert, we two sisters performed a little dance routine, with me freezing in terror on stage. Freda saved the performance by dancing around my unmoving figure, making us both look good.

Freda recalls this time:

> I remember my school years with fondness, particularly one teacher whose name escapes me. She was warm and loving to her students. I enjoyed learning and had a number of friends, all non-Jews, whose names I also don't recall—with the exception of a little girl named Jola. I was always on the plump side and learned very early how to laugh at myself, to forestall any embarrassment or hurt from being called names. I personally never felt any antisemitism, although there were Jewish girls in my class who did. I felt liked by both my teachers and fellow students.
>
> Adele and I would walk to school together every morning. Quite often our mother would be there during the day, assisting the teachers or attending a parent-teacher meeting and she would walk home with us. Our uniform consisted of a dark navy satin coat with a white collar, which we wore over our clothing. Our hair was adorned with bright white bows. In winter, to walk through the snow, we wore two pairs of shoes with coats, scarves, warm hats and gloves.
>
> From an early age I loved drawing, which was encouraged at school. I remember creating bright decorative boarders at the bottom of the pages of my exercise books. I also drew dark industrial landscapes with coal trains and heavy machinery, in line with the socialist realism of the time we were living through.
>
> I learned ballet at the Jewish Ballet School, and attended ballet camps.
>
> For a while I was a member of the Yiddish Children's Theatre, and remember being given long poems and songs to recite. As I did not speak Yiddish, these were spelled out

phonetically in Polish script, which I had to memorize. One of the songs was the famous *Papirosen* (from the Polish word papierosy) about Jewish children selling cigarettes outside the Ghetto walls.

Two Jewish periodicals were published in Dolny Śląsk, the Polish-language *Nowe Życie* and *Niderszlezji* (*Lower Silesia*) in Yiddish. By 1947 the Jewish community had established libraries, community centres, choirs and orchestras.[4]

Adele recalls:

> Our parents tried to pass on their Yiddishkeit (Jewish way of life) to us. Dad described his life in his small town and his relationship with his extended family: how most people attended prayers daily, kept Kosher and observed the Sabbath. The vibrant Jewish culture of his boyhood included Yiddish language newspapers, books and music. Some young boys studied in yeshivas (Jewish religious schools), while others, as he had, learned trades or skills necessary to survive in a small town or rural area. He told us about the youth camps he attended and his Leftist-Zionist awakening. He remembered how many Gentiles such as his family's neighbours proved to be good friends, and tried their best to help their Jewish neighbours. He described the many Jewish families who lived in abject poverty.
>
> Mum told us wonderful stories from the Torah, or described her girlhood in Kraków. She spoke of the vibrant Jewish community that had once thrived in her city. She recalled the family's celebration of Shabbat and the customs of tzedakah and mitzvoim (the joy of giving). She told us how they came together for the High Holidays, about the magnificent

synagogues and the fun of Purim. She described singing in a choir and her Zionist awakening as a member of the Akiva youth group.

Dad and Mum sometimes spoke to one another in Yiddish at home. We attended the High Holidays' services in the Synagogue. It was not possible to attend Shabbat services, since the only synagogue in Wrocław was a very long tram ride away. Mum and Dad were more traditional than religious in their observance, despite each having grown up in religious families. They always lit candles and made special dinners on Friday nights. Dad would sometimes reflect on his lack of faith. He said that he could not believe in God, given the horror of the events he had witnessed.

By the mid-1950s Wrocław's small Jewish community was well-organized, despite the huge difficulties it still faced. For example, there were very few men able to conduct prayers and the community had great difficulty finding or retaining a rabbi. Our neighbour, David Ringel, who was a cantor, often led the congregation in prayers.

It was also difficult to obtain kosher meat or other products. The community had very few resources and funding depended on the generosity of Jewish aid agencies based in the United States, Australia and Britain. Nevertheless, a community centre was established which was largely manned by volunteers. It housed a kosher kitchen and a club with a meeting place like a drop-in centre. There was the small Yiddish theatre, a youth group, Torah studies and Yiddish language classes.

Freda recalls:

> I have some vague memories of going to the synagogue for the High Holidays, all dressed up in our finery and playing with other children in the courtyard. I also remember the carp swimming around in a big bathtub in the kitchen, in preparation for our festive meal. Mum took plaited challah to be cooked at the local bakery.
>
> There were no religious icons in our school, since these had been banned by the Communist government. However, the Catholic Church continued to wield enormous influence on the population. People continued to attend church services and there were many religious shrines at various points around the city, including one in our local park. I remember watching with wonder children curtseying and crossing themselves in front of statues of Mary and Jesus which we passed on our way from school to the park.
>
> I recall having been inside a church only once. This was on a late afternoon in winter and I was in town alone with the elderly lady who sometimes looked after us. We were shopping for hats and gloves for me, but it was getting late. She was a devout Catholic and I think she needed to go to the evening service. She hesitated about taking me inside. I remember her discomfort more than the feeling of being in the unfamiliar place.

Adele remembers:

> At an early age, we became part of the 'other'. My family did not attend mass at church; did not wear crosses; and did not have Christian icons displayed at home. We did not celebrate

Christmas with relatives.

We kept our Jewishness a secret—or at least did not discuss it with our school friends. I remember one evening, in the late 1950s visiting the Jewish Club with my father. He and his friends would meet there to play cards, chess or dominoes. They would engage in political discussion or watch television, a rarity in Poland during this period. To my great astonishment, a classmate of mine walked into the Club. We were both embarrassed. I had no idea he was half-Jewish and he was just as surprised to see me there. Interestingly, although we saw each other every day at school, neither he nor I ever referred to this chance meeting.

In public, Mum and Dad conversed in Polish. Mum's Polish language skills were excellent and she was asked to join our school's parents' committee. I recall the school Principal coming to visit our apartment for a cup of tea and a chat. He had a lot of respect for Mum's intelligence and valued her contribution to the school.

During the 1950s and 60s, relations between Jews and Poles were marred by a perceived link between Jewry and Bolshevism. People who didn't like Jews anyway could feel justified for liking them even less if they were also to blame for Bolshevism. The phrase used, Żydokomuna (Judeo-Communism), was an antisemitic slur built on stereotypical assertions that all Jews had supported Communism in Poland before the War and enjoyed a privileged position afterwards. While it is true that many Jews supported Marxist ideology, seeing it as a movement that would end oppression, including their own, and some Jews did attain high office in the Communist Party of Poland, per capita their number was relatively low. For example, in pre-war Poland only 1 percent of the total Jewish population were members of the Communist Party.⁵

The Communist regime continued to use antisemitism in the same way as it had been used for centuries: to divert attention from its own incompetence and to offer the wider public a scapegoat. After his removal from the post of Party First Secretary in 1948, Gomułka wrote a letter to Stalin in which he clarified his position regarding Jews: 'Too many Jewish Communists have been appointed to responsible positions in Poland.' He further argued that as First Secretary he had opposed this because it diminished the Party's appeal to the masses. Even if there had been a shortage of Polish-born Party cadres, still his former colleagues in the Politburo had allowed too many Jews to be appointed to the administration and Party apparatus.⁶

In February 1953, the severance of diplomatic relations between the Soviet Union and Israel marked a new era in Stalin's anti-Jewish politics throughout the Soviet bloc. In Poland, Jewish community leaders were arrested, among them Jakub Egit, previously the president of the Provincial Jewish Committee of Dolny Śląsk. In his memoirs, Egit wrote that he had been accused of wanting to take Dolny Śląsk out of Poland and with the help of American organizations, to build a Jewish nation there.⁷

Adele recalls:

> **Overall, we kept a low profile and tried not to draw attention to our 'otherness', while privately retaining and celebrating our Jewish identity. Dad made one concession: he would dutifully buy a Christmas tree in an attempt to pacify his children and make us feel part of the wider community. In such ways we adapted to being Jewish in a predominantly Catholic country. If I was lucky enough not to experience open antisemitism, I knew Jewish boys at other public**

schools who were taunted and got into fist fights. I recall a Jewish girl, newly arrived in our school from the Soviet Union, whose fractured Polish irritated everybody. She was very unpopular and ostracized by the other students. I, on the other hand, felt accepted and liked by my classmates.

In 1960, aged eleven and in upper primary school, I began forming close friendships with neighbourhood children, many of whom were my classmates. I recall one Christmas trudging through the snow with two boys, carrying an enormous tree from the local market. We climbed three floors to the boys' apartment and were rewarded for our efforts by being given steaming cups of hot chocolate. It was taken for granted that my family would be celebrating Christmas too. This was, I believe, largely a result of ignorance of Jewish culture or religion. It was beyond people's imagination, unthinkable, even if they suspected we were Jewish, not to celebrate this key holiday!

Jacob's and Mina's relationship with the wider Polish community differed in various ways.

Adele explains:

Dad, the extrovert, mixed with Poles easily. His warmth and jovial nature disarmed all who met him, whether on a personal or business level. He missed his family and pre-war Wieruszów and recalled with pleasure his life there.

Growing up, while aware of the history of persecution of Jews in Poland, and critical of Polish treatment of them, Jacob did not personally experience antisemitism. After all, Wieruszów's population had been 50 percent Jewish and the two communities had largely lived peacefully with one another. Jacob had felt very much at home in his small town.

The Frankowski family, the Widawskis' immediate neighbours, remained close and trusted friends before and during the War. After it ended, they continued to support and help Jacob and Mina until our family's departure for Australia. So Jacob had a positive view of Poles, based on this close, warm friendship. He would stress that while there were Poles who had betrayed their Jewish neighbours, others had helped, even hiding Jews at great personal risk, since the penalty for doing so was arrest, Auschwitz or death.

By comparison Mina, who had grown up in a large city with a vibrant Jewish community, had very little personal contact with non-Jews. Her experiences, with her brothers being victims of antisemitic attacks before the War, had led her to mistrust Poles. Her brothers had insisted on escorting their sisters to and from the places they wanted to go. Mina had few Polish friends.

During the late 1950s and early 1960s, Mina began to involve herself with her children's school. As a member of the parents' committee she was well-liked and respected by the Principal, the teachers and fellow parents. But none of these people became her friends. She was very close to her Jewish friends and cynical about her 'acceptance by the Goyim', which she saw as born of the fact that she had excellent spoken and written Polish language skills and was a gifted public speaker. Many parents of this generation, at this time, were barely able to put a sentence together, or were illiterate, largely as a result of interrupted education or family poverty. Others came from regions of Poland where Ukrainian or Russian were spoken at home and some used dialects that Polish speakers found difficult to understand.

Despite these tensions between my Jewishness and the

culture of the wider community, by the early 1960s I had developed close friendships with a few of my school friends. We began going to a local cinema, feeling very grown-up, yet giggling all the way. Movie magazines became popular. We fantasized about Alain Delon, envied Brigitte Bardot and tried lipstick at the local pharmacy. We grew dizzy learning the hula hoop. In other words, we acted just like millions of other pre-teens. I also discovered I loved reading and the local library became a favourite stop on my way home from school.

At this stage of our lives, Dad was the main breadwinner, while Mum took care of us and our home. My favourite memory is of the welcome home each afternoon: home-made pączki or jam doughnuts which I could smell as I ran noisily up the stairs to our apartment.

There was no television and so the radio provided our main form of entertainment. I remember as little children being introduced to the wonder and beauty of classical music and the pleasure of listening to Mum's soprano voice singing along with a record. As a result, we both developed a life-long passion for music. As a family, we also tuned into favourite comedy programs. I recall Mum making up games to keep us entertained during the lengthy days of winter when the weather often forced us indoors. We would fall about laughing as we attempted to glide over the apartment's wooden floors, pretending that our old rags were ice-skates (and simultaneously ensuring the floors got a good polish!). We largely relied on Mum and each other for entertainment.

Poland's summers can be quite warm, twenty-eight to thirty degrees. Dad would regularly take Freda and me to the city centre, the market square. It was an open plaza, where I loved to walk around the many flower stands, fruit stalls and bustling cafes. Treats of an ice-cream or cream cake and a cool drink often formed part of the outing. Dad was such a sociable, outgoing and friendly man that our walks were punctuated by frequent stops to greet friends and acquaintances and have a chat. These added to the festive feeling as we moved around the square. When they were available, we bought and feasted on fresh cherries, berries, stone and citrus fruit. Many of these delicacies came from Hungary or Yugoslavia. I remember my parents' great excitement at one day finding oranges marked Jaffa, from Israel. They were very expensive, but Dad bought two for the family to share. We celebrated with every mouthful.

Mum baked delicious cakes with the summer produce, or made jam and preserves to keep us going through the winter. Sometimes Dad brought a carp home. It swam around our kitchen sink until, horror of horrors, it was unceremoniously dispatched by Dad wielding his cleaver. The first time I witnessed this 'murder', I was very distressed, However, I learned to love gefilte fish as part of our Friday night feasts.

Freda remembers:

I loved roaming around with Dad and going to visit his friends while we were out walking. My favourites were Stasio (Stanley Ryzman), who had a tailoring shop around the corner from our house, and Henry Lewkowicz who worked in a chocolate shop. We also visited a watchmaker in town and a number of friends at the Hala Targowa.

Dad also took us to the movies and, because the arts were heavily subsidised by the state, we would frequently attend one of three cinemas, such as Lalka, close to our house. The Jewish Club held frequent dances and it was there that Dad taught me how to tango. He was a soccer 'tragic' and in the absence of sons, would drag his girls to football matches.

Mum, having grown-up listening to her cousin practising the violin, loved music and took every opportunity available to expose us to it. She took us along to operettas, concerts and ballet performances. Despite my restlessness and catnaps during these, her love of music migrated into my heart.

Adele recalls:

In summer, we went for long walks along the Odra River or to a lovely public park nearby. There were free concerts in the park and people danced to live music. I remember watching Mum and Dad dancing together, enjoying each other's company on a warm summer's evening. In the winter months, the park provided opportunities for tobogganing, building snowmen and lots of snow fights.

One summer, a friend of Dad's invited us to visit his farm in Wieruszów. We stayed in his house and helped the family harvest a large field of potatoes. I loved the horses and fed them carrots and apples. Our hostess showed us how she milked her cows, how the cows' milk was turned into slabs of butter and how buttermilk and yoghurt were made. We girls went with their children to the nearby Prosna River and enjoyed the coolness of its fast-flowing waters. For city children like us, it was a memorable holiday.

Freda recalls:

We spent some of our summer holidays with other families in holiday spots such as the forests around Oborniki Śląskie or the mountains of Szklarska Poręba. We boated on the rivers, foraged for wild mushrooms and berries in the forests and trekked up mountains.

The one and only time that we made it to the Baltic coast was in 1961, during what was to be our last summer in Poland. We travelled with Stasio Ryzman and his son Alec to the small fishing town of Ustka, where we boarded with a fisherman's family. Every morning we would eagerly await his return so that his wife could fry up the herring that he had caught that morning, for our breakfast. Despite the cool weather, we took long walks on the beach, immersed ourselves in the icy salt water, and discovered the magic of the sea.

So despite the hardships which our parents endured in Poland, we girls had happy childhoods.

In the 1950s and early 1960s Mina and Jacob were creating a new life together. The background was the memory of their traumatic war experiences, loss of family and home and a political system which often required daily battles for food and the necessities of life. Their Jewish background meant constant vigilance, a feeling of being 'on guard', of keeping one's Jewishness personal and private. They knew the importance of not attracting attention by avoiding speaking Yiddish in public. They recognized the glazed-eyed look when your name or your appearance revealed your Jewishness.

Ultimately, struggling to establish a life for their family in this climate of uncertainty and non-acceptance convinced them that, as Jews, they no longer had a place in Poland. Mina and Jacob began to make plans to leave as soon as it was possible.

Top: Adele with her class and beloved teacher, Pani Szkarłowa (back row centre), 1958. 1. Adele, 2. Adele's half-Jewish school friend, 3. The only other Jewish girl in Adele's class.
Bottom: Freda in national dress to the right of her favourite teacher, 1959. Best friend Jola is second from right.

MINA & JACOB

Top: Adele and Freda in traditional Górale dress
(mountain people), Szklarska Poręba 1957.
Bottom: Adele and Freda with Mina and Jacob in
the background, Szklarska Poręba 1957.

Top: An excursion through the forests, 1957.
Bottom: From left: Alec (Stasio Ryzman's son), Jacob, Adele and Stasio, Ustka, Baltic Sea. 1961.

MINA & JACOB

Notes

1. http://fbk.org.pl/new/en/synagogue/history-of-the-synagogue/
2. Leo Kantor, *W poszukiwaniu utraconego krajobrazu* (In Search of a Lost Landscape), 2014;
   https://www.youtube.com/watch?v=dytss8MxKiw&feature=youtu.be;
   Notes from an Exhibition held at White Stork Synagogue, recorded by Freda Widawski, Wrocław, 2010; http://wroclaw.jewish.org.pl/about-community/
3. http://pl.wikipedia.org/wiki/Adolf_Rudnicki
4. Exhibition at White Stork Synagogue, 2010
5. Simon Wiesenthal, *Justice not Vengeance* (New York: Grove Weidenfeld, 1989), 209-10; Jan T. Gross, *Fear: Anti-Semitism in Poland after Auschwitz* (Princeton and Oxford: Princeton University Press, 2006), 196-97
6. Gross, *Fear: Anti-Semitism in Poland*, 213
7. Grzegorz Berendta, ed., *Społeczność Żydowska w PRL przed kampanią antysemicką lat 1967-68 i po niej*, (The Jewish Community in PRL, before the Anti-Semitic Campaign during the Years 1967-68, and After,), (Warsaw: Instytut Pamięci Narodowej IPN), 66-69

26
Emigration

In the immediate post-war years many Jews had left Poland because of antisemitic attacks. For example, after the pogrom in Kielce of 4 July 1946, more than 5,000 survivors left within twenty-four hours of the killings.[1]

Jewish community leaders hoped that the Catholic Church, which had great influence over the largely Catholic Polish population, would condemn the violence. The week after the Kielce pogrom, Cardinal August Hlond, the Primate of Poland, had issued a statement containing four points. He said that the Catholic Church opposed all murder; that 'the miserable and deplorable events in Kielce cannot be attributed to racism'; that numerous Jews in Poland owed their lives to Poles and Polish priests; and that he was not an antisemite. This statement would become the position of the Polish Catholic Church.

Other powerful authorities also took positions. The British government, while limiting the entry of Jews into Palestine, called on the Holy See to condemn antisemitism. The Vatican responded with silence.[2]

For Jews who chose Palestine as their destination, their journey was facilitated by Zionist organizations and initially supported by the Polish government. Just after the War, the Soviet Union and its satellite states were sympathetic to the plight of the Jews and supported the establishment of a Jewish state in Palestine. They saw this as weakening the British. They also believed that a future Jewish state's foreign policy would be pro-Soviet.

However, when Israel was established in 1948, Stalin's position changed. This marked the beginning of anti-Zionist, anti-Jewish and anti-Israel actions, not only in the Soviet Union but throughout the Soviet bloc, including Poland.[3]

More than 200,000 Jews left Poland in the years 1945-50.[4] Those who stayed believed promises of a just, socialist Poland. Others felt compelled to reconstruct Jewish life, even on a tiny scale, in the country where Jewish communities had existed for many centuries. Many like Mina were simply too frail, too tired, worn down by the War and their losses, to leave the country of their birth.[5]

In the winter of 1949, a friend involved in smuggling survivors across the border into Germany had urged Jacob and Mina to make the crossing with him. He was, he said, about to make his last trip. Mina, heavily pregnant with Adele, had neither the physical nor emotional strength to attempt the crossing. At that time, they chose not to leave.

Later Mina recalled the decisions they had made regarding emigration:[6]

> **People were running away across the borders, but I was sick after the War and tired of struggling and being afraid. I thought: 'I went through such hell, such danger. Where am I going to go now?'**
>
> Then later, after our children were born, I asked: 'Where will I go with such tiny children?' I put all of my love into the children. 'They are my only family. They are everything that I have.'
>
> However, with time, I came to the conclusion that: 'No,

we won't stay here. Poland is always between two powers, Russia and Germany and as history shows us, it is always in danger. No, I am not going to stay on this soil.'

Freda explains:

> Moshe Laub (Mum's father) had several siblings who had migrated to the United States in the early 1900s. After the War, they searched for any survivors. According to our American cousins, Mina's aunt Sarah Feiler discovered the fate of her family by accident. She happened to be visiting a cousin in Brooklyn in New York City on a day when he received bad news from Poland. She found him in tears. When he explained why, she realized that her brother Moshe had perished in the Holocaust.
>
> Sarah renewed her efforts to try and find out if any of Moshe's family had somehow miraculously survived the War. Through the International Red Cross, she managed to locate Mina, the sole survivor of the Laub family in Poland.

In the late 1940s and early 1950s Mina made contact with her family in the United States, hoping to migrate there. Records provided in 2013 by the Instytut Pamięci Narodowej, IPN (Institute of National Remembrance) show that Jacob and Mina had applied for an exit visa to go to Israel while they were still living in ul. Niemcewicza. The decision of 21 December 1952 was 'odm' (odmówjone), meaning that the request was denied. Although the destination is shown as Israel, we believe that their actual destination would have been the United States.

Mina recalled:[7]

> I had received papers from my family in the United States when they traced me through the Red Cross. During the War, I had no contact with these relatives. Afterwards they tried to find out who had survived in Poland from their large family.
>
> But the Poles didn't let us out; there were restrictions on migration. We didn't get the necessary exit visas, and soon I even had to hide any letters or papers from my family because we were afraid to correspond with the West.

As the Cold War between the Soviet bloc and the West escalated, restrictions on freedom of movement and travel abroad were imposed. Communications with the West were heavily censored or banned. Packages or letters from abroad were commonly treated as suspicious and routinely opened for inspection. An envelope in Mina's handwriting addressed to her aunt in the United States became part of the evidence against Jacob during his 1954 trial.[8]

Stalin died in 1953. In February 1956, Nikita Krushchev, the Soviet Party Secretary launched an attack on his rule, ushering in an era of 'de-Stalinization'. In Poland, Władysław Gomułka was appointed First Secretary of the Communist Party and given 'free' rein on domestic policy, as long as his government continued to support the Soviet Union in foreign affairs.[9]

After Gomulka's appointment, the situation for Polish Jews deteriorated, during the Polish October of 1956, when de-Stalinization began and following the struggle for the Suez Canal. Anti-Israel and anti-Jewish propaganda proliferated. Gomułka, 'encouraged' the small Jewish population to leave, with the Biuro Paszportów Zagranicznych, (Overseas Passport Office within the Ministry of Internal Affairs) starting to issue exit visas for Israel. As a result, during the years 1956-58, more than half of the Jewish population left for Israel, including most of those repatriated from the Soviet Union.[10]

MINA & JACOB

Among them were Jacob's brother Berek and his family, who left Poland in 1957 to settle in the small town of Ness Ziona, close to Tel Aviv. Jacob's imprisonment between 1954-56 forced the family to postpone any plans for migration. Once he was released, he wanted to leave for Israel, but Mina resisted the idea. Her argument against migrating there was that she was reluctant to face more war and death. She wanted to find a safe and peaceful haven for her family, far from conflict and sad memories.

In 1958, our family friends, the Frenkiels, decided to leave Poland. Despite Mr Frenkiel's high profile as a criminal lawyer and his reputation as a brilliant orator, it was made clear to him that his career was over. There was no future for him, nor his solicitor sister, in Poland.

During this period the Polish press published anti-Jewish propaganda and many Jews lost their jobs. Reluctantly, since they did not speak English and had little knowledge of Australia, the Frenkiels, helped by distant relatives in Sydney, decided to emigrate.

Mina was sad to see them leave but also excited for them, at the prospect of a new life far from Europe's problems. She was herself tired of the daily struggle to feed and clothe her children; tired of being worried and afraid; weary of hiding her religion; depressed by the grey skies and cold winters. She recalled:[11]

> The Frenkiels knew that I wanted to get out of Poland at any price. They liked me; they liked our children. They always remembered how, despite the shortages, my children were well-dressed. I put all my energy into dressing them nicely. They asked me: 'Once we arrive in Australia, if we find that we like it, would you also like to go there?' I said: 'Any place in the world! I don't want to stay in Poland.'

Not long after their arrival in Australia, Giza Frenkiel started writing to Mina, telling her what a wonderful country it was. It was a land of opportunity, peaceful and friendly, where their children would flourish. She offered to help and approached the Australian authorities for the issue of the necessary entry visas. She also lobbied the Australian Jewish Welfare Society and the American-based Hebrew Immigrant Aid Society, HIAS, for assistance with the cost of travel and first settlement.

In 1959, Mina and Jacob received the necessary papers from Australia and again applied for exit visas. The whole process took about three years and required the family to travel to Warsaw for an interview, take medical tests and obtain passports.

Adele recalls:

> I clearly remember the pleasure and joy of staying at a lovely old hotel in Warsaw and celebrating that night with a fabulous dinner. For me, the train trip to and from Warsaw was also a source of wonder: I spent hours watching the countryside through the large window.

In 1960-61 the situation for Polish Jews deteriorated further. Many were removed from government and party positions and financial control was assumed of Jewish organizations. Terms such as 'national nihilists', 'rootless cosmopolitans' and 'Zionists' were spread by Communist functionaries and the press. Jewishness in Polish Communists was frowned on and they were pressured to Polonize their names: 'Wygląd w porządku, ale co za nazwisko' ('The looks are OK, but pity about the name').[12]

It was with great joy and relief that Mina and Jacob received the news in July 1961 that they had been granted exit permits. They could leave for Australia!

MINA & JACOB

Mina recalled:[13]

We arrived in Australia in 1962. I didn't know in advance that this is really such a beautiful country. We waited quite a long time to come here. After many struggles and unsuccessful applications, we were given an exit visa.

We came to Australia thanks to our neighbours, the Frenkiels. They were our sponsors: they helped us to get visas and a place to live in Sydney. They did a lot for us!

Adele remembers:

Once all the formalities were completed, our parents busied themselves making preparations for our departure. Personal items such as furniture were sold off and Mum packed a few precious china items: two dinner sets, one a gift for the Frenkiels, and one for us. She had also commissioned a quilt-maker to fashion new bedding for our life in Australia. She knew little of the country's climate. These heavy goose-feather quilts, covered in the best damask we could afford, proved to be highly inappropriate for Sydney's mild winters! Equally, the large European pillows used in Poland were then unknown in Australia, where smaller sizes were manufactured. This proved to be another problem since it was impossible to buy replacement pillow slips. However Mum, resourceful as ever, found a solution: she made her own. Our other worldly possessions consisted of a couple of crates and a suitcase each. We set off with a few dollars in our pockets on one-way passports.

We children were told to keep our impending trip a secret. I told my school friends that we were going on holidays abroad. Jewish neighbours were trusted and goodbyes said, but no others were privy to our true destination.

Dad had come to know the Marmurs, another Jewish family scheduled to leave Wrocław for Australia. It was arranged that the two families would drive from Wrocław to Warsaw together, where they would board a train. In February 1962, we left in the middle of a cold night so as not to attract too much attention from curious neighbours.

Mum was to say later that they held their collective breaths, fearful of some last-minute problem. She said that she only relaxed once we crossed the border into Czechoslovakia.

With our migration, generations of the Widawski, Jakubowicz, Laub and Sand families' recorded presence in Poland ended.

In the years following our departure, the small Jewish community in Poland was subject to continuing persecution. This intensified after the Soviet Union and Poland broke off diplomatic relations with Israel following the Six-Day-War in 1967.

The climax came in 1968 when Gomułka in a speech alleged that Jews in Poland were a 'fifth column'. He received a standing ovation! A full-scale antisemitic campaign was then unleashed, using the media to attack so-called Zionists. Those of Jewish origin, as well as anyone who spoke out openly in support of Jews, were either dismissed from their jobs, demoted or removed from positions of influence. Many Jewish students were expelled from school or taken into the Army. Jewish institutions also suffered harassment.[14]

As a direct result of these antisemitic campaigns, approximately 20,000 of the 30,000 remaining Jews left Poland on one-way passports. Some twenty years after the Holocaust this mass exodus ended the 1000-year-old Jewish presence in Poland.[15]

From March 1968, Jewish life in Wrocław died. The last wave of emigration ended services at the White Stork Synagogue. In 1974 the authorities invoked the law on abandoned German property to expropriate the synagogue building from the Jewish congregation. It was left to decay, falling into a state of complete ruin until the mid-1990s. The remaining Jewish community was left with a small prayer room that could hold only fifty people. Restrictions placed on the religious slaughter of animals meant that the community could no longer provide its members with free Kosher meals.[16]

Over the ensuing years, the Jewish community of Wrocław 'officially' stood at forty-three. The Widawski's neighbour, Cantor David Ringel, officiated during those long, bleak decades, whenever the community had no rabbi.[17]

After the fall of Communism in 1989, and the restoration of a free and democratic Poland, Jewish religious and cultural communities across the country began slowly to rebuild. The Jewish religious community of Wrocław was set up again in 1993. On 24 September 1995, some 400 people took part in the first holiday: Rosh Hashanah. On 10 April 1996, the White Stork Synagogue was returned to the Jewish Community. By 2010, it was fully restored.

Igo Feldblum and Antonina Gurycka wrote:[18]

Poland represents my childhood for me. It is the country of my birth—but I cannot call it my 'homeland'. One yearns to return to one's homeland at any cost, like to your father.

These sentiments resonated with many families' view of their country of birth. Despite our many visits back to Poland in later years, it never felt like 'home' again.

Top: Record of applications for exit visas: Number 1 for Israel, rejected in December 1952, and number 2 for Australia, granted on 20 July 1961. Provided by IPN, Wrocław, 2010.
Bottom: Mina, Adele and Freda at the mass grave in Wieruszów,
shortly before the family's departure in 1962.

Notes

1 Grzegorz Berendta, ed., *Społeczność Żydowska w PRL przed kampanią antysemicką lat 1967-68 i po niej*, (The Jewish Community in the PRL before the Anti-Semitic campaign during the Years 1967-68, and After) (Warsaw: Instytut Pamięci Narodowej, IPN, 2009), 40; Jan T. Gross, *Fear: Anti-Semitism in Poland after Auschwitz* (Princeton and Oxford: Princeton University Press, 2006), 28-29, 43
2 Gross, *Fear: Anti-Semitism in Poland*, 134-37
3 Berendta, ed., *Społeczność Żydowska*, 40, 66-69; Gross, *Fear: Anti-Semitism in Poland*, 28-29, 43
4 Berendta, ed., *Społeczność Żydowska*, 40; Gross, *Fear: Anti-Semitism in Poland*, 28-29, 43
5 Celia Heller, *On the Edge of Destruction: The Jews of Poland between the Two Wars* (New York: Columbia University Press, 1977), 296
6 Mina Widawski nee Laub, audio testimony for the *12th Hour Project of Oral Testimonies* (Sydney: Australian Institute for Holocaust Studies, 1990); video testimony (Sydney: USC Shoah Foundation Institute, 1995), code 2526
7 Mina Widawski, *12th Hour Project of Oral Testimonies*; USC Shoah Foundation, code 2526
8 Instytut Pamięcia Narodowej, IPN (Institute of National Remembrance), Wrocław, 2010
9 https://www.britannica.com/biography/Wladyslaw-Gomulka; Anita Prażmowska, *Poland: A Modern History* (London: IB Tauris, 2010), 185
10 Berendta, ed., *Społeczność Żydowska* 57; 70; Heller, *On the Edge of Destruction*, 296
11 Mina Widawski, *12th Hour Project of Oral Testimonies*; USC Shoah Foundation, code 2526
12 Berendta, ed., *Społeczność Żydowska*, 62-63; Gross, *Fear: Anti-Semitism in Poland*, 214
13 Mina Widawski, *12th Hour Project of Oral Testimonies*; USC Shoah Foundation, code 2526
14 Notes from an exhibition held at White Stork Synagogue, recorded by Freda Widawski, Wrocław, 2010; http://wroclaw.jewish.org.pl/about-community/; Leo Kantor, *W poszukiwaniu utraconego krajobrazu* (In Search of a Lost Landscape), 2014: Ministry of Culture and National Heritage and Polish Film Institute; http://www.polishdocs.pl/en/films/1452/in_search_of_the_lost_landscape https://www.youtube.com/watch?v=dytss8MxKiw&feature=youtu.be

15 Leo Kantor, *W poszukiwaniu utraconego krajobrazu*; Josef Banas, *The Scapegoats: The Exodus of the Remnants of Polish Jewry* (London: Weidenfeld & Nicolson Ltd, 1979), 21, 23
16 http://fbk.org.pl/new/en/synagogue/history-of-the-synagogue/
17 Exhibition at White Stork Synagogue, 2010; http://wroclaw.jewish.org.pl/about-community
18 Igo Feldblum and Antonina Gurycka, *A skąd pan właściwie jest?* (But where are you actually from?), (Warszawa: Wydawnictwo Nowy Świat, 2004), 54

PART 4

Australia

27

The Journey

Our friend, Vala Marmur recalled:[1]

We met the Widawskis through my husband's cousin, Chaim. He had a stall in Wrocław's Hala Targowa and knew Jacob from there.

We left the city in February 1962, the two families travelling together by truck: Jacob, Mina, Adele and Freda Widawski; Adam, Vala, Edek and Izio Marmur; plus Adam's nephew and niece. The truck belonged to the Wrocław Film Institute, for which Adam had worked. Our suitcases went with us. The larger pieces such as the Widawskis' crates were dispatched from Dworzec Towarowy (the freight station) and we didn't see them until our arrival in Australia.

Mina recalled:[2]

We came to Australia by ship. Other migrants have horror stories of voyages from Europe. We were lucky. Our Dutch ship, the *Oranje*, was almost a Royal ship, and conditions on board were very, very good. I said: 'After what we've been through during the War, I hope we can do another trip like this in the future'—because it was lovely. We travelled by train from Poland to Genoa where we waited three days to board the ship.

The ship took four weeks to get to Australia, and we came straight to Sydney.

On boarding the train in Warsaw, the family discovered that there were some ten other Jewish families, from various Polish cities, travelling to Australia. From Warsaw, the family travelled south, via Czechoslovakia, Austria, Switzerland and into northern Italy. In anticipation of their departure for Australia, Mina had taken a few English lessons, so during the journey she acted as an 'interpreter' for the other Polish passengers. For example, as they sat in freezing air-conditioning in Italy, she tried to explain to the Italian conductor, using her best English and making it sound Italianized, that we were 'caldo', an approximation of the English word 'cold'. However, she was actually saying that we felt 'hot' in Italian, so the poor conductor was very confused!

Adele remembers the journey:

> Freda, Izio, Edek and I loved the excitement of train travel and watching the magnificent Swiss Alps and the Italian countryside through the large windows. We left the train in Genoa, a port city in the north of Italy, from where we were to sail to Australia. We had only a couple of days in this old city as we waited for our ship, but despite the February cold, relished exploring the streets. We marvelled at its buildings and the shops full of merchandise, and enjoyed gelatinos. We loved our hotel with its Baroque architecture, wall paintings and big, high beds. My only fear was that I would fall off the bed—which I duly did. The hard-tiled floor was an unpleasant landing.

Our parents left Poland with very little money, so there was not much spare cash for shopping. Thanks to the support of various Jewish organizations, we were to enjoy a wonderful trip on the *Oranje*. In 1962, our parents were both forty years old. I marvel at the courage it took to face a new beginning in Australia, a strange land, with no language skills and no family. They hoped that their friends, the Frenkiel family, as well as a few other acquaintances they knew from Poland who had also settled in Sydney, would provide them with some support and advice. Despite their understandable concerns, my parents and our fellow Jewish passengers were filled with high hopes for a peaceful life and a brighter future for their children.

The ship was a delight: mahogany panelling everywhere, friendly officers and stewards, comfortable cabins. The food, while strange to the Polish palate, was plentiful and tasty. Overall it was a far cry from those uncomfortable ships used to transport migrants during the 1940s and early 1950s. There were 242 passengers.

The ship sailed via the Mediterranean islands; the Suez Canal and the Red Sea port of Aden; then along the west coast of India to Australia. I recall my wonder at souvenir sellers approaching our ship to show and sell their exotic wares. We bought wonderful inexpensive pieces of colourful cloth and pointed shoes decorated with coloured glass.

I don't recall being sea-sick during the voyage, although I do remember that on the Indian Ocean off the coast of Western Australia the ship rose and fell over huge waves.

After a month, the first Australian port we sailed into was Fremantle. Mina and Jacob, excitedly walking around the port area, loved the balmy weather and pointed towards palm trees.

Freda remembers the beginning of the journey:

> I recall Mr Nejman coming from Brzeg to say goodbye. I have a strong memory of him sitting on a chair in our lounge, eating chicken soup from a plate perched on a tea-towel on his lap. By then the apartment had been emptied of furniture.
>
> When we arrived in Genoa, Mum and Dad bought us a beautiful blue-eyed blonde doll that travelled with us all the way to Australia. It would remain perched on Mum's bed for decades to come.
>
> For a child of ten, the trip was one huge adventure. I had left a grey landscape, Poland in mid-February with low skies and sludge on the ground, crumbling coal-stained, bullet-ridden buildings and depressed people in drab clothing. After this, to behold the splendour of the Suez Canal: palm trees, sand dunes, the bluest of blue water, was amazing. Egyptian traders in their brightly-painted boats sailed up to our ship to sell their wares, holding up mirror-covered bags and sandals sparkling in the sun. I was living in a fairy-tale!
>
> The captain and crew of our Dutch ship treated our group with kindness and respect. Although we slept in dormitories, the men separated from their wives and children, we were all well fed. Bottles of vodka were served at meals. The children were looked after in their separate dining room while the parents were free to dance and enjoy this time of 'suspended reality'. They didn't know what the future held for them in the far-off unknown land of Australia. But they could be sure that it would require hard work and tenacity. They had come through great hardships and were about to embark on yet another beginning, without support, money, or language. But they were all still young, so they might as well enjoy

themselves now.

Both Jacob and Adam were so broke that they would share their cigarettes. It was a wonderful sight watching those two strolling around the deck smoking and talking: the short, slight Jacob and the tall, muscular Adam. The bond that was forged on that journey sustained them through the first difficult years in their new country. It was to last for the rest of their lives.

Diane Armstrong wrote:[3]

She snipped off a small piece of the stem of the plant and handed it to her. 'You put in soil, in pot, in warm place. Will grow.' Could such a short piece of stalk, severed from its parent plant, put down roots in new soil, and bloom?

MINA & JACOB

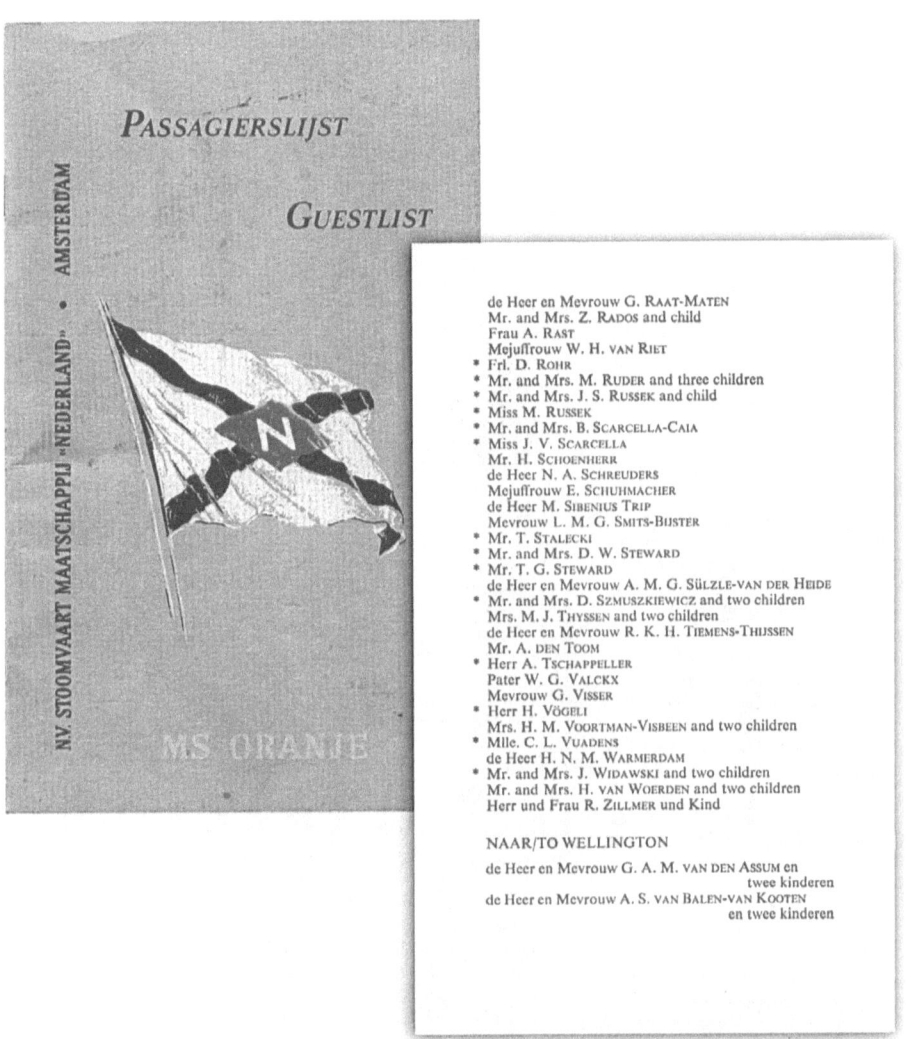

Mr and Mrs J. Widawski and two children (last bullet) listed on the *Oranje's* passenger list. Provided by Izio Marmur, 2012.

Top: Jacob's passport photo. 1962.
Bottom: From left: Jacob, Adele, Izio Marmur and Freda, Genoa, 1962.

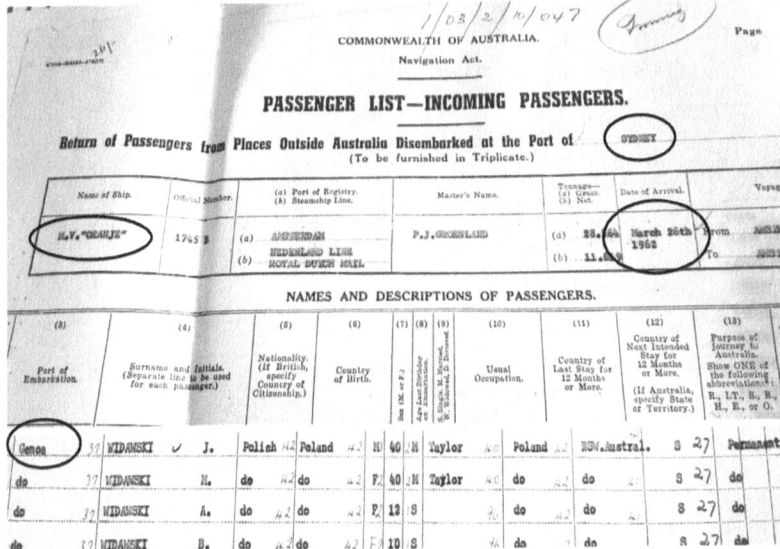

Top: On board the *Oranje*, February 1962.
Vala Marmur (second from left), Freda (covering her eyes), Mina (second from right) and Adele wearing Edek Marmur's hat (right).
Bottom: Incoming passenger list, showing that the family embarked in Genoa on the *Oranje* and disembarked in Sydney on 26 March 1962.
Provided by National Archives of Australia, 28 August 2012.

Notes

1 Vala Marmur, interview with Freda Widawski, Melbourne, 2011
2 Mina Widawski nee Laub, audio testimony for the *12th Hour Project of Oral Testimonies* (Sydney: Australian Institute for Holocaust Studies, 1990); video testimony (Sydney: USC Shoah Foundation Institute, 1995), code 2526
3 Diane Armstrong, *Empire Day* (Sydney: HarperCollins, 2011), 454

28
Settling in Sydney

The *Oranje* sailed into sparkling Sydney Harbour on 26 March 1962. Mina recalled:[1]

> For us it was a very warm welcome, because our friends, the Frenkiel family, came to greet us with flowers at Circular Quay and then took us home for dinner. Because we had no family in Australia, we were really lucky to have them. They became our family and remained our dear friends until the end of their lives. Jewish Welfare, now known as Jewish Care, arranged accommodation for us in Flood Street, Bondi. Sadly, we were separated from our friends the Marmurs, who had disembarked in Melbourne. And even though we arrived without a cent and with young children (one was ten, the other twelve), we started to build a new life.

Adele recalls:

> We said goodbye to the Marmur family as well as another couple of families who, with no direct sponsor in Australia, left the ship in Melbourne, to be looked after by the Melbourne Jewish community. The rest of our group sailed on to Sydney. We sailed into Sydney Harbour on a beautiful March day.

Mum, standing on the deck, took in the sights, the sparkling water and the sunny autumn day, and declared that this was truly the paradise she had hoped and dreamed of for so long. It was so different from the depressing grey skies of Poland.

The Frenkiel family escorted us to Bondi in Sydney's east, a suburb with a substantial Jewish population. We soon discovered Bondi Beach, but Jacob and Mina were disappointed to find that there were few cafes or restaurants where they felt happy eating. We encountered milk bars and hamburger places, which appeared strangely uninviting, the food unappetizing and 'smelly'. This was Bondi in the early 1960s.

Freda remembers:

I was in paradise! We arrived in March, with blue, blue skies, the sunshine sparkling off the chrome of highly-polished Holdens and Valiants, palm trees swaying in the breeze. I spent hours sitting in the front room looking out of the window at the passing parade.

Our family lived first in a boarding house owned by a Polish Jew, Mr Greenbaum, in Flood Street, Bondi, a pleasant tree-lined street close to a local park and the beach. It was a two-storey terrace, and our accommodation consisted of a room where Mina and Jacob slept, plus a glassed-in veranda for the children. We shared the bathroom and toilet with other tenants living on our floor, and cooked in the communal kitchen.

The other occupants were mainly Jewish migrants from Poland, although I remember the smell of Aussie sausages frying in lard, which indicates that there may have been some Australians living there too.

A few days after our arrival, Dad started work in a small clothing factory in Surry Hills, the schmatter (rag trade) district of Sydney. It was owned by a fellow Polish Jew, who Jacob soon found out was exploiting him, the new arrival, paying him less than the other tailors. But Dad persevered, biding his time, until something better came along.

Mum started doing some small sewing jobs, working from our little veranda in Flood Street. Mrs Giza Frenkiel and her sister-in-law, Janka, were among her first customers, and they recommended her to their friends. Her focus, as always was her children: she was determined that we would not become latchkey kids and that she would be there for us when we got home from school.

Adele recalls:

In 1964, Mum would bravely rent a small shop on Campbell Parade, Bondi Beach, where she began to do alterations and design made-to-measure dresses. Despite having very little English, being largely self-taught as a dressmaker and with no business experience, she was determined to make a go of the shop. Her patience and meticulous work saw her steadily increase her client base.

Meanwhile, aged twelve, I was to begin Year 7 at Randwick Girls High, while Freda was enrolled at the local Bellevue Hill Primary School. At the school I was given an IQ test in English to determine my intelligence and hence the appropriate class level. I didn't do very well because I couldn't follow the instructions and explanations. Only the mathematics section went well, the familiar symbols easy to decipher. But I was assigned to a class and my parents given full instructions on the mandatory school uniform: hat, gloves, white socks and dress. Mum, the ever-clever problem solver, visited the local department store and copied the dress from their stock, so saving some money. The other items were purchased second-hand.

Financially, life was a struggle, but we were initially helped by the Jewish welfare people and slowly, with Dad's work and Mum's sewing, things began to improve. Somehow my parents managed to feed, clothe and nurture us.

On my first day at school, one of the teachers came into the classroom wearing a Star of David around her neck. I was so excited to see her publicly displaying this iconic Jewish symbol that I couldn't wait to get home and tell my parents. Mum's eyes brimmed with tears on hearing my news: this was confirmation that she and Dad had made the right decision in coming to Australia.

Overall, I found the first few months of school very difficult. I was unable to comprehend the instructions in class and couldn't communicate with my fellow students. I had been a top student at school in Poland and the adjustment was very difficult. What saved me was meeting a handful of Polish Jewish students who had arrived some months earlier. I looked forward to the lunch break to hear a familiar friendly voice, to elicit information and ask questions. My Australian classmates, while curious about Poland, would ask me dumb questions: 'Is it near the north Pole?' This was a question that floored me. They found the food in my lunchbox different, strange and 'smelly', and quickly lost interest in me since communication was difficult.

Education standards in Poland were comparatively high: by Year 6 of primary school we had covered subjects such as chemistry, physics, science, Polish literature and grammar, social studies, mathematics (including algebra), geography, history and the Russian language. I was now attempting to come to grips with English, Australian history and a different curriculum, difficult to follow. The academic standard seemed much lower and the first year of high school covered very little of what I had already learned. My single joy was the maths lessons, where the universal symbols made it possible for me to keep up with the rest of the class.

I soon began to lose interest in school altogether and spent classes day-dreaming. My English teacher tried to help me. She gave me special homework which consisted of writing a short paragraph in English, asking me to describe my weekend or my interests and hobbies. She suggested I listen to the radio and watch television, trying to follow the sense, inflections and rhythm of the language. But overall, I found the transition very difficult and my school days were lonely. I hid my misery from my parents, assuring them that all was going well. After all, they were busy attempting to build a new life for us and did not fully understand the school system or the problems I was facing.

I missed my Mum's advice on school work and her attention. Although I managed to pass Year 7 and progress to the next year, I became a disinterested student and later, with both parents working, a truant teenager.

Freda remembers:

When Adele was sent to high school, I started at Bellevue Hill Public, a lovely small primary school within walking distance of our rooms in Flood Street. Luckily for me, in the adjoining boarding house, also owned by Mr Greenbaum, lived the Salomon family, friends of the Frenkiels from Wrocław. Their daughter Sylvia, who was my age, also attended Bellevue Hill Public. Because they had arrived a few months before us, she already spoke some English and knew her way around. A gentle girl, she took me by the hand and led me to school. Her guidance made those first few months in the strange country a lot easier to navigate. I will be forever grateful to her. The teachers at the school were also very warm and friendly. One of my best memories of that time is trying to do an exam with a group of fellow students crowding around me, helping.

Adele recalls:

Some twelve months after our arrival, having kept in touch by letter with my school friends in Poland, I told my parents in no uncertain terms that I had suffered enough of this 'vacation' and wanted to return home. Mum patiently explained that there was no going back. This strange country was to be our permanent home.

Jacob also found adjusting to living in Australia very difficult. He loathed his factory job, and his lack of English skills created a barrier and made it difficult to meet or communicate with people from the wider community. His pale complexion did not thrive in the strong Australian sun, so sunburn was a constant dilemma. Mina, on the other hand, with her olive skin, enjoyed the heat and the beach. None of the family knew how to swim or to catch the waves and surf, although Jacob knew how to dog-paddle. Soon, however, the girls learned to swim and adapted to Australian beach culture.

MINA & JACOB

Like Adele, Jacob at one point threatened to return to Poland. He missed the easy camaraderie of his friends and conversations in a familiar language. He knew and understood the system in Poland, how to work around it and to provide for his family. In Australia he felt lost and confused. Adele recalls when she was thirteen visiting a local bank with her parents. During the meeting with the bank manager, she acted as an interpreter. Jacob did not like having to rely on his daughter to smooth the way. Mina, however, made it clear that she had no intention of returning to Poland. She suggested he could return on his own if he wanted, but the rest of the family would remain in Sydney.

Mr Frenkiel came to the rescue by sharing with Jacob a personal story. In 1958, newly arrived in Australia, Joseph Frenkiel, the respected criminal lawyer, worked cleaning and sweeping railway platforms! While holding down a full-time job, he studied part-time at evening college and eventually graduated as an accountant and tax advisor. By the time the Widawski family arrived in 1962, he was working in this new profession, providing a vital service to grateful clients, many of whom, as newly arrived migrants, preferred to deal with a fellow Jew and Polish speaker.

Janka, Joseph's younger sister, also changed her career. She had been a solicitor; she became a cosmetician. Giza, his wife, taught French and German at a local private school and gave piano lessons in order to help boost the family's finances. She had never worked in Poland.

Easing their adjustment to Australia was Mina's and Jacob's membership of a large group of fellow migrants who became an extended family. Friendships were forged which continued all their lives. They reconnected with friends and acquaintances who had also migrated from Wrocław or Wieruszów, and enjoyed a vibrant social life with them. For example, the Friedman family who lived nearby in Bondi became close friends. Their three children, of similar age, were welcoming and fun. The Frenkiel family were frequent visitors, often sharing Yom Tovim and Shabbat dinners. The Lewkovich family, who had settled much earlier in Sydney, impressed with their comfortable home and obvious signs of prosperity. They demonstrated that, with hard work, Australia provided opportunities for a good life.

Slowly Jacob adjusted to life in Australia. With time our parents' language skills improved. Mina enrolled in evening English classes, while Jacob learned by listening and talking to people. They both took on additional work, doing piecework for several clothes wholesalers to supplement their income.

The family stayed in Flood Street for sixteen months, after which Jacob and Mina rented a two-bedroom flat in pleasant Edward Street, close to Bondi Beach. It was in a two-storey building of six units, owned by a Greek migrant, Nicolas or 'Nico' Tzimopoulous, who became a very good friend. Slowly Mina and Jacob furnished their three-room 'palace'. It was here that the girls grew into teenagers, did their homework, had their first crushes and learned about Zionism and a little bit more about their parents' history.

In 1966, a small semi-detached cottage next door to the apartment block was put up for sale. Mina bravely decided that they had to buy it. She approached the owner, a kind Australian man who, on learning of their past experiences, genuinely wanted to sell the house to them. He promised to wait until they could get enough money for a deposit and for the subsequent loan arrangements to go through. Jacob and Mina went frantically from friend to friend, from acquaintance to acquaintance. Finally, with a lot of generous help, including a loan from the bank as well as from Jewish Welfare, they managed to raise the necessary finance.

In this way Jacob and Mina became the proud owners of their

own Australian home. They were to remain grateful to their Australian friend for the rest of their lives. For some years after the sale they exchanged Christmas cards and visited one another's homes.

For a few years Jacob and Mina struggled financially, but slowly they began to repay the loans as they happily looked forward to a bright future for the family.

To meet the mortgage and loan repayments, Jacob realized that he needed to earn a higher wage. A cousin of Mrs Friedman's, Iche (Isaac) Fox, was working at Presto, a smallgoods factory owned by a Hungarian Jew, and through him Jacob secured a job there. The work was hard and meant standing for many hours knee-deep in water, making various types of sausage. The days were also long. Jacob rose at 4am, ready for a 5am pick-up and the long drive to the factory's premises in Leichhardt.

If the days were hard, the pay was good. There was lots of overtime and, most importantly, he could bring home meat and various smallgoods free of charge—or for a fraction of their cost in the shops. All his fellow workers were migrants: Poles, Hungarians, Greeks and Yugoslavs. English was the common language, regardless of the proficiency of the speaker, and Jacob picked up an interesting assortment of swear-words spoken in a broad range of accents.

A couple of years later, Mina moved her business to larger premises on Bondi Road. There Jacob joined her as a tailor, and together they established Mila's Fashions, making ladies 'ready-to-wear' clothes and doing alterations. The laundry in the basement of their small Edward Street home became their 'factory', where they designed and sewed beautiful garments. Mina would make the skirts and dresses and Jacob the jackets and coats. They did not grow rich, but they earned enough to take care of their family, educate their children and build a good life in their new country.

Most days there was enough time in between sewing and

manning the shop for both of them to spend some time at the beach, as well as take care of the myriad domestic jobs needed to create a warm, happy home.

Adele recalls:

> Sharing the designing and sewing and selling their clothes was very satisfying to both our parents. As a result, Freda and I learned early in life that there was no gender barrier: that either partner could take on the role of homemaker or businessperson as dictated by circumstances or as required. From our early teens, my sister and I also helped with some of the lighter household duties, as needed.

Mina recalled:[2]

> We worked as a tailor and a dressmaker. After the War I lost any desire or motivation to pursue further studies. How could I study under such circumstances? I was grateful to God simply for having survived! I had lost so much. So I turned the sewing skills that I developed through necessity in the camps to earning a living. But I also read a lot and attended English evening classes. It was still difficult for us to master English because, to support the family, we had to focus on work.
>
> At first Jacob worked in a factory and I opened a little shop, making clothes and selling them. Later I said to my husband: 'You can't work forever for somebody else—so come and work with me. Instead of my having to employ somebody, we'll work together.' Later I sold the shop on Bondi Road and we moved to Bondi Junction into the new shopping centre. We ran a shop there until our retirement.

Education was always of primary importance to Mina and she never stopped learning. In her later years, she took up Hebrew. She left numerous notebooks with lists of English and Hebrew words; commentary on books that she had read; copies of poems that had touched her; and ideas and thoughts that she wanted to record.

She recalled:[3]

> I told the children: 'We'll work very hard to support you, and to do what's in our power—but you'll have to study.' I reminded them that they had both been very good students in Poland. I corresponded for many years with the Principal of their school, because he was interested in their progress. He wrote: 'Your children were the best students in our school and I wonder what they are planning to do in the future?' So I stressed: 'We're not rich, but if you study, that will be your wealth. You will have opportunities open to you everywhere if you get an education.'

Adele remembers:

> The only disappointment occurred in 1967. Aged sixteen and having completed my School Certificate, I decided to drop out of school. Mum and Dad were devastated. They knew I was capable of more than being a hairdresser, a profession I claimed I was going to embrace. Mum attempted to make me see reason, and many discussions took place with my parents to dissuade me from this decision. I spent the next few years moving from one boring job to another, after clerical skills gained from a six-month secretarial course. The only plus during this time was that I was able to contribute a little to the family income and cover some of my personal expenses.

Finally, aged nineteen, I went back to college and completed my Higher School Certificate in twelve months of intensive full-time study, during which my long-suffering but ever-generous parents supported me financially. I did well and in the 1980s, as a mature student, completed a Bachelor of Arts in Humanities, plus a partial Diploma in Education.

MINA & JACOB

Mina in Fremantle, our first point of call in Australia, March 1962.

MINA & JACOB

Top: Giza, Joseph and Janka Frenkiel, 1974.
Bottom: The Presto Boys, from left, Iche Fox and Jacob with two others.

Notes

1. Mina Widawski nee Laub, audio testimony for the *12th Hour Project of Oral Testimonies* (Sydney: Australian Institute for Holocaust Studies, 1990); video testimony (Sydney: USC Shoah Foundation Institute, 1995), code 2526
2. Mina Widawski, *12th Hour Project of Oral Testimonies*; USC Shoah Foundation, code 2526
3. Ibid.

29
Finding a New Community

During the 1960s and 70s, Mina and Jacob developed an active social life. In Sydney, they made new friends such as David and Renia Grossman, and reconnected with Joseph Pakuła, Jacob's friend from the Poznań camps. They continued their close friendship with the Marmurs and travelled to Melbourne to see them whenever they could, usually on the overnight train, to cut costs. They also rekindled their close friendship with their camp family such as Guta and Max Procel and Felix Malinowski and his family, also now living in Melbourne.

They went out to clubs such as the Hakoah and South Sydney Juniors, and to movies and dances. But most of their socializing was done at people's home, each family taking turns to host. When it was their turn, Jacob and Mina provided sumptuous meals at a beautifully-set table laden with the very best they could buy. Over time Jacob became an expert cook, and had his favourite butchers, grocers and fruit suppliers who knew him well and chose for him the best cuts and freshest produce. Mina specialized in cakes, delicious salads, delicately-formed kreplach and pieroszki (different kinds of dumpling).

At the beach, Mina sun-bathed and swam. Jacob, hiding from the sun, played dominoes at the back of the Bondi Pavilion with fellow migrants. They walked and picnicked with friends in Centennial Park, took trips into the mountains and holidayed in Canberra.

Hersz Friedman recalled when he spoke to Freda in Sydney in 2011:[1]

> Social life was with lots of other friends who also came from Poland: the Widawskis, the Ruders, the Bigels. On Sundays we played cards in the park. We went on holidays to Blackheath together. Later we used to travel to Canberra for the Christmas break. We also used to go to Narrabeen on the Northern Beaches a lot. So social life was sharing it with other migrants: dinners together, parties, the Hakoah Club and occasionally soccer matches—although I wasn't such a fanatic as Jacob.
>
> I bought my first car sometime in 1962 and every Saturday morning—or every second week—we would go to Paddy's Market to buy a sack of potatoes, boxes of apples, pears and other fruit. We would divide them into three: for me, Jacob and another Polak.

Adele recalls:

> In the mid-1960s, we girls, now comfortable socializing in English, joined the Zionist youth group Hashomer Hatzair, largely because most of its members were fellow Jewish Poles, recent migrants, and most were known to us. In summer, camps were organized and I loved feeling grown-up, away from parental supervision for a week or so. We swam and hiked and learned camping and bush-walking and survival skills.

Freda remembers:

> Hasho provided a wonderfully safe environment for us to socialize with other youngsters with whom we shared a

common language, culture and sense of displacement. We would get together every Sunday afternoon, listen to a lecture or learn a new Hebrew song, do some Israeli dancing, play volleyball or just 'hang out'. This was the place where we learned to be proud of our Jewish heritage and of Israel and first fell in love, forming lasting bonds. With our parents busy trying to make a living in their new country, most of us had been left to our own devices, deciphering the laws of the school yard, learning a new language and succeeding academically. At the same time many of us were also going through the first signs of puberty and early adolescence. Our Hasho friends became our extended family, within which we could safely experiment, adapt and develop. And we had fun!

Mina spent what little leisure time she had reading, learning, embroidering and listening to music. Jacob loved nothing better than a long conversation with a friend, sharing tales and jokes. He was mad about soccer and a fanatic supporter of the Hakoah soccer team (later renamed Sydney City). He went to every game that they played, often travelling with the team and other 'tragics' to their regional games in Gosford, Newcastle or further afield.

Sydney City was the best team in the League at that time, due mostly to a number of its English, Irish and Scottish players. Hence the team was heavily supported by British migrants and visitors. The team bus pulling out from the Hakoah Club full of young British skinheads in their soccer regalia, side by side with their middle-aged, Jewish co-supporters presented a strange sight.

Freda remembers:

> As an adolescent discovering boys, I quickly realized that many of them would go to the soccer games with my

father and his friends. This provided me with a wonderful opportunity to be in their company, so I often 'volunteered' to go with Dad to a match. He gladly accepted, if slightly bemused by my new-found enthusiasm for the game. This love of soccer has stayed with me and will always be associated with Dad, his friends and those Sunday afternoons.

On 2 November 1967, the family was granted Australian citizenship. Mina and Jacob remembered this as the highlight of those years. It made them feel secure and accepted in Australian society, their growing fluency in English easing their way. They were certain then that they had made the right decision in leaving Poland.

The 1970s brought major changes. Freda recalls:

I married Walter Roland in 1970. He was also a Polish Jew, the brother of a close school friend. Soon after marriage we embarked on years of travel and wanderings around the world.

Mid-decade, we divorced. It was then that I rediscovered my long-lost love of drawing and started to study art, at first informally, in London and the United States, then formally at the National Art School, Sydney. This led to a Bachelor of Arts in Fine Art at the Victorian College of the Arts, Melbourne, followed by a Diploma in Education at Sydney University.

In 1984, I commenced work at the Department of Veterans' Affairs, a 'temporary job' until I could get a placement in a high school as an art teacher. I stayed at Veterans' Affairs for twenty-two years! This was primarily because of the wonderful people that I met there, colleagues who became life-long friends. I enjoyed the work of dealing with our veterans and hearing their stories echoing the conversations of my parents' friends around our dining table. In the later part of my career, I undertook staff training, developing and delivering training packages around the country. This was a hugely satisfying job which used both my art and teacher training.

Throughout those twenty-two years, I continued to paint, draw and 'doodle', holding a number of exhibitions which were well-received and gave me a lot of satisfaction. My love of art continues to this day.

But as the years progressed and Mum's and Dad's stories of their experiences during the War unfolded in more detail, I grew passionate about the need to find out more: to tell, to explain, to record. This has been my primary focus for the past few years.

Adele recalls:

When I was nineteen, I met a young engineer whose family came from India (originally from Iraq). Both our families were suspicious of one another at first, since he was a Sephardi Jew and our family is Ashkenazi. By a strange twist of fate, my Jewish teacher from Randwick Girls High, who had so impressed me with her public pride in her religion, was my future husband's aunt! I was delighted to see her again and become included in a large extended Abraham-Mordecai family. We finally convinced our parents that our differences made for an interesting mix.

Mum was aghast, however, when during the first Shabbat dinner, Morrie politely asked whether she had a pickle or something spicy to add to his gefilte fish, which he found bland and tasteless.

We were married in 1974, and the union was to last thirty-eight years. Together we produced our daughter Michelle, now a wonderful young woman. Over the years, Mina learned to make her fish less sweet and ignore our culinary differences, while Morrie learned to love my parents and their Ashkenazi food. At the same time, I learned to love his mother's wonderful curries and other Middle Eastern food.

From 1970-88, Mina and Jacob continued to run their shop, first in Bondi and then at the newly-built Bondi Junction centre. Both Freda and I helped out on an occasional basis, while at the same time establishing our careers and enjoying our personal lives.

After Morris and I married, we lived in Northbridge on the lower North Shore for several years. Having no car, Mina and Jacob travelled regularly from Bondi on public transport, often carrying special Jewish delicacies.

On a visit to Israel in 1979, we explored the possibility of becoming olim, migrants to Israel, but on our return to Sydney the idea was shelved for a number of reasons. But our daughter Michelle was conceived in Israel on this holiday.

Mum and Dad proudly welcomed their first grandchild in September 1980. Over the years as she grew up, they showered her with unconditional love and treasured the time they spent with her. When she played in school bands, they came to her concerts. They proudly shared in her scholastic achievements and attended her prize-giving nights. They thought her the most beautiful girl in the world and made sure that she knew how much they loved her.

In the mid-1980s, Morris found a job lecturing at the University of Technology as I was studying at the University of New South Wales. We moved back to the Eastern suburbs and Michelle enrolled at Moriah College. After his retirement Jacob joined the school in the early 1990s as a lollypop man or traffic warden—and loved every day there. Not only did he enjoy seeing all the children, but he could meet his granddaughter every day!

We had moved to Bronte, so we saw them for weekly Friday night dinners and Sunday picnics and outings. Every Yom Tov we spent time with both sides of the family. Mina took Michelle to the beach, and Jacob and she would take her to the Zoo or on the ferries to Manly and Luna Park. They also cooked her special delicacies. We rented cottages in the Blue Mountains and on the Central and South Coasts and stayed for long weekends—or longer during academic breaks in summer.

In May 1990, frustrated with searching for work in the private sector, I joined the New South Wales Branch of the Department of Immigration. This was intended as a short-term arrangement. Four years later, I found interesting work in the Refugee branch of the Department. I assessed refugee applications, work which involved a lot of research, provided a high level of personal satisfaction and attracted a great group of co-workers. My colleagues came from every corner of the globe. There was mutual respect, harmony and high morale. For me, helping to resettle refugees from Africa, Afghanistan or Iraq felt like coming full circle. During World War II, Jews had been shunned and banned by strict visa quotas from entering 'neutral' or safe countries. The post-war United Nations Refugee Convention now provided a framework to ensure that people fleeing persecution were given asylum or refuge by countries which were signatories to this agreement.

By the late 1990s, with the increasing numbers of boat arrivals in north Australia, I travelled to Port Hedland and

Derby in northwest Western Australia and worked in detention centres set up to process these new arrivals. While the work was very demanding, we gained a high level of satisfaction working long hours to complete our cases and see people released filled with hope for a better future in Australia. Mum and Dad were very interested and proud of the work that I was doing; we had many lively discussions about it.

Of the 200 staff in our Sydney office, there were six Jews. Overall, our work and relatively high profiles commanded a lot of respect within the Department; none of us was subjected to antisemitic comments. I certainly identified as a proud Jew, and my Director tended to fume at the leave I requested for Jewish holidays. It was always approved, his only comment being: 'I am converting to Judaism.'

In 2004, aged fifty-five, I resigned from my job. There were several reasons: firstly, Mum was gravely ill, and Dad needed help. Secondly, I had become disillusioned with the changes taking place within the Department. Our work had become highly politicized and we were subject to far greater scrutiny and 'direction' in our decision making. My last trip before retirement was to Nauru, in March 2002. Asylum seekers had been sent there as part of our new border protection policies.

Since my resignation, I continue to enjoy the company of my former colleagues and look back on my fifteen-year career with the Department with pleasure and fond memories. I was lucky to have found work which stimulated me and offered so much satisfaction. I look back with pride, for instance, to May 1999 when I worked with the Kosovo Task Force helping to process the papers and settle some 2,000 people offered refuge by Australia.

Michelle, perhaps true to her destiny, made aliyah (emigrated to Israel) in 2008 and at the time of writing is living in Jerusalem. She works as a child psychologist and has been the pride and joy of her family.

Notes

1. Hersz Friedman, interview with Freda Widawski, 2011, Sydney

Top: The Bondi Boys, with Jacob (standing) kibbitzing a domino game. From the 1993 book *Bondi*, p.87, by Robert Drewe et al.
Bottom: The Hasho Gang, 1965. Photo by Hersz Friedman. Adele (front centre) and Jack Friedman (front right).

Top: From left, Freda, Adam Marmur, Adele, Eddie Marmur, Melbourne, 1966.
Bottom: From left, the Ruders, the Friedmans, unknown couple, Mina and Jacob, New Year's Eve, 1967.

Top: Freda's and Walter's wedding, April 1970.
Bottom: Freda's exhibition at the Bondi Beach Pavilion Gallery, 1993. From left, Mary Diaz-Martinez, Eti Marmur (Izzy's wife), Mina, Jacob, Izzy Marmur (behind), Freda, Peta Stevenson, Adele.

Top: Freda delivering training with Stephen Andrews. Sydney 2005.
Bottom: Adele's and Morrie's wedding, 14 January 1974.

Top: (left) Birth of Michelle, 11 September 1980. (right) Michelle's first birthday. The joy and love in Jacob's face is boundless!
Bottom: Mina with her beloved granddaughter, 1983.

Adele's graduation, 19 April 1988.

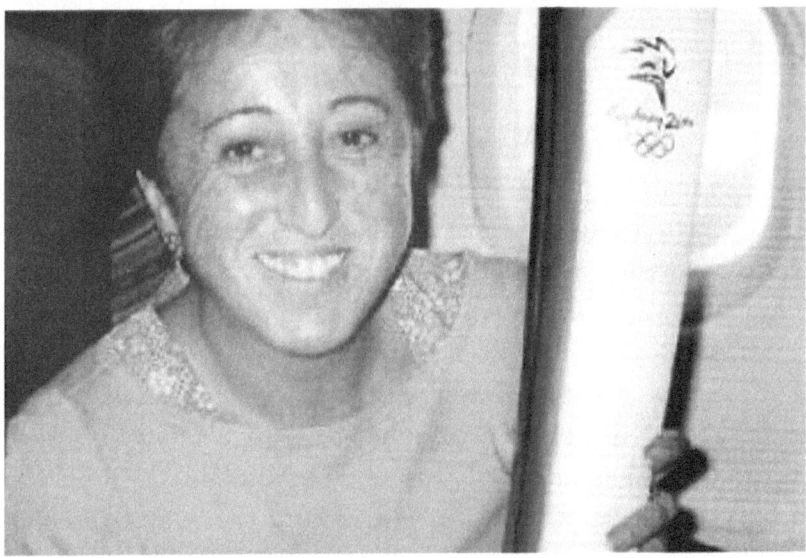

Top: Adele (second from right) with colleagues on the Kosovo Task Force, welcoming refugees arriving at Sydney Airport from Kosovo, 1999.
Bottom: Carrying the torch for the Sydney Olympics on a flight from Perth to Sydney, 2000.

30
Zachor: To Remember

In 1939 there were nine million Jews living in Europe, including Soviet Jewry (many of whom were never under Nazi rule) and the Jews of Britain and neutral countries. In 1945, some three million were left alive. That means two-thirds or some five-point-eight million Jews were murdered during the Holocaust.

For survivors, like Mina and Jacob, the years after the War were focused on rebuilding their lives. It was only once they felt stable and secure that their energies could be directed towards paying tribute to what had been lost.

The memory of those affected by the Holocaust has been honoured in a number of ways. These include the establishment of Holocaust museums in many countries, including Germany; commemorative monuments; exhibitions; the development of Holocaust studies; the formation of survivor associations; and Holocaust remembrance ceremonies, including the annual March of the Living. Most of all these memories have survived through individuals telling their stories, as we do in this book.

Survivors have borne witness by recording their testimonies; writing memoirs; sharing their stories with audiences in educational settings or museums; or by testifying in courts of law.

Mina and Jacob, like many survivors, believed that it was their duty to testify. Perhaps this was why they had been spared. They believed that the world had to be told what had happened to them, not only so that those who had died so brutally would never be forgotten but also, in some small measure, to restore justice, by bringing the perpetrators to trial. They were not seeking revenge—for how could a few years of imprisonment or even an execution compensate for the murder of so many? They sought acknowledgement that the torture, enslavement and mass murder of the Jewish people lay outside what was acceptable human behaviour. Every one of those who had been murdered had been somebody: a mother, a father, a daughter, a son, or a child who died all alone.[1]

'I am not responsible,' says the *Kapo*
'I am not responsible,' says the officer
Then who is responsible?[2]

The Nuremberg Trials were a series of military tribunals held by Allied forces under international law. They brought to judgement prominent members of the political, military and judicial leadership of Nazi Germany who planned, carried out or participated in the Holocaust and other war crimes. The first trial was held before the International Military Tribunal, between 20 October 1945 and 1 October 1946. Twenty-four defendants were indicted, of whom twenty-two were brought to trial. The defendants were each charged on one or more of four counts, including Crimes Against Humanity and War Crimes.[3]

Of the twenty-two, eleven were sentenced to death, including Hans Frank, the Governor-General of Poland, and Hermann Goering, the Reichsmarschall and Supreme Commander of Defence and Commander of the Luftwaffe. Three were sentenced to life imprisonment; two to twenty years; one to fifteen; one to ten years of imprisonment; and three were acquitted.[4]

MINA & JACOB

In December 1945, it was decided that each occupying power should proceed against Nazi criminals as it saw fit.[5] Accordingly, between 1946 and 1948 at least 1,000 former members of the Auschwitz SS were extradited to Poland and tried before the Najwyższy Trybunał Narodowy (NTN) (Supreme National Tribunal). This presided over seven high-profile cases, including that of Rudolf Höss, plus those of forty other SS officers who had worked at Auschwitz. Höss was hanged in Auschwitz on 16 April 1947. Twenty-three of the Auschwitz SS were also executed.[6]

Amon Göth, commander of the Kraków-Płaszów concentration camp, and the man responsible for liquidating the Kraków Ghetto, was tried in Kraków by the NTN from August to September 1946. Pleading guilty, he laid full blame on Hitler and his closest advisors, presenting himself as simply the unwilling executioner of their orders. But he was sentenced to death. Göth was hanged in Kraków on 13 September 1946. Neither Mina nor Jacob attended the trial, being too frail emotionally to do so.[7]

With the creation of the Federal Republic of Germany (West Germany) in 1949, the prosecution and punishment of members of the Auschwitz SS passed to its courts. Using West German judges and West German law for the first time, the history of the camp was reconstructed before a mass audience. On trial were the guards and functionaries at the lowest rungs of the Nazi hierarchy, who had carried out their job: to murder. Of the twenty-two indicted, six received life sentences, eleven were given sentences varying from three to twenty years; and two were acquitted.[8]

During the Adenauer era in West Germany, from 1949-63, a large proportion of the population opposed 'any serious efforts at post-war judicial reckoning or frank public memory'. Adenauer's main policy was to integrate rather than alienate ex-Nazis. Little action was taken in bringing the perpetrators to account.[9]

Of those directly connected with Mina's imprisonment, Paul Budin, HASAG's Director, is assumed to have committed suicide with his wife in April 1945.[10]

In 1948, twenty-five German foremen from the Skarżysko-Kamienna camp were brought to trial in Leipzig. Four were sentenced to death, two to life imprisonment and the others to prison terms of varying length. Egon Dalski, the manager of the HASAG factory in Skarżysko-Kamienna and many of his helpers were never caught.[11]

There is little information about the fate of Wolfgang Plaul, the Commandant of Leipzig, but he was never sentenced for his crimes. Of the other Leipzig officials, neither Oberka Käthe Heber nor her various assistants ever faced trial. In 1945, former guard, Elfriede Kaltofen, was tried in Poland. Arrest warrants were issued against other SS women but their outcome is unknown. Szumańska, the Lagerälteste or camp elder, was tried in Poland, but acquitted because of lack of evidence. Former guard Ingeburg Schulz was sentenced by a French military court in Reutlingen to five years in prison, which she served.[12]

In October 1958, the Zentrale Stelle der Landesjustizverwaltungen zur Aufklärung Nationalsozialistischer Verbrechen (Central Office of the State Justice Administrations for the Investigation of National Socialist Crimes) or ZStL, was formed. Its mission was to initiate and co-ordinate the prosecution of Nazi crimes. Following initial investigation and research, jurisdiction for prosecutions devolved to the Office of the State Prosecutor of the state in which the prime suspect lived.[13]

The German managers of HASAG-Leipzig were investigated by the ZStL but never indicted for their brutal treatment of the prisoners. Investigations into what had happened at Leipzig-Schönefeld ceased in 1976. The HASAG company was never held accountable.[14]

To Jacob's disappointment, no-one had been prosecuted for the execution of his mother, brother, sister-in-law and nephews, killed during the liquidation of the Wieruszów Ghetto.

Nobody has been held accountable for the exploitation of Jews in the various Poznań forced labour camps where Jacob was enslaved. In 2005, Dr Anna Ziółkowska of the Martyr's Museum in Żabikowo noted:[15]

The majority of firms that exploited Jewish labour in the Poznań area operate to this day, some of them even undertaking building projects in Poznań. The unwillingness of industry to acknowledge a moral and, most importantly, material responsibility for their participation in the exploitation of Jewish slave labour, was the cause of their silence.

So those who benefited most from the exploitation of war-time slave labourers were the owners of companies operating to the present day.[16] For example, half the shares in the HASAG business were held by the Dresdner Bank. Women such as Mina who were imprisoned in Leipzig and the other HASAG camps effectively worked for the Dresdner Bank and its partners. Every HASAG prisoner knew what many distinguished scholars seem to forget today: that they provided the owners with free manpower from which they earned huge profits.[17] Similarly, there is a direct connection between Auschwitz and its sub-camps such as Janinagrube, where Jacob laboured, and the big industrial concerns of IG Farben and Krupp.[18]

Twenty-four members of the board of directors of IG Farbenindustrie were tried at Nuremberg during May-August 1947. They were indicted on five counts including 'committing war crimes and crimes against humanity through participating in the enslavement and deportation for slave labour of civilians from

German-occupied territories, and of German nationals'. Almost half were acquitted, with the others receiving prison sentences ranging from one to eight years.[19]

Only a handful of Janinagrube's officials were brought to trial. Jacob gave evidence against Heinrich Niemeyer who had served as a guard in the camp and afterwards was in charge of prisoners during the evacuation Death March, from Gleiwitz onwards. Niemeyer was indicted for the killing of ten prisoners during that march: Indictment against Heinrich Niemeyer, StA Hannover 11 Js 5/73, and Judgement 11 Ks 1/77; AR-Z 15/70, B 162/8956.[20]

Jacob was first contacted by the Senior Public Prosecutors Office at the State Court, Hannover, on 18 December 1973. We assume that the German authorities found him through Auschwitz prisoner records and his application for restitution to the German War Claims body in 1970.[21]

He was interviewed on 16 January 1974 at the Consulate-General of the Federal Republic of Germany in Sydney. He was asked about his arrival at Janina, the conditions in the camp, the work details, accommodation, food and clothing.

Jacob was interviewed again at the Consulate-General in Sydney on 8 July 1975. He then provided details of the Death March, specifically about the shooting of prisoners. He was also shown a number of photographs of SS members for identification and was able to pick out several:[22]

> The Unterscharführer who commanded the guard detail was very much feared by the prisoners because he tortured them during the march with penalty exercises. There was also the Oberscharführer who succeeded the camp Director Baumgartner for a short time. There was Baumgartner and one of the SS who marched us to work.

Jacob subsequently appeared as a witness at a court in Hannover in 1978, 1982 and 1989. Mina accompanied him on the first two occasions and Freda on the last.

During his first court appearance on 30 November 1978, he was asked about the circumstances of his arrival in Janina, and about those working there. He was shown a number of photographs of SS members from various photo albums and identified 'the young officer of the guard duty; the second camp Director; plus, Unterscharführer Baumgartner'. When shown a number of photos from other albums of supposedly the same person at different ages, who it was suggested could have been the boxer he remembered from the kitchen, Jacob replied: 'I do not recognize him.'[23]

When asked about the Death March, Jacob restated that the group from Janina were escorted by their own guard units, and that Baumgartner had stayed with them until Gleiwitz. He stressed that although there was no shooting on the march from Janina to Auschwitz, this changed on the march from Auschwitz to Gleiwitz. He testified:[24]

> I did not see Baumgartner after Gleiwitz. The young officers of the guard detail and also the camp Director who replaced him were with us on the march. The guards were issued with machine guns. They also had rifles, pistols and carried hand grenades that were hooked into the front of their belts. Many prisoners were shot on the march. I heard these shootings. I do not know the individuals who did the shooting.
>
> The young officer of the guard detail as well as the camp Director that succeeded Baumgartner I saw until we were loaded into the rail cars. The young officer was an Unterscharführer. At that time, I could recognize the ranks of Rottenführer, Unterscharführer and Oberscharführer.

A friend, Renia Grossman, recalled Jacob's account of his first appearance in Hannover:[25]

> After Jacob came back from Germany, he told David, my husband, that when he arrived in the hotel in Hannover, they knew that 'today a Jew came to testify against a German'. He was afraid to testify and to walk around there. He was happy when he came back home, because it took a lot out of him to testify and be afraid.
>
> Jacob didn't want to talk about it much; he only told David and me. He said: 'He, the accused, is free. The trial is only a show. Nobody is sitting in jail. They are free, sitting and laughing.' And they looked at him like an enemy. He felt safe here, in Australia. In my eyes he was a hero for having gone to testify!

Mina described how, during one of Jacob's court appearances, while the court took a lunch break, the accused, Niemeyer, with his defence team, entered the same restaurant where Jacob and Mina were dining and cheekily doffed his hat to them. This was very hard for them to take. He was still out in the world, free to come and go as he pleased.

During his second court appearance, on 7 January 1982, Jacob again described his arrival in Janina and some of the officials. This time he was asked in more detail about the evacuation of the camp. He again identified the person whose photos he had been shown in Sydney as 'the officer of the guard detail'. He referred as well to others:[26]

> There also was one who was called Junge (boy), or the Bandit. He tortured people: 'lie down, stand up, lie down, stand up'. I also recall the doctor, Dr Orlik. Scharne was a writer of

protocols. I also recall a kitchen *Kapo*. He was a boxer and a big criminal.

When shown the photos Jacob identified the person who was known as the Bandit.

In February 1989, Freda accompanied Jacob to Hannover for his third court appearance. She recalls:

Despite the reported comments to David Grossman after his first appearance, when asked in 1989 if he was sure that he wanted to do this again, Dad's reaction was: 'Ah, this doesn't bother me. It's nothing. I'm fine!' However, on arrival in Hannover, when we realized that we had to share a room, the sheer relief on his face that he would not have to be alone said volumes about his real emotional state. The following are some observations that I recorded after his appearance in court:

12pm, 8 February 1989

We are sitting in the prosecutor's office, chatting amiably with the secretary about Australia while we await Dad's turn in the witness box. Mr Kasher walks in. He has just given evidence. They are introduced. Dad stands and looks deeply into Mr Kasher's eyes. They try to place one another, to find a familiar face across the distance of many years. Dad questions him: 'When were you there? Where did you work? The only Czech that I remember from the dispensary was the doctor's clerk.' 'I am that clerk,' Mr Kasher replies. They hug, while the secretary, Mr Kasher's son and I stand and watch, tears filling our eyes. A moment of recognition, of understanding.

Without knowing one another they know all that there is to know of each other in that time and place.

12.35pm, 8 February 1989

Dad sits alone at a table in the middle of a large sun-filled room. The accused sits to the left of him, wearing glasses and accompanied by two lawyers. We are all awaiting the three judges and the prosecutor.

These people are legal machines. They have a set of specific questions that need to be asked and they want quick answers. But in front of them they have a man who does not see life in terms of straight answers, straight lines. He is nervous and his voice keeps on disappearing. He is not used to the technology, the microphone he is using. He has lots to tell them but they do not want to hear it.

They are very kind, very courteous, very polite, but on the whole detached. They ask him questions, look for the key sentences in his answers which are necessary for their justice, for their defence, and then let him talk on as they drift off into their own thoughts or look at the ceiling. After all, it is lunch time. They must be hungry and bored, and here is someone telling them the most unbelievable stories about having to march kilometres to and from work! During cross-examination by the defence lawyer, Dr Pilz, this happened:

Dr Pilz: What vehicles were available when you evacuated Janina? What was available for the SS and for the prisoners. Were horses available?

Jacob: We did not have vehicles; we built sleighs. It was winter. The SS packed their baggage and the prisoners pulled them all the way.

Dr Pilz: Mr Widawski, today you are in Hannover for the second time, at least.

Jacob: I am here for the third time.

Dr Pilz: Yes. Sorry. At the earlier times, in 1978 and 1982, you were presented with the photo books I, II, III. You recognized all sorts of things—but not Niemeyer. However later, starting in 1982, you suddenly recognized Niemeyer in both photos. How come?

Jacob: I recognized Mr Niemeyer from the very first moment when I saw the photos in Sydney in the German Consulate-General. But I did not know his name because not one prisoner knew the name of the SS men! I knew the name of Baumgartner because he had come to Auschwitz to select people for Janina and he introduced himself. Otherwise, I believe no prisoner knew the names of the SS. They did not introduce themselves.

Dr Pilz: You said: 'I do not recall the name of Niemeyer. I think that because the court case is in this person's name that this person must be Heinrich Niemeyer.'

Jacob: That is what I said. I recognized the person only from the photo, but his name I did not know then. From the court case I learned that his name was Niemeyer.

At the end of the session the Judges courteously thank Jacob for attending, and me for accompanying him. We get back to the office and speak with the prosecutor, who assures me that he will let us know the results of the trial. He never did.

Today, looking back on that day in court from the vantage

point of thirty years, the most vivid image I see is the back of my father's head. He is leaning on his right hand, speaking into the microphone in German, having rejected the offer of an interpreter. He would rather testify in the language of the accused and those sitting in judgement, even if he does so badly.

He is almost totally bald and his small naked head evokes, more than his words, his total vulnerability. And yet here he is, this small elderly man who had the sheer audacity to survive the most powerful machine of destruction ever created by man. Now, some forty years later, he was on their home turf, testifying against one of the perpetrators.

On 4 May 1992, the Hannover Public Prosecutor wrote to Jacob about the possibility of his appearing again as a witness in a new hearing. Jacob advised the German Consulate-General that he would be willing to do so. There was no further contact.

In 1995 an article appeared in *Der Spiegel* about the case. It reported that Niemeyer had been sentenced to six years' imprisonment on the original charges. Following a second round of indictments in 1981, the proceedings had been suspended in the early 1990s, the defendant judged unfit for further prosecution.[27]

What we found impressive during these trials was that, despite the passage of time, Jacob was able to remember faces, events and details so clearly. What is even more commendable was that at no time was he tempted to 'stretch the truth' or embellish his testimony. He repeatedly stated: 'I don't know; I did not see,' when that was the case. His total commitment to unbiased and even-handed depiction of the accused and their actions seems particularly admirable.

Charlotte Delbo, an Auschwitz survivor, wrote about the difficulty of making the unbelievable believable:[28]

> You don't believe what we say
> because
> if what we say were true
> we wouldn't be here to say it.
> we'd have to explain
> the inexplicable

Primo Levi best expressed the gulf between now and then:[29]

> The gap exists and grows wider every year between things as they were down there and things as they are represented by the current imagination, fed by approximate books, films and myths. It is part of our difficulty and inability to perceive the experience of others, which is all the more pronounced the further these experiences are from ours in time, space or quality. We are prone to assimilate them to those 'related' ones, as though the hunger in Auschwitz were the same as that of someone who has skipped a meal.

Of over 100,000 people investigated in Germany of being suspected of committing mass murder and participating in the machinery of the Final Solution, only about 6,500 were actually brought to trial, the large majority before 1949.[30]

Of those who were prosecuted, 85 percent were convicted of 'non-lethal' crimes, generally aiding and abetting. Because racial hatred, identification of the ethnicity of victims and the program of racial annihilation were not elements central to a murder conviction, of all these convictions only a little over 7 percent related to the mass killing of Jews.[31]

This was apparently the only way for Germans to feel comfortable about themselves and to move beyond the Holocaust. They got some satisfaction out of condemning the crimes of the SS guards and others by addressing them through trials. Then they distanced themselves and considered the subject closed.[32]

What has never been fully explored was that the murder of millions of innocent victims provided a source of rich booty for the Nazi war machine, and for Germans and non-Germans alike. Every deported Jew owned something, even if it was only simple bedding, furniture or personal items such as eye-glasses and jewellery. The looting continued, as we have seen, in the death camps themselves, when the food carried for a journey, the last few precious coins, a blanket or a small suitcase or rucksack, were taken away. In Birkenau alone there were thirty barracks in which items taken from the deportees were sorted and stored.[33]

There was not a single SS man who didn't profit directly from those gassed. In addition, they sent their families hundreds of thousands of marks and foreign currency; scores of watches; kilos of gold; and dozens of diamonds.[34]

Arnošt Lustig wrote:[35]

> **He had been to Auschwitz-Birkenau for a share in the loot held in those huge stores of everything that her father, mother, grandmothers, aunts and uncles and untold others had regarded as indispensable to life, and of which they had been stripped. That, in her eyes, made something cling to him, as it would cling to Germany to the end of time.**

The mass destruction of a large part of the Jewish civilization left indelible marks on individuals, families and on the attitudes of the Jewish people as a whole. This will continue for many generations to come.[36]

In addition to Jacob testifying against Niemeyer, both he and Mina remembered in other ways. They participated in various activities associated with commemoration of the Holocaust. Not long after its establishment in 1983, they both became members of the Australian Association of Jewish Holocaust Survivors and Descendants. Attending regular meetings provided them with the opportunity to meet other survivors, people who spoke the same language as they did and who understood what it was like 'down there': sharing their stories, remembering, crying, laughing, celebrating their miraculous survival. Commemorating the Holocaust continued to be of great importance to the family.

When the Sydney Jewish Museum was opened on 18 November 1992, it provided Mina with the opportunity to bear witness on a weekly basis. She joined the ranks of the museum's volunteer guides, as a witness sharing her personal story with visitors and teaching about the Holocaust. She met many overseas visitors, some of whom became her pen-pals. She felt keenly that the guides, with their personal stories and experiences were a vital part of ensuring that the memory of the Holocaust would continue to new generations. This work gave her enormous satisfaction and she was very proud to be involved with the Museum.

Importantly, both Mina and Jacob recorded their testimonies, for their children, for the community and as a permanent record not only of the crimes committed against them, but also of the lives that had existed in Jewish Poland before the Holocaust and their destruction. For this we will be eternally grateful.

Top: Jacob and Max Kasher outside the Hannover court, 1989.
Bottom: Jacob inside the main gates of Auschwitz,
following the hearing in Hannover. Photo February 1989.

Notes

1 Israel Gutman, ed., *Encyclopedia of the Holocaust* (New York: Macmillan, 1990), 117; Yehuda Bauer, *A History of the Holocaust* (New York: Franklin Watts, 1982), 368; Arnošt Lustig, *Lovely Green Eyes* (London: Harvill, 2000), 168
2 Alain Renais, *Night and Fog*, DVD, released in France 1955 (Australia: Umbrella Entertainment, 2008)
3 Hilary Gaskin, *Eyewitnesses at Nuremberg* (London: Arms and Armour Press, 1990), 28; Harry James Cargas, ed., *Voices from the Holocaust* (Lexington: University of Kentucky Press, 1994), 99-101; Rebecca Wittmann, *Beyond Justice: The Auschwitz Trial* (Cambridge, Massachusetts: Harvard University Press, 2005), 20; https://en.m.wikipedia.org/wiki/Nuremberg_trials
4 Gaskin, *Eyewitnesses at Nuremberg*, xiii, xv
5 Wittmann, *Beyond Justice*, 23
6 http://en.wikipedia.org/wiki/Supreme_National_Tribunal
7 http://www.scrapbookpages.com/Poland/Plaszow/Plaszow03A.html
8 Bernd Nauman, *Auschwitz: A Report on the Proceedings against Robert Karl Ludwig Mulka and Others before the Court at Frankfurt* (London: Pall Mall Press, 1966), xvii; Wittmann, *Beyond Justice*, 3, 6, 95, 159
9 Wittmann, *Beyond Justice*, 23
10 Gutman, ed., *Encyclopedia of the Holocaust*, 647; *Remember for the Future: A Memorial to the Forced Labourers in Leipzig during National Socialism* (Leipzig: The Leipzig Memorial of Forced Labour), 14; Felicja Karay, *HASAG-Leipzig Slave Labour Camp: The Struggle for Survival told by the Women and their Poetry* (London, Portland: Vallentine Mitchell, 2002), 223
11 Gutman, ed., *Encyclopedia of the Holocaust*, 1,362
12 United States Holocaust Memorial Museum (USHMM), *Encyclopedia of Camps and Ghettos* 1933-45, (Washington: 2012), Vol. 1, 380; Karay, *HASAG-Leipzig*, 227-29; Ramona Bräu, interview with Freda Widawski, Buchenwald Museum, Weimar, 26 August 2010
13 Christopher R. Browning, *Ordinary Men: Reserve Police Battalion 101 and the Final Solution in Poland* (New York: HarperCollins, 1992), 144-45
14 USHMM, *Encyclopedia of Camps and Ghettos*, Vol. 1, 380; Karay, *HASAG-Leipzig*, 227-29; Bräu, Buchenwald Museum interview, 2010
15 Anna Ziółkowska, *Obozy pracy przymusowej dla Żydów w Wiekopolsce w latach okupacji hitlerowskiej (1941-45)* (Forced Labour Camps for Jews in Wielkopolska during the Years of Nazi Occupation), (Poznań: Poznań Publishing, Wydawnictwo Poznańskie, 2005), 14
16 Felicja Karay, *HASAG-Leipzig*, 234
17 Karay, *HASAG-Leipzig*, 234-35

MINA & JACOB

18 Ota Kraus and Erlich Kulka, *The Death Factory: Document on Auschwitz* (London: Pergamon Press, 1966), 216
19 Abraham J. Edelheit and Hershel Edelheit, eds., *History of the Holocaust: A Handbook and Dictionary* (Boulder: Westview Press, 1994), 442-43; http://www.jewishvirtuallibrary.org/jsource/Holocaust/WarCrime31.html
20 Indictment against Heinrich Niemeyer, StA Hannover 11 Js 5/73, and Judgement 11 Ks 1/77; AR-Z 15/70, B 162/8956, provided by the Niedersächsisches Landesarchiv, Hannover, 2013, translated from the German by Volker Spieth
21 Transcripts of Jacob's testimonies provided by the Niedersächsisches Landesarchiv, Hannover, 2013, translated from the German by Volker Spieth
22 Transcripts, Niedersächsisches Landesarchiv, Hannover
23 Ibid.
24 Ibid.
25 Renia Grossman, interview with Freda Widawski, Sydney, 2011
26 Transcripts, Niedersächsisches Landesarchiv, Hannover
27 "Justiz: Reichlich spitzfindig" (Justice: Abundantly subtle), *Der Spiegel* no.13 (1995), http://www.spiegel.de/spiegel/print/d-9176330.html;
28 Charlotte Delbo, *Auschwitz and After* (New Haven: Yale University Press, 1995), 276
29 Primo Levi, *The Drowned and the Saved* (New York: Summit Books, 1988), 128
30 Wittmann, *Beyond Justice*, 5
31 Wittmann, *Beyond Justice*, 30-31
32 Wittmann, *Beyond Justice*, 175-77
33 Martin Gilbert, *Never Again: A History of the Holocaust* (London: HarperCollins Illustrated, 2002), 122-23; Ministerstwo Sprawidliwości Główna Komisja Badania Zbrodni Hitlerowskich w Polsce (Ministry of Justice Main Commission for the Investigation of German Crimes in Poland), *Obozy Hitlerowskie na ziemiach Polskich 1939* (Hitler's Camps on Polish Soil 1939-45) (Warsaw: 1979), 36
34 Janusz Siedlecki, Krystyn Olszewksi, and Tadeusz Borowski, *We were in Auschwitz* (New York: Welcome Rain Publishers, 2000 (English translation; first published in Polish, 1946), 14
35 Lustig, *Lovely Green Eyes*, 57
36 Bauer, *A History of the Holocaust*, 368; Raul Hilberg, *The Destruction of the European Jews* (New York: Holmes and Meier, 1985), 305

31

The Golden Years

In October 1973, Freda travelled to Poland, the first of the family to return after an interval of more than ten years.

She describes her visit:

> Following an extended stay in Israel, I decided on a whim to travel to Poland. Arriving in Wrocław, I somehow found my way to our old building in ul. Kluczborska, even though I did not have a conscious knowledge of how to get there. Gripped by dread, I climbed the stairs to our landing and knocked on the Keslers' door. While waiting for them, I sat on the wide windowsill overlooking the courtyard and the crumbling building opposite. A lady walking up the stairs looked at me quizzically. I asked her whether she remembered the Widawski family who had lived there in 1962. She replied: 'Yes, they had two daughters and went to Australia.'
>
> Nothing had changed in that building in the ten years since our departure, which for me it had been a time of transformation: from childhood to adulthood.
>
> When I first entered the Keslers' apartment and met their bedridden mother, it was like coming home into my grandmother's arms. That first night, I slept in their 'study' which had an old grandfather clock mounted on the wall.

When it chimed, I suddenly realized that it had been ours. We had given it to the Keslers before we left.

I also travelled to Kraków, then to Auschwitz, where I first encountered the horrors that my parents had lived through. Then I went on to Wieruszów, where I sat and drew by the river, imagining Dad playing there as a child.

It was not just the grey streets, the lack of consumer goods or the drab people which hit home hardest during that first visit. It was the fact that my childhood friend, Renia, having made arrangements to meet me for lunch, begged off at the last minute, out of fear. As her mother explained: 'It's not that we hide the fact that we're Jewish—but you may inadvertently mention in public that you've just arrived from Israel.' There was nothing more to say and I felt very lucky to be living elsewhere.

During the years 1978-95, Mina and Jacob travelled to Europe, Israel and the United States. In Poland they visited the Frankowski family in Wieruszów and old friends and neighbours still living in Wrocław. They also travelled to Kraków and Auschwitz, to Warsaw and to other places of interest in Poland.

On their first visit to Israel, Jacob reunited with his brother Berek and his family. It had been some twenty years since the brothers had seen one another. He and Mina also met old friends from Poland, such as the Kożuch family in Netanya, and the Pankowski family in Jerusalem.

For Mina, a visit to New York in 1978 provided the opportunity to finally meet her cousins Bernice, Daniel and Seymour for the first time. Unfortunately, her Aunt Sarah had died about a year earlier. Seymour, on seeing Mina, burst into tears, because she resembled his dear departed mother so closely.

MINA & JACOB

In 1982, Jacob met up with members of the Lajzerowicz family, his cousins in Los Angeles. These were the children of his Aunt Maryia, his father's sister.

Following their retirement in 1988, they both set off on a six-month journey to Israel and Europe. In Paris they met Jacob's cousins who had left Poland as children. It had been more than fifty years since the cousins had been together, but they welcomed him and Mina with open arms. That warmth and connection between the offspring of Jacob and Ester Bajla Widawski, Jacob's grandparents, continues on to the next generation.

Freda recalls her special 1989 trip to Poland with Jacob:

> Following Dad's third appearance as witness in Hannover in 1989, we travelled to Poland. It was a wonderful opportunity for me to visit Wieruszów with Dad and to meet, as an adult, his childhood friend Józio Frankowski and family. Because of the shortage of beds, Jacob and Józio tucked themselves into bed together, as they so often had been by either of their mothers, some sixty years earlier. To see Dad walking around his home town, showing me the places of importance to him and watching him being greeted warmly by some of the locals who recognized him through the haze of time and alcohol, was moving. But we felt most deeply when we stood together at the communal mass grave where his beloved mother was likely to have been buried. This was a great privilege.
>
> One of the highlights of the trip was our visit to Zenek Frankowski, Józio's older brother. Much mystery had surrounded this man who had spent many decades living in Germany and had been imprisoned on his return to Poland in the 1970s. The last time that Jacob had seen him was to say a hurried goodbye at Wrocław Station sometime in early 1950.

Zenek had made it clear that he was going to 'disappear' and would not be able to be contacted in the future.

We travelled some 400 kilometres north to visit him. A frail, obviously gravely ill man, he spoke in the gentlest of voices and hugged me like a long-lost daughter. He and Dad sat up the whole night talking. They had a lifetime to cover. As we were saying our goodbyes, Zenek thanked me profusely for making the journey to see him. I couldn't help but reply: 'How could I not want to meet you, given what you did for my father during the War? You sent him parcels of food and clothes during those first few months in Poznań.' He broke down sobbing in my arms, repeating over and over: 'It was nothing. I didn't do anything that any normal person would not have done.'

But it was not nothing! Sadly, Zenek passed away a few months later.

A few days later, while on a train from Wrocław to Kraków on our way to Auschwitz, Dad and I shared a compartment with an elderly Polish man. He was chatting very amiably with us, very happy to share Dad's imported cigarettes, telling us about contemporary life in Poland, asking about Australia. At one point as we passed the small town of Będzin, Dad said to me in English that before the War this town had a large Jewish population. The Polish 'gentleman' remarked: 'There were many Jews in this town before the War. One good thing that Hitler did was teach the Jews how to work.' Dad looked at me, smiled ironically and said in English: 'Got it?' I replied: 'Got it.'

Walking with Dad through the gates of Auschwitz, just a week after his appearance at the court in Hannover, I was overwhelmed with pride in this little man of towering strength and courage.

In 1994 Freda accompanied her parents on what was to be Mina's last trip overseas, to Poland, France and Israel. She recalls:

> It was very special sharing this trip with my parents, particularly being with Mum in her beloved Kraków. As we walked around the old Ghetto area, Mum pointed out where she had lived with her family. We then found her pre-war apartment block. She was stunned—and very moved—to find across the street from her building a plaque dedicated to the late Dr Thon, her youth group's patron and a most revered member of Kraków's pre-war Jewish community.
>
> While in Israel we were taken on a tour of Jewish National Fund projects, as a token of appreciation for Mum's years of charitable work.

A few years later, Adele shared a trip with Jacob to Israel. She remembers:

> In 1998, Michelle was spending her gap year studying in a girls' yeshiva in the Old City of Jerusalem and we wanted to see her and to visit our other family members. This lovely April afternoon, Dad and I were enjoying our coffees on the terrace of the King David Hotel, looking towards the Old City and the Jaffa Gate. Nearby some American tourists were busy taking photographs and also having coffee. A young African American woman approached us, having noticed Jacob's 'tattoo' on his forearm. Awkwardly and shyly she asked whether this was in fact a number from Auschwitz. Her group had visited Yad Vashem Museum that morning and she had been very moved by the experience. Quick as a flash came his response: 'Darling, this is my girlfriend's telephone number.

I am getting old and forgetful.' She laughed in disbelief and after a short exchange about our mutual countries, said her goodbyes.

Later I questioned Dad. Why did you say that? Why didn't you tell her? He explained that it was unnecessary to burden this young woman with his experiences. It was too long a story to dwell on during this lovely afternoon. At seventy-eight, I think he had reached that stage in his life where he simply wanted to forget the past and not continually re-live the pain and sorrow. Or maybe, in Israel, he just wanted to live for the present day, to take joy in life.

Sadly, this was the last time the brothers would see one another. Berek passed away in 2002, aged ninety-one.

In 2003, the sisters travelled back to Poland together. Adele recalls:

This was my first visit back since we had left some forty years earlier, so I had mixed feelings about our visit. I had concerns about being there as a Jew and about being able to communicate, since my Polish language skills had become rusty. Although we sometimes spoke Polish with Mum and Dad, this happened less and less often. However, when we arrived, I was pleasantly surprised to find that I was able to communicate in Polish.

The country seemed both strange and familiar. Freda and I visited Warsaw, Kraków and Auschwitz, Wieruszów and our hometown of Wrocław.

In Wrocław, we revisited our old primary school, our apartment and the main synagogue we had attended as children with our parents. We walked through the nearby park we had both loved so much as children. Throughout,

I felt somewhat removed from my childhood experiences. There was no feeling of homecoming, but rather a strong sense of a foreign place. We loved the food so familiar to us through our parents' cooking, but could not escape the feeling of being again 'the other'.

It was emotional and very moving visiting the well-kept old Jewish cemetery in Kraków. As records show, Mina's family had first settled in the Kraków region in the eighteenth century. Unfortunately, there are no graves of those from her family.

The ruins and malicious damage to the headstones we found in the Wieruszów cemetery made me very angry at the blatant lack of respect for Jewish culture and its long history, as well as the loss of the town's Jewish life. Dad's old friend, Mr Frankowski, while guiding us through the cemetery, acknowledged that after the War, some headstones were used by the locals as foundations for their houses.

There is a monument erected in memory of those who were killed by the Nazis and to the Jewish community in Wieruszów. This was funded by the handful of Holocaust survivors now living in the United States and Israel. But overall there is indifference. No Jews now live in the town and the current Jewish population of Poland is very small.

Our emotional visit to Auschwitz included meeting a group of Israeli scouts proudly carrying the Israeli flag. We ran to them and hugged as many of these young people as we could, wishing them all 'shalom'. They were equally excited to meet two Jewish ladies from Australia.

On return we shared our impressions and experiences with Mina and Jacob. Both during our trip and on our return, despite the fact that we had found most Poles welcoming and friendly, Freda and I thanked our parents for taking us to Australia and giving us the opportunity to live peaceful and happy lives.

Over the years, Mina and Jacob had become involved in a number of ways with the Jewish community. They had both grown up believing in the dream of a Jewish homeland and were Israel's fervent supporters. Mina devoted many years collecting around her neighbourhood for Karen Kayemit, the Jewish National Fund. In recognition of 'her dedication and outstanding voluntary work for Israel', she was presented with a Blue Box Certificate on 27 August 1995. On 11 June 1996, a cluster of trees was planted in Israel in honour of Mina and Jacob, on the occasion of their Golden Wedding Anniversary.

Their retirement years were filled with outings with their children, meals with their friends, daily walks on the beach, going to the movies and attendance at community events. Mina took up yoga and swimming. She joined the Central Synagogue's SPARCS group, where she took Hebrew classes. She would discuss her homework and practise her Hebrew with Michelle, proudly reporting her progress in class to the family.

Although blessed with overall good health and a happy disposition, the years of loss and deprivation during the War had left their mark. During her years in the camps, as noted, Mina had stopped menstruating and it was a miracle that she managed to bear children just a few years later. In the early post-war years, she also suffered from inflammation of the joints, a likely consequence of the typhoid she had contracted in the Kraków Ghetto.

After years in the camps being forced to expose her body in public, in the following years she zealously guarded her privacy and would not readily undress in front of others. For a long time she refused to wear clothing made of striped material.

Another consequence of her experiences was that she hated to throw food away. She loved mouldy, smelly cheese, which she made at home by leaving farm cheese for some time in the kitchen cabinet.

Jacob also suffered physical and emotional damage from his years in the camps. He was subject to stomach ailments all his life. He had a nervous tick. Suzy Zail, in her book about her father, another survivor who had been in Jawischowitz (like Janina, a sub-camp of Auschwitz), describes an almost identical affliction:[1]

> **Apart from a nervous tic—a barely discernible tilting of his head in the direction of his right shoulder—you'd never guess my father was one of the wounded.**

As he grew older, Jacob hated being alone, especially in dark forests or the bush. He had problems sleeping and was plagued by recurring nightmares of being chased by dogs. He was always rushing, especially when he had to catch a train or a plane. He had to be early. He used his small stature and his speed to make his way to the front of any crowd.

Food became a major obsession, particularly in his later years. He loved shopping for things to eat, always choosing the freshest and best quality, and he loved cooking. His greatest pleasure was feeding his loved ones.

He continued to enjoy life. He had a continuing love affair with soccer, played dominoes on the beach and walked around town schmoozing with all and sundry. He loved to talk, and people loved to listen to him. He was on friendly terms with the butcher, the greengrocer, the fishmonger and the delicatessen staff, who all took special care of his requirements.

After retirement he worked part-time as a 'lollypop man' or

traffic warden for Moriah College, a job he dearly loved because of the opportunity it gave him to be around children, all of whom he spoiled like his own. Every Friday he bought large bags of sweets for the following week and lined his pockets with goodies for his 'kids'. This job also meant that he could see his dear grand-daughter, Michelle, every day, while she was a student there.

For the school, he provided a wonderful link with its Jewish past. He was a living memorial to what had been endured and what had been lost. In one of its promotional videos the school featured Jacob talking to Michelle, highlighting this link between the generations, the past and the present:[2]

> **This is Jacob Widawski. He has been supervising our children's safety for about eight years now. Jacob believes that Jewish education is very important, that children have to know who they are and where they come from. He has a message for the children of Moriah: 'I just want to say to the children, you never give up. Never give up!'**

In 1979, much to everyone's horror, he suffered a minor heart attack. This was followed by a second attack in 1980, leading to triple bypass coronary surgery in November 1991. His stomach problems escalated. A recurrent peptic ulcer led to gastro-intestinal bleeding, requiring blood transfusions.

The greatest shock came in July 1996, when Mina suffered a stroke. They had just celebrated their fiftieth wedding anniversary by taking a cruise in the Pacific. According to Jacob: 'Your Mum was doing exercises every morning with the young girls.' True to form, she was struck down in the swimming pool of the Hakoah Club, doing what she loved. Luckily, she was rescued by a fellow swimmer. The initial impact of the stroke was shattering. Her right side was affected, she had slurred speech, lack of balance and difficulty walking.

After intensive physiotherapy and with her steely willpower and determination, within a couple of years she was again sewing intricate tapestries with her right hand. But she never fully regained her stunning calligraphic writing style. Further, her vocal chords having been damaged, she became even more softly-spoken. This sadly ended her guiding work at the Sydney Jewish Museum, which was a great disappointment to her.

But life continued, always busy, both of them doing what they loved the most. In 2001, they celebrated their eightieth birthdays with a series of parties and a trip with their daughters around Tasmania.

A second blow came in July 2002, when Mina was diagnosed with lung cancer. Given that she was a non-smoker, the family always suspected that her cancer must have been caused by the years inhaling dust and chemicals during her slave labour in the munition plants of Skarżysko and Leipzig. It was inoperable. She was treated with radiation therapy, which bought her and her family another couple of years. But in 2004, the cancer spread to her liver.

As Mina's health deteriorated, Jacob became her loving carer, while all the while his heart was breaking. He was not able to comprehend that the unthinkable was happening, that he was losing his beloved Mina. It wasn't supposed to happen like this; he was supposed to go first.

While Mina was in palliative care, he himself needed radiation treatment for a cancerous growth on his lips. This was a terrible physical and emotional strain, but also a godsend. It gave him respite from his vigil at Mina's bedside and the tragedy that was unfolding before his eyes.

Mina passed away ten days after being admitted into Wolper Hospital, on Sunday 31 October 2004 (Cheshvan 16, 5765).

In her memory, a tree was planted by the JNF in the Yizkor

Forest in Israel; a plaque was erected in her honour in the Sanctum of Remembrance at the Sydney Jewish Museum; and a donation made in her memory by the Feiler family, her cousins in the United States, to the Memorial Sloan-Kettering Cancer Center in New York City. Condolences flowed in from friends and family in Australia and overseas, including from the Jewish Communal Appeal, the Australian Association of Jewish Holocaust Survivors and their Descendants, and the Sydney Jewish Museum.

Professor Chris Milross, her oncologist, wrote:

> **I felt a close connection with Mina from the beginning of our association. I knew a very small amount about her wartime experiences. Perhaps it was considering those awful early experiences that I was so impressed by the grace and the dignity with which she approached her cancer. She was a woman with such a beautifully balanced inner strength and peacefulness. It was my pleasure to know her and to be involved with her care.**

Jacob, Adele and Freda had lost the heart and soul of their small family. The last remaining member of Eidel and Moshe Laub's family was gone.

Jacob never recovered from that loss. Mina's death was the cruellest blow that he ever had to bear. He shuffled along as best he could: continuing to host friends to lunch at his home; going for drives with his daughters; meeting mates at the Hakoah Club for coffee and a schmooze. But the light had gone out of him. They had been so close, particularly in their later years. Friends called them 'the lovebirds'. Living without his Mina was impossible for Jacob.

At the end of 2005, after numerous tests and blood transfusions, he was diagnosed with leukaemia. His immediate reaction was to shrug his shoulders and say; 'Oh well, I'll be with Mum soon,' adding: 'As much as I love you girls, your Mum was the best thing that happened to me in my life.'

On 12 December 2005, Jacob's last remaining Wieruszów friend, Max Procel, died. He had phoned Jacob a few days earlier, saying: 'Jacob I'm going.' Jacob had responded: 'If you're going, I'm coming.' He, Freda and Adele flew out to Melbourne the next day, managed to say their goodbyes, and stayed for Max's funeral.

Jacob's final trip with his daughters was to Byron Bay, northern New South Wales, in February 2006. By then he was very weak, but he still managed to clap and dance with 'those crazy hippies' at a full moon celebration on Byron's main beach.

Towards the end of April 2006, he was taken to hospital with suspected pneumonia. His life expectancy at that stage was only 'a few days'. But true to form, he fought on for six weeks. On 21 May he even managed to leave the hospital for a few hours in order to celebrate his eighty-fifth birthday with close friends and family. It was really to say goodbye.

In the days that followed, he deteriorated day by day, until he passed away on 14 June 2006 (Sivan 19, 5766).

Adele recalls:

> A few days before his death, as I sat by his bedside, Dad began speaking to me and the staff in Yiddish, a language which he seldom used at this time. He repeatedly attempted to climb out of his bed, as though the bed's railings reminded him of being in prison or entrapped, unable to leave. He died with Freda and Michelle by his side.
>
> Michelle said, through her tears, lovingly touching the fading tattoo on Jacob's still-warm arm: 'Hey Gramps—it took them more than sixty years to get you.'

Jacob was buried next to his darling Mina. At his funeral, a number of old friends from the original 1962 migrant group were present among the mourners. A plaque was also erected in his memory next to Mina's in the Sanctum of Remembrance at the Sydney Jewish Museum.

And that's how they will remain: forever side-by-side.

Adele remembers:

I can still hear Dad's response to questions about his wellbeing with the Yiddish word uberleben, meaning to survive. Over the years, our parents' miraculous survival was the subject of constant questioning and conversations between us and other survivors.

Many factors contributed to Mina's and Jacob's survival. Physically they were both of small stature, slim and young, eighteen years old when the Germans marched into Poland. Jacob had learned from an early age about poverty, how to do without, and ways to adapt to changing circumstances. From the age of twelve, following his father's death, he had served as an apprentice in his cousin's workshop. He knew how to work hard and how to please strangers, to meet their needs. He had a great ability to charm people. His gift for languages, Yiddish and Polish as well as a smattering of German and Russian, enabled him to communicate readily with anyone. He was quick and street-smart.

By contrast, Mina's childhood had been pampered and secure, surrounded as she was by a protective, loving family. But she had courage, intelligence, great tenacity, ingenuity and perseverance. She had excellent Polish language skills, knew Yiddish and quickly learned some basic German. In Leipzig, she used her skills to make underwear out of rags and in Cavertitz she sewed dresses out of blankets. She was a proud woman who managed to keep her integrity and dignity in the midst of degradation.

Luck, of course, also played a huge part in their survival. Mina had her older sister Freüda with her in the Ghetto, where she had saved Mina's life. In Płaszów she had been a great source of comfort and support. Later, when Mina was chosen to work for the Eisenbergs in Skarżysko-Kamienna, this saved her from hard physical labour and starvation so that she had something 'in reserve' for Leipzig and the Death March. Throughout her time in the camps, the 'family' group she forged with other young women provided great comfort and support.

Similarly, Jacob's work as a handyman for the Commandant and the Guttenbrunn police station gave him access to better food. This work also protected him from hard physical labour and the guards' maltreatment. That meant that when he arrived in Auschwitz he was still in relatively good physical shape and was not immediately selected for death. With advice from Rapport Writer Scharne, he then presented himself as an experienced road builder rather than a tailor. This meant that he escaped the horrors of Auschwitz and was sent to work in the Janina coal mine.

But none of these factors would have necessarily meant survival if Mina and Jacob had not possessed that magic ingredient: their unshakeable belief in life! They never lost hope and preserved joy and love in their hearts.

Simon Wiesenthal wrote:[3]

We Jews, we eternal optimists, believed in all seriousness that survival was a possibility.

Top: Jacob with Joseph Frankowski at the Jewish cemetery, Wieruszów, 1989.
Bottom: Zenek Frankowski, 1989.

Top: (left) Mina's Aunt Sarah with her grandson, Eliot, 1954. (right) Jacob and Mina with his cousins, Isaac (at back) and Lily (far right). The lady in the middle is probably Esther, Lily's mother. Photo, LA, 1982.

Left: Mina with her cousin Seymour, Oklahoma, 1982.

MINA & JACOB

Top: Mina and Jacob with her cousins (from left), Daniel, Bernice and Barbara (Daniel's wife), Brooklyn, New York, 1982.
Bottom: Mina outside her pre-war apartment block in Kraków (left), and in front of the old pharmacy in the Kraków Ghetto: *Apteka* pod Orłem. (Pharmacy under the Eagle), now a museum. Photos 1994.

MINA & JACOB

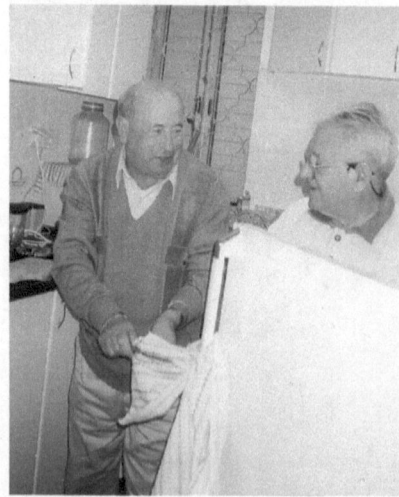

Top: Jacob and Mina with his French cousins, (from left) Myriam, Giles, Celine and Leon, Paris, 1994.
Bottom: The two brothers, Jacob and Berek, together for the last time. Ness Ziona, Israel. Photos 1998.

Top: Jacob's eightieth birthday, with Mina, family and friends, May 2001.
Bottom: Adele and Mina, six weeks before her death.
Photo September 2004.

MINA & JACOB

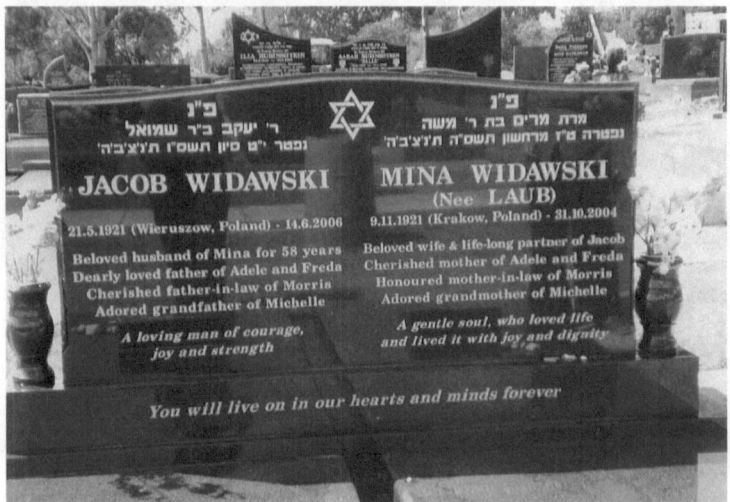

Top: Jacob with Hersz Friedman in Mullumbimby, 2006.
His daughter Helen refers to the spot as 'Jacob's bench'.
Bottom: Mina's and Jacob's graves, Rookwood Cemetery, Sydney.

Notes

1 Suzy Zail, *The Tattooed Flower* (Melbourne: Scribe Publications, 2006), 91
2 Extract from video recording, Moriah College, 1997
3 Simon Wiesenthal, *Max and Helen* (London: Granada, 1981), 67

32
Visiting the Past

Adele recalls:

In 2008, Freda, Michelle and I travelled from Tel Aviv to Warsaw. This was Michelle's first trip to Poland and we visited our birthplace Wrocław as well as Kraków and Warsaw. In Wrocław, we showed Michelle our school, the park and the neighbourhood, and walked the city's busy Market Square. We also caught up with Mr Ringel, our Jewish neighbour still resident in our building after so many years. His family had chosen not to leave Poland during the 1960s and, sadly, his parents and siblings have now passed away. He is a respected elder of the Wrocław Jewish community. We had a lovely kosher lunch together in the dining room of the beautifully renovated Synagogue. As he showed us around, memories of our time there with our parents flooded back.

We travelled to Auschwitz and visited its museum. But the focus of our trip was to participate in the March of the Living, to honour Mina and Jacob; the murdered members of both families; and all those who suffered or perished during the Holocaust.

The March of the Living began in 1988. It is an annual three-kilometre march from Auschwitz to Birkenau, symbolizing all those other marches. Some 7,000 youth and adults from fourteen nations, including representatives of the Israeli Defence Forces and Christian groups from Hungary, the Czech Republic and Poland marched with us. Wherever possible, a Holocaust survivor was at the front of each group. We walked with the Aussie contingent, joining some Holocaust survivors from Melbourne.

Michelle remembers:

As we waited in the ruins of death and humiliation for the March to start, for the 'dignitaries' to arrive, I looked across to my left and saw true dignity. A man in his fifties was sitting on the steps of the block bunkroom, a large Talmud open across his lap, learning quietly. Connecting to his soul, his people, his life-blood.

His actions were quiet, but you could have sworn you heard every word. I watched as the words and letters leapt off the page to float upwards above this place, back to the Source from which they came, bursting forth with unbridled joy and pride. They were carried on the wings of the knowledge that whatever happens in this life, truth, dignity and goodness must ultimately prevail, as my grandparents always said. We, standing there, were living proof.

Adele recalls the March:

It was a very moving experience as we marched in silence, Israeli flags waving in the wind, with the locals watching us. We congregated in an open field in Birkenau and as we gathered there, we heard the song *Eli Eli* coming from the stage that had been erected. This was a South Korean choir singing in fluent Hebrew!

The ceremony culminated in the lighting of a giant six-armed menorah, its arms representing the six million Jews murdered during the War. The most moving moment was the joint lighting of one of the candles by a Jewish male survivor and the Gentile Polish woman who had hidden him during the War.

The Israeli Chief Rabbi said Kaddish, the Mourner's Prayer, and the Israeli Army Choir sang.

Freda wrote of the March and that special time spent together in Poland:

> A very moving day. Lots of tears because our folks weren't there to march with us, but so much hope and love among the participants and dignitaries that you couldn't help but feel enriched.
>
> Following the March, we spend some time in Kraków, visiting Kazimierz, the Ghetto area and the town centre. It was very moving standing together, we two generations of Mina's descendants, in front of the house where she and her family had lived in the Ghetto. We looked up at the windows behind which Mina had watched her beloved parents herded into Płac Zgody for deportation and death.
>
> Equally meaningful was being with Michelle in front of the house where Mina had grown up and the beautiful leafy street in which she would have played, walked with her friends or listened to Dr Thon address the Akiva group.
>
> We then flew back to Israel, in time for the Yom Hatzmaut (Independence Day) celebrations! How fitting and how edifying.

MINA & JACOB

AM ISRAEL HAI! (Israel lives!).

In December 2009, a year after her visit to Poland, Michelle wrote this piece from Jerusalem:

WHEN STORIES BECOME LIFE

I cannot really remember the first time I ever heard about the Shoah (Holocaust). The word seemed to float in the background of my life like a mist, ethereal and hard to hold. I remember kids used to compare stories in the playground; whose family had the most gruesome experience, the deepest tragedy? We traded these stories like baseball cards. We did this, I believe, as a type of competition—yes—but also as a way to wake ourselves up and try to understand.

At home things were thankfully uneventful. Grandparents were the people you visited on Shabbat. They made chicken soup. They had accents and beautiful, calligraphy-like handwriting. They talked about snow and Black Forest cake. They reminisced about days after the War when food was easier to come by. Occasionally, they made a remark about a Commandant of a labour camp, or a comment on the nature of evil. But mostly, as I came to understand, they tried to live for the years before and after the pain. As the only grandchild, I was shielded from most of it. Growing up in a country that tasted of sun, surf and freedom, the whole idea was covered with a blanket of warm unreality.

I occasionally would feel a twinge of guilt for not engaging more emotionally with the totality of what they had gone through, with the experience of living it, over and above the dates and times of their stories. I believe my grandparents were overjoyed by my lack of understanding. They could not afford the luxury of such distance.

Even walking on the beach hand-in-hand on a sunny morning did not allow them respite from the memory of lost love and lost innocence. My mother and my aunt inherited some of this. Theirs was a more contained grief, surfacing in the company of their parents, at their dedication to all things 'Holocaust' and their fierce ambition to provide themselves and their loved ones with things that their parents never had. I would catch a glimpse of this dedication on my mother's return from the Jewish Museum or on late nights watching her prepare for an immigration interview with a refugee desperate for a better life. But as I turned my head back towards my own life, my group of friends and the opera-drama of the schoolyard, this awareness seemed vague and not all that important.

Nevertheless, as the years rolled by and life went on, I continued to wonder. What was my role in all of this? Finally, at age twenty-seven, I was granted the beginning of an answer. Following graduation from university I had moved to Israel and was now enjoying a blessed life there. My mother called one day to give me some news. She was coming with my aunt for Pesach and they had an idea. They wanted to take me on a trip back to Poland. We would join the March of the Living on the day it happened, but the rest they wanted to show me themselves. Ours would not be a trip of coaches and strangers singing dirges. Whatever this trip was destined to be, it would be personal.

I was initially both excited and apprehensive about the experience. However, I felt that Hashem (G-d) was finally asking me to step up and become part of the story. I was not sure if I could break through the surreal wall that I had created in order to understand a little, and then pass it on. As an only child and only grandchild, I felt the pressure to understand even more. Who would be left after me to pass on the history of their experiences? Would I be able to comprehend even a little of how they came to relate to their lives in those awful years, and what they wanted the world to understand? How could I—how could any of us—break through the vastness of words like Holocaust, camp, evil and faith, to grasp even a remote understanding of what they truly meant?

I hoped that at the very least I would come away from the trip with a bit more knowledge about my family's experience. What I was granted instead was a profound glimpse into the essence of love, faith, connection and my own identity.

You see, when you stand outside a European brownstone on a leafy street, looking up at your grandmother's childhood home, the view is very different. My mother stood holding on to me, describing the family's life before the War: cultured, classical, Jewish. It was suddenly as if I could hear Mozart played lightly on a piano by the window. I could see my grandmother, a young girl, being hoisted on to an older brother's shoulders or sitting in a living room surrounded by books, by culture, and dreaming of her own education to come. I flashed back to an image of her in later years as I had known her, sitting in a warm Bondi apartment, wearing a sky-blue tweed suit jacket and pearls, bent over a Hebrew language magazine, savouring another moment to learn something new. I began to understand a little more of her and my mother's passion for knowledge.

Another moment came as we wandered into a grocery store in Wrocław. I noticed handwriting on cakes and pastries: the same swirls and beautiful letters. My eyes filled with tears. I see her writing now, not through a judgemental child's eyes who thinks 'that's not how you write English', but from the perspective of a woman torn away from her home, and her country for no reason at all. She was a woman who had the right to take her swirls with her.

On a train through the Polish countryside, my mother described the life of my grandfather before the war. Poor. Blue-collar. Hard-working. A prankster with lots of brothers. Then 1945 brought two survivors together in a 'chance' meeting of cultures: the prankster and the lady. They were two people from different worlds who would never otherwise have had a chance to meet. They were two people who had lived through a nightmare and emerged on the other side alive, only to find themselves living in the same small town. They met. Married. Gave birth to two children. Moved to Australia. One of their children gave birth to me.

I had a sudden realization that a town that had been home to some 2,500 Jews before the War was left with only a handful of survivors, a few strangers whose names I don't know. Max Procel, a friend of the family. My grandfather.

How must we understand such living? How did he?

I gained insight into humour. Into rebirth. My grandfather, asked about the number on his arm, replied: 'It's my girlfriend's telephone number!' Laughter. Appreciation of what it takes to see what he has seen and laugh like that.

Standing in the home my mother grew up in, I could hear her laughter as she ran between her building and the next with a group of other children, backpack rocking from side to side. I wonder how such sounds would have felt to my grandparents. I am shown the sparse furniture and lack of privacy. But still I feel the love within these walls.

I remembered a story from childhood: 'Your grandmother stood at the window and watched her parents being taken away forever. Her sister ran out and gave the people water while they stood to be selected. Your grandmother hid behind the curtain and watched. She cried when they left. She never saw them again.'

'You remember that story?' my aunt asked. 'Look up.' We're standing by Number 4, opposite the square of the Kraków Ghetto, fifty metres from the square. That's the place where Mina stood and watched.

This was not some story. This was her life.

Finally we visited the site of Płaszów labour camp. I remembered that they used to sit in a circle breaking limestone into pieces for the Germans and then wheeling the pieces across the muddy fields in wheelbarrows. I remember that my grandmother was sitting next to a woman and her mother when the Commandant of the camp shot the mother in cold blood.

We arrived by hire car from our hotel. I saw the limestone still sitting in blocks. The German guard towers had been recreated for the film *Schindler's List*. I *saw*.

Through moments like this, slowly I began to understand how such big tragedies could trickle down into everything. Holocaust Memorial Day. Friends from Poland, Mr Frenkiel and Mr Procel who saved my grandfather, used to come to our table on Friday nights. I remembered Yiddish theatre on tape. Mountains of food. Love of learning and sunshine. Appreciation of the quiet life and for the goodness in people. Nightmares and stomach problems and fifty-eight years of marriage. Kindness to strangers. The kindness of my mother.

My very existence.

Through thinking about such experiences, I was taught that if you truly want to see, or relate to anything, you have to look into the details. For me, it's the same with our relationship to the universe, to spirituality, to G-d. We can find Him most intimately in a small whispered prayer, in the healing touch of divine intervention, in the wonder and beauty of our tradition and laws.

My mother once said to me that the way to glimpse any huge communal experience is to look at just one story. In our case, I am honoured to have understood a little more of the lives of two wonderful people through a few of the moments of their lives. I hope that I can continue to tell their story. I hope this leads to a greater appreciation for the tiny moments in life and for everything that Hashem sends us. Because in the end, that's what we are here for.

Michelle dedicated her words to the memory and 'ilui neshamot' of Miriam (Mina) bat Moshe and Yaakov (Jacob) ben Szmuel.

Adele and Freda have their own tribute:

We miss Mum and Dad every day. The conversations; the music we danced to, and the humour; the joy and laughter they both shared with us. Their love of life, of travel and adventure.

We remember their generosity and hospitality to all, friend or neighbour, their open attitude to strangers. Mina flirted with Adele's handsome work colleagues and young Israeli soldiers. She had a passion for, and life-long interest in current affairs and politics. Once she phoned our local branch of the Liberal Party and gave them an earful, displeased that one of their members had been rude to the then-Labor Prime Minister. Jacob and Mina supported social justice and a fair tax system for the weakest or those in need in our society.

Their Blue Box was always kept full of coins, ready to be collected. We fondly remember Friday nights and Yom Tovim: Jacob and Mina's best china, flowers and silver candles. We remember their pride in Michelle's and their daughters' academic achievements, always acknowledged. We all enjoyed our many trips together around New South Wales, to Queensland and Tasmania. We visited old friends in Melbourne, and have lovely memories of travels overseas.

Most of all we are grateful to our parents for sharing with us their life philosophy: be positive and love life; acceptance of others and an even-handed approach to their War experiences, Jacob stressing that even during the darkest years he was helped by others' humanity. We remember his generosity of spirit, which allowed him to see goodness in people during the worst of times, when so many behaved so cruelly.

We remember Mina's and Jacob's amazing ability to distinguish between the barbaric behaviour of participants, those War generations who perpetrated the crimes during the Nazi period, and those who came after, who did not. We remember our parents' incredible courage and survival skills, both during the War and later, as a young couple without family and traumatized by what they had experienced.

Their greatest gift was their unconditional love for their daughters, and later for their granddaughter.

MINA & JACOB

Adele, Freda and Michele at the March of the Living, 2008.

Adele and Freda in Płac Bohaterów Ghetta (previously Płac Zgody), the main square of the Kraków Ghetto. Photo 2008.

Michele in front of No. 10 Bogusławskiego Wojciecha, Kraków (previously Jasna Street), where Mina lived before the War. Photo 2008.

Adele and Freda with their old neighbour, David Ringel,
in the White Stork Synagogue, Wrocław, 2008.

The Descendants

Top: Adele and Michelle.
Bottom: Braha (Berek's daughter) with her daughter Anita and her son Moshe (right), Israel.

Top: Braha's daughter Inbar with her husband Avi,
son Yogev and daughter Yuval, Israel.
Bottom: Szmuel (Berek's middle son) with his daughters Dalit (left),
Lilah (right), wife Perhija and son Aaron, Israel.

Menachim (Berek's youngest son) with his son Ben, Israel.

Top: Eliot, son of Mina's cousin Daniel (second from left) with (l-r) daughter Cassie, son Andrew, daughter Michelle, son-in-law Justin, granddaughter Scarlett Eva, daughter Shayna, son-in-law Zach, United States.
Bottom: Adele and Freda with French cousins (great-grandchildren of Ester Bajla). Back row, left to right, Pierre, Gerard, Marc; front row Merylene, Dominique and Michelle. Uluru, 2018. Inset: Claude.

Acknowledgements

First and foremost, we are grateful to Mum and Dad for recording their testimonies. To Michelle Abraham our heartfelt appreciation for her unique contribution. Our gratitude is also extended to friends and strangers, who generously shared their memories—Hersz Friedman; Renia Grossman; Bella Grill; Harry Procel; the Marmur family; the Malinowski family; the Frankowski family and Grażyna Kowalczyk; David Ringel; Sigmund Józefowski; and Krystyna Marszałek. Also to those whose recorded testimonies we have used to enhance our parents' stories, especially Max Procel; Morris Shell; Issac Pankowski; Adam Malinowski; Jack Fogel and Leon Jolson.

We are also indebted to the staff of numerous institutions around the world who provided vital records. They include the Polish State Archive Offices of Kraków, Kańczuga, Kalisz, Łódź, Przemyśl, Tarnów, Wieruszów and Wrocław; the Prisoners' Information Office, Auschwitz Museum; Jewish Historical Institute (Warsaw); Institute of National Remembrance (Wrocław); the International Tracing Service, Bad Arolsen; the Leipzig Memorial of Forced Labour (Gedenkstätte für Zwangsarbeit Leipzig); the Buchenwald Museum, Weimar; and Niedersächsisches Landesarchiv, Hannover. For vital background information, the dedicated staff at Friends of Libiąż; the Museum Martyrologiczne w Żabikowie (Luboń); Museum at MESKO (Skarżysko-Kamienna); Kraków Museum-Pharmacy under the Eagle; the Galicia Museum; Yad Vashem (Jerusalem); USHMM, United States Holocaust Memorial Museum (Washington); YIVO Library (New York); Sydney Jewish Museum and the Melbourne Holocaust Centre.

We are grateful for the information relating to our family tree/ history provided by Bracha Habari and Menachim Widawski in

Israel; the Feiler family in the United States and the Nejman family in France.

For the onerous task of translating records and other vital material, our heartfelt thanks go to Volker Speith (from German); Hannah Browarnik (from Hebrew); Bracha Habari (from Yiddish) and Freda Rosenberg (from Russian).

This book would not have come to fruition without the help and guidance of the team at the Sydney Jewish Museum, led by Jacqui Wasilewsky and Professor Konrad Kwiet, but especially that of our editor Diana Giese whose skills, patience, sensitivity and support are greatly appreciated. We would also like to thank Audrey Larsen from compu-vision for her creative design.

Lastly we thank friends and family for their unfailing encouragement and support throughout this project.

www.ingramcontent.com/pod-product-compliance
Lightning Source LLC
Chambersburg PA
CBHW032121160426
43197CB00008B/479